ELIZABETH I

Queen Elizabeth I: painting on panel attributed to
Federico Zuccaro (the Darnley portrait), c.1575

JASPER RIDLEY

ELIZABETH I

The Shrewdness of Virtue

Fromm International Publishing Corporation

New York

Published in 1989 by Fromm International Publishing Corporation
560 Lexington Avenue, New York, NY 10022
by arrangement with Viking Penguin Inc.

Library of Congress Cataloging-in-Publication Data

Ridley, Jasper Godwin.
Elizabeth I : the shrewdness of virtue / Jasper Ridley.
p.   cm.
Reprint. Originally published: New York, N.Y. : Viking, 1988, c1987.
Bibliography: p.
Includes index.
ISBN 0-88064-110-X
1. Elizabeth I, Queen of England, 1533-1603.
2. Great Britain—Kings and rulers—Biography.
3. Great Britain—History—Elizabeth, 1558-1603.
I. Title.   II. Title: Elizabeth the First.
[DA355.R53   1989]
942.05'5'0924—dc19 [B]
88-29255 CIP

The miniature painting of Queen Elizabeth by Nicholas Hilliard on the half-title page
and the painting of Queen Elizabeth facing the title page are reproduced by permission
of the National Portrait Gallery.

Cover illustration courtesy of The Bettmann Archive.

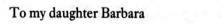
To my daughter Barbara

ACKNOWLEDGEMENTS

I am grateful to Miss Ana Attwood, Dr R. Beck, Mrs Jean Cadell, Mr Stuart Collins, Mr T. A. B. Corley, Mrs Marlies Evans, Miss Ann Hoffmann, Dr Colin Martin, Mrs Joan Owen, the late Mr Hugh Reynolds, Mrs Denise Sells, Dr Michael Smith, Major Peter Watson and Mrs Claire McAllister White for their assistance; Mr Tony Mercer for driving me to the battlefields where the soldiers of Elizabeth I fought in Belgium, Holland and France; the late Mrs Bence-Jones for her hospitality to me at Glenville Park when I was researching in Ireland; the librarian and staff of the London Library for their help on so many occasions; the staff of the British Library, the Kent County Library at Tunbridge Wells, and the Public Record Office; and my wife Vera and my son John for their help with the proofs.

Tunbridge Wells,   Jasper Ridley
6 July, 1987.

CONTENTS

CONTENTS

NOTE ON THE CALENDAR

When Elizabeth I was born, all Western Europe used the Julian calendar, which was ten days behind our modern Gregorian calendar. In England and Scotland the year began on 25 March; in France and the Netherlands on Easter day; and in Spain, Italy and parts of Germany on 1 January.

In 1582 Pope Gregory XIII promulgated our modern Gregorian calendar, which was introduced in Spain in October and in France, the Netherlands and all Catholic countries in December. Elizabeth wished to introduce it into England, but abandoned the idea in view of the opposition of both the bishops and the Puritans to a calendar which had been approved by the Pope; and the Gregorian calendar was not introduced into England until 1752. In the years between December 1582 and Elizabeth's death in 1603, the calendar in England was therefore ten days behind the calendar in France, Spain and the Netherlands; thus 19 July in England was 29 July in France, Spain and the Netherlands.

I have adopted the universal modern practice of giving the date of the year throughout in the Gregorian New Style calendar, beginning the year on 1 January. Dating the days of the month between 1582 and 1603 presents a problem. To give both dates, e.g. 19/29 July, and 28 July/7 August, is irritating to readers. There are advantages in giving all dates in the Old Style calendar, but this involves dating well-known events in France and the Netherlands ten days earlier than the date by the calendar in force there at the time and on which they have always been remembered in history. It would mean stating that William the Silent was murdered, not on 10 July, but on 30 June, 1584, and that Catherine de Medici died, not on 5 January 1589, but on 26 December 1588; while to adopt the Gregorian New Style calendar throughout would mean stating that Elizabeth died on 3 April, not on 24 March, 1603.

I have therefore dated events according to the calendar in force at the time in the country where they occurred, unless there are special reasons for doing otherwise, distinguishing all dates given in the New Style calendar by adding '(N.S.)' after the date. Where the date is given without the addition of '(N.S.)', it is given in the Old Style calendar.

[vii]

PREFACE

Elizabeth I was a controversial figure in her lifetime, and has been ever since. To her loyal Protestant subjects, she was 'the precious jewel' of the realm of England, whom God regarded 'as the apple of His eye', 'our sovereign sacred Princess, upon whose life so many lives do depend'. To her Catholic enemies, she was 'this woman hated of God and man', 'the very shame of her sex and princely name'.[1]

Elizabeth hated and feared the Protestant extremists—the Puritans—as much as, and perhaps more, than she hated and feared the Catholics; but they saw her as the national leader in the fight against the foreign Papist enemies, and, with very few exceptions, they never ventured to criticise her openly. After her death, the struggle between the Puritans and the monarchy became sharper, and the Parliamentary leaders under James I and Charles I compared the good old days of Queen Elizabeth with the tyranny of the Stuart Kings. It was not until the eighteenth century, after the Glorious Revolution of 1688, that the victorious Whigs could criticise Elizabeth, seeing her in historical perspective as a despot who nevertheless used her position to advance the cause of constitutional freedom before its champions were strong enough, in the seventeenth century, to fight for it themselves.[2] In this respect, the Whig and the Marxist interpretations of the sixteenth and seventeenth centuries broadly coincide.

But religious differences and historical perspectives are not the only factors which influence people's opinions about Elizabeth. By 1842 a writer who was a staunch upholder of the Church of England and who hated both Oliver Cromwell and James II, wrote about Elizabeth I:

> Good Queen Bess! was ever name
> So grossly misapplied;
> The scourge of man, fair women's shame,
> The vixen lived and died.[3]

Today, the religious hatreds have passed away in England and America, and the conflict between Catholics and Protestants in sixteenth-century Europe can be seen, not as a struggle between true and false religion, but as another phase in the never-ending contest in which the conservative upholders of the established order, the revolutionary youth, the martyrs, the career-

[ix]

ists, and the Foreign Offices of the great powers all played their part. The public's attitude to Elizabeth seems now to be determined largely by nationality. I have not conducted an opinion poll to discover the public reaction to her, but from my personal experience, a clear majority of the English admire her, though a substantial minority dislike her. However, an even larger majority of Scots and Irish are very hostile. To nearly all the Scots she is still the 'Jezebel, that English whore', who will never be forgiven 'for murdering our Queen',[4] though none of the actions which she sanctioned caused her more distress and remorse than the execution of Mary Queen of Scots.

Froude's twelve-volume *History of England from the Fall of Wolsey to the Defeat of the Spanish Armada*, of which nearly seven volumes are devoted to Elizabeth's reign, presented a critical view of her. Froude, who had started out with the traditional English admiration for Elizabeth, became convinced in the course of his research that all the credit for the great achievements of her reign must go to her ministers, above all to the great William Cecil, Lord Burghley, and not to her.[5] During the next eighty years, many authors agreed with Froude, including Lytton Strachey in his *Elizabeth and Essex* in 1928, while several others followed Agnes Strickland's *Lives of the Queens of England* of the 1840s in showing the waywardness and the spiteful side of Elizabeth's character and relations with her intimates.

Sir John Neale's great biography was first published as long ago as 1934, though many readers today can hardly believe it. Neale swung public opinion once more in Elizabeth's favour. He is generally regarded today as her unqualified admirer; it has been said that he was so much in love with her that he could not be really objective about her. He is not, in fact, as uncritical in his later writings, especially in his *Elizabeth I and her Parliaments*, as in the earlier, more popular, and somewhat selective biography of 1934, in which he presented her as a great national leader as well as an attractive person whose acts of cruelty must be excused by the period in which she lived, and whose apparent hesitations and vacillations were cunning and brilliant diplomatic manoeuvres—unscrupulous perhaps, but justified in the interests of England. Elizabeth Jenkins in 1958 fully shared Neale's admiration for Elizabeth. His opinion that the Queen, and not her ministers, was responsible for the glories of the Elizabethan age has been put forward even more forcibly by Paul Johnson both in his biography of 1974 and in his contribution to *Queen Elizabeth I: Most Politick Princess* in 1986. In England, Neale still reigns supreme, for Sir Geoffrey Elton's criticism has been confined to arguing that Neale exaggerated the influence and organisation of the Puritans in the House of Commons.[6] In recent years only an American biographer, Carolly Erickson, who is an erudite historian, has damned Elizabeth as a hateful shrew who made life unbearable for her unfortunate courtiers and ministers.

While writing this book, I have often been asked, always by people who have read nothing by Neale except the biography, whether I have found anything new to say about Elizabeth since Neale. This shows the extent of Neale's influence, but it is a surprising question. Apart from the fact that Elizabeth Jenkins, Edith Sitwell, Paul Johnson, and Carolly Erickson have all

written their very successful biographies since 1934, Neale's biography contained virtually no unpublished material. In this sense Neale wrote nothing
new since Froude, though this of course does not apply to Neale's other
books or to his articles in learned journals. What was new about Neale's
Queen Elizabeth was his interpretation of her character and influence, which
reversed Froude.

It is possible today for a new biographer of Elizabeth to discover at least a
limited amount of unpublished material, particularly about Ireland, a subject
which has been examined in specialised studies by a number of English and
Irish authors, but has been almost entirely ignored by Elizabeth's biographers. It is also possible to quote correctly for the first time several well-
known phrases from contemporary documents which have been incorrectly
quoted for over a hundred years. In the nineteenth century, great historians
like Froude and Motley saw nothing wrong in paraphrasing passages from
sixteenth-century letters and putting their paraphrases within quotation
marks as if they were actually quoting from the document. In many cases all
other authors have used these 'quotations' ever since.

As long as historians and biographers wish to write, and their readers wish
to read, about Elizabeth I, they will be able to find a new interpretation of the
character and the place in history of this complex, contradictory, bewildering
and fascinating woman. My Elizabeth I is not Neale's heroine, not Elizabeth
Jenkins's 'Elizabeth the Great', not Paul Johnson's 'most politick Princess',
and not the 'vixen' of the poet of 1842 and of Carolly Erickson in 1984. I see
Elizabeth as a very religious and conscientious woman, a convinced Protestant, determined to do her duty, as she saw it, to God and her people, and to
uphold the prestige and power of the absolute monarchy for this reason. She
was overwhelmed by her sense of responsibility as a Queen, which she did not
enjoy, and for which she had sacrificed her love for Leicester. This was why
she could never make up her mind what to do in moments of crisis and would
so often change her mind. Nevertheless, in the last resort it was she alone who
had to make the decisions, and she always did so when it was really necessary.
Sometimes these decisions were wrong, and had disastrous results, but on
the most important occasions, for example in Scotland in 1559, they were
right, and she deserves the credit for them.

REFERENCES

1. Neale, *Eliz. & Parliaments*, ii.193; Murdin, *Burghley Papers*, 671: *Span. Cal. Eliz.*,
   iv.41; Allen, *Admonition to the Nobility and People of England*, 54.
2. Kenyon, 'Queen Elizabeth and the Historians' (in *Queen Elizabeth I: Most Politick
   Princess*, 52–54).
3. Burke, *A General Armory of England, Scotland and Ireland* (1842 ed.), where it is a
   verse of a poem said to be written by an 'amateur herald . . . recently deceased'
   (pp. 35–36, unpaginated).
4. Antonia Fraser, *Mary Queen of Scots*, 545.
5. Williams, 'In Search of the Queen' (*Elizabethan Government and Society*, 13).
6. Elton, *The Parliament of England* 1559–1581.

ELIZABETH I

THE PROTESTANT CHILD

I N the summer of 1533, all over England and Western Europe, everyone interested in public affairs was eagerly awaiting the answer to the most important political question of the day. The kings and rulers, as they returned from the hunt, asked their secretaries about it. The ambassadors in London held back their messengers, with their saddled horses in the courtyards of the embassies, while they added the latest news in postscripts to their dispatches. The merchants, pondering on the risks of a rupture in trade relations between England and the Low Countries, discussed it with their factors. Would the expected baby of King Henry VIII of England and his new Queen, Anne Boleyn, be a boy or a girl?

The child was born at Greenwich Palace between three and four o'clock in the afternoon on Sunday 7 September. It was a girl, to the dismay of its parents, of King Henry's loyal courtiers and officials, and of the Protestants throughout Europe, and to the delight of the Pope, the Holy Roman Emperor, and their supporters everywhere, including perhaps the majority of the English people.

Twenty-five years later, the baby became Queen Elizabeth I. As far as her personality was concerned, she inherited very little from either her father or her mother. She had Henry's red hair, his intelligence, his physical energy, and his ebullient personality, but not his ability to take rapid decisions, his cold, calculating cruelty, his utter lack of conscience and his disregard of everything except his own personal advantage and pleasure. She had Anne Boleyn's vivacity and charm, but not her daring and her irresponsibility. But Elizabeth's destiny and all her actions were determined by the fact that she was the daughter of Henry VIII and Anne Boleyn – of a father who was a ruthless despot, a national leader against the hated foreigner, and a conservative in religion, but also of a mother who represented, in the eyes of her friends and enemies, subversive Protestantism, the revolutionary movement of the century.

Fifteen years before Elizabeth was born, England was a country in which

State and Church combined to regulate the lives of the people, who were forbidden to export goods, or to travel, without permits, to eat meat on the fast days, to fornicate, to wear the clothes or colours of their social superiors, or to criticise the King or his counsellors or the dignitaries or doctrines of the Church. A few dissidents, the Lollards, put forward new religious ideas; but they were arrested and tried as heretics before the ecclesiastical courts, and if they refused to recant were burned alive in the nearest market town. They were hailed as martyrs by a small number of supporters, but gained very little sympathy from most of the English people, though the ordinary Englishman was always ready to laugh at jokes about the immorality of priests, monks and nuns, and grumbled about the interference and extortions of the foreign Pope and his officials in Rome.

On 31 October 1517 Martin Luther, a monk at Wittenberg in Saxony, nailed a document to the church door in Wittenberg in which he denounced a particularly scandalous example of Papal corruption. If the Pope and the Church authorities had been prepared to accept his criticisms in a sympathetic way, nothing more might have been heard of him. But he was violently denounced as a presumptuous heretic, and this drove him to make more far-reaching attacks on the Papacy. By 1521 his followers all over North Germany were rioting and breaking images in the churches, and soon large areas of Germany and Northern Europe had repudiated the Pope's authority.

In England, Lutheranism spread rapidly among those sections of the population which were receptive to revolutionary ideas – the artisans of the towns in the economically advanced areas of south-east England, the discontented youth, and the intellectuals of Cambridge University, especially the priests and divinity students. Oxford was less affected, but here and in many other places the movement spread. The 'Lutherans', as all the dissidents were now inaccurately called, advocated new doctrines and practices in the Church, all of which had one thing in common: they denigrated the status of the priesthood, and emphasized the direct relationship between the individual layman and God.

They thought that the congregation at Mass should share the wine with the priest; they condemned the doctrine of the celibacy of the clergy and of monks and nuns, and believed that priests should marry, instead of living almost openly with a concubine, as many bishops and priests did; they denied the Real Presence, the doctrine that the priest, by his words at Mass, could transubstantiate the bread and wine into the body and blood of Christ, and they taught that Christ was only spiritually and figuratively present in the bread and wine when the congregation commemorated the Lord's Supper; they condemned images of the saints, and even the crucifix; they rejected the splendid vestments in which the Church dressed its clergy, and thought that bishops and priests should officiate in ordinary clothes. Above all, the reformers believed that all men and women should read, and accept the truth of, the Bible, and reject every doctrine and ceremony which had been added by the Church without Scriptural authority. The Church forbade ordinary laymen to read the Bible, and severely punished anyone who translated it from Latin into English; for if people read the Bible, they would argue about it, and interpret its meaning for themselves, and raise the authority of the Bible above the authority of the Church.

The young artisans and apprentices who became Protestants, as they would soon be called, were passionately devoted to their cause, and had no respect for authority or for the feelings of the conservative silent majority in England. They broke images, which were condemned as idols in the Bible, interrupted the religious processions which were often held in the streets of the towns, and desecrated the Host, for they believed that it was a wicked act of idolatry to worship a piece of bread. At Dovercourt in Essex, where a crucifix was particularly worshipped by the parishioners, four Protestants broke into the church at night, dragged the crucifix to a nearby field, and burned it. Three of the offenders were caught and hanged.[1]

It was natural that Henry VIII, with his autocratic and conservative outlook, should condemn Lutheranism and burn Lutherans. The Protestants, searching for powerful allies in their struggle against the Papacy, laid great emphasis on the duty of obedience to 'the Prince' – that is to say, the ruler of an independent sovereign state. But Henry agreed with his friend Sir Thomas More that a movement which believed that the individual should follow his conscience and not the laws of the Church would ultimately be subversive of the authority of both Church and State. 'What can be a greater duty for you and for powerful Princes devoted to Christian civilisation than to watch, and act vigorously to repress, the Lutheran faction?', he wrote to Luther's protector, the Elector of Saxony. 'There is nothing new in Luther making use of any lie to stir up the riff-raff and excite the people to hate Princes . . . The poison is producing dissension in the Church, abrogating the laws, weakening all magistrates, stirring up the laity against the clergy, and both against the Pontiff, and the people against Princes, and will certainly incite the people of Germany to declare a war for liberty . . . while Christ's enemies look on and laugh.'[2]

But Henry VIII had another problem. His wife, Catherine of Aragon, had been unable to produce a male heir. She had been six times pregnant, but only her daughter, Princess Mary, had survived for more than a few weeks. Grave dangers would ensue if a Queen were to inherit the throne. She would have to marry in order to ensure the succession. If she married a foreign prince, this would mean in practice that England would become a vassal state of her husband's country, whatever safeguards might be inserted in the marriage treaty; while if she married an English nobleman, this would almost certainly mean that the other noblemen, resenting his authority, would rise in revolt against the Queen and her husband. So Henry VIII desperately needed a son. Catherine of Aragon had been married to Henry's brother Arthur before she married Henry; and her marriage to Henry would have been illegal by the law of the Church if the Pope had not granted a dispensation allowing the marriage to take place. Would it not be possible to persuade Pope Clement VII to discover some technical flaw in the dispensation which his predecessor had granted, and to declare that Henry's marriage to Catherine was therefore void, and that Henry was free to marry another wife, who could give him a male heir?

Henry was already considering the possibility of taking this step in 1526 when he fell in love with Anne Boleyn. He was thirty-five, and she was nineteen. Her father, Sir Thomas Boleyn of Hever in Kent, had been Henry's ambassador to France and Spain, and Henry afterwards created him Earl of Wiltshire; and her sister Mary had been Henry's mistress. Henry's calculating state policy now went hand in hand with his passionate desire for Anne Boleyn.

In ordinary circumstances, the Pope would probably have granted Henry a divorce by finding some excuse or other for invalidating the dispensation of twenty-five years before; for Popes often granted divorces when reasons of state required it. But Catherine was the aunt of the Holy Roman Emperor, Charles V, who ruled Spain and the Netherlands and large parts of Italy as well as being in theory the overlord of Germany. Charles was angry with Henry, who had repudiated his alliance with Charles and joined their common enemy, King Francis I of France, in a war against him; and he put the strongest pressure on the Pope to refuse Henry's request for a divorce. The Pope, unwilling to offend either Henry or Charles, played for time, and found one pretext after another for postponing giving judgement in the divorce case for seven years.

From the beginning of the divorce proceedings in 1527, Henry had realised that if the Pope refused to grant him a divorce, there was another way: Henry could claim that the marriage of a man to his brother's widow was against the divine law, and that no Pope had the power to grant a dispensation to contravene the divine law. There was a text in the Bible which condemned the marriage of a man to his brother's widow, even though there was another Biblical text which said exactly the opposite. So Henry, for his own advantage, could adopt the Protestant tactic, which he had hitherto so strongly condemned, of quoting the Bible against the decrees of the Pope. Soon after he first asked the Pope for a divorce, he began threatening the Pope with the possibility that if he were not granted the divorce, he would repudiate the Papal supremacy over the Church and take England into schism; but he was reluctant to carry out his threat, for though he was willing to make use of the Protestants, he did not wish to encourage this subversive movement too far, and continued to burn heretics who denied the Real Presence.

In the summer of 1531, four years after he had first begun the divorce proceedings, Henry sent Catherine away from court and lived openly with Anne Boleyn as man and wife. By this time, it was being widely rumoured among the Pope's supporters in England, and at the court of the Emperor and the King of France, that Anne and her father were Lutherans. This story probably began as a Papist slander; but if Anne and her family were not Lutherans in the proper sense of the word, they sympathised with the broader anti-clericalism which was spreading in England. They had their own reasons for encouraging Henry to obtain a divorce from Catherine, and it was becoming increasingly obvious that the only way to obtain the divorce was by breaking with Rome. So they favoured the repudiation of Papal authority, and were denounced by Catherine's supporters as Lutherans; and the more they were denounced as Lutherans, the more Lutheran they became.

In January 1533, Anne realised that she was pregnant, and this forced Henry's hand. Her child might be the male heir which he needed so much, and this made it essential that he should marry Anne before the child was born. He married her very secretly at the end of January, and in April directed Parliament to pass an Act which abolished the right of appeal from the English courts to the Papal court in Rome. As the Archbishop of Canterbury had recently died, he appointed Anne's chaplain, Thomas Cranmer, who was sympathetic to Lutheranism, to be the new Archbishop, and ordered him to sit as a judge in a special court to decide whether Henry's marriage to Catherine was valid. Cranmer, who in his private correspondence with Henry made no pretence of impartiality, gave judgement that Henry's marriage to his brother's widow was void by the divine law, despite the Papal dispensation. This meant that Henry, never having been lawfully married, had always been free to marry another woman. It was then given out that Henry had already married Anne, and as it was realised that their child would be born in September, an untrue rumour was circulated that they had been married on 14 November 1532, and not on or about 25 January, which was the true date.[3]

On Whit Sunday, 1 June 1533, within a week of Cranmer's judgement, Anne was crowned Queen in Westminster Abbey after coming from the Tower of London in the traditional procession through the streets. Some of the onlookers cheered her, but most of them did not.[4]

Charles V's ambassador in London, Eustace Chapuys, had heard as early as February that Anne had secretly married Henry. By the middle of May his spies had discovered that Anne had had her dresses let out because of the pregnancy. He was convinced that Anne and her father were Lutherans, and that England was about to fall, not only into schism, but into Lutheran heresy. Encouraged by the Bishop of Rochester, John Fisher, and by other supporters of Catherine, he urged Charles to intervene by force and launch a crusade to liberate England from the heretics. Charles refused to do so, and he equally firmly rejected the idea that he should impose economic sanctions against England, which would have hit the important trade in wool and other commodities between England and the Netherlands. But he continued to urge the unfortunate Pope to give judgement for Catherine in the divorce case and to pronounce censures against Henry, though the Pope was convinced that he would make himself ridiculous by issuing bulls which he would be unable to enforce. On 11 July, at Charles's insistence, he reluctantly issued a bull declaring that Henry was unlawfully cohabiting with Anne Boleyn, and that any child born of their union would be illegitimate.[5]

In England, all news of the Papal bull was suppressed, and a propaganda campaign was launched to prepare the people for the break with Rome and the birth of the lawful heir to the throne. It was very important for Henry that Anne's child should be a boy. Not only did he need the male heir for whom he had been waiting for so long, but he and his supporters had argued that Catherine's failure to produce a surviving son was a proof that God had condemned their marriage. A few days before the child was born, he asked the physicians and the astrologers whether it would be a boy or a girl. They all assured him that it would be a boy. In view of this good news, he ordered that an especially splendid tournament should be held to celebrate the birth of the Prince. He told the French ambassador that he had not yet decided whether to call his son Henry or Edward.[6]

As the time for Anne's delivery approached, the wildest rumours were circulating in England and abroad. It was reported in Flanders that Anne had given birth to a monster. Another report in Flanders was that the child was stillborn.[7]

When it was known that the child was a girl, Henry's opponents did not conceal their satisfaction; but Henry did not allow the public to see his disappointment. As soon as Anne was delivered on the afternoon of 7 September, the Te Deum was sung in the London churches, and arrangements were made for a splendid christening.

On Wednesday morning, 10 September, the child was carried by the old Duchess of Norfolk in a procession to the church of the Franciscan friars at Greenwich in which all the dignitaries of the realm took part, including the Lord Mayor of London and the city corporation, who had arrived by barge from London in their scarlet robes and collars accompanied by forty of the leading citizens of London. The walls all along the route from the palace to the church had been hung with arras, and the path along which the dignitaries walked two by two was strewn with rushes. In the church, which was richly adorned in crimson and gold, the child was christened at the silver font by Stokesley, the Bishop of London. Cranmer was godfather, and the old Duchess of Norfolk and the Lady Marquis of Dorset were godmothers. The foreign ambassadors in London did not attend the christening. Chapuys had been shocked to hear a rumour that the baby would be given the name Mary, so that she would replace Queen Catherine's daughter, Princess Mary, in name as well as in rank; but the report was untrue, and the child was christened Elizabeth.[8]

Orders were sent to the bishops, and transmitted by them to the clergy, that the people must pray for the King and Queen and their daughter, the Princess Elizabeth. Henry was determined that all his subjects should accept Elizabeth as the heir presumptive to the throne until it pleased God to send a son to him and Queen Anne. He expected Catherine of Aragon and his daughter Mary to comply like obedient subjects. As he had never been lawfully married to Catherine, she was to be regarded only as the widow of Arthur, Prince of Wales, and was therefore no longer to be addressed as Queen, but as 'the Princess Dowager'; and as the marriage was void, Mary was illegitimate, and was to be called, not Princess Mary, but 'the King's daughter, the Lady Mary', while Anne Boleyn was 'the Queen' and Elizabeth 'the Lady Princess'. To Chapuys and the Pope's supporters, and to many of Henry's subjects, Catherine was still 'the Queen' and Mary 'the Princess'. Anne was 'the concubine', and Elizabeth 'the little bastard'.

Catherine and Mary refused to renounce their titles. Henry made it clear that if they complied he would treat them well, but that if they refused he would force them to obey by harsh treatment. He subjected them to a policy of deliberate provocation to test their obedience and break their spirit. A few weeks before the birth of Elizabeth, he ordered Catherine to send him the costly christening shawl which had been used at Mary's christening, seventeen years before, for Elizabeth's use at her christening. Catherine refused to hand it over.[9]

Elizabeth was set up in an impressive establishment at Hatfield in Hertfordshire, in the care of Lady Bryan, who was Anne Boleyn's aunt. When she was three months old, Henry ordered that Mary should be separated from her mother and sent to live at Hatfield as one of Elizabeth's ladies-in-waiting. Mary indignantly refused to recognise Elizabeth as a princess, and claimed that she alone was the Princess. She was treated almost as a prisoner at Hatfield, and confined to her room at the top of the house. When Henry visited Hatfield in January 1534, and made a great fuss of Elizabeth, he refused to meet Mary, though he had once been very fond of her.[10]

From time to time, Elizabeth was moved from Hatfield to the King's palaces at Greenwich and Eltham. On these occasions she was carried in a litter, having pride of place among the travellers, while Mary was forced to follow her in another litter to show her inferior status. When she refused to go, she was dragged to her litter by force, and after this, on the advice of Chapuys, with whom she was in secret communication, she submitted after making a formal protest.[11] Her greatest grief was that she was not allowed to write to her mother or receive letters from her.

In March 1534 Parliament passed the Act of Succession, which compelled every subject, when required to do so, to swear that he believed that the children of Henry and Anne Boleyn were the lawful heirs to the throne. Refusal to take the oath was punishable with life imprisonment. The oath was put to everyone in a position of authority in England, by the justices of the peace to the masters of households, and by the masters of households to their family and servants. Many thousands of people took the oath; only a handful refused and suffered imprisonment. These included Bishop Fisher, Sir Thomas More, and a number of monks. Henry was proclaimed Supreme

Head of the Church of England, and later in the year an Act of Parliament enacted that it was high treason to deny any of the King's titles, thus making it a capital offence to deny that he was Supreme Head. In the summer of 1535, Fisher, More and the Carthusian monks were executed under this statute, though Henry, in his usual manner, countered his action against the Papists by almost simultaneously burning fourteen Anabaptists as heretics for denying the Real Presence.

All over the country unpaid informers – zealous Protestants or spiteful neighbours – denounced Papist sympathisers whom they had overheard speaking, in inns or in churchyards after Mass, against the King and his policy, or more often against Anne Boleyn. Reports came in to the authorities of people who were saying that Anne Boleyn was a whore who should be burned at Smithfield. When a woman at Watlington in Oxfordshire was successfully delivered of her child, she praised the midwife, telling her that she was worthy to be the midwife to a Queen of England. The midwife said that she would be very pleased to be midwife to a Queen like Queen Catherine, but not to Queen Anne, who was a harlot. A few weeks later, John Hilsey, a friar who had become a Protestant and was soon afterwards appointed Bishop of Rochester, pursued two friars through Somerset, Devon and Cornwall, and eventually caught them at Cardiff. They had been preaching in favour of Papal supremacy wherever they went. When someone asked them if Princess Elizabeth had been christened in hot or cold water, they said that she was christened in hot water, but that it was not hot enough.[12]

Henry was aware of the popular hatred of Anne Boleyn, and of the discontent which followed the wet summer and bad harvest of 1535. He was worried at the renewed threat of foreign intervention after the outburst of indignation throughout Europe at the execution of Fisher. But the death of Catherine of Aragon in January 1536 opened up the possibility of an improvement in Henry's relations with the Emperor. As Catherine was dead, Henry would now be free to marry again, whether or not he had been lawfully married to Catherine. Soon after her death, Henry's Secretary of State, Thomas Cromwell, held secret talks with Chapuys on the possibility of a rapprochement with Charles V. Chapuys told Cromwell that though the world would never recognise Anne as Henry's lawful wife, they might be prepared to recognise a new wife.[13]

Henry was turning against Anne. She was behaving in a provocative way, insulting her uncle the Duke of Norfolk, poking fun at the French ambassador to his face, and making jealous scenes with Henry when he paid attention to other women. She had failed to produce a male heir; after two miscarriages, she gave birth to a son, but he was stillborn. A few months earlier, Henry had fallen in love with Jane Seymour, the daughter of a Wiltshire gentleman.

On May Day 1536, Anne was arrested and charged with high treason for having committed adultery with five men and having plotted to assassinate the King. Her lovers were said to be Sir Henry Norris and two other gentlemen of her household; her young lute-player, Smeaton; and her own brother, Viscount Rochford. They were all sent to the Tower. The acts of adultery were alleged to have been first committed in 1533. According to the prosecution, Anne had fallen in love with Norris, and planned to murder Henry. Her two-year-old daughter, Princess Elizabeth, would then become Queen, and Anne would rule as Regent for Elizabeth and marry Norris. Although Norris was her chief lover, she had had casual affairs with the others, who had agreed, in return for her favours, to help her and Norris murder the King.[14] Smeaton pleaded guilty, perhaps out of spite because Anne had repulsed him; the others denied the accusations, but were found guilty at their trial. They were all executed.

As Henry and the authorities in England had now accused Anne of adultery, it is not surprising that her old Papist enemies hastened to assert that Elizabeth was not only a bastard but was not even Henry's bastard. Chapuys wrote that it had been proved that Norris was her father. In the Netherlands, more far-fetched rumours were circulating; it was said that Elizabeth was the child of a peasant whom Anne had casually met. The foreign Papists made much of the story, which was untrue, that Anne had been caught in bed with her lute-player; but despite what has been written by several modern writers, no one seems to have suggested that Smeaton was Elizabeth's father.[15]

Two days before Anne was beheaded, she was divorced from Henry after a secret two-hour hearing before Cranmer. Henry had decided to marry Jane Seymour as soon as Anne was dead, and wished to bastardise Elizabeth as well as Mary so that there would be no rival claimants to challenge the right of the children whom he hoped to have by Jane Seymour. It was not easy to find a pretext for holding that Henry's marriage to Anne had always been void. The first plan was to prove that Anne had entered into a precontract of marriage with the Earl of Northumberland before she married Henry, which would have invalidated her marriage to Henry; but Cranmer had investigated this question in 1533 before Henry married Anne, and had held that there had been no precontract with Northumberland. So he now had to fall back on the argument that, under ecclesiastical law, Henry's marriage to Anne was illegal because Henry had had sexual relations with her sister Mary. As this was discreditable to the King, the reason for the divorce was kept secret.[16]

Both Catholics and Protestants saw the fall of Anne Boleyn as a great defeat for the Reformation. They were convinced that Henry would now legitimise his daughter Mary and restore her to her position as heir presumptive to the throne, and would halt the advance towards Protestantism which had taken place in the last three years, even if he did not again acknowledge the Pope's authority. But Henry surprised everybody. Instead of legitimising Mary, he pressed her more vigorously than ever to admit that she was a bastard, and after he had threatened to send her to the Tower, and even to put her to death, if she refused, she at last gave way, and signed a grovelling submission. She was then allowed to come to court, and received with favour by Henry and his new Queen.

The new Act of Succession of July 1536, two months before Elizabeth's third birthday, enacted that both Mary and Elizabeth were bastards. Elizabeth no longer had the title of Princess, but was 'the King's daughter, the Lady Elizabeth', just as Mary was 'the King's daughter, the Lady Mary'. But Mary, who was aged twenty, held a more prominent position than Elizabeth. While Mary was at court, Elizabeth was brought up at Hatfield in the care of Lady Bryan. Her nurse and governess was Katherine Champernowne.

On 25 June 1536, an order reconstituted the households of Mary and Elizabeth. It was certainly no coincidence, in that age when the number of servants in a household was a great status symbol, that Mary was given forty-two servants, and Elizabeth thirty-two.[17]

THE LADY ELIZABETH

LIZABETH was aged thirty-two months when her mother was beheaded, and cannot have remembered anything about it. We do not know if she remembered Anne, who had not seen very much of her baby daughter when she was Queen. Nor do we know when Elizabeth was first told that her mother had been executed as an adulteress and a traitor. Modern biographers have imagined the little girl wondering about her mother's fate, growing up in a household where Anne Boleyn was never mentioned, but gradually learning or guessing the truth from overhearing the occasional unguarded phrase and the whispered gossip of the ladies of the household. But this ignores the nature of Henry VIII's régime. It is much more likely that Elizabeth, as a child, was subjected to the barrage of propaganda which was being put over by preachers week after week in churches throughout the realm. Elizabeth would have been clearly told that she was a bastard and that her mother was a wicked woman, even though she was not required, as Mary had been, to sign documents acknowledging her bastardy.

Elizabeth was undoubtedly taught that the King her father was the Supreme Head on earth of the Church of England; that the Bishop of Rome had no more authority in England than any other foreign bishop; that her sister, the Lady Mary, was a bastard because the marriage of a man to his brother's widow was against the law of God; and that she herself was a bastard, because the marriage of her mother to her royal father was void, for reasons which it did not please the King's Majesty to disclose but which had been held to be sufficient by the Archbishop of Canterbury and other learned men.

Modern writers have probably also misunderstood Elizabeth's attitude to her father. They have pointed out that while she very rarely spoke about her mother she was always praising her father and boasting that she was her father's daughter. But the biographers who picture the little girl being fascinated by the boisterous personality of her powerful father may have overlooked the nature of her admiration for Henry VIII. Elizabeth was taught to obey and admire Henry because he was the King, and that she, like all other subjects, must never question his actions or go against his wishes, but must always accept 'It is the King's Majesty's pleasure' as the conclusive argument which justified every action.

In the year after the execution of Anne Boleyn, the bishops issued their official statement of Church doctrine which was popularly called 'the Bishops' Book'. In the commentary on the fifth commandment, 'Honour thy father and thy mother', it explained that this commandment meant that the subject must love the King, as the father of all his subjects, and it expressly stated that a Christian must love the King more than he loved his natural father.[1] Elizabeth would have been brought up to feel that it would be almost sinful if she loved Henry VIII because he was her father, and not because he was the King.

In October 1537, when Elizabeth was just four, Jane Seymour gave birth to a son, and at last Henry had a male heir. The Prince was christened at Hampton Court, and was given the name Edward. Cranmer and the Duke of Norfolk were the godfathers, and Mary was godmother. Elizabeth held the 'richly garnished' chrisom cloth, but she herself 'for her tender age' was carried by Jane Seymour's brother Edward and by Lord Morley. After the ceremony, Mary, Elizabeth and Lady Herbert of Troy carried the baby Prince's train as they walked out of the chapel royal.[2] Twelve days after the birth, Queen Jane died of septicaemia. Mary, as chief mourner, rode behind the hearse in the funeral cortège from Hampton Court to Windsor; but Elizabeth was not required to take part in the funeral.[3]

In January 1540 Henry married Anne, the sister of the Duke of Cleves. The seventeenth-century Italian author, Leti, who wrote a biography of Elizabeth, published the text of a charming letter which she wrote, at the age of six, to Anne of Cleves. Unfortunately, there are good grounds for doubting if the letter is genuine, at least in the form in which Leti published it; but she would certainly have been capable of writing a suitable letter to Henry's new Queen. When the King's secretary, Wriothesley, met her at Hertford Castle in December 1539, he wrote that she behaved with the gravity of a woman of forty.[4]

Henry was disgusted with Anne of Cleves. He reluctantly agreed to marry her, but six months later he divorced her, beheaded Thomas Cromwell, who had urged him to marry her, and intensified the persecution of Protestants. He married Katherine Howard within a fortnight of obtaining his divorce from Anne of Cleves. Elizabeth met Katherine Howard on several occasions, and in May 1541 she spent some days with her at Chelsea.[5] Two months after Elizabeth's eighth birthday, Henry discovered that Katherine had committed adultery, and she and her lovers were executed.

On 12 July 1543 Henry married Katherine Parr. In the sixteenth century, royal weddings were normally private affairs, in the presence of only a few witnesses; but Prince Edward, Mary and Elizabeth were among a number of lords and ladies of the court who attended Henry's marriage to Katherine Parr in the chapel royal at Hampton Court.[6]

Katherine Parr was the daughter of a knight of Westmorland. When she was very young, she married the aged Lord Borough, but he died leaving her a widow at the age of seventeen. She then married Lord Latimer, who as one of the leading noblemen in Yorkshire was involved in the Pilgrimage of Grace, the great Catholic revolt against Henry's religious policy and the dissolution of the monasteries. But Henry pardoned him, and he died a few years later, leaving Katherine a widow for the second time. She was in love with Sir Thomas Seymour, Jane Seymour's younger brother; but the King decided to marry her, and she had of course no alternative but to agree. She became Queen of England at the age of thirty-one. Henry was fifty-two.

For the first year after Katherine's marriage to Henry, Elizabeth was not often at court, but spent part of the time in the household of her brother Prince Edward, with whom she became close friends. The royal children moved between Hatfield, Hertford, Hampton Court and other royal residences; and both of them, and Mary, were invited to the family supper party which Henry gave in Hyde Park before he left for the siege of Boulogne in July 1544.[7]

Elizabeth now held the recognised position of the King's bastard daughter. Royal bastards were a well-known phenomenon in sixteenth-century Europe, though normally their bastardy came about in a more obvious and less controversial way than in the case of Mary and Elizabeth. They were honourably treated, and placed very high in order of precedence at court; and provided that they clearly recognised that they could not succeed to the throne and did not claim to be the equals of the King's legitimate children, they could rise to the greatest eminence. Royal bastards like the Earl of Moray, the illegitimate son of James V of Scotland, and Margaret of Parma and Don John of Austria, the bastards of the Emperor Charles V, were appointed to act as Regents in Scotland and the Netherlands during the minority, or absence abroad, of the King. Royal bastards were useful instruments in diplomatic marriage negotiations, for they could be offered as brides or bridegrooms to important foreign rulers who were not quite important enough to be invited to marry the King's legitimate children.

Elizabeth was only three when the Privy Council discussed, at their meeting on 3 April 1537, the possibility of her marriage to some suitable foreign prince.[8] It was the usual practice to negotiate marriages of royal infants from the earliest age, though by the ecclesiastical law the marriage could not take place until the child was twelve, and marriage contracts were often broken, on some pretext or other, if new diplomatic alignments took place before the marriageable age was reached. But there were special circumstances which did not normally arise in the case of Mary and Elizabeth. Though Mary had been made a bastard by the English Act of Parliament, all foreign Catholic rulers recognised her as the legitimate daughter of Henry and Catherine of Aragon, and accorded her the title of Princess; while Elizabeth was not only a bastard, but the daughter of the infamous Lutheran adulteress, Anne Boleyn, and perhaps not Henry's child at all.

This last factor ceased to matter in the course of time, as the exigencies of international diplomacy made both Charles V and Francis I eager to make an alliance with Henry. When the Duke of Norfolk held informal talks with the French ambassador in the summer of 1541, he said that he would never suggest that King Francis should marry his son to the daughter of a woman like Anne Boleyn.[9] But Norfolk bitterly hated Anne and all Protestants, and admitted to the ambassador that, as he was Anne Boleyn's uncle, he was particularly eager to show that he had no sympathy for her and no wish to help her child. Everyone else, including the foreign rulers, came to accept Elizabeth as an eligible royal bastard.

In 1538, soon after the death of Jane Seymour and before Henry married Anne of Cleves, Henry entered into negotiations with both Charles V and Francis I about possible marriages for himself and his two daughters. There were discussions about his marrying Charles's niece, the Duchess of Milan, or Mary of Guise or some other French lady of high rank. His daughter Mary was considered as a possible bride for Charles's son, Prince Philip of Spain, or for Francis's son, the Duke of Orleans. Henry suggested that Elizabeth should marry slightly less eminent husbands – the son of Charles's brother, King Ferdinand of Bohemia, or Emmanuel Philibert, Prince of Piedmont, the son of the Duke of Savoy. A few years earlier, Charles and his ambassador would have regarded as an insult any proposal that a Habsburg Prince should marry 'the little bastard'. But now Charles hoped to enlist Henry as his ally against France. Chapuys politely said that he could not discuss a possible marriage 'to the King's daughter by Anne Boleyn' because she was too young.[10]

When Elizabeth was nine, Henry wished to negotiate a marriage for her which would have had far-reaching repercussions and might have brought her for the first time into conflict with her future enemy, Mary Queen of Scots. In 1542 James V of Scotland, encouraged by his minister Cardinal Beaton, went to war with Henry; he posed as the champion of the Roman Catholic Church against the heretical realm of England. His armies crossed the Border, but were routed at Solway Moss. James died a fortnight after this disaster, leaving his daughter, Mary, who was only six days old, to succeed him as Queen of Scots.

Henry at first pursued a conciliatory policy towards Scotland. He tried to bribe the Scottish noblemen to support his proposal that Mary Queen of Scots should marry his son Prince Edward and should immediately be sent to

England to be brought up at his court. He offered the biggest bribe to James Hamilton, Earl of Arran, who became Regent of Scotland for the infant Queen. On 4 April 1543 he wrote to Arran, telling him that he had a daughter called the Lady Elizabeth, who was 'endowed with virtues and qualities agreeable with her estate', and that he would be prepared to condescend to her marriage with Arran's son. When this letter was read to Arran by Henry's ambassador, Sir Ralph Sadler, Arran was so overwhelmed by the honour that he took off his cap and expressed his gratitude; but it was a condition of the offer that Arran's son should be sent to be educated at Henry's court, which would in practice have made him a hostage for Arran's conduct. Arran avoided giving a direct answer to the proposal.[11]

As Arran, after four months, had still not committed himself, Henry made him an even more tempting offer. He wrote on 4 August that if the little Queen of Scots were sent to France, or married anyone except Prince Edward, he would recognise Arran as King of Scotland on condition that Arran's son married Elizabeth and came at once to live at the English court.[12] But anti-English feeling was rising in Scotland, and Arran told Sadler that unfortunately it was politically impossible for him to accept Henry's offer. In September the people of Edinburgh rose in indignation and repudiated the treaty which their representatives had signed for their Queen's marriage to Prince Edward. Henry sent his armies to ravage Scotland. They burned every house in Edinburgh except the castle, and on nearly every moonlit night for two years raided and burned the towns, villages, farms and abbeys along the Border in the Merse and Liddisdale.

Two years later, Elizabeth's name was associated for the first time with another of her future enemies, Philip II of Spain, who in 1545 was aged eighteen and Regent of Spain for his father Charles V during Charles's absence in the Netherlands. He had already been married, but his wife had recently died. In October 1545, Henry made tentative proposals for a marriage treaty with Charles. He suggested that the Emperor, who was a widower, should marry Mary; that Prince Edward should marry Charles's daughter; and that Elizabeth should marry Philip of Spain. Charles could not contemplate the marriages with Mary or Elizabeth as long as they were officially illegitimate. Elizabeth was also suggested as a bride for the King of Denmark's brother, the Duke of Holstein; but nothing came of the negotiations.[13]

Elizabeth's honourable position as a royal bastard was clearly recognised. At court the Lady Elizabeth's Grace came third in order of precedence among the ladies, after the Queen's Majesty and the Lady Mary's Grace, but before the Lady Anne of Cleves and the Lady Margaret Douglas, the daughter of Henry's sister the Dowager Queen of Scotland by her marriage to the Earl of Angus. When Francis I's sister Margaret, Queen of Navarre, wished to please Henry, she asked the English ambassador to send her the portraits of Mary and Elizabeth; and an eminent foreign physician, wishing to thank Henry for his favours, inquired after the health of his Queen, his son Prince Edward, and his two 'sweet daughters'.[14]

Although Elizabeth was sometimes at her own home at Hatfield, she was usually in Katherine Parr's household at court, being included among 'the Queen's ordinaries accustomed to be lodged within the King's Majesty's house'.[15] Katherine Parr, who was the most intelligent of Henry's six wives, probably had a greater influence than anyone else in forming Elizabeth's character and outlook. For four years, while Elizabeth was between the ages of eleven and fifteen, she spent much of her time with her stepmother.

Katherine was probably chiefly responsible for her excellent education. Most women, including girls of aristocratic families, received no academic education, and often never learned to read or write; but Henry VIII's daughters were among a number of notable exceptions to this rule. Elizabeth learned to speak and write perfectly in French and Italian, very fluently in Latin, and moderately well in Spanish and Greek. She became well-read in religious and classical literature, as well as learning the sewing, dancing, riding and deportment which were the necessary attributes of all high-born young ladies. Her sewing was particularly neat, and she sometimes gave garments which she had sewn herself to Prince Edward in the usual exchange of gifts on New Year's Day.

Despite the fact that Katherine Parr's former husband had been involved in the Pilgrimage of Grace, she herself had strong sympathies with Protestantism. She became Queen at the height of a new drive against the Protestant heretics. It was directed by Stephen Gardiner, the Bishop of Winchester, who was the leader of the conservative faction in Henry's Council; but though the Protestants blamed Gardiner for the persecution, it was authorised by Henry as part of his usual policy of striking alternatively, and often simultaneously, at the Papist traitors who challenged his position as Supreme Head of the Church in his realm, and at the Protestants with their new ideas which were unpopular with the majority of Englishmen and subversive of all authority. From time to time, a new royal decree would suppress the placing of candles before the images of saints, or some other established practice of the Church; then another decree would forbid anyone to challenge some other established doctrine or ceremony. The people were compelled to go as far, and no farther, than Henry ordered at any particular time; anyone who went either too far or not far enough was severely punished.

In the spring of 1543, Henry issued a new formulary of faith, which was known as the King's Book, and was more Catholic than the Bishops' Book which it replaced; and the reading of the English Bible was drastically restricted, because bible-reading was said to encourage arrogance, dissension, and 'carnal liberty'. No one was allowed to argue about the meaning of a passage in the Bible, or to read it aloud to other people; and no man under the rank of gentleman, and no woman of any rank, was allowed to read the Bible even privately to themselves.

Gardiner and his supporters aimed at Protestants in high places. They denounced Cranmer as a heretic, but Henry protected him. They found a group of heretics at Windsor, which included a canon of the chapel royal and one of Henry's musicians, as well as two citizens of the town. They were accused of denying the Real Presence, though almost the only evidence against one of them was that he had looked around the church during Mass, instead of gazing adoringly at the elevated Host. They were burned in the park at Windsor, within sight of the castle, a week after Henry married Katherine Parr.[16]

But the new Queen's household was a secret nest of Protestant heresy. She could do nothing to stop the persecution, but very cautiously she could try to ensure that her stepchildren, who might one day be King or Queen of England, were brought up to be sympathetic to the Protestants. She was unable to influence Mary, who was only four years younger than she was herself; but both Prince Edward, aged six, and the Lady Elizabeth, aged ten, could be moulded by Protestant tutors. Sir John Cheke was appointed to supervise the education of the royal children, and he chose Roger Ascham as Edward's tutor and William Grindal as Elizabeth's. Cheke, Ascham and Grindal were all secret Protestants.

Destiny had marked Elizabeth, even before she was born, to be the champion of the Protestant cause. It was her presence in Anne Boleyn's womb which had made Henry take the plunge at last in January 1533 and decide to repudiate the Papal supremacy. From the day of her birth, she had been acclaimed by the Protestants as the lawful heir to the throne, and reviled by the Papists as the bastard of the Lutheran concubine. But by the time that she was old enough to learn about religion, the Catholic reaction was in full swing, and it was thanks to Katherine Parr and the tutors that she became a devout Protestant. Through all the twists and turns of her diplomacy when she was Queen, and the ambiguities of her religious policy, she never wavered in her sincere devotion to the Protestant religion.

Her faith was very different from her father's. Henry VIII attended Mass five times a day, spending a few minutes in the chapel royal in the intervals between hunting and banqueting; he kept the fast days, and observed the ceremonies of the Catholic Church, always 'creeping to the Cross' on Good Friday. But while he observed these outward forms of religion, he changed his religious policy, encouraged Anabaptists abroad and persecuted them at home, burned Protestant heretics and had Catholic abbots hanged, drawn and quartered, only for his own selfish ends, to advance the interests of his diplomacy, to fill his treasury, or even to satisfy his personal pleasure. Elizabeth, unlike Henry, had a conscience, and sometimes made great personal sacrifices in order to do her duty to God and to her people.

In 1545 the authorities became aware of the activities of Anne Askew, who was the wife of a Lincolnshire gentleman named Kyme, but shocked the officials by leaving her husband and using her maiden name. She moved to London, where she secretly distributed Protestant books, and may have had contacts in the Queen's household. After being arrested and let off with a warning, she was imprisoned in the Tower in the summer of 1546 and savagely tortured in an attempt to force her to confess that several ladies of high rank were implicated in her heretical activities; but she endured the rack with great courage, and would neither recant nor reveal the names of her accomplices. On 16 July she was carried to Smithfield and fastened to the stake in a chair, as she could not stand after the racking, and was burned with two other heretics.[17] The authorities believed that three ladies of the Queen's privy chamber were heretics: Katherine's sister Anne, the wife of Sir William Herbert, who in Edward VI's reign was created Earl of Pembroke; her cousin, Lady Lane; and her stepdaughter, Lady Tyrwhit, who was the daughter of Katherine's first husband, Lord Borough.

According to John Foxe in his *Book of Martyrs*, Gardiner and his colleague Wriothesley, the Lord Chancellor, persuaded Henry to order that these three ladies, and the Queen herself, should be arrested and charged with heresy. Foxe, who seems to have had reliable inside information, describes how Katherine angered Henry by arguing with him about theology, and that Henry then agreed to Wriothesley's suggestion that she and her ladies should be sent to the Tower. But Henry's physician, Dr Wendy, who was a Protestant sympathiser, got to hear of it, and warned Katherine. She ordered her ladies to get rid of their banned heretical books, and went to the King, humbly apologising for having contradicted him in argument, and admitting that he had been right. Henry then rescinded the order for her arrest, and reviled Wriothesley for having dared to advise it.[18]

We do not know the date of this incident, but if, as seems probable, it was during Anne Askew's last imprisonment in the summer of 1546, Elizabeth was in Katherine's household at the time. She was nearly thirteen, and no longer really a child. Girls developed early in the sixteenth century, and princesses learned at an early age the art of self-preservation at the court of Henry VIII. They learned how to be humble, obedient, and completely submissive on the surface; how to lie, and use deceitful devices, including the faked secret letter which they knew would be intercepted by the authorities, in which they wrote what they wanted the King to think that they really believed; and they learned to admire the martyrs who, unlike themselves, did not submit and dissemble, but openly bore witness to their beliefs and to the true Protestant faith, and endured torture and death in the fire. They had a guilty conscience about the martyrs, even though they could try to justify their own submission by the well-known argument that a man should not try to run before he can walk, and must not be so presumptuous as to seek

[34]

martyrdom until he was sure that God had called him to make the ultimate sacrifice for His cause. They knew that the blood of the martyrs is the seed of the Church.

⟫ 3 ⟪

THE LORD ADMIRAL

I N the autumn of 1546, Henry made another turn. Less than six weeks
after he had burned Anne Askew for denying the Real Presence, he
announced at a supper party that he intended to repudiate the Real
Presence and abolish the Mass, which would be replaced by a Protestant
communion service. He did not, in fact, carry out his intention during the
remaining five months of his life; but he destroyed the Catholic faction in his
Council, driving Gardiner from court and arresting the Duke of Norfolk and
his son, the Earl of Surrey, on a charge of high treason. Surrey was beheaded,
but Henry died on the night of 27 January 1547 before he had time to sign
Norfolk's death warrant.

A month before his death he had made his will, in which he exercised the
power which had been granted to him by Parliament of naming his successor
to the crown. He bequeathed the throne to his son Prince Edward, and failing
him and his issue, to any children whom he might have by Katherine Parr or
by any future wife; failing them, to his daughter Mary and her issue, on
condition that she did not marry without the consent of his executors; and in
default of Mary and her issue, to Elizabeth, subject to the same restraint on
marriage. After Elizabeth and her issue, it was to pass to Lady Jane Grey and
her sisters, the grandchildren of Henry's sister Mary and her husband the
Duke of Suffolk.

Henry appointed sixteen executors, and directed that they were to form a
Regency Council during Edward's infancy. Thirteen of them were Protestant
sympathisers. One was Jane Seymour's brother Edward, Earl of Hertford,
who had distinguished himself as the commander of Henry's armies in
Scotland. He immediately took charge, and pushed the other executors into
the background. Two days after Henry's death he rode to Hertford, where
the nine-year-old King was staying, and took him to Elizabeth's house at
Hatfield. Here he told both the royal children that Henry had died, and they
showed the appropriate grief.

Within a few weeks, Edward Seymour was created Duke of Somerset and

Lord Protector for the infant King. He relaxed the severities of Henry's government, and the new reign began in an atmosphere of hope and freedom. This freedom went to the head of the London Protestants, and the impetuous young heretics began to break the images in the churches and to desecrate the Host. Somerset and Cranmer, who guided his religious policy, would not tolerate this anarchy, and insisted as strongly as they had done under Henry VIII on the duty of obedience to the royal authority. They firmly ordered the Protestants to make no innovations in religion till the Lord Protector and his Council introduced official changes. They made it clear that they would punish disrespect to the Sacrament; but images were abolished within a few weeks, and other Protestant innovations were introduced later in the year.

When Parliament met, the Heresy Acts, under which heretics could be burned, were repealed; and by the spring of 1549, Cranmer had promulgated the Book of Common Prayer, in which the Latin Mass was replaced by the communion service in English, and the doctrine of transubstantiation and the Real Presence was officially condemned as erroneous. Catholics who refused to attend the new English service were to be fined, and for repeated offences could be sentenced to short terms of imprisonment. This was the only persecution which they suffered; but despite the repeal of the heresy statutes, two Protestant Anabaptists were burned as heretics in the reign of Edward VI for denying the doctrine of the Trinity.

Under Somerset and Cranmer, the Church of England officially adopted doctrines for which Protestants had been burned as heretics by Henry VIII; but the government propagandists continued to praise Henry as a great King, and claimed that they were merely carrying further the policy which he had initiated before his death. They blamed Gardiner, not Henry, for the persecution of Protestants in Henry's reign. On the other hand, Gardiner and the Catholics who opposed the Protestant innovations also claimed to be pursuing Henry's policy. Only a handful of Protestant extremists, and an equally small number of secret Papist sympathisers, condemned Henry as a cruel tyrant. Most Englishmen admired him as the patriot King who had ravaged Scotland and captured Boulogne. This attitude of officialdom and of the people must be borne in mind in assessing Elizabeth's attitude to her father after his death. Whatever her real feelings about him may have been, she would in any case have thought it prudent and proper to glorify his memory and to express her great grief at his death.

Somerset's younger brother, Thomas Seymour, had also risen to prominence during Henry's last years, though he had not reached the heights which Somerset himself had attained. He had been a favourite of Henry's, and had distinguished himself as a soldier on land and sea. At Edward VI's accession he was created Lord Seymour of Sudeley and appointed Lord High Admiral of England. He was the kind of dashing, impetuous braggart who appeared not only as a character in Shakespeare's plays but also in real life in Tudor England. His contemporaries rightly called him ambitious, but he did not scheme to gain political power in order to further his religious beliefs, or even primarily, like most courtiers, to enrich himself, but out of a desire for adventure and success. He was not on good terms with his brother the Lord Protector, and the rivalry between the brothers played a big part in Thomas Seymour's rise and fall.

He was probably in love with Katherine Parr, and she was certainly in love with him, before she married Henry VIII. Now that Henry was dead, she was again a widow; but the remarriage of a Queen Dowager was always thought to be shocking, and was dangerous for her new husband. Thomas Seymour nevertheless married Katherine Parr within four months of Henry's death; but before doing so, he apparently considered the possibility of marrying Elizabeth instead. Elizabeth was developing into a handsome young woman, with a tall, stately figure and a clear skin, though she lacked the fair complexion which was so favoured by her contemporaries. She had a fine head of red hair, and beautiful hands which she displayed to great effect. The Lord Admiral fancied the idea of not only marrying an attractive bride but of impressing and shocking the courtiers and the people by winning the hand of a royal Princess who, though she was still officially illegitimate, was third in line to the throne under the terms of Henry VIII's will.

Leti published the text of a delightful proposal of marriage which Seymour wrote to Elizabeth, and an even more delightful reply from Elizabeth refusing him.[1] They are models of how a passionate wooer should propose to a princess, and how a demure young lady should courteously refuse him; but the letters are of very doubtful authenticity, especially as Elizabeth stated, when the matter was investigated two years later, that she had heard a rumour that Seymour had thought of marrying her before he married Katherine Parr, which would have been a very misleading statement if she had in fact received a written proposal of marriage from him.

Soon after Thomas Seymour married Katherine Parr, Elizabeth went to live with them in their household in Chelsea. It is difficult to be sure just what happened between Elizabeth and Seymour in Chelsea, because all the evidence about it comes from statements made by people who were prisoners in the Tower after Seymour had been arrested on a charge of high treason, and who therefore wished to curry favour with the government and to shield themselves and their friends. But they are probably true enough. According to these statements, Thomas Seymour flirted with Elizabeth under the eyes of his wife, and engaged in boisterous and amorous play with her. He used to come into her room early in the morning, when she was still in bed, and try to kiss her and slap her on the buttocks; when she retreated further into the great bed to escape him, he came into the bed after her. Although she rose earlier in the morning, so as to be dressed and working at her writing desk by the time he arrived, he most improperly came into her room in his dressing gown and slippers.

At first Katherine Parr did not object to her husband's frolics with

Elizabeth. On one occasion, when Seymour chased and caught Elizabeth in the garden, Katherine helped hold her while Seymour cut her dress into strips, so as to get a look at her body and underclothes. But she was not so pleased when she came into a room one day and found Elizabeth in Seymour's arms, while he kissed her passionately.[2] She realised that the affair was becoming serious, and also realised, as did the ladies of her household, that there was a risk of a dangerous scandal. She decided that Elizabeth must be sent away, and Elizabeth and her servants moved to a house in Cheshunt before returning to Hatfield.

We do not know what Elizabeth felt about Thomas Seymour and his behaviour. Several of her modern biographers have suggested that her decision in later life to live and die a virgin Queen was due to the fear of sex which Seymour's brutal lovemaking had aroused in her; while one writer of an older generation believed that her flirtations with the men at her court were the result of her moral sense having been perverted by Seymour's debauchery.[3] It is impossible to psychoanalyse Elizabeth, nearly four hundred years after her death, on the evidence of frightened witnesses in a treason investigation. We can only guess that Elizabeth was both stimulated and frightened by Seymour's amorous advances, and that she was also very conscious that if the rumours about their antics began to spread, she might be in a very dangerous situation.

It was during her residence in Katherine Parr's household that Elizabeth first became acquainted with William Cecil, a young man of twenty-seven who was Somerset's secretary and MP for Stamford. He was a well-read intellectual, as familiar with the classical studies of the humanists as with law and divinity; and he was sympathetic to Protestant doctrines, and had written a preface to a religious tract, *The Lamentations of a Sinner*, by Katherine Parr. Elizabeth had got to know him before August 1548, when her governess, Kate Ashley, wrote to Cecil to ask his help in arranging the exchange of an English prisoner-of-war in Scotland. Elizabeth added a postscript to Cecil which she signed: 'Your friend Elizabeth'.[4] Two years later, she appointed Cecil to supervise the management of her property at a salary of £20 a year, which is about £10,000 in terms of money today; and he continued to perform the duties of this office in his spare time after he became Secretary of State a few months later.

Katherine Parr became pregnant by Thomas Seymour. On 31 July 1548 Elizabeth wrote her a respectful letter praying for her safe delivery. She playfully wrote that she hoped that Seymour 'shall be diligent to give me knowledge from time to time how his busy child doth; and if I were at his birth, no doubt I would see him beaten for the trouble he hath put you to.'[5] But in September, a few days after Elizabeth's fifteenth birthday, Katherine Parr died in childbirth at the age of thirty-six. Her baby also died.

Thomas Seymour immediately resumed his attentions to Elizabeth. He offered her the use of his London house, and suggested that he should visit her at Hatfield. Her ladies persuaded her that this would be unwise; but rumours grew about a forthcoming marriage between them. When Elizabeth was asked by her cofferer, Thomas Parry, whether she would consent to marry Seymour if the King's Council permitted it, she refused to reply, and asked him why he wanted to know.[6]

On 17 January 1549 the Lord Admiral was arrested on a charge of high treason at the orders of his brother the Lord Protector. He was accused of plotting to overthrow the Lord Protector and the Council and to seize the King's person; and one of the thirty-three charges against him was of planning to marry Elizabeth 'by secret and crafty means . . . to the danger of the King's Majesty's person'.[7] He was sent to the Tower. Kate Ashley and Parry were also sent to the Tower, accused of being Seymour's accomplices in the plot to marry Elizabeth; and Kate Ashley's husband was sent to the Fleet prison. Elizabeth herself was held under house arrest at Hatfield. Somerset and the Council sent Sir Robert Tyrwhit to interrogate her.

Elizabeth was in a difficult situation. She obviously did not wish to say anything which might incriminate Seymour, her servants, or herself; but she must not, by obstinately refusing to answer questions, arouse suspicion, or risk being accused of contempt of the King, the Lord Protector, and the Council. When Tyrwhit told her that Mrs Ashley and Parry had been sent to the Tower, 'she was marvellously abashed, and did weep very tenderly a long time'; but she told him nothing. He warned her that, being but a subject, she might find herself in a dangerous position, though if she made a full statement, the Lord Protector would deal leniently with her on account of her youth. He tried to blacken Kate Ashley's character, and to encourage Elizabeth to save herself by throwing the blame on her; but he failed, and wrote to Somerset: 'In no way she will not confess any practice by Mistress Ashley or the cofferer concerning my Lord Admiral; and yet I do see it in her face that she is guilty, and do perceive as yet she will abide more storms ere she accuse Mistress Ashley'.[8]

At her second interrogation, Tyrwhit decided to use gentle methods, and felt that he was more successful, especially after he had told her that Mrs Ashley had been released from the Tower and was confined under house arrest in Westminster. 'All I have gotten yet is by gentle persuasion', he wrote to Somerset. 'I do assure your Grace she hath a very good wit and nothing is gotten of her but by great policy'.[9]

After further questioning, Tyrwhit persuaded Elizabeth to sign a statement; but she admitted only that Mrs Ashley had told her that Seymour wished to marry her, both before he had married Katherine Parr and after her death, and that she knew that rumours were circulating about her and him. She asked Somerset to suppress the new rumours that she had been sent to the Tower and that she was pregnant by Seymour, for 'no such rumours should be spread of any of the King's Majesty's sisters, as I am, though unworthy'.[10]

Somerset and the Council appointed Lady Tyrwhit to replace Kate Ashley as Elizabeth's governess. Elizabeth was very angry, and told Tyrwhit that Mrs Ashley was her governess and she would have no other. When he told her that the Council insisted that his wife should be her governess, 'she took the matter so heavily that she wept all that night and lowered all the next day'.[11] This was the first of many recorded cases in which she reacted to a crisis by weeping and indulging in outbursts of anger. Those who observed her, and future historians, often assumed that she was play-acting as part of a tactical ploy. If it was a tactic, it was an unsuccessful one, for it usually created a bad impression, and sometimes landed her in serious difficulties, at least in the short run. The truth was that Elizabeth was an emotional woman, and often acted on impulse, and not from cunning political calculation.

Elizabeth soon changed her mind about Lady Tyrwhit, and came to like her. She often changed her mind.

On 7 March, after Kate Ashley had been in detention for six weeks, Elizabeth wrote to Somerset and asked him to be merciful to Kate and her husband.[12] The Ashleys and Parry were soon released; but Thomas Seymour was condemned as a traitor by Act of Parliament without being allowed to appear in his own defence, and was beheaded on 20 March. According to Leti, Elizabeth commented, on the day of Seymour's execution: 'This day died a man with much wit and very little judgment'.[13]

Somerset did not survive for long after he sent his brother to the block. In the summer of 1549 a formidable Catholic revolt broke out in Cornwall and Devon in protest against the church services in English which had been introduced by the Book of Common Prayer; the rebels demanded the restoration of the Catholic Mass and the burning of Protestant heretics. At the same time a rebellion against land enclosures broke out in Norfolk, where many of the people were Protestants. The government suppressed both the revolts; but the nobility and the landowning class thought that Somerset's liberal policy had encouraged the discontent, and in October the Lord Protector was overthrown by his colleagues on the Council. He was replaced as the King's chief minister by John Dudley, Earl of Warwick. Somerset was sent to the Tower, and though he was released a few months later and restored to his seat on the Council, Warwick was only biding his time. In January 1552 Somerset was beheaded as a traitor.

Warwick's government continued Somerset's Protestant policy, and carried the Reformation still further. The Book of Common Prayer of 1549 was followed by the second Book of Common Prayer of 1552, which made more drastic innovations in the church services. Many of the bishops, though they had accepted the repudiation of Papal supremacy under Henry VIII, opposed the Protestant doctrines and practices which were introduced under Edward VI, and were imprisoned and deprived of their sees. These included Gardiner, Heath, and Bonner, the Bishop of London, who had been an active persecutor of Protestants in Henry's reign.

The most troublesome opposition came from the Lady Mary. She was brave, obstinate, intolerant, incapable of compromise, convinced that she was right and her opponents wrong, and determined, at whatever cost, to adhere to her opinions and force others to accept them. A devout Catholic and rigid conservative, she believed that the established Church and all the traditional values which State and Church had upheld for ages past, were threatened by the new subversive Protestant religion which the emissaries of Satan had spread throughout Christendom. She was afraid of no one, not even of her formidable father; and she had only submitted in 1536, after he had threatened her with death if she continued to resist him, because her friend, the Emperor's ambassador Chapuys, had with difficulty persuaded her that the Pope and the Emperor believed that a feigned submission was the proper course for her to pursue.

If she had been prepared to defy Henry VIII for three years, she was not likely to be intimidated by the quarrelling counsellors of the infant Edward VI. She did not admit that she believed in Papal supremacy, but took her stand on Henry VIII's religious settlement, denying the right of counsellors to introduce innovations in religion during the King's infancy. When the Book of Common Prayer was introduced and the Mass suppressed, she refused to comply, and her chaplains continued to celebrate Mass in her houses in Hertfordshire, Essex and Norfolk. The chaplains, and she herself, laid themselves open to prosecution under the Act of Parliament and to fines and short terms of imprisonment; but Charles V threatened to go to war if Mary was prevented from having Mass in her house.

Warwick at first gave way, but in August 1551 at last decided to be firm with Mary. He sent the Lord Chancellor and other Privy Councillors to Mary's house at Ruthall in Essex to inform her that she must obey the law in future. She shouted defiance at them from the window of the house as they stood in the courtyard below, and taunted them with the mildness of their laws against Catholics, which would never deter her chaplains. 'The pain of your laws is but imprisonment for a short time, and if they will refuse to say Mass for fear of that imprisonment they may do therein as they will; but none of your new service shall be used in my house.'[14] Three officers of her household were arrested, but she herself remained free, and continued to hear Mass in secret in her house throughout Edward's reign.

Warwick and the Council had no such trouble with Elizabeth. She happily accepted all the Protestant innovations which were introduced. Although the government did not publicise their difficulties with Mary, it became known in London that Mary was a Catholic and Elizabeth a Protestant. This reputation for Protestantism was probably a more important factor than her young and graceful appearance and personality in making her very popular with at least one section of the population of London.

It did not endear her to her sister. Mary already had reason to feel resentment against Elizabeth, the baby whom she had been forced to serve as a lady-in-waiting in the time of Anne Boleyn. Now Elizabeth, by becoming a Protestant, was offending not against herself but against God.

For nearly a year after the execution of Thomas Seymour, Elizabeth lived quietly at Hatfield; but in January 1550, three months after the fall of Somerset, she came to court and was received with great favour; in Mary's absence, she took precedence over all other ladies in the land. The Emperor's ambassador, van der Delft, wrote to Charles that though Princess Mary was too virtuous to be loved by those who wished to exterminate religion, Lady Elizabeth was more to their taste.[15]

Elizabeth remained high in favour with the new régime. By November 1550 Scheyvfe, who had replaced van der Delft as Charles V's ambassador, was reporting to Charles's sister, Mary of Hungary, the Regent of the Netherlands, that Warwick was thinking of divorcing his wife so that he could marry Elizabeth and reign with her as King and Queen after Edward's death. When Elizabeth came to court again in January 1551, escorted by her household servants and a hundred horsemen of the King's guard, Scheyvfe reported that she was treated very honourably by the Council because she had adopted the new religion and had become a very great lady. The French and Venetian ambassadors called on her, and Scheyvfe thought that it would be tactful if he visited her too; but he was told that she was with the King and could not receive him.[16]

She made a good impression on the devout Protestants by dressing more soberly than many of the other ladies at court. The Protestant propagandist, John Foxe, remembered and wrote approvingly more than ten years later that she had avoided extravagances in dress at the festivities at Hampton Court and Whitehall on the occasion of the visit of Mary of Guise, the Queen Dowager of Scotland, when she travelled through England on her journey from France to Scotland in the autumn of 1551. 'When all the other ladies of the court flourished in their bravery, with their hair frowsened, and curled, and double curled, yet she altered nothing, but, to the same of them all, kept her old maidenly shamefacedness'.[17]

She was aged eighteen, and there were many rumours in 1551 about possible marriages. There was talk of her marrying Jean de Bourbon, Duke of Enghien, the brother of Antoine de Bourbon, who had married Jeanne d'Albret and later acquired the title of King of Navarre; but only a few weeks later, the prospective husband was said to be the Duke of Aumale, the brother of the Duke of Guise. The King of Denmark's son was another possibility. But there were rumours that Elizabeth did not wish to marry. In March 1552, when she rode through London with her escort to visit Edward VI at St James's, Scheyvfe wrote that William Herbert, Earl of Pembroke, who was a prominent member of the Privy Council and had recently become a widower, had proposed marriage to Elizabeth, but that she had refused him.[18]

It was perhaps because of her troublesome attitude about marriage that she fell from favour with the King and Northumberland. In the spring of 1552 she was in great favour with Edward, to whom she had always been close when they were children, and was being treated with all honour by Northumberland and his ministers; but a year later Edward and Northumberland decided to exclude her from the crown.

Edward VI, at the age of fifteen, was very intelligent, very determined, and very Protestant; but he knew that he was dying of consumption. He was alarmed at the prospect of being succeeded by Mary, who was heir to the throne under the terms of Henry VIII's will, and he and Northumberland worked out a plan to exclude her and leave the crown to Lady Jane Grey, who was the granddaughter of Henry VIII's sister Mary and who had married Northumberland's son, Lord Guilford Dudley, though under the provisions of Henry VIII's will she came only third, after Mary and Elizabeth.

In May 1553, after consulting no one except Northumberland, Edward confronted his counsellors with a document which he had drawn up, bequeathing the throne to Jane Grey and after her to her sisters. The document stated that Edward's two half-sisters, Mary and Elizabeth, were excluded because they were both illegitimate, as Henry VIII's marriages to Catherine of Aragon and Anne Boleyn had been declared void by the ecclesiastical courts; and even if they had been legitimate they would be excluded, because of what was said to be an ancient custom in England, that Kings could not be succeeded by relatives of the half-blood. The document stipulated that if Mary and Elizabeth accepted these provisions, they were to be paid an annuity of £1,000 a year and a gift of £10,000 when they married.[19]

When Edward ordered his counsellors to subscribe the document, they were reluctant to do so. The Judges thought it was illegal, because it contravened the terms of Henry VIII's will, which had been given force of law by the provisions of an Act of Parliament. But the counsellors eventually agreed to sign after Edward had passionately exhorted them to do so in a series of private talks with them from his sickbed; and once the Council had agreed, there was no difficulty in persuading the Judges, the Lord Mayor of London, and other dignitaries to sign.

Edward died at Greenwich on 6 July 1553. Four days later, Jane Grey was proclaimed Queen in London; but Mary took refuge in Framlingham Castle in Norfolk, and called on the people to support her cause. Charles V and the ambassadors whom he had sent to England were convinced that Northumberland, with the forces under his command, would quickly suppress all opposition and capture Mary. But she rejected their advice to submit to Queen Jane, and to their surprise and delight the people rallied to her support. Within a few days she was joined by 40,000 men at Framlingham. The crews of the ships that Northumberland sent to the Norfolk coast, to prevent her escape by sea to the Netherlands, mutinied and went over to her side; and when Ridley, the Protestant Bishop of London, preached against her at Paul's Cross in London, and denounced her and Elizabeth as bastards, he was shouted down by the crowd.

Protestants as well as Catholics supported Mary. Hooper, the staunchly Protestant Bishop of Gloucester and Worcester, urged his congregation to fight for Mary, because she was the rightful Queen, and many Protestants all over the country gave her at least passive support. The Protestants had become disgusted with Northumberland's corruption and the way in which he used Protestant innovations in religion as an excuse to enrich himself; and they remained true, at great cost to themselves, to the Protestant doctrine which they had been preaching for thirty years: the Christian must not rebel against the King, the Lord's anointed, but must passively submit to martyrdom if this was the King's will.

Northumberland assembled an army and marched against Mary; but when he reached Cambridge he heard that a majority of the Privy Council in London had carried out a *coup d'état* and ended the reign of Queen Jane nine days after she had been proclaimed. On 19 July two of the Privy Councillors, the Earl of Arundel and Lord Paget, both of whom were Protestants, persuaded their colleagues to go over to Mary's side, and ordered the Lord Mayor to proclaim Mary as Queen at the cross in Cheapside. 'There was such a shout of the people', wrote a Londoner in his diary, 'with casting up of caps and crying "God save Queen Mary!" that the style of the proclamation could not be heard . . . All the people and citizens of the city of London for so joyful news made great and many fires through all the streets and lanes within the said city, with setting tables in the streets and banqueting also, with all the bells ringing in every parish church in London, till ten of the clock at night, that the inestimable joys and rejoicing of the people cannot be reported.'[20]

When Northumberland heard about the events in London, he decided to submit, and himself proclaimed Mary as Queen in the market place in Cambridge. It was at least forty-eight hours too late to save his head. Mary promptly sent a gentleman to arrest him and take him to the Tower. During the next week, many of Jane's supporters went to Framlingham to acknowledge Mary as Queen. She pardoned most of them, but a few were arrested. On 26 July Northumberland's son, Lord Robert Dudley, was taken to the Tower with Bishop Ridley, where they joined Northumberland and Lord Robert's brothers and Jane herself.[21]

What did Elizabeth do during the nine-day reign of Queen Jane? It seems certain that, as so often at times of crisis, she did nothing. Leti published a letter which he says she wrote to Jane's Council, protesting against Edward's devise of the crown to Jane;[22] but as the letter contains errors of fact which she would not have made, and as there is no record in the Council minutes of such a letter having been received or of any action being taken about Elizabeth, it is unlikely that she wrote and sent the letter. According to the historian William Camden, who is a reliable contemporary authority, she refused to accept the legacy of £1,000 per year which Edward had bequeathed to her under his devise, until she had heard what Mary would do about her legacy;[23] and she apparently claimed illness as a ground for remaining inactive at Hatfield while Mary and Jane fought for the crown. She had nothing to gain, and could only lose, whatever the result of the struggle. If Jane and Northumberland won, England would remain Protestant, and Elizabeth could continue to live comfortably in retirement and worship according to her beliefs, but she would be for ever excluded from the throne. If Mary won, Henry VIII's will, and her right under it, would presumably remain in force, but a sister who hated her and would persecute her religion would come to power.

She waited for ten days after the issue had been decided, and then on 29 July rode to London escorted by a thousand horsemen. After spending the night at her town residence of Somerset Place in the Strand between London and Westminster, she rode with her escort through the city next day and out at Aldgate on her way to meet Mary, who was slowly advancing from Norfolk. On 3 August Mary entered London in triumph with her supporters; Elizabeth rode next behind her. They passed the Tower, where Gardiner, the Duke of Norfolk, and other Catholics were still in the prisons where they had been confined by the Protestants in Edward's reign, along with the new intake of Protestant supporters of Jane Grey. Mary pardoned the Catholic prisoners as she passed the Tower, and immediately appointed Gardiner to be her Lord Chancellor.[24]

Mary was received with great enthusiasm as she rode through London, where the streets had been decorated with banners bearing the slogan 'Vox populi vox Dei'.[25] It was the greatest defeat which had ever been inflicted on the Protestant cause in Europe.

⟫ 4 ⟪

THE TOWER

W HEN Edward VI became King, the Lord Protector and Council ordered the Protestants to make no religious innovations and to obey the law which enforced the Catholic doctrines and practices until they were altered by the proper legal means. Mary adopted a different policy. She did not recognise the validity of any law that violated the doctrines of the Catholic Church, and she announced that the law which forbade the Catholic service of the Mass, and punished those who celebrated and attended it, was not to be enforced. One judge, who claimed that he was bound to enforce this law until it was repealed by Parliament, was arrested at Mary's orders.[1]

At court, the Catholic Mass was celebrated in Mary's chapel royal, and was attended by all the courtiers except Elizabeth and Anne of Cleves. Mary spoke to Anne of Cleves, who thereafter attended Mass; but when she urged Elizabeth to come to Mass, Elizabeth said that she was a Protestant, and that it would be against her conscience to go to Mass until she was converted to the Catholic religion. Her absence from Mass was noted, not only by the Emperor's ambassador, Simon Renard, and by the French ambassador, Antoine de Noailles, but by everyone at court, and news of it spread in London.[2]

Charles V had advised Mary to submit to Northumberland, but he was not slow to take advantage of her miraculous triumph. He had done all he could to help her during her twenty years' ordeal, and he was now to gain his reward. He proposed that Mary should marry his son, Prince Philip of Spain. Mary was thirty-seven, and her strong religious feelings made her recoil in disgust at the idea of sex; but she was prepared to do her duty to the Church by marrying Philip in order to provide an heir to the throne.

Charles considered the marriage of Philip and Mary to be his greatest diplomatic triumph during his thirty-seven years' reign. For most of those years he had been at war with France, and he and Francis I had continually tried to win England over to their side. Now the Queen of England would be

[47]

his devoted daughter-in-law, who signed her letters to him 'Your most humble daughter, sister and cousin, Mary'; and England was firmly on his side against King Henry II of France.

Charles and Renard gave Mary two pieces of advice: to execute as traitors all the leading supporters of Jane Grey, and anyone who threatened, or might threaten, her position; and to do nothing to force the Catholic religion on her people. She should have Mass celebrated in the chapel royal for herself and her court, but should publicly declare that she would make no change for the time being in the established Protestant religion. She should only introduce changes very gradually and cautiously when the opportunity presented itself.[3] Charles was persecuting Protestants with great severity in the Netherlands; but he thought that if Mary tried to enforce Catholicism too soon on the English people, they would rebel and blame the Spaniards, which would endanger the marriage alliance between Philip and Mary.

Mary refused to follow his advice on either point. Northumberland and two of his closest associates were executed in August; but she refused to put to death Jane Grey and her husband Guilford Dudley, or any of the other prisoners, and she pardoned nearly all Jane's supporters. On the other hand, she insisted, at whatever cost, on enforcing the immediate conversion of England to Catholicism, for though she was prepared to pardon offences against herself, she would not pardon offences against God. She would at once reinstate the Catholic religion as it existed at the time of Henry VIII's death, and as soon as possible reunite the realm to Rome. Charles prevented her from doing this immediately by refusing to give an exit permit to Cardinal Pole, who after twenty-five years of exile was preparing, in a monastery in Northern Italy, to return to England as Papal Legate.

Mary reluctantly agreed to issue a proclamation on 12 August in which she announced that though she hoped that her subjects would follow her advice and become Catholics, she would not compel them to do so by force.[4] But the young Protestant hotheads in London reacted to the illegal restoration of the Mass and the Catholic propaganda with the usual suicidal folly of extremists, and played right into Mary's hands. On the day after the proclamation, Sunday 13 August, Dr Bourn preached at Paul's Cross. He was the Catholic chaplain of Bonner, who had been released from prison and restored to his old position as Bishop of London. When Bourn praised Bonner in his sermon, a mob of furious Protestants shouted him down, and one of them threw a dagger at him, but missed. Two eminent Protestant clergymen, John Rogers and John Bradford, intervened and escorted Bourn to safety. The authorities retaliated by arresting Rogers and Bradford, whom they accused of inciting the riot.[5]

There were more arrests of 'seditious preachers' before the end of the month, and prominent Protestants were rounded up throughout the country. In the first week of September the aged Protestant preacher, Latimer, who was living in retirement in Warwickshire, was ordered to appear before the

Privy Council. The counsellors sent him to the Tower 'for his seditious demeanour' at the hearing. The normally cautious Archbishop Cranmer, who had reluctantly agreed to sign King Edward's devise of the crown to Jane Grey, was so moved to indignation at the illegal celebration of the Mass that he wrote a declaration against it, which was printed, apparently without his permission, and circulated in London. He was sent to the Tower.[6]

A violent propaganda campaign was launched against the Protestants in official and semi-official pamphlets. Married priests and their wives were singled out for particularly fierce attacks. Their marriages were regarded as void and their wives as harlots; and the propaganda portrayed not only the wives of Protestant priests but all Protestant women as shameless hussies who fornicated with every Protestant man they met, and were presumptuous enough to have ideas of their own about religion.[7]

The Protestants who had supported Mary against Jane Grey now turned against her in less than a month; and Elizabeth reaped the benefit of her inaction and neutrality during the struggle between Jane and Mary. The many Protestants who had been disgusted with Northumberland, and thought that Jane was his pawn, had an alternative princess to whom they could look for leadership against both Northumberland and Mary – a princess who was known to be a Protestant and was refusing to go to Mass in the chapel royal. The situation was dangerous for Elizabeth. Before the end of August Renard wrote to Mary and warned her not to trust Elizabeth, as she was a Protestant. 'She seems to be clinging to the new religion out of policy, to attract and win the support of those who are of this religion, if she decides to plot. We may be mistaken in suspecting her of this, but at this early stage it is safer to forestall than to be forestalled'.[8]

It was in this atmosphere, with leading Protestants being arrested nearly every day, that Elizabeth asked for an audience with the Queen. Mary made her wait for two days, and then received her in a gallery in the palace at Richmond. Elizabeth went on her knees to Mary, and said that she had been brought up as a Protestant, but asked for Catholic books which would show her the error of her ways. Mary said that she hoped that Elizabeth would come to Mass in the chapel royal on 8 September, the Feast of the Nativity of the Virgin Mary; and Elizabeth, after asking to be excused on the grounds that she was ill and was suffering from stomach pains, eventually agreed to come, and attended Mass for the first time on the feast day.[9]

Mary, Gardiner and Renard did not believe that she was sincere. They interpreted her initial refusal to go to Mass, and her subsequent conversion, as a clever political tactic designed to save herself while encouraging the Protestants to think that she was a convinced Protestant at heart. Gardiner told Renard that 'they had been at Lady Elizabeth to overcome her and draw her from her error', and that she had agreed to go to Mass, but that they thought that 'she is dissembling, the better to play her game'.[10] Their fears were confirmed when Elizabeth did not go to Mass on the next Sunday after the Nativity of Our Lady;[11] but this was only a last spasm of resistance, for after this she attended regularly.

Elizabeth's conversion, whether sincere or no, was useful to Mary, for the Queen had summoned Parliament to meet in October so that religion could be changed and the Mass re-established by statute; and she was expecting opposition from MPs. Noailles wrote to Henry II that though it was thought that Elizabeth had gone to Mass 'more for fear of the danger and peril which were facing her than from good devotion', Mary had since then shown her every favour, because she knew that the news that Elizabeth had gone to Mass would be a great help in persuading Parliament to vote in favour of re-establishing the Catholic religion. Renard had the same thought. He wrote to Charles V on 9 September that her attendance at Mass on the Feast of the Nativity of Our Lady, even if she was dissimulating, would nevertheless be an example which would 'promote religion still further.'[12]

Twenty years before, Mary had resisted Henry VIII for three years before submitting when threatened with life imprisonment and perhaps with death; and she had never given in to the pressure in Edward VI's reign to attend the Protestant religious service. Elizabeth gave in to Mary after less than six weeks. But their positions and their characters were different. When Mary faced persecution, she knew that the Emperor supported her, and that she could rely on the secret advice of his ambassador; and she knew that large sections of the population, almost certainly a majority, agreed with her. She was absolutely convinced that her persecutors were instruments of the Devil and that she was right in maintaining the religion in which she had been brought up as a child and which had existed in England for a thousand years. Elizabeth had no powerful foreign prince to support her. She was popular with many Protestants, but some of them had supported Northumberland's plan to oust her in favour of Jane Grey and had denounced her as a bastard. She could not be sure that the Protestant religion in which she believed was the only true religion. It was, after all, the 'new learning', as the Catholics called it, contravening the accepted doctrines of the older generation. Elizabeth herself and all other subjects had gone to Mass seven years before, for her revered father, the glorious King Henry VIII, had attended Mass all his life and burned the Protestants who reviled it.

Elizabeth was not the stuff of which martyrs are made, and she was not a religious bigot like her sister. If she resisted, she faced the prospect of a far more terrible fate than Mary could have feared under Edward VI or even under Henry VIII. Elizabeth could not taunt Mary, as Mary had taunted Edward's Privy Councillors, with the mildness of the laws which punished religious dissidents only with fines and short terms of imprisonment. A refusal by Elizabeth to go to Mass might be treated as heresy; and though the heresy statutes had not yet been re-enacted, she knew how Catholic sovereigns treated heretics. She could not be sure that even her rank would save her from the fire. It is not surprising that at a time of rising anti-

Protestant hysteria and in her unenviable situation she capitulated and went to Mass on that first and fatal occasion on 8 September 1553.

Mary was crowned in Westminster Abbey on 1 October, after the traditional coronation procession from the Tower. The service included all the old ceremonies of the Catholic Church. Elizabeth, who rode in a coach with Anne of Cleves in the procession immediately behind the Queen's coach, was given precedence over all other subjects at the coronation and the banquet. She was the first to take the oath of allegiance to the Queen; but Renard believed that she had not taken the oath sincerely, and was in secret contact with the French ambassador. He repeatedly warned Mary that Elizabeth was dangerous, and he had little difficulty in persuading her, for she made it clear to him that she hated Elizabeth as the child of Anne Boleyn.[13] She said that she did not trust Elizabeth, though Elizabeth had assured her that she had not dissembled when she went to Mass, and 'was very timid, and trembled, when she spoke' to her. Renard wrote to Charles that he 'placed a different interpretation on her answer and her trembling'.[14]

King Henry II of France found his national interests in conflict with his religious principles. He was a devoted Catholic who persecuted Protestants more consistently and severely than his father Francis I. He had established a special tribunal, the *Chambre ardente*, in imitation of the Spanish Inquisition, which developed refinements of cruelty in the punishment of heretics. Protestants who were prepared to make a public recantation at the stake were merely burned alive; those who refused to recant were tortured before they were burned, and their tongues were cut out to prevent them from proclaiming their heresy as they suffered in the flames. Sometimes heretics were suspended over a slow fire and left to roast to death. But Henry II realised that Mary's accession in England was a diplomatic victory for Charles V which would make England the permanent ally of the Emperor, and which, by adding England to Charles's territories in the Netherlands, Italy and Spain, completed the encirclement of France. He instructed Noailles to congratulate Mary on her decision to restore in her kingdom 'the honour of God and His holy Catholic faith and true religion', but at the same time to try to prevent her marriage to Philip of Spain; and he gave political asylum to English Protestants in France.[15]

When Parliament met in October, it passed an Act which enacted that Henry's marriage to Catherine of Aragon had been lawful, that their divorce was illegal and had been procured by the wicked advice of Thomas Cranmer, and that Mary was legitimate. As the new Act contained no mention of Elizabeth, and did not repeal the provisions of the Act of 1536 which declared that she was illegitimate, she remained, unlike Mary, a bastard in law; but this did not affect her right to succeed to the crown under Henry VIII's will. Renard thought that a new Act should be passed to exclude Elizabeth from the crown. Charles went further, and suggested that if Elizabeth had been plotting with the French ambassador, as Renard had reported, she should be put under surveillance, as it might then be possible to find reasons for sending her to the Tower.[16]

But Mary's Council was divided. It consisted of two sections whom Renard called the Catholics and the heretics,[17] and who today would be called the Hards and the Wets. The Catholics were Gardiner, Bourn, and the former officers of Mary's household – Rochester, Waldegrave and Englefield – all of whom, like Gardiner, had been imprisoned under Edward VI. The heretics were the Earls of Arundel, Pembroke and Sussex; Lord William Howard, the Lord Admiral, who was a cousin of Anne Boleyn and Elizabeth; and Paget and Petre. The 'heretics' had all been members of the Privy Council under Edward VI and Queen Jane, and had signed the orders sending Gardiner and the Catholics of Mary's household to prison; but it was they who had carried out the *coup d'état* which had placed Mary on the throne, and she could hardly govern the country without them.

They were happy that religion should be restored to the position at the end of Henry VIII's reign, and to see fanatical Protestant artisans burned, along with any of their former colleagues in the government, the Protestant bishops, who obstinately refused to recant their heresies at the command of their new sovereign, Queen Mary, like all sensible persons were doing. They also wished to renew the old alliance with Burgundy and the Low Countries by the marriage of Mary to Philip of Spain. They were even prepared, though less enthusiastically, to support the re-establishment of Papal supremacy. But they were against the restoration of the monasteries and the return of the monastic lands which so many gentlemen and speculators had bought from Henry VIII after the suppression of the houses; they were against the forfeiture of the lands of the wealthier Protestant gentlemen and merchants who had fled abroad to escape the persecution; and they opposed any move against the popular and charming Lady Elizabeth, since she had had the sense to go to Mass and, by implication at least, to recant her Protestant heresies. She should not be antagonised, for she was the heir to the throne under Henry VIII's will if Mary died without children; and this was quite possible, even if she married Philip of Spain, for not many women over thirty-seven bore children in the sixteenth century.

They were prepared to give Elizabeth the benefit of the doubt, to assume that her revocation of her heresies was sincere, and to solve her problem not by imprisoning her, but by according her honourable treatment at court and marrying her to some reliable Catholic husband who would keep her in order. One possibility, which had already been suggested in Henry VIII's reign, was Emmanuel Philibert, Duke of Savoy, who was becoming one of Charles V's foremost generals. Another was Don Carlos, Philip of Spain's son, who was a child of eight, but only twelve years younger than Elizabeth; this was not an insuperable obstacle to a diplomatic marriage.[18]

Another possible husband was Edward Courtenay, whose short life was sacrificed throughout to the exigencies of Tudor power politics. He was aged eight when his father, the Marquess of Exeter, was arrested, tried and beheaded for high treason under Henry VIII in 1538, partly perhaps because of his descent from the Yorkist line, but chiefly because of his link with the Papist sympathisers and the family of Cardinal Pole. The Marquess's brilliant and scheming wife, Gertrude, who had played a leading part in the plot to foist Jane Seymour on the King and bring down Anne Boleyn, was also arrested, but was soon afterwards released; but their son Edward was held prisoner in the Tower for the rest of Henry's reign and throughout the rule of Somerset and Northumberland, from the age of eight till he was twenty-three. Mary released him when she arrived at the Tower on her journey from Framlingham.

Courtenay, being a sixteenth-century nobleman, probably never imagined that he would now be able for long to lead a carefree life as an ordinary young man. He soon found that he would be as much a political pawn under a Papist Queen as under a schismatic or a heretic King. Mary, who was a close friend of his mother, appointed her to be one of her ladies-in-waiting, and granted Courtenay the title of Earl of Devon. She also toyed with the idea of marrying him to Elizabeth, for he was a good Catholic, or alternatively of trying to persuade Parliament to revoke Henry VIII's will and make Courtenay, not Elizabeth, the next heir to the throne. But when she noticed that Courtenay was becoming friendly with Elizabeth at court, she at once became suspicious.[19]

John Clapham, who was an official at court in the last years of Elizabeth's life and a friend of Lord Burghley, wrote in an unpublished manuscript a few months after Elizabeth's death that she had been in love with Courtenay at the court of Edward VI, and that one of the reasons why she never married was because of her disappointment at being unable to marry Courtenay.[20] This statement is at least partly inaccurate, for Courtenay was in the Tower throughout the whole of Edward's reign, and first met Elizabeth at Mary's court. His story is probably merely an unfounded popular rumour; but Elizabeth and Courtenay became at least good friends at court in the autumn of 1553. Not unnaturally, Courtenay reacted to his release from his long imprisonment by leading what his contemporaries, and nineteenth-century historians, called 'a dissolute life'; and Elizabeth's undoubted physical attractions were probably the chief reason why he became interested in her. But Mary and Gardiner were sure that Courtenay and Elizabeth were in league with the French ambassador and hatching plots to overthrow Mary, to break the alliance with the Empire and Spain, and to reign together as King and Queen.

Renard referred the decision to Charles V. If Elizabeth married Courtenay, would this tame her and persuade her to become a Catholic supporter of the Queen and the Spanish alliance; or would it give her a powerful ally in Courtenay and his tenants in the West country, and provide an additional incentive to both of them to usurp the crown? And why was Elizabeth becoming so friendly with Courtenay? Was it because she knew how close his mother was to the Queen, and hoped to elicit State secrets through her and Courtenay which she could pass on to Noailles and Henry II?

Charles, as usual, took no hasty decisions, but coolly considered the advantages of pursuing a harsh or a lenient policy towards Elizabeth. Even Mary, for all her hatred of Elizabeth, was prepared to consider the possibility of dealing with her by kindness, as long as she went to Mass. When Renard yet again warned her to be on her guard against Elizabeth, she told him that though she strongly distrusted Elizabeth, she was not displeased at the friendship between Elizabeth and Courtenay; for if Elizabeth persuaded Courtenay to plot with Noailles, Courtenay would certainly let slip the secret to his mother, who would at once tell Mary. But Renard wrote to Charles that he found it difficult to persuade Mary to hide her loathing for Elizabeth, because she felt so bitter about the way in which Anne Boleyn had treated Catherine of Aragon and herself. She subjected Elizabeth to petty slights at court, and forced her to yield precedence to Margaret Douglas, the Countess of Lennox, and to Jane Grey's mother, the Duchess of Suffolk.[21]

Many members of Elizabeth's household were Protestants, and some of them may have been more deeply involved in Protestant and French plots than was Elizabeth herself. But two of her servants took a different course. At the end of November they approached Paget and told him that as their duty to the Queen transcended their loyalty to their mistress, they felt obliged to reveal that Elizabeth was plotting with the French ambassador. Paget, for all his sympathy for Elizabeth, did not dare conceal this information, and told not only Mary and his fellow-counsellors, but also Renard. On investigation, it transpired that Elizabeth had merely been in touch with a French Protestant preacher who had come to England as a refugee from persecution in Edward VI's reign. Mary had issued an order deporting all the foreign Protestant refugees, and had informed the foreign rulers when they would be arriving in their territories, so that they could be arrested and burned as heretics in their native countries. According to her servants, Elizabeth had urged this French preacher not to obey the deportation order, but to remain in England.[22]

Mary and Renard were undecided as to whether Elizabeth should be kept at court or sent back to her houses in Hertfordshire. At court it would be easier for her to plot with Courtenay, but it would also be easier to keep her under observation at court than in her own household. At the end of November, Mary moved from Whitehall to Hampton Court, and soon afterwards Elizabeth asked permission to go to her manor at Ashridge near St Albans. Before she left, her supporters in the Council, Paget and Arundel, warned her to be very careful not to be involved in any plots. She assured them that she had become a Catholic not from hypocrisy or from fear but from sincere conviction, and that she would prove this by taking some Catholic priests with her to Ashridge and dismissing any member of her household who was suspected of heresy. She strongly denied having had any contact with either the French ambassador or any English heretics. She also had a farewell meeting with the Queen. She asked Mary not to believe any false accusations against her without first giving her the opportunity to clear herself in a personal interview with the Queen. Mary granted her request, and gave her a sable fur as a parting gift.[23]

Soon after Elizabeth arrived at Ashridge, she wrote to Mary and asked her to send copes, chasubles, crucifixes, patens, and other gear for use at Mass in her chapel.[24] All these had been suppressed by the second Book of Common Prayer and were anathema to the Protestants. Renard was sure that Elizabeth was dissembling; but before jumping to this conclusion we should remember that the Mass now had legal sanction, because the Act of Parliament which abolished the second Book of Common Prayer and restored the Mass was about to come into force; that after 21 December it would be a criminal offence for anyone to refuse to go to Mass; that Elizabeth was always amenable to pressure and liable to change her mind; and that even when she was Queen of Protestant England she shocked the more extreme Protestants by having a crucifix in her chapel and by insisting on the retention of ecclesiastical vestments. What she was not prepared to do was to turn against her friends, which any unscrupulous Machiavellian intriguer would have done; and despite her promise to Mary to dismiss any member of her household who was suspected of heresy, she did not do so.

Instead, she wrote an unsigned letter to her cousin, Katherine Knollys, who was the daughter of Mary Boleyn by her first husband Sir William Carey. Lady Knollys and her husband Sir Francis Knollys were zealous Protestants who had emigrated rather than go to Mass.

Relieve your sorrow for your far journey with joy of your short return, and think this pilgrimage rather a proof of your friends than a leaving of your country. The length of time and distance of place separates not the love of friends, nor deprives not the show of goodwill. An old saying, where *bale* is lowest, *boot* is nearest; where your need shall be most you shall find my friendship greatest.

She signed the letter 'Your loving cousin and ready friend, Cor Rotto.'*[25]

The Protestant extremists had learned nothing. They did all they could to provoke the Queen and the Catholics. The corpse of a dog, with its head shaved like a priest and a rope around its neck, was thrown into the Queen's presence chamber, with a written note that all priests should be hanged like the dog.[26] Encouraged by Henry II, they planned an insurrection to prevent the marriage of Mary to Philip of Spain and what they regarded as the subjection of England to the foreign yoke. They planned to safeguard the national independence and the Protestant religion by deposing Mary and

* 'Broken Heart'.

making Elizabeth Queen, after which she would marry Courtenay. The centre of the plot was Kent, which, after London, was the most Protestant part of England, and the leader was Sir Thomas Wyatt of Allington near Maidstone, the son of the poet and diplomat of Henry VIII's court. Wyatt wrote to Elizabeth and Courtenay, telling them of his plan to put them on the throne. The letters were intercepted by the government's spies, who also intercepted the correspondence between the plotters and Noailles; but they could not discover any letter from Elizabeth or Courtenay to either Wyatt or the French ambassador.

By the middle of January 1554, Mary, Gardiner and Renard had full knowledge of the planned insurrection, but allowed the plotters to think that they were undetected so that the rebel heretics could reveal themselves and be destroyed. Meanwhile Mary heard that Elizabeth was about to move with her household from Ashridge to another of her houses at Donnington in Berkshire.

On 25 January Wyatt and his supporters rose in revolt at Rochester. Next day, Mary wrote to Elizabeth informing her of the revolt and ordering her to come to court, where she would be safer at this dangerous time than at either Ashridge or Donnington.[27] On the same day, Noailles wrote to Henry II and explained that the plotters had begun the revolt two months earlier than they had intended because Courtenay had prematurely revealed the plot,

. . . assuring you, Sire, that Master Thomas Wyatt, who is one of them, has not failed his friends in his promise to take the field, which he did yesterday with forces which are increasing every hour . . . Lady Elizabeth has moved thirty miles further away to another of her houses, where, it is said, she has already assembled her supporters, often receiving letters from this Queen because of their suspicions about her. I have obtained a copy of a letter which she wrote to the Queen, which I have had translated into French and herewith enclose.[28]

His letter was intercepted by Mary's officers. Here at last was the evidence for which Mary, Gardiner and Renard had been waiting and hoping. Noailles had known about Wyatt's rising in advance, and he was in touch with Elizabeth; for how otherwise could he have obtained a copy of her letter to Mary?

Their suspicions were confirmed when the officers of Elizabeth's household wrote in reply to Mary's summons that Elizabeth was too ill to travel to court, though they invited Mary to send her own physicians to verify her illness. Mary sent Dr Wendy and Dr Owen, who confirmed that Elizabeth really was ill; and there can be very little doubt that she was, for whether she decided to submit to Mary or to join the rebels, the worst thing that she could do was to stay at Ashridge and neither obey the order to come to court nor try to escape. But no one wished to accept the obvious and true explanation; and while Renard was convinced that she was pregnant, having led an immoral life like her mother, Noailles believed that she had been poisoned by Mary's agents, and was dying.[29]

Wyatt and his seven thousand followers marched on London. This time far fewer Protestants were prepared to fight for Mary, though some of them still believed that it was their duty to defend their 'Prince'. In London, the rebels had many sympathisers. Two of them told a story of the ghost in the wall, where if anyone cried out 'God save Queen Mary!' the wall was silent, but to the cry 'God save the Lady Elizabeth!' the wall answered 'So be it'; and when the wall was asked 'What is the Mass?', it replied 'Idolatry'.[30] Charles V offered Mary the aid of his Spanish soldiers in the Netherlands. Gardiner advised her to refuse the help of the hated foreigners, and to leave Protestant London and take refuge in Oxford.

Mary rejected the conflicting advice of both of them. She refused Charles's offer of help, but stayed in London, and going to the Guildhall called on the people of London to protect their Queen against the traitors. The citizens who heard her were stirred to admiration for her courage, and rallied to her defence. Wyatt advanced to Ludgate, but his attack on the gate failed, and he was driven back, and defeated and taken prisoner in Hyde Park. Mary had once again triumphed over the rebels and heretics.

Elizabeth was now in a very dangerous situation. This second insurrection had convinced Mary that the Emperor was right when he advised her to show no mercy to the rebels, and within a week Jane Grey, her husband and her father had been beheaded under the sentence of death which had been passed on them three months earlier, but which Mary had hitherto refused to carry out. She put all her trust in Charles and Renard, with whom she had long talks in her closet late at night when none of her Council were present; and her emotional hatred of Elizabeth and Renard's cold, calculating diplomacy drove them both to reach the same conclusion. When Renard consulted Charles about what Mary should do with Courtenay and Elizabeth, Charles wrote on 31 January that Courtenay might be sent on some diplomatic mission to his court at Brussels, but that he agreed with Renard and Gardiner that Elizabeth should be sent to the Tower.[31]

By the middle of February, Wendy and Owen had reported that Elizabeth was well enough to travel, and Mary ordered three members of her Council – Lord William Howard, Sir Edward Hastings and Sir Thomas Cornwallis – to bring her to St James's in a litter which she sent to Ashridge. Whether by coincidence or otherwise, these three were all members of the faction in the Council which was sympathetic to Elizabeth. They travelled in slow stages because of Elizabeth's illness, taking five days to travel the thirty-three miles, and staying the night at Redbourne, St Albans, Mimms and Highgate. The crowds gathered to see her pass through London. Renard complained that Elizabeth, who was dressed in white, drew back the curtains of the litter to show herself to the people, and that she looked pale and arrogant to hide her vexation.[32] But was there any calculation here, or was she just a young woman who was ill, frightened and defiant?

She was held for nearly a month in her rooms in the palace while Mary and the Council considered the possibility of placing her under house arrest in the charge of some member of the Council; but as no councillor was eager to accept the responsibility of guarding her, it was eventually decided to send her to the Tower, though this was strongly opposed by many of the councillors. Mary ordered the Earl of Sussex and another councillor* to take her to the Tower by barge, as this was thought safer than taking her through the streets where her Protestant supporters might attempt to rescue her. When Sussex and his colleague told Elizabeth that she must go to the Tower, she was very distressed, and asked for an audience with the Queen. As this was refused, she asked permission to write to Mary before they embarked in the barge; and Sussex, despite his colleague's opposition, insisted that pen and paper should be brought for Elizabeth.[33]

In her letter, Elizabeth reminded Mary of her promise, the last time they had met, not to allow her to be condemned without a chance to clear herself in a personal talk with Mary.

If any ever did try this old saying that a King's word was more than another man's oath, I most humbly beseech your M. to verify it in me and to remember your last promise and my last demand that I be not condemned without answer and due proof, which it seems that now I am for that without cause proved I am by your Council from you commanded to go unto the Tower, a place more wonted for a false traitor than a true subject ... I have heard in my time of many cast away for want of coming to the presence of their Prince; and in late days I heard my Lord of Somerset say that if his brother had been suffered to speak with him, he had never suffered, but the persuasions were made to him so great that he was brought in belief that he could not live safely if the Admiral lived, and that made him give his consent to his death. Though these persons are not to be compared to your Majesty, yet I pray God that evil persuasions persuade not one sister against the other, and all for that they have heard false report and not hearken to the truth known. Therefore once again kneeling with humbleness of my heart, because I am not suffered to bow the knees of my body, I humbly crave to speak with your Highness, which I would not be so bold to desire if I knew not myself most clear as I know myself most true. And as for the traitor Wyatt, he might peradventure write me a letter but on my faith I never received any from him; and as for the copy of my letter sent to the French King, I pray God confound me eternally if ever I sent him

*Foxe, who tells this story, does not identify this other councillor. It has usually been assumed that it was Gardiner, but if so, it is very strange that Foxe did not name him; and Sussex would not have ventured to overrule Gardiner's decision.

word, message, token or letter by any means, and to this my truth I will
stand in to my death.

After finishing the letter, she drew long diagonal lines across the remaining
blank spaces on the paper, so that no one could add a forged passage and
make out that it had been written by her. Then she added at the foot of the
letter: 'I humbly crave but only one word of answer from yourself. Your
Highness's most faithful subject that hath been from the beginning and will
be [to] my end, Elizabeth.'[34]
She took so long writing the letter that they missed the tide, and had to wait
for the next tide at midnight; but as Sussex and his colleague feared that she
might escape if they landed at the Tower wharf in the dark, they decided to
hold her for one more night at Westminster and take her to the Tower next
morning, on Palm Sunday, when the people of London would be at Mass and
could not take part in any demonstration or rescue bid. Renard believed that
Elizabeth had asked permission to write to Mary with the deliberate plan of
wasting time so that it would be impossible to take her to the Tower that night.
If he was right, we would have to believe that the erasures, corrections and
verbal omissions in the letter were signs, not of her nervous agitation, but of
the most cunning play-acting. If she wrote the letter as a tactic, it was
unsuccessful; and the tone of the letter, which fell far short of the cringing
plea for mercy which would have been expected from a prisoner on the way to
the Tower, can have done her no good. Mary was furious with Sussex and his
colleague for allowing Elizabeth to write to her. She said that they would
never have dared to do it in her father's time, and she wished that he could
return for a day to teach them a lesson.[35]
Elizabeth was taken by barge from Westminster to the Tower on the rainy
morning of Palm Sunday, 17 March 1554. She landed at the gate that later
became known as 'Traitors' Gate', but at that time was simply called 'the
watergate'. Elizabeth paused for a moment outside the gate and sat down on a
stone, though it was damp from the rain. The Lieutenant of the Tower, Sir
John Bridges, said to her: 'Madam, you were best to come out of the rain,
for you sit unwholesomely'. 'It is better sitting here than in a worse place',
replied Elizabeth, 'for God knoweth, I know not whither you will bring me'.[36]

THE HEIR TO THE THRONE

FOR two months, Elizabeth was held as a prisoner in the Tower, where she was confined in a suite of four rooms. Her servants were allowed to attend on her, but she was permitted to see no one else, and elaborate precautions were taken to prevent her from communicating with any of the other prisoners. At first she was strictly confined to her prison, but later she was allowed to walk in a little walled garden where none of the other prisoners could speak to her. A four-year-old child, the son of one of the warders of the Tower, came every day to her prison to bring her flowers; but after a while he was discovered, and was told that he would be whipped if he visited her again. He came to the walled garden when she was walking there, and, slipping in through the gate, hurriedly told her that he could not bring her any more flowers. She said nothing, but smiled, to show him that she understood.[1]

The Queen and Council were discussing what to do with her. Renard strongly advised Mary to put her to death, for if she did not do so now, the opportunity would never recur. 'It seems to me that she ought not to spare Courtenay and Lady Elizabeth on this occasion', he wrote to Charles V, 'for while they are alive there will always be plots to raise them to the throne, and it would be just to punish them, as it is publicly known that they are guilty and so deserve death'.[2] Gardiner agreed with Renard; but there was strong opposition from Paget and Lord William Howard and their faction in the Council.

Paget, playing a skilful political game, now appeared as an enthusiastic supporter of Mary's marriage to Philip, and tried to ingratiate himself with Renard. He told him that he was addressing him not as a foreign ambassador but as the Queen's closest confidant in pointing out to him how inadvisable and impossible it was to have Elizabeth executed. There was not enough evidence to convict her of high treason if she were put on trial, for the rebels who might have been persuaded to give evidence against her had escaped abroad. The most that could be proved against her was misprision of treason – the failure to report treason which she knew was taking place – and this was punishable only by life imprisonment, not by death. These difficulties could be surmounted if Parliament passed an Act of Attainder condemning her as a traitor and sentencing her to death without trial by Act of Parliament. But Paget assured Renard that there was no hope of persuading either the House of Commons or the House of Lords to pass an Act of Attainder against Elizabeth. He thought it would be wiser to marry Elizabeth to Emmanuel Philibert of Savoy or to some other foreigner, though he suggested a ruler of an inland territory far from the coast, like Baden, with no port from which she and her husband could send agents to intrigue in England.[3]

In May, after Elizabeth had been two months in the Tower, Mary ordered that she was to be taken to the royal manor of Woodstock in Oxfordshire and confined there under house arrest. Sir Henry Bedingfield, who was a member of the Privy Council, and Lord Williams of Thame were sent with an escort of a hundred horsemen to guard her on the journey. Williams was a typical sixteenth-century gentleman who had loyally served Henry VIII and the governments of Edward VI as well as Mary, and always adapted his religion to comply with the orders of his Prince. Mary had just rewarded him for his services by creating him a peer. As Sheriff of Oxfordshire he was required during the next two years to supervise the burning of Latimer, Ridley and Cranmer at Oxford; but he showed great consideration to the heir to the throne on the journey from the Tower to Woodstock.

On 19 May they left the Tower and travelled to Richmond by water without landing anywhere, for Mary was anxious to avoid any demonstrations by the citizens of London in Elizabeth's favour; but her departure from the Tower was known in the city, and a rumour spread that she had been set free, to the great joy of the people.[4]

The move from the Tower to house arrest at Woodstock was at least a slight improvement, and suggested that mercy might perhaps eventually be shown to her; but when Elizabeth was removed from the Tower by her armed escort, she feared the worst. When they landed at Richmond she said to Lord Williams 'This night I think to die'; but he assured her that she was in no danger. Next morning they rode to Windsor. As they crossed the river at Richmond they encountered a small group of Elizabeth's servants who were standing there to get a glimpse of her. She told one of her guards to go to them 'and say these words from me, *Tanquam ovis*,' like a sheep to the slaughter.[5]

She stayed the night at the Dean of Windsor's house, and on the third day of their journey travelled fifteen miles to High Wycombe. As they passed Eton College the boys came out to see her, and crowds assembled in the villages along the route. They welcomed Elizabeth, and threw wafers and other gifts of food into her litter as she passed. At first she gratefully accepted the gifts, but later had to refuse them as she had received so many edibles. She stayed the night at High Wycombe at the house of Sir William Dormer.[6]
That evening, Bedingfield wrote to Mary an account of their journey and of Elizabeth's reception in the villages, 'by which, if it shall please your Highness to peruse, you shall right well perceive, among the other matters therein

mentioned, that men betwixt London and this place be not good and whole in matters of Religion.'[7]

On 22 May they went on to Lord Williams's own house at Thame. As they approached Woburn they saw a labourer waiting on the top of a hill, a quarter of a mile outside the town, to see Elizabeth pass by. Bedingfield spoke to him and 'found him a very Protestant'.[8] This worried Bedingfield, and he questioned the people at the market in Woburn and High Wycombe, and found that most of them were Protestants. He thereupon reported to Mary that this was the fault of Lord Russell, the Earl of Bedford's son, who had used his local influence to advance the Protestant cause.

The interest in the villages was as great as it had been on the previous days' journeys. At Aston, where the people came out to greet Elizabeth, four men went to the church and rang the bells in Elizabeth's honour. Bedingfield and Williams had them arrested and taken to the local jail. Williams, with his wife, his gentlemen and his servants, treated Elizabeth with great honour in his house at Thame. This displeased Bedingfield, who had to remind them that she was a prisoner who had offended against the Queen.

On the fifth day of their journey they reached Woodstock, after encountering more demonstrations in Elizabeth's favour in the Oxfordshire villages.[9] At Woodstock, Elizabeth was to be in Bedingfield's charge, and he received precise instructions from Mary herself as to how he was to treat his prisoner. Elizabeth was to be entitled to walk in the garden whenever she wished at all reasonable times of the day; but Bedingfield himself was to be with her on these walks. She was to receive no visitors or letters, and not to write to, or communicate with, anyone; but Bedingfield could permit visitors whom he considered suitable to speak to her in his presence. He was to treat her with the respect which was due to her rank, but she was not to have a cloth of state above her chair at dinner, to which she would have been entitled if she had been a Princess.[10] She had several of her own servants to wait on her, but they were carefully watched, and within a week of her arrival at Woodstock Mary had ordered that one of her women was to be removed, because she was 'a person of an evil opinion'.[11]

Bedingfield did not wish to alienate the heir to the throne more than was necessary, but he was even more determined not to displease the Queen and to carry out his instructions to the letter. His guiding principle was not to take the slightest decision himself. At Woodstock he referred every request from Elizabeth to the Queen or Privy Council, which meant that some time elapsed before any of them was granted.

When she asked for books, there was a long delay. She asked for an English Bible, and for two books by Cicero and the Psalms of David in Latin, and was eventually allowed to have them, after the Council had ordered Bedingfield to examine them carefully to make sure that there was no secret message hidden between the pages of the books. She asked to be allowed to have her tutor John Picton at Woodstock, so that she should not forget the foreign languages which he had taught her in her youth; but this request was refused by the Council, because they did not have enough information about his character and record. They also rejected her request to be allowed to walk in the park of the palace as well as in the garden.[12]

She attended Mass, and made no difficulty about complying in religious matters. At first her chaplain conducted the service in her chapel in English; but when Mary sent instructions to Bedingfield, in October 1554, that the services should henceforth be in Latin, Elizabeth obeyed at once, and ordered her chaplain not to say prayers in English in future.[13]

She felt the strain of her confinement at Woodstock. She fell ill. Her face swelled up. Sometimes she wept, and sometimes she made angry scenes. On one occasion there was a fire in her apartments, but Bedingfield and his men arrived in time to extinguish it. The Protestants believed that it had been an attempt to murder Elizabeth, but this was obviously untrue.[14]

Once she asked permission to write to the Queen. When it was granted, she wrote a letter which has not survived but which did her cause no good. It was probably a catalogue of complaints. It angered Mary. Renard wrote that it was a bold and insolent attempt at self-justification, and that she addressed Mary throughout the letter as 'you', never as 'your Highness' or 'your Majesty'. After receiving the letter, Mary wrote to Bedingfield that it revealed Elizabeth's pride and obstinacy and the insincerity of her protestations of loyalty. In future Bedingfield was to refuse her permission to write to Mary; if she had any requests to make to Mary, she was to tell Bedingfield, and he himself must write the letter.[15]

At other times Elizabeth was in calmer mood. One day she scratched with a diamond on a window pane:

Much suspected by me,
Nothing proved can be,
Quoth Elizabeth, prisoner.[16]

While Elizabeth was at Woodstock, important events took place in England. In July 1554 Philip of Spain arrived at Southampton and married Mary in Winchester Cathedral. He reigned jointly with Mary as King and Queen, and was known throughout Europe as 'the King of England'; but it was a term of the marriage treaty that they should govern England through native-born ministers. Philip's Spanish courtiers, and all other Spaniards in England, were repeatedly ordered to be courteous and tactful towards the English; but the ill-feeling grew stronger every day. 'The English hate us Spaniards worse than they hate the Devil, and treat us accordingly', wrote one of Philip's gentlemen. 'They rob us in town and on the road.' Soon afterwards, this gentleman wrote again: 'We Spaniards move among the English as if they were animals, trying not to notice them; and they do the same to us.'[17]

In November 1554 Cardinal Pole arrived as Papal Legate, and the realm was reunited to Rome. After Pole and the government had announced that the monasteries would not be restored and that the owners would be left in possession of the monastic lands which they had purchased from Henry VIII, Parliament agreed to re-enact the heresy statutes, and the burning of the Protestant heretics began in February 1555. But the situation was different from what it had been twenty or thirty years before, when a handful of Protestant extremists who denied the most sacred doctrines of the great majority of the English people had been burned at the orders of their great King Henry VIII who had led them to victory in his wars against the French and Scots. Now a Spanish King and an Italian Pope were burning bishops who had held high office under Edward VI for holding doctrines which the younger generation had been taught for six years were the official doctrines of the Church of England. It was largely a question of the generation gap. The Venetian ambassador, Michiel, thought that no Englishman under thirty-five was really a Catholic at heart.[18]

Rogers was the first to suffer. Before he died, he asked permission to have a farewell meeting with his wife; but Bonner, the Bishop of London, refused to allow him to see his 'harlot'. He was burned at Smithfield in London on 4 February 1555.[19] Renard was worried at the public reaction. He wrote next day to King Philip:

Sire, the people of this town of London are murmuring about the cruel enforcement of the recent Acts of Parliament on heresy which has now begun, as was shown publicly when a certain Rogers was burned yesterday. Some of the onlookers wept, others prayed to God to give him strength, perseverance and patience to bear the pain and not to recant, others gathered the ashes and bones and wrapped them up in paper to preserve them, yet others threatening the bishops ... Your Majesty will also consider that Lady Elizabeth has her supporters, and that there are Englishmen who do not love foreigners.[20]

A few days later, Hooper was burned at Gloucester, where he had been the bishop. It was a terrible burning, for the faggots were damp and burned slowly. He was seen to move in the fire after both his legs had been burned off, and took three-quarters of an hour to die. In March Ferrar, the Protestant Bishop of St Davids, was burned at Carmarthen.[21]

After Elizabeth had been at Woodstock for eleven months, Mary ordered that she was to be brought to court. This was another improvement in her position, and she owed it to Philip. Even if she could have been put to death in the immediate aftermath of the Wyatt rebellion, it was certainly impossible now; and as she could not be executed, she had better be reconciled to Philip and Mary. But her rehabilitation was to be a gradual process. When she arrived at Hampton Court on 29 April 1555, she was ordered to stay in her apartments. She was not invited to take part in any of the court functions, and though she was allowed to receive visitors, few of the courtiers ventured to call on her. Cardinal Pole's apartments in the palace were almost next door to hers, but he never invited her to visit him and did not see her during the four months that she was at Hampton Court in the summer of 1555. Her friend Courtenay had left court the day before she arrived; he had been sent on a nominal diplomatic mission to Charles V in Brussels as a way of getting rid of him.[22] From there he went on to Italy, where he died soon afterwards at the age of twenty-six.

Shortly before Elizabeth's arrival at court, Mary announced that she was pregnant. She said that she had felt the child move in her womb on the first occasion on which she saw Pole when he arrived as Papal Legate; and she was convinced that she was carrying the heir to the throne who would ensure that England remained true to the Catholic faith. Almost from the beginning her ladies-in-waiting were sure that she was imagining it; but on 30 April, the day after Elizabeth arrived from Woodstock, a Te Deum was held in St Paul's, and all the London churches rang their bells in celebration of the joyful news. It was reported in Flanders and Spain that the baby had already arrived, and was a boy; and the Princess Dowager of Portugal, who was Regent in Spain for her father Charles V during his absence, wrote and congratulated Mary on the birth of her son and heir.[23]

If Mary was right about her pregnancy, the baby was expected in June, and for two months England and Europe waited in suspense. In Hever Castle today, there is a layette which, according to tradition, was made by Elizabeth for Mary's baby. It consists of a coif, a pair of little shoes, two jackets, two bonnets, some collars and sleeves, in white satin, or in silk, and a flannel jacket, all very delicately sewn. The written records about the layette have been lost, so the truth of the tradition cannot be verified;[24] but it is not impossible that Elizabeth, who was a skilful needlewoman, made the tiny garments during May and June 1555 while she was confined, almost as a prisoner, in her apartments at Hampton Court. We can only imagine her thoughts as she made the garments for the baby who might end her chance of ever becoming Queen and might ensure the destruction of Protestantism in England.

Everything turned on the birth of Mary's child. Renard wrote to Charles V on 14 June:

> Sire, everything in this kingdom depends on the Queen's delivery . . . If God is pleased to grant her a safe delivery, things will take a turn for the better. If not, I foresee disturbance and a change for the worse on so great a scale that the pen can hardly set it down. It is certain that the order of succession to the crown has been so badly arranged that Lady Elizabeth comes next, and that means heresy again, and religion overthrown.[25]

No baby came. Soon everyone knew that Mary had never been pregnant, and almost certainly never would be pregnant, though no official announcement was ever made about the non-arrival of the heir whose advent had been publicly celebrated at the end of April. Everyone now felt, like Renard, that the future was Elizabeth's, even though she was still confined in disgrace to her apartments at Hampton Court.

In May Kate Ashley and Elizabeth's Italian tutor Castiglione were arrested on a charge of being in possession of heretical books. But they were released after a few weeks; and for Elizabeth herself, things seemed to be slowly improving. On two occasions, Mary received her in audience, and was not unkind.[26]

Elizabeth also met King Philip at court, and it was to him that she owed the change in her position. By the summer of 1555 it was clear to Philip that Mary would not have a child; and though she was only thirty-nine, her health was not good. Under Henry VIII's will, Elizabeth would succeed to the throne at her death. After Elizabeth, the next heir would be Mary Queen of Scots, the granddaughter of Henry VIII's sister Margaret. Mary Queen of Scots was living at the French court and was engaged to marry Henry II's son, the Dauphin Francis. If Mary Queen of Scots became Queen of England, it would make England the ally and vassal state of France, and be a great defeat for Spain and the Empire. Philip preferred Elizabeth, for all her heretical sympathies, to Mary Queen of Scots, the King of France's daughter-in-law. He and Renard therefore used their influence with Mary to prevent her from depriving Elizabeth of the crown, and tried to win Elizabeth's goodwill in the hope that the ancient friendship and common interests between England and Burgundy would lead her to pursue a pro-Spanish policy when she became Queen.

Though Philip certainly befriended Elizabeth at court, we know nothing about their personal relationship. Later writers have stated that he was in love with her, and that she played on his feelings for her in order to gain his protection against her sister's hatred. This is not impossible, for Elizabeth was a more attractive woman than the embittered and fading Mary. But Philip's attitude to women is even more puzzling than Elizabeth's attitude to men. According to contemporary gossip, and to Protestant propaganda throughout the centuries, he often pursued women, including the ladies at Mary's court; but the confidential reports of his closest servants suggest that he had a horror of sex which his lascivious father, Charles V, had hypocritically implanted in him in his youth.[27] There is no evidence of Philip's personal feelings for Elizabeth. We know that he protected her and had political motives for doing so; and it is impossible to say whether he also had personal reasons for helping her.

Elizabeth knew that she owed much to Philip, and was not ungrateful. In later years, when their relations were at their worst, she acknowledged that he had protected her in Mary's reign,[28] and through all the years of hostility and war she never quite forgot it. She always thought of Philip a little differently from the way in which her loyal Protestant subjects regarded him. For them, Philip was the foreign despot who in Mary's reign had instigated the burning of the martyrs; for Elizabeth, he was the man who had been kind to her at Mary's court.

On 20 August Philip left England to take part in the proceedings in Brussels when Charles V abdicated in his favour as ruler of the Netherlands; some months later, Charles likewise transferred his kingdom of Spain to Philip. Elizabeth went with Mary and all the court to see Philip embark at Dartford; but while Philip and Mary rode through the streets of London and travelled overland to Dartford, Elizabeth went by barge, perhaps because Mary did not wish to give the Londoners an opportunity to demonstrate in her favour as they passed. After Philip had left, Mary and Elizabeth moved to Greenwich. On 4 September Elizabeth joined Mary and all the court in taking part in a special fast day on which they received a pardon which the new Pope, Paul IV, had granted to all men to celebrate a Jubilee year. Elizabeth stayed at court for another six weeks before asking permission to go to her own house at Hatfield. Mary allowed her to go, and gave her gifts at her departure.[29] Elizabeth was free, rehabilitated, and, for the moment, safe.

Three weeks later, her enemy, Gardiner, died. Noailles reported that the Queen regretted his death as much as the majority of her people rejoiced at it. But the burnings went on. In October, two more Protestant bishops, Ridley and Latimer, were burned at Oxford. Latimer was quickly suffocated by the smoke, but Ridley had a long, agonising death.[30] Eighty heretics had been burned in the last eight months. In June 1555 a Protestant preacher, Thomas, Bryce, began to record the deaths of the martyrs in a poem which expressed the feelings of many Protestants:

When worthy Watts with constant cry
Continued in the flaming fire;
When Simson, Hawkes and John Ardite
Did taste the tyrant's raging ire;
When Chamberlain was put to death,
We wished for our Elizabeth.
When blessed Butter and Osmande
With force of fire to death were brent;
When Shitterdon, Sir Frank and Bland,
And Humphrey Middleton of Kent;
When Minge in Maidstone took his death,
We wished for our Elizabeth.[31]

Bryce continued to record the deaths of the martyrs – in Dartford, Chichester, Reading, Uxbridge, Norwich and Coventry. In March 1556 Archbishop Cranmer was burned after he had recanted, although hitherto heretics who recanted had always been spared, unless they were relapsed heretics. At the stake he repudiated his recantations, and said that his hand should be burned first, because it had signed the recantations. The authorities published his recantations and suppressed all mention of his repudiation of them; but it soon became known throughout the country that he had died a Protestant.[32]

> When constant Cranmer lost his life,
> And held his hand unto the fire;
> When streams of tears for him were rife,
> And yet did miss their just desire;
> When Popish power put him to death,
> We wished for our Elizabeth.[33]

In June 1556 Kate Ashley and other members of Elizabeth's household were again arrested. Mary sent Sir Edward Hastings and Sir Francis Englefield to warn Elizabeth about the 'licentious' behaviour of some of her servants. She ordered Sir Thomas Pope to go to Hatfield and purge the establishment there. Kate Ashley was again released, but was dismissed from Elizabeth's household and told that she must make no attempt to get into contact with Elizabeth.[34]

The danger for Elizabeth was not over, and the burnings continued. The persecution was particularly fierce in London, where 'bloody Bonner' was hated by the Protestants because of the number of his victims, the floggings and tortures which he inflicted on his prisoners, and the brutal and mocking way in which he behaved at the trials. Now that the prominent Protestant bishops and divines had suffered, the victims were mostly artisans and labourers. Many of the martyrs were women; some were very old, and others youths of under twenty. A woman aged twenty-two, who had been blind from birth but had become a skilful rope-maker, was burned at Derby, and a lame old man and a blind man at Stratford-at-Bow.[35]

> When Margaret Eliot, being a maid,
> After condemning in prison died;
> When lame Lamarock the fire essayed,
> And blind Aprice with him was tried;
> When these two impotents were put to death,
> We wished for our Elizabeth.[36]

In July 1556 some English Protestant refugees in France, under the protection of Henry II, sent a wretched youth named Cleobury, who had had several convictions for burglary, to impersonate Courtenay in Essex and Suffolk, though Courtenay was in fact living quietly in Venice. Cleobury proclaimed Courtenay and Elizabeth as King and Queen in several villages before he and his handful of supporters were arrested.[37] When Elizabeth was informed about this by Sir Thomas Pope, she expressed her indignation in a letter to Mary on 2 August:

When I revolve in mind, most noble Queen, the old love of Paynims [pagans] to their Princes, and the reverend fear of Romans to their senate, I cannot but muse for my part and blush for theirs, to see the rebellious hearts and devilish intents of Christians in name, but Jews in deed, towards their anointed King . . . Much it vexed me that the Devil oweth me such a hate as to put me in any part of his mischievous instigations, whom, as I profess him my foe (that is, all Christians' enemy) so wish I he had some other way invented to spite me . . . And like as I have been your faithful subject from the beginning of your reign, so shall no wicked person cause me to change to the end of my life . . . Your Majesty's obedient subject and humble sister, Elizabeth.[38]

It would be wrong to assume that this letter was entirely hypocritical. Elizabeth had been brought up at Henry VIII's court to condemn rebels who revolted against their Prince, and when she became Queen she was always reluctant to help revolts by foreign rebels, even when it was in her interests to do so.

Mary at least pretended to believe Elizabeth's protestations of loyalty, and the influence of Philip and Renard continued to protect Elizabeth. But Philip was eager that she should marry Emmanuel Philibert of Savoy, which would give him an excellent hold over England when Elizabeth became Queen. In the autumn of 1556 he pressed again for the marriage. At the end of November Elizabeth came to London, probably in order to persuade Mary not to marry her to Emmanuel Philibert. She rode from Hatfield escorted by two hundred horsemen dressed in red coats with borders of black velvet, and was cheered by the people as she passed through the city by Smithfield, Old Bailey and Fleet Street to her London residence at Somerset Place in the Strand. She had an audience with Mary, and was received by Cardinal Pole, whom she met for the first time. When it was known that she was at Somerset Place, many lords and gentlemen called on her. The Venetian ambassador decided to visit her, but found that she had already left, for she returned to Hatfield after only a week, again riding with her escort through the city and provoking fresh demonstrations of support.[39]

She was still at Somerset Place on 30 November, the second anniversary of the re-establishment of Papal supremacy. Pole had proclaimed the anniversary as a new holy day, the Feast of the Reconciliation, which was to be celebrated every year to all eternity; and he and all the courtiers attended a great ceremony in Westminster Abbey on 30 November 1556. The Queen was too ill to go. It would be interesting to know whether Elizabeth attended, but neither her presence nor her absence are recorded.[40]

War had once again broken out between the Habsburg rulers and the King of France. By the end of 1556 King Philip's armies were fighting the French in Italy. England joined in on Philip's side, and Scotland on the side of France. It brought Mary into conflict with the Pope, the ferocious octogenarian Paul IV. He was determined to expel the Spaniards from Italy, and supported France in the war. He excommunicated Philip, and appointed a new Papal Legate in England to replace Pole. Philip announced that anyone who published the Papal bulls in his territories would be punished by death, and Mary refused to allow the new Legate to enter England. Pole sadly realised that it was a situation from which only the heretics could benefit.[41]

In March 1557 Philip paid a second visit to England, in order to enlist English support for his war with France. Elizabeth came to court and met him again, and he again put forward proposals for her marriage. His plan was for her to marry Emmanuel Philibert, who would reign with her as King and Queen of England, and for Emmanuel Philibert to cede Nice and other parts of Savoy to him in return for his part in arranging the match with Elizabeth. Apart from Emmanuel Philibert, he suggested another possible suitor, Alexander Farnese, the son of the Duke of Parma and Margaret, the illegitimate daughter of Charles V. Alexander later became Elizabeth's greatest enemy after Philip of Spain himself, and the commander of the army which was ready to invade England with the Spanish Armada in 1588; but when he visited England with his mother in the spring of 1557, and met Elizabeth at Mary's court, he was suggested as a possible husband for her, though he was only twelve and she was twenty-four.[42]

Mary declared war on France. The declaration was made in the traditional way; an English herald was sent to the French court at Rheims to issue the challenge to the King. Henry II burst out laughing, and said: 'What a state I am in when a woman challenges me to war'.[43] The idea of a woman sovereign still seemed strange in the sixteenth century, though Charles V had for many years governed the Netherlands through his aunt and his sister, Margaret of Austria and Mary of Hungary, and Philip II would soon appoint Margaret of Parma to follow them as Regent in Brussels.

In July, Philip left England with ten thousand English soldiers who joined his Spanish troops in the Netherlands and invaded France. He won a great victory at St Quentin, thanks largely to the generalship of Emmanuel Philibert, and then proceeded to take the town by storm, though it was valiantly defended by Gaspard de Coligny, the Admiral of France. The double victory at St Quentin was duly celebrated in England with Te Deums, bell-ringing, and bonfires in the streets; but it did not make a national hero of Philip, and the success was soon followed by disaster. On 31 December 1557 a French army under Francis, Duke of Guise, invaded the Marches of Calais; within four days the castle of Guisnes had fallen, and on 7 January the town of Calais surrendered. The whole of the English territory, which had been held as a bridgehead in France for two hundred and ten years, and was so important for English pride, commerce and strategy in peace and war, had been lost in a week and was in the hands of the French.

The defeat caused great ill-feeling between the English and their Spanish allies. A Spanish army had remained inactive at Gravelines, less than fifteen miles away, while Guise was overrunning the Marches of Calais; and while the Spaniards blamed the English for not holding out longer in Calais, the

English accused the Spaniards of dilatoriness in coming to their aid.[44] In July 1558 the Spaniards under Count Egmont won another victory over the French near Gravelines, but they made no attempt to follow up their victory by recapturing Calais. Instead, they made a truce with the French until Christmas, and opened peace negotiations at Cateau-Cambrésis on the borders of France and the Netherlands.

Philip and Mary were becoming more and more unpopular in England. The inflation of the last years of Henry VIII continued to rise, and caused prices to double in ten years. Beef and butter both now cost fourpence a pound, and two eggs one penny, which caused great dissatisfaction, though the daily wage of an agricultural labourer had risen from fourpence to sevenpence a day.[45]

The burnings continued unabated during 1557 and 1558. Nearly every month a heretic was burned at Smithfield, and in Kent village after village provided a martyr.

When two at Ashford with cruelty
For Christ's cause to death were brent;
When not long after two at Wye
Suffered for Christ his testament;
When wily wolves put these to death
We wished for our Elizabeth.[46]

The people, at least in the south-east where most of the burnings took place, sympathised increasingly with the victims. There were demonstrations of support for the heretics by the spectators at the burnings. Mary issued a proclamation that any bystander who showed sympathy for a heretic at an execution was to be arrested and flogged. When seven Protestants were burned at Smithfield in June 1558, the sheriff read out the proclamation as soon as the people had assembled; but this did not prevent a great demonstration of support for the martyrs. Books and leaflets attacking the government were circulating illegally in England. Mary issued a proclamation that anyone who came across one of these publications was to burn it immediately and that failure to do so would be punished by death under martial law.[47]

In July 1558 the Protestant Bembridge was burned at Winchester. The crowd at the burning rioted, put out the flames, and dragged the half-burned Bembridge from the stake, demanding that the execution be respited. The sheriff agreed, removed Bembridge to prison, and asked the Council for instructions, as Bembridge had now offered to recant. Mary ordered that he was to be brought to the stake a second time and burned, whether he had recanted or not, and she imprisoned the sheriff for a few months for having postponed the execution without authority.[48]

But Mary could not harm Elizabeth, and Philip supported her more strongly than ever. In April 1558 Mary Queen of Scots married the French Dauphin in Notre Dame in Paris; and with France at war with Spain, it became more essential than ever to prevent the Queen-Dauphiness from succeeding to the throne of England. In January 1558 Philip sent a new ambassador, the Count of Feria, to England, with instructions to do all he could to win Elizabeth's goodwill. Elizabeth came to court in February, after again riding through London with her escort,[49] and was received by Mary. It was the last time that the sisters met.

The only danger which now confronted Elizabeth was that she would be forced to marry. Philip still favoured her marriage to Emmanuel Philibert; but Paget and the moderates in the Privy Council pointed out that there might be trouble from the people if Elizabeth were married to a foreigner and sent abroad. The King of Sweden, Gustavus Vasa, hoped that Elizabeth would marry his son Prince Eric, who later became King Eric XIV. When a Swedish envoy came to England in the spring of 1558 to negotiate a commercial treaty, he wrote to Elizabeth and suggested that she might marry Prince Eric. He had not asked Mary's permission to make the proposal to Elizabeth; and Elizabeth was able to get out of any involvement with Eric by informing Mary, who scolded the ambassador for having approached Elizabeth without first consulting her.[50]

In October Mary fell ill, and it became generally known that she was dying of cancer of the ovary at the age of forty-two. Her grief and depression were made worse when she heard of the deaths of Charles V and Mary of Hungary; all the champions of the Catholic Church seemed to be departing in the autumn of 1558. Philip sent his confessor Fresneda to England to urge Mary to send a message to Elizabeth recognising her as heir to the throne. Mary refused, and broke out in rage. She told Fresneda that Elizabeth was not her sister or the child of Henry VIII, but the daughter of an infamous woman who had outraged the Queen her mother and herself. Fresneda persisted, and at last Mary agreed to do as he asked; but two days later she changed her mind, and again refused.[51]

The Queen lay dying, but the burnings continued. At the beginning of November, three men and two women were condemned as heretics at Canterbury. The Archdeacon of Canterbury, Nicholas Harpsfield, who had been dividing his time between writing a hagiographical biography of Sir Thomas More and energetically burning Protestants in the diocese of Canterbury, was determined to burn these last five heretics before Mary died, and hurried down from London to Canterbury to expedite the execution. They were burned on 10 November. Other Protestants awaiting death in the jails in London and Salisbury were more fortunate. There was no time to burn them before Mary died.[52]

On 10 November, Feria rode to Brockett Hall near Hatfield to visit Elizabeth, who was staying at the house of her tenant, Sir John Brockett. She received him graciously, and invited him to have dinner with her and Lady Clinton, the Lord Admiral's wife. 'During the meal', he wrote to Philip, 'we laughed and enjoyed ourselves a great deal.' Afterwards she sent everybody out of the room, except for two or three of her women who understood only English, though Feria did not state in what language their conversation took place. He assured her of Philip's brotherly love for her. She replied that she was grateful to Philip for his intervention on her behalf when she was a prisoner, and for this reason, and because of the ancient friendship between England and Burgundy, she intended to preserve the alliance with him. She also said that she would never make peace with France unless Calais were restored to England. But Feria was uneasy. He believed that she would steer a neutralist course between France and Spain; and he was particularly worried that so many of her friends and ladies were heretics. He wrote to Philip that 'she is a very vain and clever woman'.*[53]

While Mary was dying at St James's, Pole was dying in Lambeth Palace. They sent each other messages of sympathy. Both of them sent messages to Elizabeth. Mary asked her, as a last request, to preserve the Catholic religion when she became Queen. Pole's secretary, Priuli, wrote that she promised not to introduce any changes in religion;[54] but it is more likely that she gave an ambiguous reply which conveyed this impression without definitely committing herself over her future religious policy.

Mary died at seven o'clock in the morning on 17 November, a day which would be celebrated for over a hundred years as Queen Elizabeth's Accession Day. The Privy Councillors at St James's rode at once to Hatfield to inform Elizabeth. According to tradition, they found her sitting under an oak tree in the park, reading the Bible in Greek. It is unlikely that she was sitting under a tree, reading, on a November day; but perhaps she was taking a brisk walk in the park, and they found her near the tree.

At seven o'clock in the evening, Pole died, twelve hours after Mary. It was the end of a reign, the end of an era, and the end of the burnings. In three years and nine months, two hundred and twenty-seven men and fifty-six women had been burned for heresy, nearly three times the number in the previous hundred years; but the five Canterbury martyrs were the last victims.

When last of all, to take their leave,
At Canterbury they did consume,
Who constantly to Christ did cleave,
Therefore were fried with fiery fume,
But six days after these were put to death
God sent us our Elizabeth.[55]

*The account of this conversation in Froude (*History of England*, vi.93–94) and in Neale (*Queen Elizabeth*, 61) is misleading.

※ 6 ※

THE CORONATION

On the afternoon of 17 November, Nicholas Heath, Lord Chancellor and Archbishop of York, informed the Houses of Parliament that Queen Mary had died and had been succeeded by Queen Elizabeth. He then praised the qualities of the late Queen, especially her devotion to the Catholic Church.[1]

But what would the new Queen do about religion? The Catholics feared the worst, for she was regarded by the Protestants as the head of their party; but when party leaders come to power they do not always fulfil the hopes and fears which they aroused when in opposition, and it was still possible that Elizabeth might realise the serious political drawbacks of making England Protestant once more. The members of Mary's Privy Council, who had proclaimed Elizabeth as Queen, were Catholics; and so were the bishops, the justices of the peace, and the majority of the English people, whatever might be the view of the inhabitants of London and Kent and of the activists of the younger generation. A reversion to Protestantism would cause even greater difficulties abroad. All Englishmen, whatever their religion, wished above all to recover Calais, and this could only be achieved with the help of their Spanish ally. It was not the time to antagonise Philip by imposing heresy on the realm.

But strategical considerations were not the only factors involved. The new Queen was a young woman of strong emotions, strong religious feelings, and strong likes and dislikes. Whatever Protestant and Catholic theologians might say, she loved the crucifix which Protestant enthusiasts condemned as a graven image. She loved the splendid vestments of the clergy, which had been suppressed by the Protestants under Edward VI; and she shared the prejudices of so many of her subjects against married priests and their wives. But she hated the Mass and the elevation and adoration of the Host, which implied belief in transubstantiation and the Real Presence. This had been, in the most literal sense, the burning issue for the last forty years; nearly every martyr who had been sent to the stake under Henry VIII and Mary had been condemned as a 'sacramentary' for denying the Real Presence, even if he had also been accused of other heresies. Now England was ruled by a Queen who, however conservative she might be in other matters and however cautious in her approach to religious change, was a convinced sacramentary. She had not been prepared to testify to her hatred of the Mass during her sister's reign, and to suffer martyrdom for it; but she hated it all the more because of her forced submission and silence during these last five years, and as a result of that submission and silence she was now in a position where she could hit it hard.

Elizabeth was clear on one point: any religious changes must be introduced in a lawful and orderly way under the royal authority. There must be no riots, no destruction of churches, and no attacks on Catholic preachers by Protestant mobs. She immediately issued a proclamation in which, after stating that it had pleased God to vest the crown in her 'by calling to His mercy out of this mortal life, to our great grief, our dearest sister of noble memory', the late Queen Mary, she ordered the people not to make any unauthorised alteration in religion, on pain of unspecified 'punishment'.[2] Cardinal Pole's secretary, Priuli, was relieved, and wrote to Venice that it was clear that Elizabeth would uphold the Catholic religion in England, as she had promised Mary that she would do.[3]

She then nominated her Privy Council. She reappointed thirteen councillors who had been members of Mary's Council, but also appointed new councillors who had not held high office under Mary. They were Lord Russell, now the second Earl of Bedford, who had been arrested at the time of Wyatt's insurrection but had later fought in Philip's army at St Quentin; her cofferer Thomas Parry, who had been in trouble over the Thomas Seymour incident and during her imprisonment at Woodstock; and Sir William Cecil, whom she appointed as her Secretary of State. A month later, she appointed Katherine Parr's brother, Sir William Parr, as a Privy Councillor, after restoring him to his title of Marquess of Northampton of which he had been deprived after he had been sentenced to death, and pardoned, for his part in supporting Jane Grey against Mary. In January, she gave office to the most ardent Protestant of them all, Sir Francis Knollys, the husband of her cousin Katherine, after he returned from Germany, where he had lived as a refugee. She appointed him as Vice-Chamberlain of the Household, Captain of the Guard, and a member of the Privy Council.

Cecil had held the office of Secretary of State under Somerset and Northumberland, but after extricating himself from his involvement with Jane Grey, he had been pardoned but down-graded by Mary. She had sent him to escort Cardinal Pole from Brussels to London when Pole returned to England as Papal Legate, and Cecil and Pole became friends, probably because they both enjoyed reading Plato and Cicero and other works of classical literature. He conformed and went to Mass, and spent most of his time at his house at Wimbledon; but as MP for Stamford, where he had another residence, Burghley House, he attended Parliament and spoke in the House of Commons against a proposal to freeze the rents payable to any Protestant landowner who had gone abroad as a refugee. The bill was defeated, and Sir Anthony Kingston, who had organised the opposition to it, was sent to the Tower; but Cecil escaped with a warning.[4]

It was no more common in the sixteenth than in the twentieth century for gentlemen living quietly in the country to be suddenly appointed to hold high office in the government. Elizabeth and Cecil had obviously kept in touch during the last months of Mary's reign. No correspondence between them at this time has survived. If they wrote to each other, they were no doubt careful to destroy the letters. It would ordinarily have been as risky for anyone in Cecil's position to visit Elizabeth in Mary's reign as to write her politically compromising letters; but since 1550 Cecil had been surveyor of Elizabeth's property, and his official duties as surveyor may have given them the opportunity, rarely and very discreetly, to discuss their plans for the future, though on at least one occasion he thought it wiser to avoid meeting her.[5]

Cecil was neither a martyr nor a revolutionary by temperament. He had no wish to burn at the stake, to suffer on the rack, or to undergo long terms of imprisonment, and he had no intention of rebelling against his Catholic Prince. But he was a convinced Protestant, and from 20 November 1558 he placed all his abilities for forty years at the service of Elizabeth and the Protestant cause. They were great abilities. With his cold judgement, he nearly always succeeded, though sometimes with difficulty, in controlling Elizabeth's emotional decisions, and he was a great Foreign Secretary.

On 22 November Elizabeth left Hatfield and moved towards London, taking up residence at the Charterhouse near the Barbican just outside the city walls. The Lord Mayor and city dignitaries came out to Highgate to meet her; but when Bonner, the Bishop of London, the most hated of all the persecutors – fat, jovial, coarse and brutal – approached with the rest to kiss her hand, she snatched it away and turned from him in disgust. After six days at the Charterhouse she entered London, riding through the Barbican and Cripplegate, along London Wall to Bishopsgate, and by Leadenhall Street, Gracechurch Street and Fenchurch Street to Mark Lane and Tower Street to the Tower, all the streets having been regravelled for the occasion. She was given a tremendous reception by the people as she passed. The London Protestants, who had cheered her during her days of disgrace in Mary's reign, now cheered her as Queen.[6]

But her first thought was to hold the London Protestants in check till she had decided what to do about religion. This could best be done through the Sunday sermons at Paul's Cross, the pulpit in the churchyard of St Paul's Cathedral where preachers appointed by the government expounded official policy to large crowds who stood in the open air in all weathers to hear the latest government propaganda line. The first preacher of the new reign was Dr William Bill, the former Master of Trinity College, Cambridge, who had been dismissed from his office by Mary when she came to the throne; two Catholic Fellows of the college had given him no time to obey the Queen's order and had forcibly ejected him from his seat in the college chapel. He suffered nothing worse under Mary, living quietly in the house of his kinsman, the rector of Sandy in Bedfordshire.

Bill was a very suitable spokesman for Elizabeth to choose to restrain the zeal of the Protestants, and in his sermon on Sunday 20 November he exhorted all supporters of the true Protestant religion to obey the law and make no changes in the established religious practices for the time being; but his reference to Protestantism as the 'true religion' alarmed John Christopherson, the Bishop of Chichester, who had been chosen to preach at Paul's Cross on the following Sunday. In his sermon, Christopherson attacked Bill, saying that what he had called the 'true religion' was heresy.

Elizabeth told Christopherson that he had been chosen to preach restraint, not to incite hatred of heretics, and she placed him under house arrest. He would probably have been released before long, but he died in confinement a fortnight later.[7]

Elizabeth arranged for Mary to have a funeral worthy of a Queen of England, and appointed John White, the Bishop of Winchester, to preach the funeral sermon. He was a devout Catholic, who had got into minor difficulties under Edward VI and had persecuted Protestants under Mary, having been president of the court which tried and sentenced Ridley for heresy. He chose as his text Eccles. iv.2: 'I praised the dead more than the living', and spoke of Queen Mary's rare devotion, and how her knees had grown hard from her constant kneeling in prayer. 'She has left a sister to succeed her, a lady of great worth, whom we are bound to obey also, for "a living dog is better than a dead lion" . . . but I must still say, with my text: "I praised the dead more than the living", for certain it is, "Mary chose the best part."'

He then warned the people against the great perils which confronted them. 'I warn you, the wolves be coming out of Geneva and other places of Germany, and have sent their books before, full of pestilent doctrines, blasphemy and heresy, to infect the people'. If those whom God had placed to keep watch and ward upon the walls failed to give warning when the wolf came towards the flock, 'then shall the more mighty be more mightily scourged, and the blood of the people be required at their hands'.

Elizabeth did not like White's sermon, and could not overlook his comparison of the dead and living Queens. She ordered him to stay under house arrest in his palace in Southwark, but released him after a month.[8]

Elizabeth, at Somerset Place in the Strand, was consulting with her advisers about how to deal with the problems which faced her, particularly the problem of how far and how fast to go in changing religion. An elderly clerk to the Privy Council, Armagil Waad, who as a young man had sailed to Newfoundland, wrote a paper on the difficulties which confronted the

Queen. He advised caution in introducing religious changes; glasses with small necks could not be filled by pouring in the liquid quickly, for they would then refuse to receive the liquid, but the glasses could be filled if the water was poured in slowly.[9]

Richard Goodrich, a lawyer and government official with strong Protestant sympathies, also impressed on Elizabeth the need for caution in introducing religious change. He thought that the Heresy Acts, under which the Protestant martyrs had been burned, should be repealed. The Queen could do away with the elevation of the Host in her chapel royal, to which she so strongly objected; she could permit the Litany, homilies, and certain prayers to be read in English, as had been done towards the end of Henry VIII's reign; and she could 'wink' at the marriage of priests without legalising it. But she should not introduce any other religious changes for the time being.[10]

Elizabeth decided to go at least as far as Goodrich advised. She spent Christmas at Whitehall, and on Christmas morning Owen Oglethorpe, Bishop of Carlisle, celebrated Mass in her chapel. During the service, in the usual manner, he held up the Host for adoration. Elizabeth ordered him to lower it, for she would have no elevation in the chapel royal. As Oglethorpe refused to comply and held it high, the Queen rose and walked out.[11] The Catholics were shocked. If any woman had spoken and acted as she had done in a church during Mass six weeks before, she would have been burned as a heretic; but on 27 December she issued a proclamation which declared that the Litany, the Lord's Prayer, the Ten Commandments and the lesson for the day should be read out in English at all church services.[12]

The coronation was to be held in the middle of January; but who would crown Elizabeth? With the see of Canterbury vacant on Pole's death, Heath, as Archbishop of York, was the obvious choice; but he told Elizabeth that as she had refused to worship the elevated Host in her chapel on Christmas Day, he regarded her as a heretic and would not crown her Queen. Several other bishops were invited to crown her, but all refused. Eventually the Bishop of Carlisle agreed to do so. When his brother bishops reprimanded him for deserting them and agreeing to crown a heretic, he said that he had only agreed reluctantly because he feared that if every bishop refused, it would drive Elizabeth into the arms of the heretics.[13]

Feria was becoming more and more disgusted with Elizabeth. 'What can you expect from a country governed by a Queen, a young girl who, although sharp, has no prudence, and is every day standing up against religion more openly? The kingdom is entirely in the hands of young people, heretics and traitors, and the Queen does not favour a single man whom Her Majesty who is now in Heaven would have received . . . The old people and the Catholics are dissatisfied, but dare not open their mouths'.[14] Feria had fallen in love with Jane Dormer, the daughter of a very Catholic English family who had been one of Queen Mary's ladies-in-waiting. He married her a fortnight after writing this letter, and his wife encouraged his misgivings about the new Queen.

But Feria had to think first and foremost of King Philip's interests, and felt that these would best be served if Philip were to marry Elizabeth. Philip would then remain King of England and would bind England firmly to the alliance with Spain and the Netherlands, and he might perhaps be able to restrain Elizabeth from promoting heresy. There was one difficulty. Philip's marriage to the sister of his dead wife was illegal by the law of the Church; but as his armies had decisively beaten the Pope's in the recent campaign in Italy, there was little doubt that he would be able to persuade the Pope to grant a dispensation for the marriage to take place. Henry II of France, who had guessed that Philip would wish to marry Elizabeth, had already instructed his agents in Rome to do their best to prevent the dispensation from being granted.

Philip had returned to Brussels after his successful campaign in France. He wrote to Feria that he did not wish to marry Elizabeth because she was a heretic; but he reluctantly authorised Feria to make her a proposal of marriage.[15] Perhaps Philip was not being quite frank with his ambassador. Elizabeth was attractive, and Philip, despite his apparent aversion to women and his pious dread of sex, may well have lusted in his heart for her, though he would certainly have concealed this from his ambassador and himself, and made out that his only reason for proposing marriage to her was his sense of duty to God and his subjects. The impression that he gave to Feria, that he was virtuously offering to sacrifice his feelings by marrying the heretical Queen, may have been as distorted as the picture which the sixteenth-century English writers drew of the lascivious Spanish villain lusting to deflower the virtuous English Virgin Queen.

Feria made a formal proposal of marriage to Elizabeth on Philip's behalf. She thanked him, and said that she was deeply honoured, but refused, as she did not wish to marry and would always remain a virgin. According to Camden, who later became a friend of Cecil's and was in a good position to discover what had occurred at court in 1559, Philip wrote Elizabeth a love-letter proposing marriage, and when she refused him, he renewed his proposal in other love-letters. Camden says that the letters were ardent and eloquent, and that Elizabeth was so delighted with them and with 'the manners and behaviour of so great a King' that she read them aloud to her courtiers. Philip might have written such letters, or had them written for him, because, though everyone knew that diplomatic marriages between princes were made for reasons of cold power politics, it was good form to pretend that they were love-matches, and to act out a charade of a romantic Prince ardently wooing a bashful Princess.

Camden wrote that Elizabeth's courtiers, seeing her so pleased with Philip's love-letters, began to worry, 'fearing lest the tender and young spirit of Maid, often moved, might easily condescend' to Philip's desires. They therefore thought out an argument to convince Elizabeth that she must refuse Philip. If she married Philip under a Papal dispensation, she would be recognising the Pope's power to allow a marriage which was prohibited by the Word of God; if the Pope could allow a widower to marry his deceased wife's sister, he could allow a widow to marry her deceased husband's brother; the Papal dispensation for the marriage of Henry VIII and Catherine of Aragon would therefore be valid, their marriage lawful, Henry's marriage to Anne Boleyn void, and Elizabeth a bastard.[16]

The coronation took place on Sunday 15 January 1559. Three days before, Elizabeth came by barge from Whitehall to the Tower, and on the Saturday drove in her carriage through the streets of London from the Tower to Westminster, in the traditional procession which was always held on the day before the coronation. It was always a great occasion for Londoners, with the Mayor and Aldermen and the Masters of the livery companies in their robes of office, and the children of the hospitals for the poor turning out to salute the sovereign with pageants, reading of verses, and general rejoicing. But the coronation procession of 14 January 1559 was something more than this: it was a great Protestant demonstration of enthusiastic support for Elizabeth. In the pageant in Gracechurch Street, showing 'the Uniting of the Two Houses of Lancaster and York', the Queen's ancestors were shown, with not only 'the valiant and noble Prince King Henry the Eight' but also 'the right worthy lady Queen Anne, wife to the said King Henry the Eight and mother to our most sovereign Lady Queen Elizabeth that now is'. The fifth and last pageant at the Conduit in Fleet Street showed how God had chosen the woman Deborah to be the judge and restorer of the house of Israel after the Israelites had long been oppressed by Jabin the Canaan King.

Elizabeth ordered her carriage to stop at each pageant and spoke words of thanks and encouragement to the performers and the surrounding crowds. At Cheapside she smiled happily when someone called out to her 'Remember old King Henry VIII!' This was the voice of a typical Englishman who revered the memory of the great King who had defeated the French and the Scots and defied the foreign Pope; but a few yards further on, at the pageant at Little Conduit in Cheapside, she saw one of the performers holding up a copy of the English Bible which people had been imprisoned for reading in the days of old King Henry VIII. She asked what the book was, and when they told her that it was the English Bible, she said 'that she would oftentimes read over that book'. She asked to have the book, and sent a gentleman to fetch it, but was told that arrangements had been made for a child to deliver it to her 'down by a silken lace'. When she received it from the child, she took it in both hands and pressed it to her breast. As she left the city boundary at Temple Bar, a child handed her a poem praising her as the Deborah who would restore Truth in place of Error.

Next day, Elizabeth was crowned in Westminster Abbey. The ceremony took place with all the traditional features, and Oglethorpe administered the oath to her in the usual form. After he had crowned her, a Mass was held in Latin; but the celebrant, her chaplain, spoke the words of consecration in English and did not elevate the Host.[17]

❧ 7 ❧

THE PROTESTANT REALM

P ARLIAMENT met ten days after the coronation. The elections had taken place without any of the usual pressure from the government. The normal practice was for the mayors in the boroughs and the sheriffs in the counties to be given the names of the candidates whom the sovereign hoped would be chosen as their MP, and the small number of voters – not more than a few hundred in each constituency – normally complied with the sovereign's wishes. This practice had been adopted at every general election in Mary's reign. Elizabeth gave no indication to the electors in December 1558 as to whom she wished them to elect as their MP, and left the choice entirely to them.[1] She had perhaps a special reason for doing this. The great question for her first Parliament would be to settle religion, and a completely free election would give her some idea as to what those classes of her subjects who had the vote – the merchants in the towns and the country gentlemen – felt about the religious controversy. Many Protestant sympathisers were elected as MPs, including a number of refugees who had just returned to England from their exile in Germany and Switzerland. It was clear to Elizabeth and Cecil that the House of Commons would support an immediate and radical alteration in religion. The House of Lords, with the forty-three peers and the sixteen bishops and the one remaining abbot, was likely to be much more difficult.

Before dealing with the religious settlement, the House of Commons asked the Queen to marry so as to provide an heir to the throne. In her reply, Elizabeth stated that she had no intention of ever marrying, 'and in the end, this shall be for me sufficient, that a marble stone shall declare that a Queen, having reigned such a time, lived and died a virgin'.[2]

Parliament then dealt with religion. With nearly all the bishops refusing to crown the Queen and almost openly hinting that she was a heretic, Elizabeth had no alternative but to turn to the Protestants who were cheering her so enthusiastically. She would have to create a completely new bench of bishops. They would have to be Protestants, and though she would be able to find a few eligible Protestant clergymen who, after being deprived of their benefices, had lived quietly in England under Mary, she would have to include those who had escaped abroad and had lived as refugees in the more radical atmosphere of the cities of Germany and Switzerland. There was no moderate party left among the leaders of the Church in England; there were only persecuting Papist Catholics and embittered anti-Catholic Protestants. Almost the only moderate in religion was the Queen herself, who was a moderate not so much because she believed in moderation as a principle or a tactic, but because of her own religious preferences. But a Queen who would not tolerate the elevation of the Host and was a sacramentary had no choice but to rely on the Protestants, whatever she felt about crucifixes, married priests and vestments.

The government introduced a bill which abolished Papal supremacy and declared that Elizabeth, like Henry VIII and Edward VI, was 'Supreme Head under God of the Church of England'. The bill was opposed by several of the Catholic bishops in the House of Lords; Heath, after stating that the Queen was 'as humble, as virtuous and as godly a mistress to reign over us as ever had English people here in this realm', insisted that as St Paul had declared that a woman could not be an apostle, a shepherd, a doctor or a preacher in the Church, she could not be its Supreme Head.[3] A compromise was reached: the Queen was to be called, not Supreme Head, but 'Supreme Governor of the Church of England'; the penalty for refusing to take the Oath of Supremacy was not to be death for the first offence, as it had been under Henry VIII, but merely loss of office; and the punishment for asserting the Papal supremacy was to be a fine for the first offence, life imprisonment for the second offence, and death only for the third offence.

In the House of Commons, John Story, the member for Downton in Wiltshire, strongly opposed the bill for the supremacy. He was an able Catholic doctor of civil law who had been counsel for the prosecution at Cranmer's trial for heresy. He said in the debate that he did not regret the part that he had played persecuting hectics in Mary's reign. 'I wish for my part that I had done more than I did ... I threw a faggot in the face of an earwig at the stake at Uxbridge as he was singing a psalm, and set a bushel of thorns under his feet ... and I see nothing to be ashamed of, nor sorry for.' But he had often told the bishops in Queen Mary's time that they were too busy persecuting the common people, 'chopping at twigs. But I wished to have chopped at the root, which if they had done, this gear had not come now in question'.[4] Everyone knew that by 'the roots', Story had meant the Lady Elizabeth, now Queen.

Eventually, the bill abolishing the Papal and restoring the royal supremacy passed both the House of Commons and the House of Lords. In the Lords, it passed on 18 March 1559, the Saturday before Palm Sunday, by 33 votes to 12, with all the bishops and two temporal peers voting against the bill. On the Wednesday in Holy Week, Elizabeth issued a proclamation ordering that on

Easter Day the communion in every church was to be administered to the congregation in both kinds, as had been done in the days of King Edward VI, because large numbers of the nobility, the gentry and the common people were unwilling to receive communion in any other way. The proclamation stated that if any parish priest refused to administer the wine to the congregation, the people were to go to another church.[5]

There seems to be no doubt that Elizabeth, after issuing this proclamation on 22 March, intended to go to the House of Lords two days later on Good Friday, give her royal assent to the Supremacy Bill, and dissolve Parliament, postponing any further statutory religious alteration to the next Parliament, which was unlikely to be summoned for some years. But she changed her mind, and instead of dissolving Parliament adjourned it for ten days until after Easter without giving her consent to the Supremacy Bill, so that the whole question of introducing Protestant Church services throughout the realm could be dealt with later in the session. Sir John Neale has shown that she must have taken this decision between the late evening of 23 March and 1 p.m. the next day. He believed that she was influenced not only by her need to rely on the Protestant clergy in the face of the opposition of the Catholic bishops, but by the news, which had reached London a few days earlier, that peace between England, France and Spain had been signed at Cateau-Cambrésis and that there was no longer any immediate danger of invasion from France.[6]

The peace negotiations, which had been carried on chiefly by Cardinal Granvelle for Philip and the Cardinal of Lorraine for France, developed into hard bargaining about the exchange of frontier towns in Flanders and in the duchy of Milan, though both cardinals were eager for Philip and Henry II to unite against the heretics throughout Europe. Lord Howard of Effingham and the other English delegates at the peace talks demanded the return of Calais; but eventually Elizabeth reluctantly agreed that the French should retain Calais for eight years, and then return it to her on 2 April 1567. Philip and Henry agreed to an exchange of the frontier towns, and that Philip should marry Henry's daughter Elizabeth of Valois. In April England and Scotland made peace. The treaty provided that they would not invade each other's territories or give help to each other's enemies, rebels, traitors, murderers, thieves, or robbers. Fugitives from justice would be extradited within twenty days. The Scots agreed to dismantle the fortifications at Eyemouth on the coast near the Border at Berwick.

When Feria informed Elizabeth that Philip was to marry Princess Elizabeth of Valois, she said that he could not have been very much in love with her if he would not wait more than four months for her to change her mind after her first refusal. Feria assured her that she could always count on Philip as a faithful ally.[7]

On the other hand, Feria clearly told Elizabeth that Philip would be deeply shocked at the religious changes which were being introduced, and that the consequences might be serious for her. She asked him if the danger would come from the King of France or from Philip, and he hastily assured her that no danger would come from Philip, who would do nothing but give her good advice. She said that she wished to have friendly relations with all foreign Princes, and that she would merely restore religion to the state it was in at her father's death; but she had in fact already gone further than this in her proclamations about religion. Feria reminded her that Henry VIII had burned Lutherans, and said that all the 'poltroons' who were now preaching to her were either Lutherans or Zwinglians.[8]

The third Book of Common Prayer was drawn up by a commission of Protestant divines, and given force of law by the third Act of Uniformity. It was not as Protestant as the second Book of Common Prayer of 1552, but more radical than the first Book of Common Prayer of 1549, and abolished the Catholic Mass and restored the Protestant communion service. Elizabeth would have preferred it to have been less Protestant in some respects. Some years later, she told her Archbishop of Canterbury, Matthew Parker, that she only agreed to the new Prayer Book because it retained the old ceremonies of the Catholic Church.[9] But apart from their vocal members in the House of Commons, the Protestant party had influential advocates at court: the Earl of Bedford, Knollys, Parry; her childhood friend Lord Robert Dudley, whom the gossipmongers were naming as a possible husband for her; Sir Nicholas Throckmorton, who, though not a member of the Council, was a friend of Elizabeth's and had been in secret touch with her during Mary's reign; and Cecil.

The Uniformity Bill was debated in Parliament throughout April, and passed both Houses. In the House of Lords, it was carried by a majority of only three votes, with all the bishops and nine temporal peers voting against it. The bill reinstated the Protestant clergy who had been deprived of their benefices for heresy or marriage under Mary. The controversial question of the marriage of priests, which was unpopular with the Queen as well as many of her subjects, was dealt with very tactfully. It was legalised by the simple and silent process of repealing the section of the Act of Mary's Parliament which had prohibited it, without making any reference to what the section contained.[10]

The same policy of tactful silence was adopted in dealing with Elizabeth's bastardy. She had been bastardised after the execution of Anne Boleyn by the Act of 1536, which had never been repealed, though this did not affect her right to succeed to the crown, which was regulated by Henry VIII's will. During the Parliament of 1559 it was decided, after a good deal of thought by Elizabeth's counsellors, not to repeal the Act of 1536 and legitimise Elizabeth. This was done largely on the advice of Sir Nicholas Bacon, the Lord Keeper of the Great Seal. He argued that as Elizabeth was in any case entitled to succeed to the crown under Henry's will, there was no point in reopening old controversies by looking into the events of 1536. Instead,

Parliament quietly passed a bill which enabled Elizabeth to succeed to her mother's property, notwithstanding any forfeiture imposed by law or by previous statutes.[11]

This was in line with Elizabeth's policy of preserving the unity between the Protestants and the older generation of Catholics who had supported Henry VIII against Rome and the foreigners. Henry's role as a persecutor of Protestants must be played down as far as possible; he was to be remembered as a patriot King who, like his daughter the present Queen, had opposed Popery. In the Acts of Parliament of 1559, he was always referred to as 'Her Majesty's dearest father the late King Henry VIII'. Edward VI was 'Her Majesty's dearest brother the late King Edward VI'. Mary was merely 'the late Queen Mary'.

Elizabeth gave her royal assent to the legislation and dissolved Parliament on 8 May.

Feria was becoming more and more disturbed at the religious developments in England 'since this woman became Queen'*[12]. The most depressing thing for Feria was the attitude of his master. Philip ordered him to try to persuade Elizabeth not to reintroduce heresy into England, but if he failed, and religious conflict broke out in England, Feria was to remain neutral; he was to encourage the Catholics, but was also to remain on good terms with the heretics. Only if it was clear that the Catholics were the stronger party was Feria to give them financial aid, and even then he must continue to use fair words to the heretics to prevent them from calling in the French, 'which is the thing principally to be avoided'.[13] It is clear that what Philip really feared was that if the English Catholics made a successful counter-revolution in England, they might depose Elizabeth and invite Mary Queen of Scots, the wife of the French Dauphin, to become Queen. The rivalry between the Habsburgs and the Valois, which had prevented Catholic Europe from uniting against Henry VIII, was now once again, as Cardinal Pole had foreseen, creating a situation from which only the heretics could benefit.

In May, Philip recalled Feria, and appointed Alvaro de la Quadra, Bishop of Aquila, to succeed him as ambassador in England. Feria's English wife followed him two months later to Philip's court in the Netherlands. Before leaving, she had a farewell audience with Elizabeth, though Feria had advised against this. Elizabeth kept her waiting for quite a long time in the anteroom. According to the Catholic writer, Henry Clifford, who knew Jane Feria when she was an old woman, she was not even offered a chair while she waited, though she was seven months pregnant. Then Quadra arrived, and made an angry scene, for he was indignant that the wife of a Spanish nobleman should be kept waiting.

Cecil wrote to the English ambassador at Philip's court giving his version of the story. The Queen had been unable to see the Countess of Feria

* . . . 'despues que esta es Reyna.'

immediately, as she was otherwise engaged, so the court officials had invited the countess to wait in a private room; but she had insisted on waiting in the anteroom. When the Queen received her, they had spoken together in a most friendly way; and the countess, unlike the Spanish ambassador, had made no complaint at all. This is confirmed by Feria, who wrote to Quadra that Jane had patiently endured the indignity in silence, though he himself was very angry about it.[14]

Jane joined her husband in the Netherlands, and next year they went to Spain. She never returned to her native country. For fifty years her house in Madrid provided hospitality for English Catholic refugees, and was the centre of the faction at the Spanish court which pressed most strongly for decisive action against heretical England.

All the bishops refused to take the oath of supremacy recognising Elizabeth as Supreme Governor of the Church of England. When the third Book of Common Prayer came into force on St John's Day, 24 June 1559, they refused to officiate at the services; in St Paul's, Bonner insisted on continuing to celebrate the old Catholic Mass. In September, Elizabeth appointed the Protestant, Matthew Parker, as Archbishop of Canterbury to fill the vacancy caused by Pole's death. No bishop would agree to consecrate him, and the government had to find three old Protestant bishops of Henry VIII and Edward VI, who had been deprived of their sees by Mary and were too old to be restored to them, to officiate at Parker's consecration.

The Council sent Bishop White of Winchester and Bishop Watson of Lincoln to the Tower, and Bonner to the Marshalsea prison. Kitchin, the Bishop of Llandaff, was eventually persuaded to sign a written declaration acknowledging the royal supremacy instead of taking the oath, and he was allowed to continue in office. All the other bishops were deprived of their sees, and either imprisoned or placed under house arrest. They were replaced by new Protestant bishops.[15]

Feria derived some comfort from the fact that whereas only Bishop Fisher of Rochester, Sir Thomas More and a few monks had opposed Henry VIII's Act of Supremacy in 1535, now all the bishops were opposing Elizabeth's religious policy.[16] This was indeed a new development. The open opposition of the bishops in Parliament was something that would have been impossible under Henry VIII or Mary. The awe-inspiring Henry, taking care not to antagonise the feelings and prejudices of his subjects, had played off the Protestants and the Catholics against each other, both in his Council and in the country; he had in the first place only asked his bishops to repudiate the Papal supremacy, not to accept Lutheranism and Zwinglianism; and he crushed the slightest opposition by beheading, by burning and by hanging, drawing and quartering his opponents. The bishops did not fear a young woman of twenty-five as they had feared the terrible King her father.

Queen Mary, too, had been a woman; but she was supported by the ecclesiastical hierarchy which for centuries had believed and taught that their authority must not be questioned; and Mary, like her father, inflicted terrible punishments on her religious opponents. Elizabeth, introducing the new religion, supported largely by the youth, and acting through spokesmen who six months before would have been burned as heretics, aroused far more opposition and dealt with it far more leniently than Henry or Mary. The Catholic bishops in 1559 knew that they were risking nothing worse than a few months in prison or under house arrest and being deprived of their bishoprics.

The firm opposition of the Catholic bishops compelled Elizabeth to depend on the Protestants in a way that Henry VIII had never had to do. While Henry used the Protestants to achieve his selfish personal aims, Elizabeth was to a considerable extent used by the Protestants, who often had to coax, flatter and patiently win her over to a Protestant policy which she had first, instinctively and tempestuously, rejected.

By temperament, too, she was very different from Henry and Mary. Henry, under a show of false bonhomie, planned the destruction of his opponents with the cool, calculating cruelty of Machiavelli's Prince; Mary consigned them to the flames with the cold fanaticism of a religious bigot. When anyone opposed Elizabeth, she raged, shouted abuse at them, slapped their faces, and usually did nothing more, or at the worst sent them to prison for a very short while. Her petulant outbursts of anger were probably an expression of her frustration and sense of impotence, compared with the power which her father and sister had wielded. Her maids of honour might be frightened of arousing her anger, but her counsellors never feared that they would suffer evil consequences if they annoyed or opposed her.

But ultimately everything depended on her. If Mary had still been alive, the bishops would have been burning Protestants in the summer of 1559; but in fact they were being imprisoned and ousted from their sees by the Protestants because the Queen was now the daughter of Anne Boleyn, the step-daughter of Katherine Parr, the pupil of Ascham and Grindal, and the friend of Cecil, Robert Dudley, Parry, and Francis and Katherine Knollys.

JOHN KNOX

THREE days after Elizabeth gave her royal assent to the religious legislation, a Protestant revolution broke out in Scotland. England and Scotland took different roads to Protestantism. In England the Reformation was imposed lawfully and peaceably by the royal authority under the leadership of Elizabeth; in Scotland, it was achieved by a revolt of the nobility, the gentry and the common people under the leadership of John Knox.

In barren, isolated and backward Scotland, the moral degeneration and unpopularity of the Catholic Church had gone much further than in England. Corruption, nepotism and absenteeism, which were causes of complaint in England before the Reformation, were endemic in the Catholic Church of Scotland. Most parishes had no parson, but only an underpaid curate. By the beginning of the sixteenth century, Protestant groups had sprung up in the port of Dundee, which carried on a busy trade with the Netherlands, Germany and Scandinavia, and among the peasants and fishermen in Ayrshire and the south-west. A few Protestants were caught and burned as heretics; but the persecution was more spasmodic and inefficient than in England, because respect for law and order, and the power of the central government, were much weaker in Scotland.

When King James V and his Chancellor, Cardinal Beaton, went to war with Henry VIII and claimed that they were fighting for the Pope and the Holy Catholic Church against the English heretics, the cause of Protestantism in Scotland became closely linked with the English invader. In the short run, this made the Protestants unpopular in Scotland; in the long run, as the hatred of the government and the Church increased, it forged a new friendship with the English.

In May 1546 some Scottish Protestant gentlemen, eager to revenge the martyrdom of the Protestant preacher George Wishart, broke into St Andrews Castle and assassinated Beaton. They then proceeded to hold the castle and asked Henry VIII for help. Henry sent a fleet to supply them with victuals, and after his death Somerset marched into Scotland; but before he could reach St Andrews, the castle surrendered to a French fleet. After this, things did not go so well for the English and their Protestant allies. A French expeditionary force defeated the English at Haddington, and a French fleet took the four-year-old Mary Queen of Scots to France. Her mother, the French-born Mary of Guise, governed Scotland as her Regent.

Knox, who had joined the murderers of Beaton in St Andrews Castle, was taken prisoner by the French when the castle fell, and served for nineteen months as a slave in the French galleys before being set free and sent to England in exchange for a French prisoner-of-war. He became well known at the court of Edward VI as a vigorous Protestant preacher and critic of the moderate policy which Cranmer and the bishops were pursuing. At Mary's accession he fled abroad with his English wife and mother-in-law, and after staying for some months in Dieppe and Frankfort he settled in Calvin's Geneva. He was a brilliant polemical writer with a lively sense of humour which was rare among sixteenth-century Protestants, and he combined a rigid devotion to principle and the international Protestant cause with a shrewd political instinct and a sense of the realities of power politics. On several occasions he acted as an English spy in Scotland,[1] and was regarded by the Scottish Catholics as a traitor to his country; but he knew that the success of the Protestant cause in Scotland depended on English diplomatic and military support.

During his years of exile in Dieppe and Geneva, in Mary Tudor's reign, he developed a theory of the justification of revolution against Catholic sovereigns. It went far beyond Calvin's tentative suggestions that in certain exceptional circumstances, if the Prince refused to reform religion, his nobles, like the *ephors* in ancient Sparta, were justified in acting on his behalf. Calvin put forward his theory with the situation in France in mind, where Princes of the Blood like the King of Navarre and the Prince of Condé and other powerful nobles became Protestants in the 1550s. Knox, in pamphlets addressed to the nobles and common people of Scotland, called on them to rise in revolt against their Catholic Queen and government.[2]

In the summer of 1558, Knox published in Geneva his book, *The First Blast of the Trumpet against the Monstrous Regiment of Women*, which should be translated into twentieth-century English as 'against the unnatural government of women'. He argued that by the law of God a woman was not entitled to rule as a sovereign, and therefore no woman ruler should be obeyed. At the same time Knox's colleague, Christopher Goodman, an English Protestant refugee from Leicestershire, published his book in Geneva, *How Superior Powers ought to be obeyed*, which asserted that no Papist sovereign who violated the laws of God by supporting idolatry – that is to say, the Mass – should be obeyed, and that his subjects were justified in overthrowing him by revolution. These two books aroused the greatest indignation, not only throughout Catholic Europe, but also among the Protestants, who hastened to dissociate themselves from Knox and Goodman.

Knox had no personal prejudice against women, and was very popular with them. He twice married a young woman of a higher social rank, and had a group of devoted women followers with whom he had religious and political discussions. But he could not resist the temptation of pandering to male prejudice at a time when several of the most oppressive Catholic rulers happened to be women. His *First Blast of the Trumpet* was written against Mary of Hungary, who had been Charles V's Regent in the Netherlands; against Mary Queen of Scots and her mother the Queen Regent, Mary of Guise; and first and foremost against Mary Tudor, Queen of England. He completely overlooked what many people in England knew, that Queen Mary was dying and would soon be succeeded by the Protestant Queen Elizabeth. The fact that a man as politically shrewd as Knox could make such an error shows how easy it is for a refugee to be completely out of touch with events at home. Knox could only see that the Lady Elizabeth had gone to Mass and had compromised with idolatry at a time when the brave martyrs were dying at the stake for their faith. He did not realise that she was the hope and heroine of the suffering Protestants in England.

Knox pointed out the anomaly, which was to continue for nearly four hundred years after his time, by which a woman was ineligible to hold any office in public life except that of Head of State. Nearly everyone else in 1558 accepted this anomaly because they believed that the general rule of the inferiority of women was overruled, in this exceptional case, by the principle of the divine right of Princes. If it pleased God to ordain that a King should have a daughter and no sons, it was His will that a woman, though by her sex an inferior creature, should be His representative in the kingdom, the 'Prince' whom all must obey without question. Elizabeth herself completely shared this point of view. She stated on several occasions that although she was only a weak woman, and as such an inferior creature, she had nevertheless been chosen by God to be a Queen. She would have been very surprised to learn that some of her modern biographers have suggested that she resented Knox's attack on her sex. What she resented was his attack on her status as a Queen, and on the principle of the divine right of hereditary sovereigns.

When Elizabeth became Queen, and Knox realised that she was a Protestant, he wrote to Cecil and offered to proclaim that she was an exception to his doctrine about women rulers and was a Deborah chosen by God to lead His people to salvation;[3] but his position was unacceptable to Elizabeth. Knox believed that she could be an exception to the accepted doctrine of the inferiority of women because she was a Protestant; Elizabeth thought that she was an exception because she was a Queen.

Goodman's book was as shocking as Knox's. Matthew Parker, whose moderate Protestantism would have made him an unqualified success with Elizabeth if he had not been married, explained the reasons why he, like Elizabeth, was alarmed at Goodman's doctrine 'that it is lawful for every private subject to kill his sovereign ... if he think him to be a tyrant in his conscience'. Parker thought that if the tenant and the servant began 'to discuss what is tyranny, and to discuss whether his Prince, his landlord, his master is a tyrant, by his own fancy and collection supposed, what lord of the Council shall ride quietly-minded in the streets among desperate beasts? What master shall be sure in his bedchamber?'[4]

When Knox heard of Mary Tudor's death, he travelled from Geneva to Dieppe, and asked permission to come to England. It was refused, for Elizabeth was incensed about the *First Blast of the Trumpet*; so he sailed direct to Scotland. On 11 May 1559, he preached at Perth, and denounced Popery to an enthusiastic crowd. As soon as he had finished preaching, a Catholic priest appeared in the church and began celebrating Mass. A young Protestant boy shouted words of protest against the Mass; a priest boxed the boy's ears; and an indignant crowd of Protestants, after smashing the images in the church, ransacked the monasteries in the town. The Congregation, as the Protestants' organisation was called, was joined by some of the most powerful lords in Scotland, including Lord James Stewart, the illegitimate half-brother of Mary Queen of Scots. They assembled their forces at Perth, while in Ayrshire and elsewhere the Protestant lairds suppressed the monasteries, and the Catholic Mass, in their territories.

Ten days after the riot at Perth, a very different event took place in Spain. A great act of faith (*auto da fe*) was held at Valladolid on Trinity Sunday. King Philip was in the Netherlands, but his fourteen-year-old son, Don Carlos, attended; it was his first public engagement as Prince of Spain. Nine men and four women, some of them of high rank, including the King's confessor and the Lord Treasurer's daughter, and two men of Jewish parentage, were burned for heresy or Judaism. Those who recanted and declared their devotion to the Catholic faith were strangled before being burned. Those who refused were gagged to prevent them from speaking, and burned alive. The Inquisition in Spain issued a new decree that no son or grandson of a heretic could hold any position at court or in national or local government administration, or become a merchant or the apprentice of any tradesman or craftsman.[5]

Within a week of the outbreak at Perth, Cecil and Elizabeth were involved. As the Queen Regent assembled her forces, including the French garrison of 1,500 men who were stationed in Scotland, and marched on Perth, Sir William Kirkcaldy of Grange, who had been one of the assassins of Cardinal Beaton, wrote to Cecil to ask the English government to help the Scottish Protestants. Cecil was chary of becoming involved until he was sure that the revolutionaries had a good chance of success, but he at once sent Sir James Croft, the Governor of Berwick, to the Congregation at Perth as an unofficial observer. We do not know if he consulted Elizabeth about this decision or about the other steps which he planned to take about Scotland in the summer of 1559. Probably he merely told her at this stage that it would be desirable to send Croft to Perth to find out what was happening.

When the Queen Regent's troops reached Perth, they found the forces of the Congregation so strong that they made a truce with them. Cecil told Croft to warn the leaders of the Congregation of the dangers which they would run if they made the truce and were taken in by the false promises of the Queen Regent. But at this very time, Elizabeth's commissioners met the Queen Regent's in the church at Upsetlington (today Upper Settle) in Yorkshire, and confirmed the peace treaty which had been agreed at Cateau-Cambrésis, with the clause by which both parties agreed not to help each other's rebels.

The truce at Perth broke down within a few days; both sides accused the other of violating it. After sacking the abbeys and suppressing the images and the Mass in the archiepiscopal seat at St Andrews, and burning the famous abbey of Scone near Perth, the Congregation entered Edinburgh in triumph on 29 June. The Queen Regent and her forces retired to Leith, intending to hold the fortress till reinforcements arrived from France. Lord Erskine, the Captain of Edinburgh Castle, remained strictly neutral and refused to surrender the castle to either side.

On the day after the Congregation entered Edinburgh, King Henry II of France was fatally wounded in a tournament at Vincennes, and died on 10 July. The new King was his fifteen-year-old son, Francis, and he and his sixteen-year-old wife were now Francis and Mary, King and Queen of France and Scotland. Mary's uncle, the Duke of Guise, at once took over the government of France. The Queen Mother, Catherine de Medici, who had had no political influence during her husband's lifetime, was completely excluded from public affairs.

The Guises, of the family of Lorraine, with their castle at Joinville and their large estates in eastern France, were a remarkable family. The eldest brother, François de Lorraine, Duke of Guise, the victor of Calais, was the most successful of the French generals, an able statesman, and the King's Lieutenant in his own province of Champagne. Even his enemies paid tribute to his courage, ability and courtesy; but to the Protestants he was the 'Tiger of France'.* The second son, Charles, Cardinal of Lorraine, Archbishop of Rheims, and bishop of several other dioceses, had been Henry II's Foreign Minister. The third, Claude de Lorraine, Duke of Aumale, was the King's Lieutenant in Burgundy and a competent soldier. The fourth son, another

---

* Although the Protestants from the beginning applied the designation 'the Tiger of France' to Guise, a careful study of the famous pamphlet of 1560, *Epître envoyée au tigre de la France*, shows that it was addressed, not, as is usually stated, to Guise, but to the Cardinal of Lorraine.

François de Lorraine, also a cardinal, was Archbishop of Sens, and known as the Cardinal of Guise to distinguish him from his brother the Cardinal of Lorraine. Louis de Lorraine held the influential office of Grand Prior of the Order of the Knights of Malta. René de Lorraine, Marquis of Elboeuf, was Admiral and Commander-in-chief of the French navy. Their sister, Mary of Lorraine, had married King James V of Scotland and was the mother of Mary Queen of Scots, and Queen Regent of Scotland. Two other sisters were abbesses of important nunneries, and divided their time between their religious devotions and engaging in political intrigue on behalf of their family.

They were a powerful and united clan with great ambitions for the advancement of their house; but there is no reason whatever to believe that up to this time, in 1559, they had ever been disloyal to the King of France. They were all sincere Catholics and determined to use their abilities and power in the interests of their King and the Catholic Church against the enemies of France and against the heretics.

The Duke of Guise began the new reign by burning some Protestants in prison in Paris, who had been condemned as heretics, but whose execution had been postponed by Henry II because of the influence of the King of Navarre and the Prince of Condé. A new law was passed, which enacted that if anyone failed to denounce to the authorities a person whom he suspected of being a heretic, he himself was to be burned, even if the person whom he failed to denounce was not in fact a heretic. This made it possible to burn Protestants who had sheltered a Catholic *agent provocateur*.[6]

Elizabeth had sent an ardent Protestant, Sir Nicholas Throckmorton, as her ambassador to France. He was a relation of Katherine Parr. He was present in the crowd at the burning of Anne Askew which he watched in silent horror and anger. He was implicated in Wyatt's rebellion and was prosecuted for high treason; but though the judge summed up strongly against him, he was acquitted by a London jury. Mary promptly sent the jurors to prison to punish them for their perverse verdict, and kept Throckmorton in the Tower despite his acquittal. Later he was released, and became a close confidant of Elizabeth at Hatfield. Was he perhaps the chief go-between, acting as the contact between her and Cecil, during the last months of Mary's reign?

Throckmorton was typical of the new kind of diplomat whom Elizabeth was selecting. In the days of Henry VIII and Edward VI, the men who were employed in carrying out a Protestant policy were bishops, deans, and other diplomats and officials who had been brought up as Catholics; and though they did their duty out of obedience to their King, their heart was not really in it, for they felt a little frightened at what they were doing in challenging the doctrines which had been accepted almost universally for centuries. Under Elizabeth, the ambassadors and agents of the Protestant government were men like Throckmorton who had seen the martyrs burn at the stake and had known some of them. Their Protestant zeal was only slightly modified by the responsibility of office; and they served a Queen who was at least half-sympathetic to their doctrines, and who might restrain, but would not thwart, their Protestant enthusiasm. When Throckmorton met Mary Queen of Scots and the Duke of Guise, and exchanged courtesies and compliments with them, he did so in order better to serve the Protestant cause and crush the hated Catholic persecutors.

The news of the fall of Edinburgh to the forces of the Congregation, and the Queen Regent's withdrawal into the fortress of Leith, reached Paris while Henry II was dying of his wound. The new government of Francis II and the Guises immediately prepared to send reinforcements to reconquer Scotland for the King and Queen and the Catholic faith. By August, Throckmorton was sending reports to Cecil about the fleet that the French were fitting out to sail to Scotland with soldiers before the end of November.

As the news of the revolution in Scotland spread through Europe, many Protestants rejoiced at the victory of the Congregation; but some were worried. In November 1559 Parker wrote to Cecil: 'God keep us from such desolation as Knox have attempted in Scotland, the people to be orderers of things'.[7] Parker did not know that already on 8 July, as soon as Cecil heard that the Congregation had taken Edinburgh, he had written to Croft that the Scottish Protestants must be encouraged 'with all fair promises first, next with money, and last with arms ... Ye must keep them in comfort that this realm neither may nor will see their ruin.'[8]

In ordinary circumstances it would not have been easy to persuade Elizabeth, with her belief in the rights of Princes, to support the Protestant revolutionaries in Scotland against their lawful sovereign within six weeks of the signing of the Treaty of Upsetlington, when her commissioners had agreed that she would give no aid to Scottish rebels. But Elizabeth was very angry that Mary Queen of Scots had adopted the arms of England; and the success of the revolution in Scotland would bring great advantages. Apart from any feelings of religious solidarity with the Scottish Protestants, their victory would be a victory for the pro-English party. For the first time in history, England would have an ally, not an enemy, on her northern frontier; English influence in Scotland would be unchallengeable, and French influence there would be destroyed.

Cecil thought out a way of presenting the issue which would overcome Elizabeth's scruples and enable her to justify her action to sixteenth-century public opinion. Starting from the principle that 'it is against God's law to aid any subjects against their natural Princes', he then proceeded to give plausible reasons why she should do precisely this. He argued that the Congregation in Scotland were not rebels; they were loyal to their Queen, and objected only to the action of the Queen Regent in bringing in French soldiers, and in trying to subjugate the realm of Scotland to France. They were justified in resisting the Queen Regent, because she was not a Prince, but a subject of her daughter.

Cecil then proceeded to argue that the presence of French troops in

Scotland constituted a threat to English security, and that Elizabeth was therefore entitled to take steps to drive them out in alliance with those Scots who were loyal to their Prince but also objected to the presence of the foreigners. Moreover, ancient records showed that on several occasions in the twelfth and thirteenth centuries the Kings of Scotland had sworn allegiance to the Kings of England as their feudal overlords; so if Elizabeth helped the Scottish Protestants she would not be helping them against their Prince, but she, their superior Prince, would be preventing an inferior ruler, Mary Queen of Scots, and her Regent, from violating the interests of the Prince by calling in foreign soldiers.[9] These arguments seem to have won over Elizabeth, though she and Cecil decided not to mention the English overlordship of Scotland, which would have been politically embarrassing for the Congregation.

It would be difficult for Elizabeth to justify intervening in Scotland if she were asked to do so only by 'private men', by a laird like Kirkcaldy of Grange and the seditious preacher, Knox. The invitation would have to come from noblemen and persons in authority, who, though loyal to their Queen, were authorised by their status to act in their Queen's true interests against her disloyal Regent. The obvious person was James Hamilton, the heir to the throne of Scotland after Mary Queen of Scots, who, as Earl of Arran, had formerly been Regent of Scotland, and whom Henry II had created Duke of Châtelherault in France in an attempt to win him over to the French side. He was supporting the Queen Regent. His son James, Earl of Arran, whom Henry VIII had proposed sixteen years before should marry Elizabeth, was in France, where he had come under the influence of the French Protestants. Elizabeth and Cecil decided that he must be brought from France to Scotland, and that he should have a secret meeting with Elizabeth on the way.

As it was obvious that the Guises would wish to prevent Arran from going to Scotland, Elizabeth and Cecil ordered Throckmorton to arrange for him to go to Geneva and through Germany to Antwerp, where he embarked for England. He reached London on 28 August, and hid in Cecil's house in Westminster. Next day he was taken secretly to Hampton Court and spoke to Elizabeth in the palace garden. Cecil wrote to Throckmorton in code about Arran's arrival and meeting with the Queen, and then, in an uncoded passage in the same letter, wrote that the rumour that Arran was in England was quite untrue, for in fact he was now at Cologne and was planning to travel to Scotland via Denmark. After staying only two nights in London, Arran left for Scotland, and had safely arrived at his family house at Hamilton by the middle of September.[10]

Mary of Guise discovered that Croft had been encouraging the Congregation to revolt, and Noailles raised the matter with Elizabeth. She thereupon wrote a personal letter to Mary of Guise in which she denied that any of her servants were in contact with the Congregation in Scotland. When Mary of Guise replied that the Congregation were openly boasting of English support,

Elizabeth replied that this was untrue, and that she was surprised that the Queen Regent should believe allegations made by rebels against her, a Queen.[11]

This was deliberate diplomatic lying; but Elizabeth was anxious if possible to avoid an open breach with Scotland and France, and to remain on friendly terms with all foreign states. In August, Philip II left the Netherlands never to return, leaving his illegitimate half-sister, Margaret, the Duchess of Parma, as his Regent in Brussels. He travelled by sea to Spain. Elizabeth, hearing of his intended journey, sent instructions to her officers in all the counties from Kent to Cornwall that if Philip was forced by adverse weather to put in to any English port, on his journey, he was to be received with the greatest honour.[12] Philip did not avail himself of her offer of hospitality, and sailed straight to Laredo.

Elizabeth made a further gesture of goodwill towards Philip when she banned some plays and pageants which were being performed at fairs and theatres, in which Philip, the Pope, and other foreign Catholic sovereigns were attacked and ridiculed; and Quadra was consoled when Elizabeth ordered that the jewelled crucifix and the silver candlesticks, which had been removed from the altar in her chapel royal by her eager Protestant chaplains, should be restored. Throckmorton and other Protestants were displeased about this, and wondered whether it meant that Elizabeth was about to abandon the Protestant cause; but the English ambassadors were ordered to spread the news about the crucifix and candlesticks at the courts of the Catholic sovereigns to whom they were accredited.[13]

VICTORY IN SCOTLAND

THROCKMORTON, and the other agents whom Cecil had sent to spy in the ports of Normandy, reported throughout the autumn of 1559 that reinforcements were being sent to Scotland in small units; that the Marquis of Elboeuf was preparing to sail from Calais on 30 November with ten ships and a thousand men to Leith; and that the Grand Prior would go with a larger force in the spring. Cecil told the Scottish Protestants to act quickly, and to attack the French garrison in Leith before the reinforcements arrived. He told them that their only chance of success lay in capturing Leith before 20 November.[1] The Lords of the Congregation thereupon ordered their forces to assemble at Hamilton on 15 October in order to march on Leith. At the suggestion of Cecil's agents, they issued a proclamation in the name of Francis and Mary, King and Queen of Scots, removing Mary of Guise from her office as Regent which she had abused by trying to subjugate Scotland to France; and they called on the people to take up arms against her and the French soldiers.[2]

The Congregation asked the English government for money to pay for the victuals and wages of their forces. This was not an easy request for Elizabeth to grant, for Armagil Waad had warned her, at her accession, that she was in a precarious financial position, and had urged the need for strict economy in government expenditure. But Cecil persuaded her to send money to the Scottish Protestants. At the beginning of October, she sent £3,000 to Sir Ralph Sadler at Berwick, with orders to him to deliver £1,000 at once to the Congregation, and to let them have the remaining £2,000 at his discretion, if he thought that this was necessary. In order to disguise the source of the money, £1,000 was sent in the form of 3,157 French crowns, each worth 6s.4d., and one English silver crown of 5s.8d. to bring the total up to £1,000. Elizabeth told Sadler that he must tell the Congregation that the money had been provided by him and some of his friends who sympathised with their cause, and not by her or her government. She also told him to impress on the

Lords of the Congregation that she would abandon them if they did not capture Leith without further delay.[3]

At the end of October, Sadler, hearing that the Lords of the Congregation had sold their plate to raise money for their forces, decided to send them immediately the £1,000 in French crowns. The Scottish Protestant, the laird of Ormiston, came to Berwick to fetch the money, and left with it on 31 October. As he passed Haddington, he was waylaid by James Hepburn, Earl of Bothwell, who, though a Protestant, had quarrelled with the Lords of the Congregation and was supporting the Queen Regent. Bothwell let Ormiston go, but kept the money. When Ormiston reported to the Lords of the Congregation that Bothwell had robbed him of the money, they sent a force at once to Bothwell's castle of The Hermitage in Liddisdale to recover it; but Bothwell was warned that they were coming, and left the castle with the money a quarter of an hour before they arrived.[4]

This was a serious setback for Elizabeth and the Scottish Protestants; not only had £1,000 been lost, but the Queen Regent now had proof that Elizabeth was helping the rebels, for although the money was in French crowns, Ormiston had brought it from Berwick, so it obviously came from the English government. Sadler and Croft decided to send them another £1,200, hoping that this time the money would arrive safely, though they were unable to change it into French crowns at Berwick, and had to send it in gold. Then came news of a further disaster. The French garrison at Leith had sallied forth against the advancing Protestant forces and defeated them so effectively that the demoralised Protestants evacuated Edinburgh on 8 November and withdrew to Stirling, where their morale was restored by a rousing sermon from Knox.

The Congregation now made a formal appeal to Elizabeth for help, in a letter which was signed, not by Knox or 'private men', but by the foremost noblemen of Scotland. Cecil had told them, through Sadler and Randolph, just what they should say in the letter.[5] They wrote that as loyal subjects of their King and Queen they wished to defend their country against the foreign soldiers who were threatening to invade it, and asked the help of the Queen of England, 'as the Prince planted by God next to us and within one land and sea'.[6] Not every Scot thought of the French, their partners in the 'old alliance', as foreign invaders, and of their 'ancient enemies of England' as friendly neighbours in the same island; but the Scottish Protestants would soon succeed in persuading many of their fellow-countrymen to see the situation in this light.

Cecil particularly impressed on his agents at Berwick and on the Lords of the Congregation how necessary it was that Knox should be kept out of the picture. On 31 October he wrote to Sadler and Croft: 'Of all other, Knox's name, if it be not Goodman's, is most odious here, and therefore I wish no mention of him hither'.[7]

Cecil was convinced that Elizabeth must now take the risk of openly sending military aid to the Congregation, though he was fully aware of the difficulties which this would involve. The Queen was in debt, owing £60,000 more than she was able to pay. The navy had been run down, and many ships were in need of repair. Apart from a handful of men in the Border garrisons, there was no standing army, and it would take some time to raise an army in the usual way through the nobles and gentlemen in the counties. There was a shortage of trained officers with experience of warfare, and some of the noblemen and gentlemen who would have to lead the army were thought to be Catholic sympathisers.[8] Could England, in these circumstances, take the risk of being involved in a war against France, which had four times the population of England and more experienced captains? And if so, what would be the attitude of the King of Spain? He could not be expected to help Elizabeth to make Scotland Protestant. The most that could be hoped for was that he would stay neutral; but there was always the possibility that he might unite with the Guises to crush the Protestants in Scotland and England.

That wise statesman, Sir Nicholas Bacon, the Keeper of the Great Seal, thought the risks were too great. Cecil thought that they must be taken. Only Elizabeth could decide. According to Cecil, she discussed the problem with a small group of advisers, consisting of himself, the Earl of Pembroke, Lord Clinton the Lord Admiral, the Marquess of Winchester 'and few other'.[9] Some time in November she decided not to intervene in Scotland.

Cecil wrote her a letter which is as near to a threat of resignation as it was possible for a sixteenth-century minister to make. He assured her that he would never pursue a policy of which she did not approve, but that as he was sure that her decision about Scotland was wrong, he could not carry it out efficiently, and therefore asked her to transfer him to other duties, in which he would of course be ready to serve her.[10] Perhaps it was partly because of this letter that Elizabeth changed her mind, as she had done in March 1559 about dissolving Parliament, and as she was to do so often in times of crisis in the future. She may also have been influenced by Throckmorton, who returned from the French court on leave to take part in person in the discussions and to throw his weight in favour of Cecil's interventionist policy.

At the beginning of December, she decided in favour of armed intervention in Scotland. She would at once send the veteran naval commander, William Winter, to Scotland through the stormy mid-winter seas to take supplies to the Congregation and to guard the mouth of the Forth to prevent any French reinforcements from reaching Leith. If the Queen Regent's forces or the French opened fire on Winter's ships, he was to fire back, but was to say that he was acting on his own initiative and not on orders from Elizabeth. She would follow this up as soon as possible by sending a land army under the Duke of Norfolk and Lord Grey of Wilton to invade Scotland from Berwick and march on Leith.[11]

She then gave audience to Quadra. She told him that the French were sending an army to conquer Scotland as a preliminary to invading England from the north; the French troops were obviously not coming merely in order to suppress the rebellion of the Congregation, for as the French forces which were already in Leith had defeated the Congregation and compelled them to evacuate Edinburgh, it was clear that there were already sufficient troops in Scotland to suppress the revolt, and the reinforcements must be coming for another purpose. She told Quadra that she was sure that the King of Spain, as her ally, would agree that she was justified in taking measures to defend her realm, and she asked for his help against their common enemy, the French.[12] She did not say anything about religion to Quadra; but she told Mont, her ambassador to the German Lutheran Princes, to tell the Princes that the French intended to massacre the nobility and gentry of Scotland, especially 'such as hath shown themselves to understand the knowledge and light of the Gospel'.[13]

Quadra was indignant. He was sure that Elizabeth's real motive for intervention in Scotland was to destroy the Catholic faith there, as a first step in her design to overthrow it throughout Christendom.[14] When Margaret of Parma, Philip's Regent in the Netherlands, and her counsellors received Quadra's report of his talk with Elizabeth, Cardinal Granvelle spoke very bluntly to Challoner, the English ambassador in Brussels. He warned him that King Philip would not break his new friendship with France in order to rescue Elizabeth from the danger into which her folly would lead her, and taunted him with the military weakness of the English, who would never be able to stand up against the French single-handed: was there any fortress in England, he asked, which was strong enough to withstand bombardment by cannon for one day?[15] Challoner was so shaken by the reaction of Margaret and Granvelle that he added his voice to those of Elizabeth's counsellors who were opposing Cecil's policy. 'A young Princess cannot be too ware', he wrote to Cecil. 'Let the time work for Scotland, as God will . . . and when we are stronger, and more ready, we may proceed with that, that yet is unripe.'[16]

But Challoner and Cecil might have been comforted if they had read the letter that Margaret of Parma wrote to King Philip on 7 December. It was strongly critical of Elizabeth's policy in Scotland. Elizabeth was rushing into a war with the French in order to help the Scottish heretics. The French would undoubtedly win, and would conquer England, which would be as great a disaster for Philip as if they captured Brussels, for if the French held Dover as well as Calais they would control the Straits and interrupt the sea-route between the Netherlands and Spain and the trade with the Indies. But the only remedy which she could suggest was for Philip to send an envoy to Elizabeth to warn her that he would not give her any help against the French, in the hope that this would frighten her into abandoning her plan to intervene in Scotland.[17]

Despite all the indignation of Margaret and Granvelle against Elizabeth, it is clear that what they feared was not her victory in Scotland, but her defeat there. They did not think it possible that she could beat the French, and were still obsessed by the French menace to the Netherlands. They so greatly underestimated Elizabeth's power that they did not regard her as a potential threat to themselves in her own right; and the only step which Margaret suggested should be taken against her was to threaten her with their neutrality.

Perhaps Elizabeth was taken aback by the extent of Quadra's disapproval, or influenced by Challoner's warning, for she evidently nearly changed her mind again. This is clear from the fact that about ten days before Christmas the whole question was reopened and discussed at a full meeting of the Privy Council at Whitehall, at which Bacon made a long speech, giving his reasons for opposing intervention in Scotland. It did not alter Elizabeth's decision, for on 16 December she sent Winter his instructions, which were drafted by Cecil. But yet another effort was made by the opponents of intervention. The question was discussed again at a meeting of the Council on 24 December. Bacon, Winchester, Petre, Mason, Wotton and the Earl of Arundel opposed intervention; Northampton, Pembroke, Clinton, Howard of Effingham, Parry, Rogers, Knollys, Cave and Sackville agreed with Cecil. After a long discussion, Bacon, Winchester, Petre, Mason and Wotton came over to the majority view. Only Arundel persevered in his opposition to the very end.

The report of the discussion was endorsed by Cecil: '24 December 1559. The opinion of the Council. 28 December. Not allowed by the Queen's Majesty'. This certainly suggests that, although all the councillors except Arundel had finally agreed with Cecil at the meeting on 24 December, Elizabeth again changed her mind on 28 December, rejected their advice, and decided against intervention. If this is in fact what happened, she was too late, because Winter had sailed from Gillingham with a fleet of fourteen ships at 9 a.m. on 27 December.[18]

The weather was dreadful. There were fierce gales in the North Sea all through December. The Marquis of Elboeuf's fleet of twelve ships was due to sail from Le Havre and other ports at the mouth of the Seine to reach Calais by 30 November, where they would take on board 5,000 soldiers and several pieces of cannon, and arrive at Leith by 16 December. More ships would follow, taking a total of 10,000 men to Scotland by Candlemas (2 February). But the strong north-east winds prevented the fleet from leaving the mouth of the Seine for several days. When at last they were able to reach Calais and to proceed towards Scotland, they ran into heavy storms, and four ships were lost off Emden. Many dead bodies were washed ashore in Zeeland. The gales were still blowing in January, when Elboeuf himself sailed for Scotland with a new fleet. He managed to get within sight of Scotland, but was unable to get closer, and was eventually forced to return to France.[19]

Captain Winter, too, encountered the gales. He arrived at Yarmouth twenty-nine hours after leaving Gillingham, but when he sailed north from Yarmouth he was driven back by strong winds and forced to stay in port at Yarmouth for seventeen days. He was able to leave at last on 14 January, but two days later encountered an even heavier gale off Flamborough Head in which he lost all his boats, and twelve of his ships were dispersed. But only three of them were too damaged to proceed, and on 22 January he reached the mouth of the Forth with eleven of his fourteen ships. He remained there, supplying the forces of the Congregation with victuals and arms, and periodically exchanging shots with the French artillery in the forts at Leith, while the French and the Congregation waged a savage guerrilla war along the banks of the Forth in Fife and West Lothian.[20]

On 27 February, the Duke of Norfolk met the Scottish Protestants' representatives at Berwick and signed a formal treaty between Elizabeth and the Duke of Châtelherault, 'second person of the realm of Scotland', and the lords associated with him. It declared that Elizabeth, being satisfied that the Scottish lords were loyal to their sovereign lady, the Queen of Scots, and to her husband the French King as long as he was married to her, was making the treaty with them, 'moved by princely honour and neighbourhood for the defence of the just freedom of the Crown of Scotland from conquest'. The original draft of the treaty referred to Châtelherault and the lords associated with him 'for the maintenance of the Christian religion', but these words were deleted from the final version of the document.[21]

Cecil had informed his officers that the Queen would be satisfied if the army assembled at Newcastle by 22 January and was at Berwick ready to cross the Border on 25 January.[22] But preparations took longer than expected, and it was not until 29 March that Lord Grey led 9,000 men into Scotland. By the middle of April they were besieging Leith. Mary of Guise, who was very ill with dropsy, had left Leith and retired to Edinburgh Castle under the protection of Lord Erskine, who still remained strictly neutral.

To a twentieth-century observer, the decisive events of the spring and early summer of 1560, which were to have such far-reaching results for the future history of Britain and of Europe, look like a drama played out in slow motion, as diplomatic and military action moved at the pace of sixteenth-century transport. But time was the essential factor in the situation, with both sides acting as fast as they could before their enemy could overtake them.

The French preparations to send a much larger fleet, with many more reinforcements, to Scotland in the spring as soon as the weather made navigation easier, were checked by the Conspiracy of Amboise. A group of French Protestants planned to slip into the castle of Amboise on the Loire, where the court was in residence, and kill the Guises and hold the King and Queen as prisoners while a Protestant government was established. The Catholics were convinced that the King of Navarre and the Prince of Condé were implicated in the plot, and that it had been masterminded by Throckmorton. There is no evidence that Navarre and Condé were involved, and we can be almost certain that Throckmorton did not know anything about the plot until it was discovered by the authorities and suppressed, for his letters to Elizabeth and Cecil, though full of confidential information in code about other secret matters, make no reference to the Protestant conspiracy until he wrote on 7 March 1560 to tell Cecil that the plot had been discovered.[23]

The Duke of Guise took the necessary steps to round up the conspirators. Some of them barricaded themselves in houses in the town of Amboise, but surrendered when Guise's officers promised to spare the lives of all except the ringleaders. Some days later, a government council declared that in view of the gravity and extent of the conspiracy, which had not been appreciated when the pardon was offered to the rank-and-file, the pardons were revoked, and absolution would be granted by the Church to those officers who broke their promise to spare the lives of those who surrendered. Hundreds were publicly executed in the castle and town of Amboise, some of them in the presence of Francis II and Mary Queen of Scots.[24] Most were hanged, some were drowned in sacks in the Loire, and a few were broken on the wheel, the court having sentenced the criminal to be fastened to a wheel, have his arms and legs broken, and left there 'to live in pain and repentance . . . as long as it pleases God to give him life.'

On 24 March, while the executions at Amboise were still going on and five days before Lord Grey invaded Scotland, Elizabeth issued a proclamation against the Guises. She stated that she had no quarrel with King Francis and Mary Queen of Scots, who, she was sure, had no hostile designs against her, but that since the death of Henry II the family of Guise, taking advantage of the youth of the King and Queen, and ignoring the wishes of the Princes of the Blood, had seized power in France. It was only the Guises who were plotting to conquer Scotland and threatening her security. She therefore called on all her subjects to refrain from committing acts of hostility against the French King's subjects.[25] Elizabeth's proclamation was an unprecedented step, for Princes did not normally publicly denounce a subject of another Prince.

The Cardinal of Lorraine, seeing the Conspiracy of Amboise as proof of the existence of an international Protestant plot to overthrow the Catholic faith throughout Christendom, asked King Philip to send troops to Scotland to help the French to suppress the Protestant rebellion there and crush heresy's fountain-head in Elizabeth's England. It is significant that Feria and Quadra, who had both been ambassadors in England, were the only two Spanish statesmen who were enthusiastically in favour of such a policy. The Duke of Alva, who had been fighting the French for thirty-five years, had no wish to help them out of their difficulties in Scotland. In any event, Philip had other worries. The provincial Parliaments in Spain were urging him to take action against the Turks in the Mediterranean, for the Turkish navy was seriously interfering with the trade between Spain and Italy.[26]

Instead of sending an army to help the French in Scotland, Philip offered to mediate. He suggested that he should send a special envoy, the Sieur of Glajon, from the Netherlands, and that the King of France should send the Bishop of Valence, to join Quadra and Noailles at Elizabeth's court, and try to settle the problem of Scotland by peaceful means. Elizabeth agreed to the proposal in order to gain time. When Glajon reached London at the beginning of April, he discovered that since he had received his instructions from Philip, Lord Grey had invaded Scotland and was in action against the French at Leith. He therefore proposed that Elizabeth and the French should agree to a truce for fifty days while the negotiations took place in London.[27]

When Glajon first asked for an audience with the Queen, he was told that she could not see him because she was ill, and that Cecil would discuss the question with him. He and Quadra told Cecil that King Philip was incensed that Elizabeth was helping the rebels and heretics in Scotland, and warned him that this might become a precedent; surely Elizabeth would not wish foreign Princes to help rebels in England who rose in revolt against her religion? Cecil replied that the Congregation in Scotland were not rebels, that religion had nothing to do with it, and that Elizabeth's only object in Scotland was to defend her realm by forestalling a threatened French invasion of Scotland. He said that in view of this threat from the French, Elizabeth would not agree to a truce which would give the French the opportunity to increase their forces in Scotland, and she expected the King of Spain, as her ally, to support her in this. When Elizabeth eventually agreed to give audience to Glajon and Quadra, she repeated the same arguments.[28]

Quadra and Glajon said that if her only object in intervening in Scotland was to prevent a French invasion of England, King Philip would indeed agree to help her against this danger. He would do so by sending 5,000 Spanish troops to Scotland. They would suppress the rebel heretics and uphold the royal authority of the Queen of Scots, and at the same time would prevent the French forces in Scotland from invading England. Philip would thus be rendering a great service to Elizabeth, for he would not only protect her kingdom from invasion, but would show the world that she had not intervened in Scotland in order to help the rebels and heretics. Elizabeth and Cecil said that they were most grateful for Philip's offer, but could not accept it, because the Spanish troops would not stay in Scotland permanently, and once they were withdrawn the danger from the French would revive. Elizabeth also tried to complicate the issue by arguing that the fortification of Eyemouth by the French in Scotland, and the quartering of the English leopards on Mary Queen of Scots' coat-of-arms, were breaches of the treaties of Cateau-Cambrésis and Upsetlington; and she demanded the immediate return of Calais, and damages in money, as compensation for these breaches of the treaty.[29]

As the French had accepted Glajon's proposal for a truce, and the English had rejected it, the Cardinal of Lorraine asked Philip to send his troops to Scotland without delay. During April, Elizabeth and Cecil received alarming reports from their agent in Antwerp, Thomas Gresham, that 4,000 Spanish troops were converging on the port, where seven ships were ready to take them to Scotland. But on 25 April Throckmorton sent more encouraging information from Amboise; after speaking to the Spanish ambassador there, and intercepting letters from Guise and the Cardinal of Lorraine, he was sure that King Philip would not send troops to Scotland, and that the soldiers in Antwerp would be sent to fight the Turks in Tripoli. Philip had in fact heard that the Turkish Admiral Pialé – a Croatian Christian who had been taken as a child and educated as a Moslem in the Sultan's harem – had made a surprise attack on Philip's fleet at anchor in the Island of Jerba off Tripoli, and had sunk sixty-five ships and killed or captured 13,000 Spaniards. In view of the Turkish menace, Philip had neither men nor money to spare to fight heretics in Scotland. At the beginning of June Gresham wrote that the ships and troops in Antwerp would sail for Spain, not Scotland.[30]

Elizabeth and Cecil decided to press ahead in Scotland, and sent orders to Lord Grey to take Leith without delay. On 7 May an attempt was made to capture Leith by assault; but the scaling ladders which were used in the attack were not long enough, and the soldiers found themselves stranded six feet short of the top of the ramparts. The attack was repulsed, the English losing a thousand men killed and wounded. They suffered even heavier losses through disease in their trenches surrounding Leith.[31]

Cecil was afraid that the setback at Leith might again make Elizabeth change her mind. When the news reached London, he wrote to Throckmorton at Amboise: 'God trieth us with many difficulties. The Queen's Majesty never liketh this matter of Scotland'. But Elizabeth decided to send more men, money and artillery to Leith at once. Cecil had obviously not found it easy to persuade her to do this. 'I have had such a torment herein with the Queen's Majesty as an ague hath not in five fits so much abated'.[32]

But the French garrison at Leith was running short of provisions, and there was no help coming from France. Elizabeth and Cecil then thought of another way to gain time. They suggested that the negotiations should take place in Newcastle or Edinburgh instead of in London. Cecil himself was appointed to be one of the commissioners to take part in the talks, and he set out for the north on 30 May, having obtained instructions from Elizabeth to him and his fellow-commissioners which he himself had drafted. They were to insist that all French troops and officials should be withdrawn from Scotland, and that the question of religion should be settled by the Scottish Parliament, not by Mary Queen of Scots.[33] This last demand violated the principle that had been accepted throughout Christendom for the last thirty years, by Henry VIII, Charles V and Philip II, and by Elizabeth herself – that it was the right and duty of the Prince to decide which religion his subjects should adopt.

Cecil and his colleagues reached Edinburgh on 17 June. A week before, Mary of Guise had died of dropsy in Edinburgh Castle. On 6 July the Treaty of Edinburgh was signed. The French agreed to withdraw from Scotland and to leave the Scots to settle their own religion. In return, the English withdrew their demand for the immediate return of Calais and compensation for Mary

Queen of Scots' assumption of the English arms, and agreed to dissolve the alliance between Elizabeth and the Lords of the Congregation. These concessions by the English made it possible for the French to claim that it was a compromise peace. In fact, on all the essentials, it was a complete victory for Elizabeth and the Protestant cause. On 15 August, the Scottish Parliament met and passed the necessary legislation to make Scotland a Protestant and Presbyterian state. The Mass was suppressed, and anyone who celebrated or attended it was to suffer fine and imprisonment, and, for the third offence, death.

It is typical of Elizabeth's waywardness, changeability and lack of perspective that, having succeeded in obtaining her objective when every statesman in Christendom had thought this was impossible, she was dissatisfied that she had not gained even more. She wrote to Cecil and his fellow-commissioners urging them to break off negotiations if they did not obtain compensation from the French for the adoption of her coat-of-arms.[34] But it was in fact the greatest success which she achieved during her reign – greater even than the defeat of the Spanish Armada, which was only a defensive victory. The events of 1560 destroyed French domination and the power of the Catholic Church in Scotland, and, despite occasional appearances to the contrary, made English influence permanently predominant in Scotland.

When we consider all the successes, and also the hesitations, vacillations and missed opportunities, of later years, Elizabeth must first and foremost be given the credit for having won the victory in Scotland at the age of twenty-six and in the second year of her reign. There were hesitations and vacillations, too, in 1559 and 1560, but ultimately the decision to defy both the great powers and take the risk of intervention was hers alone; and it was the right decision. But in one respect the success was unsatisfactory from Elizabeth's point of view. The intervention of her army and navy had made it possible for the Scottish Parliament to force their sovereign, against her will, to accept the religion of Knox and Goodman, and created a Presbyterian state where the Church was governed, not by the Prince and his bishops, but by a democratically elected General Assembly. Eighty years later, a revolution broke out in this Presbyterian state which led to a King of England being beheaded by his subjects on the balcony of Elizabeth's palace at Whitehall. The triumph of 1560 was a victory for England and a victory for the Protestant cause, but not in every sense a victory for Elizabeth.

LORD ROBERT

DURING the first two years of her reign, Elizabeth had successfully transformed England into a Protestant state and had won a victory in Scotland for England and Protestantism. Then, in the moment of victory, she was confronted with a new crisis which threatened the very existence of her throne and the Protestant cause. It arose because Elizabeth had fallen madly in love with her Master of the Horse, Lord Robert Dudley, and was behaving in a most irresponsible manner.

Lord Robert was a few months older than Elizabeth. He was born in 1532, when his father, John Dudley, was rising in favour at the court of Henry VIII, though Robert's grandfather, Edmund Dudley, had been executed when Henry first came to the throne as a scapegoat for the unpopular financial policies of Henry VII. Before Henry VIII died, John Dudley had become Viscount Lisle, and under Edward VI Earl of Warwick, Duke of Northumberland and ruler of England. Robert was brought up at court, and knew Elizabeth when they were children.

When he was seventeen, he married Amy Robsart, the daughter of Sir John Robsart of Siderstern in Norfolk. It was a few months after Warwick had won the gratitude of the local gentry by defeating Kett's peasant revolt in Norfolk, and had led the *coup d'état* which overthrew Somerset. In the sixteenth century, the marriages of the nobility and gentry were usually arranged with the main object of advancing the family fortunes financially and socially. By this standard, marriage with the daughter of a Norfolk country gentleman was not a good match for the son of the most powerful nobleman in England, though Lord Robert was a great catch for the Robsarts. Robert must have been very much in love with Amy in 1550.

After the nine days' reign of Jane Grey, Northumberland and his five sons were sent to the Tower. Northumberland and Jane's husband, Guilford Dudley, were beheaded, but John, Ambrose, Robert and Henry Dudley were pardoned, apparently because King Philip was persuaded to intervene on their behalf. Amy Dudley asked and obtained permission to visit Robert in the

Tower, and showed every sign of being a devoted wife. In due course, the four brothers were released from prison, though John died soon afterwards. Ambrose, Robert and Henry joined King Philip's army during the war in France, and served with distinction at St Quentin, where Henry was killed, but Ambrose and Robert survived. Robert, after returning to England, was close to Elizabeth during the last difficult months of Mary's reign. When she came to the throne, he was at once appointed Master of the Horse at the age of twenty-six.

He spent most of his time at court, with his sister, Lady Mary Sidney, the wife of Sir Henry Sidney of Penshurst in Kent; she was one of Elizabeth's ladies-in-waiting. Amy Dudley did not live at court. It was usual for the wives of courtiers, unless they themselves were in attendance on the Queen at court, to live in their husbands' country houses and manage their estates; but Amy spent her time in the houses of her relatives in Norfolk and Lincoln-shire, though by 1559 she was usually living at the house of her kinsman Mr Hyde at Denchworth in Berkshire, or at Cumnor Hall in Oxfordshire, a few miles north of Abingdon, which Lord Robert had leased on a short tenancy. Lord Robert visited her there and at Denchworth from time to time.

Robert was tall, strong and handsome. He was a splendid horseman, and excelled at jousting. Elizabeth, who was determined to maintain an impress-ive court despite her financial difficulties, held tournaments on the feast days, as Henry VIII had done and other Kings continued to do for another generation. In the absence of a male sovereign to play the leading part in the jousting, Lord Robert Dudley was the most prominent champion at the tournament.

By the spring of 1559 it was obvious to all the courtiers and the foreign ambassadors that Elizabeth was very much attracted to Lord Robert. She was a good rider and enjoyed hunting, and spent a great deal of time hunting with her Master of the Horse. Cecil sometimes found that she was away hunting with Robert when he wished to consult her about State affairs,[1] though her absence may not have been entirely unwelcome to him while he was secretly negotiating with Knox and directing foreign policy during the revolution in Scotland. Rumours began to circulate that she wished to marry Robert, and that this was the reason why she refused to marry Philip of Spain, the Archduke Charles, the King of Sweden, or any other suitor.

She created Robert a Knight of the Garter. She granted him the right to export wool without a licence. She gave him a present of £12,000 – about £6,000,000 in terms of 1987 prices – to cover his expenses as Master of the Horse.[2] It was quite usual for courtiers who were high in favour to receive gifts of this kind from their sovereign, but when the sovereign was a woman it always provided ammunition for the gossipmongers. What was more alarm-ing was that the Queen was always talking about Lord Robert. She took every opportunity to praise his virtues and good looks, and if anyone criticised him, she defended him enthusiastically and scolded his detractors. She praised him as a real man, not one 'who would sit home all day among the cinders'.[3]

Lord Robert's rooms in Whitehall were on the floor below the Queen's. One day he complained that they were damp. She immediately ordered that he should move to rooms on the same floor as her own, and next door to hers.[4] The rumours spread.[5]

One evening Elizabeth had supper at Robert's house at Kew, and afterwards rode back to her palace at Richmond by torchlight, escorted by Robert's servants. On the way she talked to the torchbearers, telling them what a wonderful man their master was, and that she would make him greater than any member of his family had ever been. One of the servants told a friend what the Queen had said. The friend thought that she must be intending to make Lord Robert a duke. No, said the servant, she means to marry him. The servant and his friend were summoned before the Privy Council. They admitted that they had done wrong in spreading this false rumour, and deserved severe punishment.[6]

But worse stories than this were in circulation. It was said that Lord Robert was the Queen's lover, that she had given birth to his illegitimate child, and that he was intending to poison his wife so as to be free to marry the Queen. Before Feria left England, he had heard that Amy Dudley was dying of cancer of the breast, and that Lord Robert and the Queen were only waiting for Amy's death before getting married.[7]

Kate Ashley knew Elizabeth well enough to speak to her frankly, to tell her about the rumours, and to warn her of the consequences of her indiscretions. Elizabeth said that the stories were ridiculous. She assured Kate Ashley that she had never had sexual relations with Robert, and asked how anyone could imagine that such a thing were possible when she was surrounded by her ladies-in-waiting at all hours of the day and night. Then, as if resentful of the fact that the presence of her ladies placed a restraint on her freedom of action and on her power, she added that 'if she had ever had the will or had found pleasure in such a dishonourable life – from which may God preserve her! – she did not know of anyone who could forbid her'.[8] Even with the qualification, this statement was a little tactless.

For all her brave words, Elizabeth knew that she was not as free to indulge in love affairs as Henry VIII had been. A Queen, even a Queen regnant, was not a King. Society had double standards in its view of sexual immorality by men and women, and by Kings and Queens. A King could slip unobtrusively into the bedrooms of the ladies-in-waiting at court, or could visit incognito, on a hunting expedition, the attractive wives or daughters of noblemen, tradesmen, millers and peasants. A Queen was not only under constant observation by her ladies and servants, as Elizabeth had said, but if she took a lover, without the benefit of twentieth-century methods of contraception and twentieth-century medicine, she ran a very good chance of becoming pregnant and even of dying in childbirth.

A Protestant Queen had to be particularly careful, for the Catholics were waiting for the opportunity to pursue their usual theme of the immorality of Protestant women. The shoemaker-poet, Miles Huggarde, writing in Mary's reign, had accused the Protestant 'London ladies' of encouraging their husbands to be martyrs in order to get them out of the way so that they would be free to amuse themselves with their lovers, of copulating promiscuously in Protestant churches and elsewhere with the Protestant men, and of acts of lesbianism with other Protestant women.[9] Elizabeth, as Anne Boleyn's daughter, was particularly vulnerable to slanders of this kind. The charges of adultery for which Anne had been executed had been gleefully accepted by the Catholics as proof of Protestant immorality, and in Mary's reign they believed the rumours about the sexual misconduct of Anne's heretical daughter Elizabeth, who had inherited the vices of her Lutheran mother. If they could convince the people that Elizabeth was committing adultery with Robert Dudley, it could severely damage the Protestant cause in England and throughout Christendom, and perhaps bring Elizabeth down.

Quadra, who repeated all the gossip about Elizabeth and Robert to Philip II and Margaret of Parma, thought that it might be worth while to make a friend of so influential a person as Lord Robert, though Robert was an ardent Protestant. Quadra found Robert's reaction encouraging. Robert said that he would always be ready to do a service to the King of Spain, as he owed his life to him in Mary's reign. Both Robert and Lady Mary Sidney told Quadra that they were in favour of a marriage between Elizabeth and Archduke Charles, but Quadra thought that this was only a blind to hide the fact that Robert was planning to murder his wife and marry Elizabeth himself.[10]

Cecil was very worried. He felt that he was losing the Queen's favour and was having difficulty in gaining access to her presence, and believed that Robert was prejudicing Elizabeth against him. He even went so far as to confide in Quadra, hoping that the ambassador would use his influence with Elizabeth to restrain her infatuation for Robert. With Elizabeth's behaviour becoming more and more indiscreet, Cecil himself forgot his usual discretion. Soon after he returned from Edinburgh, he spoke most imprudently to Quadra about Robert; he said that Robert was a menace who would be better in Paradise than here on earth, and that he feared that Robert would try to poison his wife. The day after this conversation with Cecil, Elizabeth coolly mentioned to Quadra when returning from the hunt that Amy Dudley had died.[11] She had been staying at Cumnor Hall, and had told the servants that they could have the afternoon off to go to Abingdon Fair. During their absence she was visited by two of Robert's servants. When Amy's servants returned from the fair, they found her lying dead at the foot of the stairs with a broken neck.

A coroner's inquest returned a verdict of accidental death, Amy Dudley having fallen downstairs. Many people believed that she had been murdered by her husband's agents when they called at the house while Amy's servants were at the fair, and that they broke her neck and put her corpse at the bottom of the stairs to give the impression that she had fallen down the stairs. It has sometimes been suggested that she committed suicide because of her distress at the rumours which had been circulating about her husband and the Queen.[12] It is very unlikely that Robert murdered her. Sixteenth-century England was not one of those societies in which noblemen could kill their wives with relative impunity. If Robert and Elizabeth had any plans to get rid of Amy, they are much more likely to have hoped that Archbishop Parker, like Cranmer in Henry VIII's time, would be prepared to twist the law to grant Robert a divorce from his wife.

Throckmorton was appalled when the news reached him in Paris. He wrote to Cecil that though he liked and respected Lord Robert, his duty to the Queen compelled him to warn Cecil, and to write frankly to Elizabeth herself, that if she married Lord Robert, the situation would be disastrous and irremediable. He urged Cecil to do all he could to prevent the marriage, 'for if it take place, we shall be *opprobrium hominum et abjectio plebis* [a disgrace to mankind and despised by the people]. God and religion, which be the fundamentals, shall be out of estimation; the Queen our sovereign discredited, contemned and neglected; our country ruined, undone, and made prey'.[13] He wrote to Chamberlain, the ambassador in Madrid, that though the news from England was that Amy Dudley had accidentally broken her neck, everybody in France believed that it had been broken for her on purpose.[14]

Elizabeth drew back from the brink. As on so many other occasions, after acting foolishly and causing her advisers great anxiety, she reached the right decision just in time. She decided not to marry Robert, and cooled her attitude towards him, at least on the surface. She abandoned for the time being her plan to create him Earl of Leicester. She is said to have reacted angrily when they brought her his patent of nobility for her to sign, cutting it in half with a knife.[15] Was she angry with him? Angry with those who had falsely accused him of murder? Angry with herself for her rash conduct? Or angry at her impotence, at her inability to marry the man she loved?

She did not disgrace Lord Robert. He stayed at court, and drew closer to the Spanish ambassador, assuring him that he desired friendship with King Philip, as an ally against their enemies the French.[16] Cecil returned to full favour with the Queen, and by the autumn of 1560 was directing English foreign policy in the complicated but hopeful situation which had developed as a result of the English and Protestant victory in Scotland. The Lords of the Congregation wished to strengthen their ties with England by a marriage between Arran and Elizabeth, but Elizabeth refused to marry Arran.[17]

Her relations with Mary were strained. When the news of the signing of the Treaty of Edinburgh reached Francis II and Mary in France, they refused to ratify it, or to abandon Mary's use of the English royal arms. The Cardinal of Lorraine asked how Elizabeth could object to this when she herself quartered the French *fleur-de-lys* on her coat of arms. Throckmorton explained that this was different; the Kings of England had borne the French *fleur-de-lys* for more than two hundred years, and everyone knew the reason for their historic claim to it, whereas Mary's use of the English royal arms was a new thing, to indicate her right to the English throne because Elizabeth was not the lawful Queen.[18]

On 6 December 1560 Francis II died at the age of sixteen of an inflammation in his ear. He was succeeded by his ten-year-old brother Charles IX, and this transformed the situation in France. The Queen Mother, Catherine de Medici, who had exercised no influence at all during the reigns of her husband and her eldest son, now became Regent for Charles IX. The Guises left court, and returned to their estates in Champagne. Mary was as effectively excluded from political power in France as Catherine had been in Francis's reign. When Throckmorton spoke to Catherine about the refusal to ratify the Treaty of Edinburgh, she said that he must discuss this with Mary, because the French government had no interest in what happened in Scotland. This meant that, at least for the time being, Elizabeth had nothing to fear from the French where Scotland was concerned.

Mary and the Guises decided that she should return to Scotland, which she had last seen thirteen years before as a girl of five. She prepared to sail with an impressive escort of ships, and accompanied by several of her Guise uncles, in the summer of 1561. As usual when travellers went from France to Scotland, she asked Elizabeth for a safe-conduct to land in England in the event of her ship being forced by weather into an English port.

Elizabeth announced that as Mary's refusal to ratify the Treaty of Edinburgh showed her unfriendly attitude towards her, she would not grant Mary a safe-conduct to land in England.[19] Mary decided to sail without the safe-conduct, hoping that in the fine summer weather it would not be necessary to seek refuge from storms in any English port. She said to Throckmorton that she hoped the wind would not drive her on to the English coast, but that if it did, Elizabeth could then do what she wished with her. 'And if she be so hard-hearted as to desire my end, she may then do her pleasure, and make sacrifice of me. Peradventure that casualty might be better for me than to live; in this matter, quoth she, God's will be fulfilled'.[20] Throckmorton assured her that if she would ratify the Treaty of Edinburgh, Elizabeth would gladly grant her a safe-conduct and be her friend;[21] but he wrote to Cecil: 'If you mean to catch the Queen of Scots, our ships must search and see all, for she means rather to steal away than pass by force'.[22]

Mary sailed from Calais on 14 August. Elizabeth made no attempt to intercept her, and after a calm and uneventful voyage she landed safely at Leith five days later.

DEFEAT IN FRANCE

I N August 1559, as Elizabeth travelled on her summer progress between her palaces in the vicinity of London, moving from Eltham to Nonesuch near Ewell and to Kingston, she fell ill with what was probably malaria and what her contemporaries called a tertian fever. Throckmorton, who knew her well, wrote to Cecil that she should change her diet, stop travelling, and 'refrain her appetite'.[1] She quickly recovered, for it was not the plague, the sweating sickness, smallpox, or measles, the killer diseases of the sixteenth century; but it reminded her counsellors that the religious settlement in England, the success of the Congregation in Scotland, and all the hopes of the Protestants in Europe depended on the continuation of one life. If she should die, who would succeed her? The Papist Mary Queen of Scots? Lady Katherine Grey, the sister of Lady Jane Grey, who was ostensibly a Protestant, but who had been visited by the Spanish ambassador and, according to him, was sympathetic to the Catholic faith? Or would it be possible to bypass them both in favour of that zealous Protestant, Henry, Lord Hastings, a descendant of Edward IV's brother the Duke of Clarence?

The problem would be solved if the Queen would marry and have a child; but she refused all her suitors. In the summer of 1559 she was being wooed by King Eric XIV of Sweden and the Archduke Charles of Austria, the son of Charles V's brother, the Holy Roman Emperor Ferdinand I. King Eric sent his brother the Duke of Finland to her court, and Archduke Charles sent his Chamberlain, Baron von Beuner. She kept the Duke of Finland and Beuner with her for many weeks, telling them both that she was honoured by their master's proposal, but was resolved to die a virgin. So the succession problem remained.

Elizabeth had trouble with Katherine Grey. Katherine fell in love with Somerset's son, Edward Seymour, Earl of Hertford, and asked Elizabeth's permission to marry him, for by an Act of 1536 it was high treason to marry a member of the royal family without the consent of the sovereign; but

Elizabeth refused to allow the marriage. This was probably because she feared that if the heir to the throne were to marry and have children while she herself remained unmarried, this would encourage her opponents to depose her and make Katherine Queen in her place. In the summer of 1561 it was discovered that Katherine was pregnant, and in due course she gave birth to a son. She said that she had secretly married Hertford, and that he was the father of her child. Hertford admitted this, but neither he nor Katherine would name the priest who had performed the secret marriage, for he was liable to severe punishment.

Elizabeth sent Katherine and Hertford to the Tower. Intent on discrediting the heir to the throne and her baby, she insisted that there had been no marriage ceremony performed between Katherine and Hertford, and that their son was illegitimate. She appointed a commission under Archbishop Parker to investigate the matter. The commissioners found, as Elizabeth wished, that there had been no marriage. From Hertford's point of view, this at least had the advantage of saving him from a prosecution for high treason.

After Katherine gave birth to her son in the Tower, she remained there as a prisoner. Hertford was also imprisoned in the Tower, and the Lieutenant of the Tower, in contravention of Elizabeth's orders, allowed them to live together as man and wife. As a result, Katherine gave birth to a second son in 1563. Elizabeth was furious, and ordered that Katherine be removed from the Tower and placed under house arrest in the custody of her uncle, Lord John Grey, at Hanworth in Middlesex, while Hertford remained in the Tower. When the plague broke out in London, he was moved to the house of his stepfather, Sir Francis Newdigate, in Essex. He and Katherine never met again. She died, before she was thirty, in 1568. After her death, Hertford was released from custody, and lived on until 1621.

Katherine's sister, Lady Mary Grey, had the misfortune to come next after Katherine and her legitimate children in the line of succession to the throne. She was very small – almost a dwarf; but she fell in love with the Queen's Sergeant-Porter, Thomas Keys, a gentleman of Folkestone, who was exceptionally tall and at least twenty years older than Lady Mary. When Elizabeth discovered, in 1564, that they had been secretly married, she imprisoned Keys in the Fleet and confined Mary in the houses of various noblemen. She tried to persuade Grindal, the Bishop of London, to declare the marriage void; but he said that this would be difficult. No one believed that the marriage, so inappropriate in view of their difference in rank, age and height, was due to anything except Keys's ambition; but Mary was devoted to her husband, and insisted on signing her letters 'Mary Keys'. Keys died in prison in 1571, and Mary was soon afterwards released. She survived her husband by seven years.

Two more lives had been ruined in the interests of the State. Elizabeth, having sacrificed her own love to save her throne, had no hesitation in forcing Katherine and Mary Grey to do the same.

It seemed for a moment in 1560 as if the bitter religious rift in Christendom might perhaps be healed by compromise. The savage old Pope Paul IV had died in 1559, and his successor, Pius IV, was much more conciliatory. He planned to reconvene the General Council of the Church which had been meeting at Trent since 1545, and to invite the Protestant states to send envoys to discuss the possibilities of Church reform and reunification. He wrote to the Protestant Princes of Germany inviting them to send representatives to Trent. He was more cautious in his approach to Elizabeth, who would be a more important gain than any of the German Princes. He decided to send his invitation to Elizabeth through Philip II, whom he asked to request Elizabeth to receive his Nuncio, Parpaglia, who had met her when he was in England during Mary's reign. Parpaglia would then formally invite her to send representatives to Trent. He enclosed a letter to Elizabeth in which he urged his 'very dear daughter in Christ' to reject 'evil counsellors that love not you but themselves and serve their own lusts' and to 'show yourself obedient to our fatherly persuasions and wholesome counsels'.[2] Philip, as usual, was slow to take action, and because of this, and the time taken by the posts in carrying letters, it was nearly a year before the Pope's request was transmitted to Elizabeth by the Spanish ambassador in London.

A more cynical Catholic than Pius IV was also experimenting with a policy of compromise. Catherine de Medici went regularly to Mass, but was no Catholic zealot, and had no aim except to maintain the power of her children and the royal house of Valois. She wished to preserve internal peace and avoid religious conflict in France, and was prepared to use any means to achieve this. As long as the Protestants were only a handful of religious idealists, of university intellectuals and artisans and peasants, this could best be done by savagely persecuting them; but when the King of Navarre, Condé and Coligny were converted to Calvinism, and the Protestants in whole areas of France could worship safely under the protection of the armed retainers of the powerful Protestant lords and Princes of the Blood, it was no longer possible to crush them by persecution. She tried to win them over by bribery, and succeeded in persuading the King of Navarre to become a Catholic again by holding out hopes to him that if he did, Philip II might agree to restore to him his Spanish kingdom of Navarre which had been overrun by the Spaniards fifty years before and held by the Kings of Spain ever since. But Navarre's wife and brother, Jeanne d'Albret and Condé, as well as Admiral Coligny, remained staunchly Protestant; and Queen Jeanne, taking her seven-year-old son, Prince Henry of Navarre, left her husband and established herself in the south of France.

Catherine de Medici decided to try the experiment of offering the Protestants religious toleration. She began by repealing the decrees which made them liable to be burned for heresy, and convened an assembly of Catholic and Protestant churchmen at Poissy to discuss a possible comprom-ise of their religious disagreements. She followed this by granting religious toleration to the Protestants, allowing them to hold church services, unmolested, in any part of France.[3]

Unfortunately, the experiment of religious toleration came too late or too soon. It was too late to placate the Protestants, after they had endured forty years of cruel persecution; and it was too early to be acceptable to Catholic extremists and to the Protestants, who had not yet been exhausted and sickened by another thirty years of civil war and massacres. All the local *Parlements*, including the *Parlement* of Paris, refused to promulgate the royal decrees which granted toleration. Large sections of Catholics, especially the lower classes in Paris, indignantly rejected the idea of tolerating the heretics – the 'Huguenots', as their enemies called them; while the Protestants, interpreting the grant of toleration as a sign of Catholic weakness, pressed home their advantage and intensified their attacks on Catholic churches and images.

At Blois and elsewhere, the Protestants seized the Catholic churches by force, destroyed the images and pictures, and used the buildings as Protestant places of worship. In Paris, the Protestants, unable to find any churches where they could worship, held a great prayer meeting in the fields outside the town. The Catholics locked the gates and refused to readmit them to the city; so the Protestants stormed the gates and forced their way in after fighting in which several men on both sides were killed. No one seemed to know how the fighting started at Montpellier, but about a hundred Protestants and a hundred Catholics were killed. Many Protestants were executed at Toulouse. In Languedoc the Protestants murdered a prominent Catholic official. At Angers the Catholic priests distributed pistols and other weapons to the people and told them to kill the 'Huguenots'.[4]

The Protestants were encouraged in their new boldness and aggression, not only by Catherine de Medici's policy of toleration, but also by Elizabeth's success in Scotland. The victory of the Congregation with English support made a great impression throughout Europe, and the fears of the French and Spanish governments that it would encourage heresy and sedition in their countries proved to be justified. Peter Martyr in Zürich hailed it as a great victory for Protestantism.[5] Admiral Coligny said to Throckmorton that everyone in France realised that the Protestant successes were due to Elizabeth, and told him: 'Do you not see (say they) within these two years since she came to the crown of England, that religion is not only planted in her own realm but also in the realm of Scotland by her means?'[6] In the mountains near Nice the Protestants destroyed the churches and rose in revolt against the Catholic Duke of Savoy; and next year there were Protestant riots and destruction of images in King Philip's territories in the Netherlands.[7]

Elizabeth and Cecil now did what they had been so careful to avoid doing during the revolution in Scotland, and openly proclaimed that they were championing the Protestant religion in every country of Christendom. Cecil gave a clear indication of the new line in his letter to Throckmorton of 15

January 1561. 'The care must be to advance that cause which we profess, that is the knowledge of Christ against the Antichrist of Rome; besides the time serveth well in that realm [France] to begin the conquest . . . Now were the time for Calvin and all such noble men as have fetched their knowledge from thence, to impugn and repress the tyranny of the Papists'.[8] Two months later, Cecil wrote to Randolph in Scotland: 'Her Majesty seeth daily no amity or intelligence betwixt one country and another so sure as that which is grounded upon unity and consent in Christian religion'. He added that they should be greatly encouraged by events in France, where the fierce persecution of Protestants had been replaced by religious toleration.[9]

In January 1561, Elizabeth sent the very Protestant Earl of Bedford to the French court to congratulate Catherine de Medici on the accession of the young Charles IX and to assure her that Elizabeth wished to maintain friendly relations with France. Bedford also told Catherine that Elizabeth believed that true Anglo-French friendship could only flourish if both realms adopted the same religion, and he therefore suggested that Catherine should go beyond the grant of toleration to the Protestants and make France a Protestant state.[10] Bedford and Throckmorton were also instructed to encourage the French Protestants to be stalwart in furthering the Protestant cause and to assure them of English support. On 6 May 1561 Elizabeth wrote to Throckmorton, in a letter drafted by Cecil, and told him to assure Coligny of her 'constancy and determination to advance the honour of Almighty God by maintaining of the truth of the Gospel of His Son Jesus Christ, by whose mighty power and singular favour we have been miraculously preserved and brought to this estate.'[11]

Elizabeth and Cecil, flushed with success, were in no mood to respond to conciliatory overtures from the Pope and to send representatives to the Council of Trent. When Quadra at last officially asked Elizabeth, on King Philip's behalf, to receive the Papal Nuncio and to give favourable consideration to his invitation to the General Council, the Privy Council advised her to refuse to permit the Nuncio to enter England, and not to send representatives to the Council of Trent; for no good could come from a General Council which was convened by the Pope.[12]

Elizabeth and Cecil watched Mary Queen of Scots suspiciously. Since her return to Scotland she had taken no step against the Protestants. She was advised by her half-brother, Lord James Stewart, who had been the most active of the leaders of the Congregation during the revolution; she created him Earl of Moray, and in effect allowed him to govern Scotland in her name, and to enforce the laws against the Catholics. She herself attended a Catholic Mass in the privacy of her chapel royal, but anyone who celebrated or attended Mass elsewhere was severely punished. Protestant bullyboys periodically attacked and wounded her Catholic priests with complete impunity. But she had a secret meeting with two Jesuits who were sent to

Edinburgh by the Pope, and she wrote to the Duke of Guise that she was determined to use her position as Queen of Scotland to further the interests of the Catholic Church as far as she was able in very difficult circumstances.[13]

Mary assured Randolph of her desire to have friendly relations with Elizabeth, and sent her able secretary, William Maitland of Lethington, to London to repeat these assurances to Elizabeth herself. Lethington said that Mary recognised Elizabeth as the lawful Queen of England, but that she herself was the next heir after Elizabeth's death, and he asked Elizabeth to state publicly that she recognised Mary as her successor, as this would cement the friendship between them. Elizabeth refused. 'Ye think that this device of yours should make friendship between us, and I fear that rather it should produce the contrary effect'. Kings did not like their heirs, and often hated their sons for this reason; if she were to name Mary as her heir, she would come to hate her as King Charles VII of France had hated his son Louis XI, and as Francis I had hated Henry II. But there was a more important objection to recognising Mary as her heir.

'I know the inconstancy of the people of England, how they ever mislike the present government and have their eyes fixed upon that person who is next to succeed . . . *plures adorat solem orientem quam occidentem* [most of them worship the rising not the setting sun].' She said that she had experienced this herself during her sister's reign, when many people would have been prepared, if she had given them any encouragement, to set her up in Mary's place; but some of those who had supported her when she was the Lady Elizabeth had turned against her when she became Queen, because their hopes of advancement had been disappointed. If she were now to name the Queen of Scots as her successor, 'we might put our present estate in doubt. I deal plainly with you, albeit my subjects, I think, love me as becomes them, yet is nowhere so great perfection that all are content'.[14]

Mary proposed that she and Elizabeth should meet. A meeting of sovereigns in the sixteenth century took as long to arrange, and was as fraught with political implications, as a summit conference in the twentieth century. Their ministers considered carefully which sovereign would gain most from the meeting, and, if it was to take place, which sovereign should have the prestige of being the host, how far each should travel to meet the other, and which of them should be in the place of honour on the right when they walked side by side. Cecil, in his usual way, jotted down the advantages and disadvantages of a meeting with Mary. It might shake the Protestants' faith in Elizabeth if she agreed to meet a Papist Queen; but if Mary was eager to meet Elizabeth, particularly if she came to England, it would be a sign of Elizabeth's power. If the meeting took place, where should it be held? There was no question of Elizabeth going to Scotland; but how far into England should Mary come? She herself suggested that the meeting should take place at Newcastle; the English preferred York or Nottingham. It was reported that

Mary was so eager for the meeting that she would be prepared to come to London if necessary.[15]

On 1 March 1562 the Protestants held a prayer meeting in a barn at Vassy in Champagne. It was in Guise's territory, and when he heard about the prayer meeting he rode over to Vassy at the head of a body of soldiers. He ordered the Protestants to stop their prayer meeting and disperse. They refused, shouted abuse at Guise, and threw stones at him and his men. One stone hit Guise and cut his head. He then gave the order to fire, and his soldiers killed forty and wounded sixty men, women and children.*[16]

The Protestants denounced the 'massacre of Vassy', and Condé and Coligny demanded from Catherine de Medici that Guise should be prosecuted for murder. Guise replied that he had the legal right to administer justice in his province of Champagne, and had judicially punished the Protestants at Vassy for their defiance of the law. He then came to Paris with a large escort of soldiers. He was loudly cheered by the people as he entered the city, and a fund was opened for subscribers to contribute money to Guise to finance a war for the Catholic cause. Catherine de Medici was powerless as both Catholics and Protestants prepared for civil war.[17]

A few days after Guise entered Paris, he invited Throckmorton to visit him. The Tiger of France was at his most affable. He said that his niece, the Queen of Scotland, was most eager to improve her relations with the Queen of England and to have a personal meeting with her. Some of her Scottish advisers were against the meeting because they did not trust Elizabeth and because they thought it would be derogatory to Mary's honour if they met on English soil; but Guise said that he himself was strongly in favour of the meeting, and realised that it would have to be in England. He merely hoped that Elizabeth, out of consideration for Mary's position, would agree to its being held as near as possible to the Border. Throckmorton then turned the conversation to the events at Vassy. Guise said that he regretted what had occurred, but the Protestants had been very insolent and menacing.[18]

Elizabeth decided to meet Mary, and it was agreed that the meeting should take place at Nottingham early in September. The officials began to make their preparations for the meeting. The captain of Norham Castle was warned to prepare to receive the Queen of Scots on her first night in England, and the wives of the noblemen of Yorkshire were ordered to welcome her with a prescribed number of ladies and servants in their retinues.[19] But in France the preparations were for civil war. Condé seized Orleans for the Protestants, and destroyed all the images in the Catholic churches there; in Blois the Catholics drowned Protestant women and children with stones

---

*These are Throckmorton's figures in his letter of 14 March 1562. Later Protestant propagandists wrote that between six and seven hundred had been killed at Vassy; but Throckmorton is not likely to have understated the number of victims.

around their necks. By June, Guise had raised an army of 7,000 men, and Condé one of 5,000, and both sides set about obtaining mercenaries. Elizabeth asked the German Lutheran Princes not to allow any of their subjects to enlist as mercenaries in the Catholic army; but German mercenaries joined Condé's forces, and Philip II sent 4,000 Spanish mercenaries to fight for Guise.[20]

Catherine de Medici decided to throw in her lot with the Catholics, who were obviously the stronger side, and offered to make peace with Condé on terms which revoked the edict of toleration and banished all Protestant preachers from France.[21] When Condé refused, she appointed the turncoat King of Navarre as commander-in-chief of the King's forces to suppress the Protestant insurrection, with Guise as second-in-command and the real leader.

Elizabeth decided to support the Protestant cause in France. She ordered Throckmorton to give every encouragement to Condé and to urge him to take resolute action; 'let him remember that in all affairs second attempts be ever more dangerous than the first'.[22] This advice turned out to be truer than Elizabeth realised.

She declared that she had no quarrel with the French King but only with the Guises, who, taking advantage of the King's youth, were pretending to act in his name in order to further their own designs. She told the French ambassador that as her neighbour's house was on fire, she was acting to extinguish the fire before it spread to her own house. Cecil, in a memorandum to her, warned her that if the Catholics won the civil war in France, it would be the signal for an armed uprising by the Papists in England.[23] He believed it was essential to give military aid to Condé, 'whom Almighty God maintains as His champion'.[24]

Elizabeth decided to send 6,000 soldiers to France. Two thousand would hold the port which the English called Newhaven and the French Havre de Grâce, and which today is Le Havre; four thousand would be sent to help the Protestants hold Rouen and Dieppe. She agreed to lend Condé 100,000 crowns, and, as security for the loan, he granted her temporary occupation of Le Havre.[25] Elizabeth and Cecil were conscious that Le Havre would be a useful bargaining counter for them to hold in their efforts to recover Calais, which under the Treaty of Cateau-Cambrésis was not due to be returned till 1567, but might perhaps be acquired sooner in exchange for the English withdrawal from Le Havre after the Protestants had won the war. It was originally agreed between Elizabeth and Condé's representatives that Le Havre should be garrisoned only by English troops; but afterwards, unfortunately, as it turned out, the English garrison was reinforced by some French Protestant soldiers.

Elizabeth's advisers all felt that in view of the imminent outbreak of the civil war in France, she would have to postpone her meeting with Mary Queen of Scots. Apart from the fact that it was inadvisable for her to go so far from

London during an international crisis, at a time when the heavy rains of a very wet summer had made the roads almost impassable, she should not demoralise the French Protestants by meeting the Guises' niece at such a time. But Elizabeth would not agree. She summoned a meeting of the Privy Council to discuss the matter, and took the unusual course of attending in person. Against the unanimous advice of all the councillors, she insisted on meeting Mary. On 6 July she confirmed that she would meet Mary at York or Nottingham between 20 August and 20 September.[26]

Then the news came from France that the fighting had actually begun in the civil war, and under pressure from her councillors Elizabeth changed her mind and very reluctantly agreed to postpone her meeting with Mary. On 15 July she ordered Sir Henry Sidney to go to Edinburgh to tell Mary that in view of the situation in France she could not meet her this summer, but would be very pleased for the meeting to take place in York, Pontefract or Nottingham on any date between 20 May and 31 August next year. Mary said that she was most disappointed that the meeting had to be postponed.[27]

Elizabeth instructed Sidney to emphasise one aspect of the situation in France which particularly shocked her – the part played by the Parisian lower classes in supporting the Catholic cause. 'An edict was published in Paris, giving authority, by express words, to the common people to kill and cut in pieces all such as had broken any church or houses, or that kept them company; an order never heard before, to give to the common people the sword, by means whereof many horrible murders were daily and yet be committed by the rash vulgar sort and headless people, without regard to estate or degree; yea, or without regard of fault known or tried.' She told Sidney to make it clear to her sister of Scotland that the thing which distressed her most about the events in France was 'the impeaching of the great desire which we have to see our said sister this present summer'.[28]

The war in France was fought with great savagery. As Guise's brother, the Duke of Aumale, advanced through Normandy, he hanged every Protestant pastor whom he captured, and in several of the towns and villages his troops killed all the Protestants, including the women and children. Condé spared the lives of the Catholic civilians, but hanged all the Catholic soldiers whom he took prisoner. In the south, the Protestant leader, the Baron des Adrets, was less discriminating, and massacred all the Catholics in every place where he passed. At Toulouse, not far from the Baron's district of operations, the Catholic bishop, believing that the large Protestant population of the town was about to seize Toulouse and kill the Catholics, decided to forestall them, and persuaded the Catholics to kill all the Protestants in the town, more than a thousand in all.[29]

The English troops under the command of Robert Dudley's brother Ambrose, who had been restored to his father's title of Earl of Warwick, landed at Le Havre on 4 October, and were greeted with great enthusiasm by the local inhabitants, many of whom were Protestants. The Privy Council ordered Warwick to expel from the town any Catholic who sympathised with the enemy, but to do so without cruelty.[30] English soldiers also joined the Protestants who were holding Dieppe and the great city of Rouen, which was a busy trading centre and a Protestant stronghold.

Catherine de Medici protested against the English intervention, which she claimed was a breach of the Treaty of Cateau-Cambrésis. She tried to take advantage of the English intervention and of the presence of the German mercenaries in Condé's and Coligny's army by calling on all Frenchmen, both Catholics and Protestants, to unite against the foreigners, who were using the mask of religion to cloak their national ambitions. She claimed that it was not a religious war, but a revolt inspired by the foreign enemies against the authority of the young King. She offered a pardon to all Frenchmen who would join the royal forces and help to expel the foreigners, and again offered religious toleration to the Protestants.[31]

On 10 October, as Guise led the greater part of his forces against Rouen and the war in France entered its most critical stage, Elizabeth, who was at Hampton Court, complained that she was feeling unwell. She decided to have a bath, but afterwards caught a chill, and next day had a high temperature. Two days later, her physicians realised that she had smallpox; she rapidly worsened, and on 16 October they told the Council that her life was in grave danger, and that she would probably die within the next few days. Cecil hurriedly came from Westminster to Hampton Court, and the Privy Council discussed what should be done about the succession, for the Protestant cause in Europe could collapse at once if Elizabeth died.

During those critical days when Elizabeth lay close to death, the most influential faction at court, including Cecil, Robert Dudley and the Earl of Pembroke, were determined to put aside Mary Queen of Scots, Katherine Grey and Margaret Douglas, and have Henry Hastings, who was now Earl of Huntingdon, as King. Quadra reported to Philip II that the Protestants had decided to proclaim him King as soon as Elizabeth died, and that Lord Robert Dudley, whose sister had married Huntingdon, was assembling a large force of soldiers who would support Huntingdon.

On the night of 16 October, the physicians believed that Elizabeth would die within a few days at the latest; but next morning she was much stronger, and by 25 October she was out of bed, and worrying only about the possibility that her face would be permanently disfigured by the pockmarks. As it turned out, her face escaped unscarred; but Lady Mary Sidney, who nursed her throughout her illness, caught the smallpox from her and was seriously disfigured for the rest of her life.[32]

On 26 October Rouen fell at the third assault, after the King of Navarre had been killed and Guise wounded in the attack. Guise ordered that all the English soldiers who were taken prisoner should be hanged, but he spared the lives of the French prisoners. After the disaster at Rouen, the Protestants at Dieppe decided to surrender, and the English garrison at Dieppe could not stop them. By the surrender terms the lives of the defenders were spared.[33] Only Le Havre in Normandy still held out, though further south Condé held Orleans, and he captured Chartres and Etampes as he advanced to within six miles of Paris.

Elizabeth and Cecil had been taken aback by the surrender of Dieppe, and it aroused all their English suspicions of the French, including the French Protestants. They became even more suspicious when Throckmorton wrote to them from Condé's camp that Condé and Coligny had met Catherine de Medici on 2 December at a mill just outside the Faubourg St Marceau to discuss peace terms. Condé, who had not informed Elizabeth about the peace talks, agreed with Catherine that the Protestants should be permitted to worship in certain parts of France, and that they would unite with the Catholics to demand the withdrawal of all foreign troops from France; but the peace talks broke down because Catherine refused to agree to two of Condé's demands – that the government should pay the wages due to his German mercenaries, and that the property of his supporters which had been confiscated and given to Catholic gentlemen should in every case be restored to them.[34]

On the day that Condé met Catherine de Medici, Cecil drafted a letter from Elizabeth to Warwick in which she said that she was worried that there were so many Frenchmen in Le Havre, particularly French soldiers, and that it would be desirable if Warwick could get rid of them.[35] A few days after he received this letter, Warwick heard that Aumale's army was on its way to Le Havre to besiege the town. He was very ready to believe the story which someone told him that there was a plot by some of the French Protestant soldiers in the garrison to betray the town and open the gates to Aumale. He ordered all his 2,000 English soldiers to be on watch that night, and informed Beauvoir, the commander of the French Protestant soldiers, that none of them must leave their lodgings during the night, 'for if they did, they should be well assured to feel the smart of it'. Beauvoir protested strongly against this mistrust of him and his soldiers, and was particularly distressed when Warwick suggested that it would be better if all the French Protestant soldiers left Le Havre, for he pointed out that as both Rouen and Dieppe had fallen, the French Protestants would have nowhere to go, and would be exterminated by the Catholic enemy. In the end, he reluctantly agreed to accept the curfew.[36] On receiving Warwick's report of his talk with Beauvoir, Cecil ordered Warwick to expel all Frenchmen, both civilians and soldiers, from Le Havre, if possible with Beauvoir's agreement, but if necessary by compulsion.[37]

On 19 December the Catholics under Guise met the Protestants under Condé and Coligny in a major battle outside Dreux. At least 15,000 men on each side took part, and between 6,000 and 10,000 were killed or wounded, including several of Guise's generals. Condé was taken prisoner, but Coligny led the defeated Protestants in an orderly retreat towards Orleans.

Guise besieged Orleans; but on 18 February 1563, while he was riding some miles behind the lines, he was shot in the back by a Protestant gentleman, the Sieur Poltrot de Méré, who had hidden behind a hedge and waited for him. Guise died six days later. Poltrot confessed, under torture, that Coligny had paid him to assassinate Guise, which Coligny vehemently denied. Poltrot was sentenced to be torn to pieces by horses.

The death of Guise made it easier for the Protestants to accept Catherine's peace terms. The Cardinal of Lorraine and Guise's other brothers withdrew from court and again returned to Joinville, with Guise's twelve-year-old son Henry, the new Duke of Guise; and Condé, as a prisoner, was under a strong temptation to accept generous peace terms. By the Treaty of Orleans of 10 March 1563 the Protestants were granted the right to preach in all the towns which their armies held on that date, in four other towns in each district which the King would allot to them, and on the lands of any nobleman who allowed it. These rights were not to apply to Paris, where no Protestant preaching or services of any kind would be allowed. Condé was appointed commander-in-chief of the King's army, while Coligny remained as Admiral and commander of the horse.[38]

Elizabeth informed Condé and Coligny that it seemed to her that they had used religion merely as a road to power and to get rid of their rivals. But Condé announced that as commander-in-chief of the King's army he would go to Le Havre to take command of the operations against the English invaders. Catherine de Medici wrote to Elizabeth, in Charles IX's name, that as Elizabeth had said that she was intervening in France to protect him from the tyranny of the Guises, now that the Guises had left court and the troubles in France were over, she should withdraw from Le Havre. Elizabeth told the French ambassador that she would only give up Le Havre in exchange for the immediate return of Calais.[39]

At Le Havre, the 4,363 English soldiers prepared to fight to the end. All the French soldiers and male civilians were expelled from the town. Warwick insisted that they had been treated as fairly as possible, for those who could not remove all their goods by the appointed date were allowed more time to leave. The French ships which had returned from their annual fishing expedition to Newfoundland were seized and sent to English ports. New resentment was caused when Warwick rounded up between two and three hundred French women from the outlying villages and forced them to carry logs and earth into Le Havre for use as bulwarks in the defence of the town.[40]

But food supplies were dwindling, and plague was spreading in Le Havre. By the middle of July it had reduced the effective garrison to about 2,800 fit men, and though 700 fresh troops were sent from Portsmouth, this left only 3,500 to face a French army of over 20,000 which was advancing on Le

Havre; and the English had only 300 shots of cannon left. So Elizabeth decided to evacuate Le Havre. She ordered Warwick to negotiate the surrender with the French commander, and told him that she had taken this decision because the safety of her soldiers meant more to her than any town. By the terms of the surrender, which was signed on 28 July, the English were to leave Le Havre and deliver it to the French King's Forces within six days. They could take all their stores and equipment with them, and were to return all the French ships and other property which they had seized. Prisoners on both sides were to be released without ransom. Warwick wrote to Elizabeth that the terms were much better than he had expected.[41]

The soldiers returned from Le Havre bringing the plague with them, and it spread in the south of England. It was one of the worst epidemics of the century. In London, 17,000 people died, about one in six of the total population of the city.*[42] The Spanish ambassador, Quadra, was one of the victims. But the plague was not the only disaster which followed from Elizabeth's decision to intervene in the French civil war. When the time for the return of Calais arrived in 1567, Catherine refused to hand it over, arguing that the English had repudiated the Treaty of Cateau-Cambrésis by seizing Le Havre, and that France was therefore no longer bound by the terms of the treaty. Elizabeth, having taken Le Havre in the hope that it would enable her to recover Calais four years earlier than had been agreed, found that, as a result, she did not recover it at all, and since 1558 Calais has never been an English town.

The outcome of the English intervention in France was a disaster for the Protestant cause in Europe. Elizabeth felt that she had been betrayed by the French Protestants, and remembered it for the rest of her life. It destroyed her faith in foreign Protestants. She decided that never again would she go to their assistance; and though she did, in fact, send troops to help them on several occasions in the future, she always did so reluctantly, belatedly and inadequately.

*The estimates of the population of London vary. It was probably about 50,000 in 1500, 100,000 in 1560, and 200,000 in 1600.

THE TOLERANT QUEEN

T HERE had been many religious changes during the lifetime of the older generation among Elizabeth's three million subjects, but in one respect things had not altered. Whatever religion might be imposed on the people for the time being, the sovereign had always required everyone to accept it, and to adopt no other doctrine or religious practice. Elizabeth was determined to adhere to this principle, and not to indulge in the experiment of religious toleration, as Catherine de Medici had done with such unfortunate results in France. Camden wrote that Elizabeth decided 'to suffer and tolerate but one and the self-same religion through the whole realm, for fear that diversity of religion should kindle seditions betwixt and among the people of England'.[1]

But religious uniformity was enforced with different degrees of severity at various times. A middle-aged man in 1560 had seen Church and State, in his youth, enforce the doctrines of the international Catholic Church by spasmodically burning a few Protestant heretics. Some years later, a bishop had been beheaded and several abbots hanged, drawn and quartered for continuing in their devotion to the Pope, while Protestants were still burned if they denied the Real Presence. For six years under Edward VI, Catholic bishops were imprisoned and deprived of their sees for rejecting Protestant doctrines, but no one was burned except two Protestant extremists who denied the doctrine of the Trinity. In Mary's reign, Protestants were burned, on average, at the rate of one every five days.

Under Elizabeth, uniformity was again enforced in the mild manner that had been adopted in the days of Edward VI. The Catholic bishops were deprived and imprisoned, and a small number of religious dissidents, including a few parish priests, were sent to the Tower, the Fleet, or the Marshalsea prisons; but compared with the persecutions of Henry VIII and Mary, Elizabeth's government was very lenient to religious dissenters.

When reports reached the Privy Council of people who refused to go to church, or who celebrated or attended the Catholic Mass, the offender was summoned to appear before the Council. There he was questioned, and attempts were made to convert him. If he remained obstinate, he was ordered to be imprisoned in the house of his diocesan bishop or of some other important Protestant churchman, where the bishop and other learned divines had lengthy discussions with him. If, after several months, he still remained unshaken, he might then be summoned to appear again before the Privy Council, and sent to the Tower, the Fleet or the Marshalsea. The Privy Council did not often take such stringent action. If the offender was sent to prison, the discussions with Protestant divines would continue, for the Council sent orders to the Lieutenant of the Tower or the Warden of the Fleet or the Marshalsea to allow certain learned divines, whom they named, to have access to the prisoner at all times. A very few prominent Catholics were kept in prison in this way for many years; but if the prisoner fell ill, or some influential friend could persuade the authorities that confinement in prison was injuring his health, the Council would order him to be moved from the prison to the house of some reliable Protestant, or even to his own house, where the discussions with the Protestant divines would continue.

If, after a few weeks or months in prison or under house arrest, the offender showed signs of submission and repentance, he was usually set free on condition that he reported to the Privy Council whenever the Council met, which was normally three or four times a week. This was of course a nuisance for the delinquent Catholic, for he had to attend at the Council chamber, day after day, perhaps for several months before he was told that he need no longer report and should go home and behave himself in future. But it was not a very heavy punishment for people who, when they themselves had been in power, had sentenced their religious opponents to be burned alive.

This leniency to the Papists angered Goodman, who had gone from Geneva to Scotland with Knox and found more sympathy and more scope for his talents in revolutionary Scotland than under Elizabeth in his native country. In October 1559 he wrote to Cecil from Edinburgh, complaining of the half-hearted measures taken in England to carry through the Reformation. He condemned the crucifix and candles in the Queen's chapel, the omission of some of the more Protestant passages in the 1552 Prayer Book from the Prayer Book of 1559, the observing of certain saints' days, and the maintaining of 'lordly bishops'; but he protested above all against 'suffering of the bloody bishops and known murderers of God's people and your dear brethren to live, upon whom God hath expressly pronounced the sentence of death, for the execution whereof He hath committed the sword in your hands who are now placed in authority'.[2]

It was not merely a case of the more extreme Protestants demanding vengeance on their persecutors, and of Elizabeth being ready to forgive them. Their attitude to the Papist bishops showed the fundamental difference between the view taken by Goodman and by Elizabeth on the duty of obedience to the Prince. For Goodman, the bishops and other royal officers who had obeyed the orders of 'wicked Mary' and had been the instruments of her cruelties against God's saints, deserved the extreme punishment for these offences against God. Elizabeth would not punish men who had burned Protestants at the orders of their Prince. Their activity in Mary's reign would not be held against them, and they would be punished only if they now disobeyed the orders of their new Protestant Queen.

Even when the Protestants could prove that their persecutors had been guilty of some illegality in Mary's reign, Elizabeth would take no action against them. At the height of the persecution in the summer of 1556, the authorities burned a young woman in Guernsey as a heretic, because, in her ignorance of the law, she did not claim her right, as a pregnant woman, to have the death sentence commuted. When she was burned at the stake, the heat of the fire caused her to have a premature delivery, and a baby boy came out of the womb and fell on to the burning faggots. One of the spectators rushed forward and dragged the baby out of harm's way; but the bailiff ordered it to be thrown back into the fire, where it was burned with its mother.

In 1562 the relations of the family brought a charge of murder against the bailiff and his officers because they had illegally burned the baby, who had not been condemned as a heretic. The bailiff argued that he had not broken the law, as the baby was included in the sentence for heresy passed against its mother because it was in her womb at the time. Elizabeth cut short the legal arguments, and stopped any further proceedings, by granting a pardon to the bailiff and his officers for any crimes which they might have committed in burning the baby.[3] She did not wish to encourage any proceedings against officials for their actions in Mary's days which might have aroused feelings of insecurity and resentment among them.

The outcome of the prosecution of the bailiff of Guernsey was still pending when John Foxe published the first edition of his *Book of Martyrs* in 1563. The publication of the book was one of the most important events in Elizabeth's reign, for this powerful Protestant propaganda work had a profound effect on the feelings of Englishmen for the rest of the reign and for the next three hundred years. Foxe, who had been a refugee in Switzerland during Mary's reign, returned to England when Elizabeth became Queen, and spent four years travelling all over the country, interviewing people who had been present when the martyrs suffered, and taking copies of the official records of the trials and interrogations of many of them, and of the letters which they wrote from prison to their wives and friends during their last days. Within four years he had incorporated all this information into a book, the first English edition of his *Acts and Monuments of these latter and perilous days touching matters of the Church*, which his friend John Day the printer published in London in 1563. It became known almost immediately as the 'Book of Martyrs'. The Catholic writers abroad attacked the accuracy of the book, but there are only a very few errors in it, including an occasional confusion of names.

The *Book of Martyrs* had an extraordinary impact. It brought home to the readers that individual men and women, including some very old and some very young, had endured the torments of the fire at the orders of Catholic bishops and judicial officers, for the personal responsibility of the Catholic Queen herself was not emphasised, out of respect for royalty and Elizabeth's family. It was not necessary for Foxe to write a book to remind the Protestant congregations in London or the inhabitants of the villages in Kent, Essex, Sussex and Suffolk about the fate of their colleagues and neighbours who had been burned at the stake; but in the other parts of England, where only a very small number of victims had suffered, the *Book of Martyrs* may have played an essential part in reminding the people of what had happened when Popery reigned.

One section of the book dealt with 'the miraculous preservation of the Lady Elizabeth, now Queen of England, from extreme calamity and danger of life in the time of Queen Mary her sister'.[4] There was no mention of the fact that Elizabeth had gone to Mass, but only of the dangers which she ran because of the machinations of Gardiner and the other wicked counsellors of Queen Mary. Foxe's account placed Elizabeth among the victims of the persecution, and this linked the Queen to the Protestants and the Protestant cause.

In 1570, Foxe published the second edition of the *Book of Martyrs*, with a great deal of new material which had been supplied to him since the publication of the first edition, and with some omissions. The second edition was published in two large volumes with a total of 2,315 pages and three and a half million words – more than four times the length of the Bible.* It was reprinted, with a few alterations, in 1576 and 1583, and, after Foxe's death, in 1596 and four times in the seventeenth century. A shortened version was published in 1589, with a dedication to Walsingham.

We do not know why some passages were deleted in the second edition. It is certainly significant that the strictures on Henry VIII for the bullying manner in which he presided at the heresy trial of the Protestant martyr, Lambert, were cut out in 1570.[5] Foxe's 'most dear sovereign, Queen Elizabeth, our peaceable Salome',[6] to whom he dedicated both editions, cannot have liked the criticism of her royal father, or wished to emphasise so strongly that he had persecuted Protestants.

In 1571, Convocation ordered that copies of the second edition should be placed in every cathedral along with the English Bible. Many parish churches also acquired copies, as did all the Oxford and Cambridge colleges, and many vicars read extracts from the *Book of Martyrs*, as well as passages from the Bible, during the lesson. During the naval war with Spain, the Council ordered that all sea-captains should have a copy on board ship and should read it regularly to their crews. Nothing could have been better calculated to

---

* Modern editions incorporate both the first and second editions in eight volumes, giving a total of over four million words.

increase their determination to fight the cruel Catholic enemy. Drake sometimes translated passages from the book for the benefit of his Spanish prisoners-of-war.

As the Protestants in 1563 read in Foxe's book of how Bonner had mocked and gloated over the martyrs whom he sentenced, and of the boy of eight who was whipped to death in Bonner's prison because he spoke up in defence of his father who had been arrested as a heretic,[7] they could at least derive satisfaction from knowing that Bonner was in prison in the Marshalsea for refusing to take the oath of supremacy and to celebrate the new Protestant service prescribed by Elizabeth's third Book of Common Prayer. But they wanted sterner measures to be taken against him and the other Catholic bishops. When Elizabeth's second Parliament met in January 1563, it enacted a more severe statute which made it a capital offence to refuse to take the oath of supremacy when required to do so for a second time after an earlier refusal and conviction. Elizabeth allowed the legislation to pass, but did not enforce it. When the oath was put a second time to Bonner in prison, he made a technical objection to the procedure adopted, and the authorities took no further action against him, though he was kept in the Marshalsea till his death in 1569.[8]

The Protestants would have been less perturbed about Elizabeth's failure to take firm action against the Catholic bishops if they could have been sure that there was no danger of these bishops ever returning to power and burning them once again; but they could not be sure of this while Mary Queen of Scots was claiming the throne and was next in line of succession by hereditary descent, if not by Henry VIII's will. The danger had come very near in October 1562 when Elizabeth was ill with smallpox, and the Parliament of 1563 presented a petition to Elizabeth, asking her to name her successor and to introduce legislation to give effect to this. When they asked her to name a successor, they meant that she should name a successor other than Mary Queen of Scots and thereby exclude Mary from the succession.

Elizabeth, in her speech in reply, put forward her usual line that her inferiority as a woman was eclipsed by her position as a Queen. 'The weight and greatness of this matter might cause in me, being a woman wanting both wit and memory, some fear to speak, and bashfulness besides, a thing appropriate to my sex. But yet, the princely seat and kingly throne wherein God (though unworthy) hath constituted me, maketh these two causes to seem little in mine eyes'.[9] She then said, at some length, that she would consider their request, but gave them no answer. According to Quadra, she was very angry with the MPs.[10]

She refused to name her successor and exclude Mary Queen of Scots. Apart from the fact that she believed, as she had told Lethington, that it would encourage plots against her if she named a successor, she wished to retain a free hand in her negotiations with Mary; and she obviously resented the attempts of MPs to arrange who their next sovereign should be, instead of dutifully accepting and obeying the Prince whom it pleased God to give them.

A majority of both Houses of Parliament, and Cecil, Bacon, and other members of the Council, favoured the claims of Lady Katherine Grey. But Elizabeth was determined not to nominate Katherine, who in her eyes had committed the unpardonable offence of either marrying Hertford without her consent or committing fornication with him and giving birth to illegitimate children. The sexual aspect of the situation was a very black mark against Katherine in Elizabeth's eyes.

John Hales, an ardent Protestant who held a minor office in the government administration, wrote an anonymous pamphlet in which he argued that Katherine and Hertford were lawfully married, that their children were legitimate, and that if the Queen died childless, Katherine and the children were the heirs to the throne under Henry VIII's will. Elizabeth ordered that Hales be sent to the Tower and prosecuted for sedition. Then she changed her mind, and did not proceed with the prosecution. Hales remained for some time in the Tower until his imprisonment was changed to house arrest in his own house in Coventry.

There was trouble, too, with some of the Protestants in London, with the 'Puritans', as they were now called for the first time, because they wished to purify the Church from the 'dregs of Popery' which they believed were still to be found in the Protestant Church of England. Many of the preachers at Paul's Cross spoke on this theme; there seemed to be as many critics as defenders of the existing practices among the preachers there. The Bishop of London, Grindal, who had to some extent come under the influence of the Protestant extremists during his exile in Germany and Switzerland in Mary's reign, was zealous enough in dealing with Dutch Anabaptists in London, but less vigorous than the Queen would have wished towards other Protestant nonconformists. The most serious clash came on the question of ecclesiastical vestments, which had divided the Protestants in Edward VI's reign. Two eminent Protestant divines, Laurence Humphrey and Thomas Sampson, objected to the wearing of vestments, and believed that the clergy should wear the clothes ordinarily worn by laymen.

In January 1565 Elizabeth decided that firm action must be taken against Humphrey and Sampson and the Protestant nonconformists in London. She wrote to Archbishop Parker that 'diversity, variety, contention and vain love of singularity' must be stamped out, as they were displeasing to God, as well as being troublesome to herself and dangerous for the peace and welfare of her realm.[11] In March, Humphrey and Sampson were summoned to appear before Parker, Grindal and other bishops, who ordered them to submit on the vestments issue. Humphrey reluctantly agreed to do so, and returned to his duties at Magdalen. Sampson refused to comply, and Elizabeth ordered that he be dismissed from his office as Dean of Christ Church and placed under house arrest. He was released from confinement after a few months, and unofficially informed that no action would be taken against him if he appeared without vestments outside the college, provided that he always wore them in Christ Church. Within two years he was appointed Warden of Wigston College in Leicester, and by 1570 he was a canon of St Paul's in London as well as a lecturer at Whittington College there, although he never submitted on the question of vestments. Things had certainly changed since the days of Henry VIII and Mary; even under Edward VI, Hooper had been treated more severely than this when he refused to wear vestments.

Parker was reluctant to begin a prosecution of Puritans in London, and knew that Grindal, as the diocesan bishop, was even more reluctant. Parker tried to warn Elizabeth what would happen if she insisted on enforcing the law about vestments; many of the London clergy, including some of those most loyal to her and most opposed to Popery, would go to prison rather than violate their consciences by wearing vestments. Elizabeth said that in that case she would send them all to prison. So Parker had no alternative, and took steps to enforce the law. Not long after this, he saw a clergyman at court, who was not wearing vestments, being received with every sign of favour by Elizabeth. He felt that she had pushed him into taking action against the Puritans, and had then let him down, leaving him to incur the unpopularity and the reputation of being a persecutor of Protestants.[12]

On Ash Wednesday 1565, Alexander Nowell, the Dean of St Pauls, preached before the Queen. Nowell was another refugee who had returned from Germany after Mary's death more Protestant than when he left England. In his sermon, he denounced idolatry and images, and then made an oblique criticism of the crucifix and candles in Elizabeth's chapel. Elizabeth interrupted him. She called out loudly 'Do not talk about that!'; but Nowell went on with his sermon. She called out again, even more loudly, 'Leave that, it has nothing to do with your subject, and the matter is now threadbare'. Nowell spoke a few more words, and then abruptly ended his sermon, and Elizabeth walked out, looking very angry. The new Spanish ambassador, Guzman de Silva, reported to Philip II that the Protestants who had witnessed the incident were in tears, but that the Catholics rejoiced.[13]

Nowell may have been very dejected, but he remained Dean of St Paul's. On the only recorded occasion when Henry VIII interrupted a preacher's sermon, the preacher* left England as soon as possible, and did not return during Henry's lifetime.[14]

The Protestants were alarmed about the way in which the Queen behaved towards Anthony Browne, a judge of the Court of Common Pleas. The readers of Foxe's *Book of Martyrs* could read of three cases in Mary's reign when Mr Justice Browne had shown great zeal in rounding up heretics in

* Friar William Peto.

Essex and committing them for trial before Bonner's ecclesiastical court;[15] but when Elizabeth became Queen, he continued on the bench, scrupulously enforcing the law against Catholics. In 1564 he wrote a treatise in reply to the book in which Hales had supported Katherine Grey's claim to the throne. Browne argued that Mary Queen of Scots was the heir to the throne of England if Elizabeth died childless. To the dismay of the Protestants, Elizabeth did not order Browne's arrest or dismissal from the bench, and in 1566, when Hales was still confined under house arrest, she knighted Browne for his services to her and her predecessors.[16]

Where was Elizabeth heading? Was she planning to hand over the realm, after her death, to Mary Queen of Scots? The answer to these questions was to be found in Scotland, not in England.

MARY QUEEN OF SCOTS

I T is not unusual for a great power, after suffering a diplomatic or military defeat at the hands of another great power, to react by exercising its authority more firmly in its own backyard. Elizabeth reacted to her defeat in France by tightening the screw on Mary Queen of Scots. If she could not recover Calais, she would not lose Scotland, or allow any other power to get a foothold there. She would never again become involved in a crusade for the Protestant cause, and would have nothing more to do with foreign Protestant rebels; she would control Scotland by having a friendly and submissive Queen there.

The relationship between Elizabeth and Mary Queen of Scots has fascinated people for four hundred years, and their characters have often been contrasted. But in many ways they resembled each other. Both were cultured, intelligent and brave. Both could be wilful and obstinate, though Elizabeth was slow to reach decisions and often changed her mind, whereas Mary was over-hasty in deciding and acting. Both had charm, which they could exercise over those who met them, and especially over men. Both were sincerely religious, and both betrayed the religion to which they adhered for tactical reasons – Elizabeth when she went to Mass in her sister's reign, and Mary when she allowed Moray and the Protestants to use her name to crush the Catholics in the north of Scotland and to execute the Gordons. Neither of them was sexually promiscuous or very amorous by nature, and both of them fell madly in love, Elizabeth only once in her life, and Mary perhaps twice.*
Both behaved foolishly when they were in love, but Elizabeth drew back from the brink just in time, while Mary fell right into the pit.

The greatest difference between Elizabeth and Mary was that Elizabeth was Queen of England, and Mary was Queen of Scotland. Elizabeth was Queen of a prosperous, powerful and disciplined kingdom, and Mary was

---

* Mary certainly fell in love with Darnley. There is strong evidence that she also fell in love with Bothwell, though her biographer, Antonia Fraser, argues persuasively that she did not.

Queen of a poor, weak and lawless one. Elizabeth had loyal counsellors, and Mary's counsellors were traitors.

Mary repeatedly declared her great desire for friendship with Elizabeth. As Elizabeth had said that the French civil war had made it necessary to postpone her meeting with Mary until the summer of 1563, Mary and her ambassador in London raised the question of the meeting as the spring approached. But the French civil war continued, and Elizabeth was more deeply involved in it than ever. Elizabeth and Mary therefore agreed that if the war in France had ended by 30 June 1563, they would meet at York in August. But on 30 June the English troops were being particularly hard pressed at Le Havre, and it was not till 28 July that Warwick agreed to surrender the town. The meeting of Elizabeth and Mary was postponed for another year, and it was provisionally agreed that it should take place at York in the summer of 1564.[1]

Elizabeth thought out a way of ensuring that Mary remained friendly. She proposed that Mary should marry Lord Robert Dudley. From Elizabeth's point of view, the plan had three advantages. It would mean that Mary's husband, the King of Scots, would be someone whom she could absolutely trust. It would confer a great honour on a man whom she dearly loved but could not honour by marrying herself; and it would end the continuing rumours that Robert was her lover and that she intended to marry him. She first broached the subject in a conversation with Mary's ambassador, Lethington, in March 1563.[2] The suggestion seemed so extraordinary to Lethington that he treated the matter as a joke.

Within a month of the débâcle at Le Havre, Elizabeth made a more formal approach to Mary about her marriage. This was prompted by reports which Elizabeth had received that the Cardinal of Lorraine, when he visited the Emperor Ferdinand at Innsbruck, had suggested a marriage between Mary and the Emperor's son, the Archduke Charles. There were other rumours that the Cardinal was planning for Mary to marry her brother-in-law, Charles IX of France, after the necessary Papal dispensation had been obtained, or Philip II's son, the Infante Don Carlos, or her cousin, young Henry, Duke of Guise.[3]

On 20 August 1563 Elizabeth sent instructions to Randolph about Mary's marriage. She and Cecil took great care over the wording of the instructions. They were drafted by Cecil, then corrected by him, and afterwards corrected again by Elizabeth herself. They began by expressing appropriate sentiments. The first and most important point to be considered was that Mary should marry a man whom she could love; the second, that the marriage should be acceptable to her subjects; the third that it should not be harmful to the interests of England. The instructions then stated that this third point was the only one on which it would be proper for Elizabeth to express an opinion, and that she would therefore consider Mary's marriage solely from this point of view. Although Elizabeth was sure that Mary had no hostile intention towards her, it could nevertheless appear to be a threat to English interests if she were to marry a powerful foreign Prince, and if she did, this would make it impossible for Elizabeth to persuade her Parliament to recognise Mary as her successor if she died childless. Elizabeth therefore hoped that Mary would marry an English nobleman, 'some person of noble birth within our realm . . . *yea, perchance such as she should hardly think we could agree to*'. These last words, which Elizabeth underlined in Cecil's draft, were a hint that she had Lord Robert in mind, and clearly implied that she would be doing Mary a great favour by agreeing to her marriage with him. It was extraordinarily insensitive of Elizabeth to think that Mary would consider it an honour to be offered a man who was generally thought to be Elizabeth's lover.

She added that if Mary would not agree to marry an English nobleman, then her marriage to 'some other noble person of any other country, being not of such a greatness as suspicion may be gathered that he may intend trouble to this realm, might be allowed; for ye shall always rest upon this argument, that neither we nor our country, having regard to the late attempts intended when she was married to the French King, can think any mighty Prince a mete husband for her'.[4]

It was firm language, though no doubt Randolph modified it a little when he transmitted the message to Mary. She accepted it without apparent annoyance, and made no comment except to say that she had never heard that the Cardinal of Lorraine was thinking of marrying her to Archduke Charles or to anyone else. Randolph raised the matter again with Mary.[5] At Christmas 1563 the festivities in Mary's palace of Holyroodhouse in Edinburgh were very gay, but Mary fell ill with a pain in her side, and when she discussed her marriage with Randolph on the Feast of St Stephen, she received him in bed. She said to the Earl of Argyll, who was also present, that 'Randolph would have me marry in England'. Argyll asked jokingly: 'Is the Queen of England become a man?'[6] There was a sting behind the joke, a reminder to Randolph that the only Englishman whom Mary might properly marry would be a king of England.

When Randolph told Moray and Lethington that Elizabeth hoped that Mary would marry an Englishman, they asked him whether Elizabeth had any particular person in mind. In obedience to Elizabeth's instructions, Randolph did not mention Lord Robert's name, but said that Elizabeth naturally left the choice to Mary. They would not take the hint, and Randolph would not mention a name. Eventually he was forced to do so, and in March 1564 he said that Elizabeth hoped that Mary would marry Lord Robert Dudley. They were not enthusiastic, and said that Lord Robert, though of noble blood, was not a nobleman himself, and had been attainted in blood through his father's conviction for high treason.[7] Elizabeth told the Scots that she proposed to overcome their first objection by making Lord Robert a peer, and she created him Earl of Leicester in October 1564. Neither Mary, Moray nor Lethington mentioned their real objection to Leicester – that he was generally supposed to have been Elizabeth's lover and to have murdered his wife.

The proposal for a marriage with Lord Robert had a chilling effect on the plan for a meeting between Elizabeth and Mary, which was put forward for the third time in the spring of 1564. This time it was Mary's turn to postpone the meeting. On 4 June, her Privy Council informed Randolph that it would not be possible for the meeting to take place that summer.[8]

By the autumn of 1564, Moray and Lethington seemed to be less hostile to the idea of Mary marrying Leicester, and Randolph began to hope that they might be persuaded to agree.[9] But it was not to be. Apart from other objections, Leicester himself was not eager. He did not wish to leave the English court, where he enjoyed so much influence with Elizabeth, to live in faraway Scotland, even with the title of King of Scots.

Leicester was a handsome man, and if he had gone to Scotland and met Mary, and she had fallen in love with him and married him, the history of England and Scotland would have been different. A marriage to Leicester would have been the best solution for Mary. Her only chance, in her very difficult situation, was to accept the position of a pro-English Queen of a Protestant kingdom. Leicester might have persuaded a loving wife to abandon all attempts to use her position on behalf of the international Catholic Church; and, being well known as an ardent Protestant and the Queen of England's great favourite, he might have persuaded the Scottish Protestants to allow Mary to have her Mass in private, and to call off their attacks on her priests. But Mary did not marry Leicester, and, though no one knew it at the time, she lost her last chance to save herself from the disasters which increasingly overtook her as she became trapped in a predicament from which there was no escape.

Lady Margaret Douglas, the Countess of Lennox, was a Catholic, and had been sent to the Tower by Elizabeth for plotting with the English Catholics and the Spanish ambassador; but she had afterwards been released from the Tower, and was now at Elizabeth's court and apparently enjoying the Queen's favour. She and the English Catholics were hatching a plot for Mary to marry Margaret's son, Henry Stewart, Lord Darnley, who was a Catholic and through his mother was in line to succeed to the English throne, though they had both been by-passed in Henry VIII's will. If he were to marry the Queen of Scots, it would greatly strengthen the Catholics in both Scotland and England. Darnley, like his father and mother, was living in England, and an elaborate scheme was thought out to get him to Scotland. First Lennox asked Elizabeth for a licence to go to Scotland in order to persuade Mary to give him back his lands in Scotland which he had forfeited for supporting Henry VIII in the wars against the Scots. Elizabeth not only granted him permission to go, but wrote to Mary, asking her to restore his lands.[10]

In the autumn of 1564, Lennox asked Elizabeth to allow his son Darnley to join him in Scotland. Elizabeth's first reaction was to refuse; but after Mary had written to ask her to accede to the request, she gave him a licence to go on an indefinite visit, and he arrived in Edinburgh in February 1565. Randolph had just written to Cecil to warn him that it would be most undesirable for Darnley to come, but his letter crossed with one from Cecil telling him that both Cecil and Leicester had advised Elizabeth to let him go, and that she had agreed and he was now on his way. Randolph could only accept the situation with deep misgiving.[11]

Darnley, who was probably aged eighteen in February 1565[12] and four years younger than Mary, was very good-looking, with a frail, sensitive appearance which obscured a vicious and violent streak in his character. Mary fell in love with him almost at first sight. This destroyed any possibility of her agreeing to marry Leicester, and within six months she had married Darnley, with fatal results for them both.

Cecil had discovered three years before that Margaret Douglas was plotting to marry Darnley to Mary,[13] and he and Elizabeth ought to have realised that this was why Darnley had asked permission to visit Scotland. Their contemporaries, and historians ever since, have speculated as to why they allowed him to go, just when Mary seemed at last to be on the point of agreeing to marry Leicester. Camden thought that it was Leicester's doing, and that Leicester hoped that if Darnley went to Scotland, Mary would marry him, so that Leicester himself would not have to marry her and would be free to marry Elizabeth. There is some evidence to support this view, and that Cecil, despite what he wrote to Randolph, agreed only reluctantly to Darnley's going to Scotland.[14]

Mary's marriage to Darnley turned out to be such a disaster for her that many contemporary Scots, like some scholars today, believed that the marriage was arranged by Elizabeth with diabolical cunning; that Elizabeth badgered Mary to marry Leicester, and allowed Darnley to go to Scotland, in order that Mary, as a reaction to Elizabeth's pressure, would marry Darnley and destroy herself by doing so. But very few statesmen are as subtle as this, and Elizabeth was the last person to plan and patiently carry out so complicated a manoeuvre. The fact is that Elizabeth committed a great blunder by allowing Darnley to go to Scotland. She either did not realise that if Darnley went there he would probably marry Mary, or else she failed to appreciate the fear and fury that the marriage would arouse among the Scottish Protestants. She did not foresee that it would lead her into the situation that she wished above all to avoid, in which she would be forced to incur the risk, the expense, and the disapproval of her fellow-sovereigns by helping Protestant rebels to revolt against their lawful Prince.

Randolph realised that Darnley's return to Scotland had had disastrous results. 'To whom this may chiefly be imputed', he wrote to Leicester, 'what crafty subtlety or devilish devise hath brought this to pass, I know not; but woe worth the time (and so shall both England and Scotland say) that ever the Lord Darnley did set his foot in this country'.[15]

The Scottish Protestants were very alarmed when Darnley arrived, and the most alarming factor in the situation was that Elizabeth had allowed him to come. Was she abandoning the Protestant cause and the Congregation in Scotland? A few days before Darnley reached Edinburgh they heard that Elizabeth had issued her order to Parker to force the English Puritan clergy to wear vestments. Moray and Lethington were so indignant that they wrote to Elizabeth to protest at this concession to Popery, which had much encouraged the Catholics in Scotland.[16] On 29 April 1565 Randolph wrote to Cecil that if Elizabeth had stopped Lennox and Darnley from coming to Scotland, 'Her Majesty might have been void of that suspicion, which is now almost universal of Her Grace, that the sending of my Lord Darnley home was a thing done of purpose, to worse end than I am willing to give in writing'.[17] In their private correspondence with each other, Elizabeth's diplomats and statesmen commented on her policy with a fearless candour which would have been unthinkable in the days of Henry VIII.

Elizabeth and her Council now realised that if Mary married Darnley, it would be the signal for an attempted Catholic counter-reformation in Scotland, and perhaps in England too, and would utterly discredit Elizabeth and the English alliance in the eyes of the Congregation. She decided to send Throckmorton to Scotland to warn Mary that the marriage would be 'unmeet, unprofitable, and perilous to the sincere amity between the Queens and their realms'.[18] But after his audience with Mary, Throckmorton realised that nothing he could say would have any effect, for she had fallen in love with Darnley, although Darnley was behaving extremely badly and was showing the vicious side of his nature; on one occasion, he drew his dagger and threatened to stab a member of Mary's Privy Council who had brought him unwelcome news. Throckmorton wrote to Elizabeth that the only way in which she could prevent the marriage was to send a powerful army to the Border and threaten war.[19]

Elizabeth refused to send troops to the Border, but she encouraged the Scottish Protestants to resist the Darnley marriage. She ordered Randolph to tell them that she considered them to be loyal servants of their Queen, and that 'we do not only allow, esteem and commend them herein, but do determine . . . to proceed the very same way in all our actions to maintain the same.'[20]

On 26 July Mary married Darnley. It was the invariable practice in the sixteenth century for the husband of a Queen regnant to be given the courtesy title of King, just as the wife of a reigning King was always called 'the Queen', though in neither case did this confer any royal power on the consort. Darnley – King Henry, as he was now named – could not exercise any royal power until Mary and her Parliament granted him the Crown Matrimonial, making him joint sovereign with her, as Philip of Spain had been when he was married to Mary Tudor; but this she would not do.

By August, the Lords of the Congregation who had led the revolution of 1560 were again assembling their forces under the leadership of

Châtelherault and Moray. Mary and King Henry, whom Elizabeth and the English diplomats insisted on calling 'the Queen's husband', raised an army and marched against them. The rebels thought that Elizabeth would help them, as she had done in 1560. Randolph wrote that they expected eight or ten thousand pounds to pay their forces; and on 15 September, after they had retreated to Dumfries with Mary in hot pursuit, they warned Elizabeth that they would be lost unless 3,000 men arrived by 4 October, and earlier if possible.[21]

Elizabeth sent £3,000 to the Earl of Bedford at Berwick, and told him to send on £1000 at once to the Lords of the Congregation; but she told them that she could not send them any military help, as this would mean going to war with Mary, which she was not prepared to do. Her official line was that she much regretted the clash in Scotland, and would do her best to persuade Mary that the Lords of the Congregation were loyal subjects whom Mary should pardon.[22]

As Mary marched on Dumfries, the rebels dissolved their army, and the leaders fled across the Border and reached Carlisle on 14 October. From there they went to Newcastle, and wrote to Elizabeth asking permission to come to her in London and present their case. Elizabeth, who knew that her actions were being closely observed by the French and Spanish ambassadors, Paul de Foix and Guzman de Silva, wrote to Moray and the Scottish lords at Newcastle ordering them not to come to her presence. But Moray had forestalled her; leaving his colleagues in Newcastle, he rode quickly down the Great North Road, and met Elizabeth's messenger carrying the letter to him and the lords between Royston and Ware, only thirty miles from London. After reading her letter, he wrote to her from Ware, and asked, as he had come so far, to be allowed to plead his case before her; and she agreed to grant him an audience.

He arrived in London on 22 October, and, according to the Spanish ambassador, had a secret meeting that evening with Elizabeth and Cecil. His official audience took place next day. Elizabeth invited Foix to be present. At first he declined, because he thought that if Moray, in excusing himself, said anything against Mary, he would have to reply to Moray, and he did not wish to become engaged in an argument in the Queen's presence; but Elizabeth assured him that if Moray said anything against Mary, she would immediately have him thrown into prison. Foix then agreed to attend, and Moray was brought in. As he knelt before Elizabeth, she upbraided him for his wickedness in rebelling against his Queen, speaking to him in French, and translating into French his replies in Scots for Foix's benefit. She said that she would never help a rebel to revolt against his sovereign, because she knew that God would then punish her for this by inspiring her people to rebel against her. Moray protested that he and his colleagues were Mary's loyal subjects, and had only taken up arms because Mary's advisers threatened their lives. After discussing the matter with her Council, Elizabeth agreed to intercede with

Mary on behalf of Moray and the others. Meanwhile she granted them asylum at Newcastle.[23]

Mary refused to pardon them. She found out that they had obtained 3,000 crowns from England, and, pretending to believe that Randolph had paid it to them without authority from Elizabeth, she ordered him to leave Scotland. He denied that he had given money to Mary's rebels, and the money had in fact been sent to them by Bedford. Elizabeth wrote to Mary that Randolph had been unjustly accused, and that she was therefore expelling Mary's ambassador in London, Melville, as a reprisal, though she regretted having to do this, as she had no complaint about Melville's conduct. Randolph delayed his departure as long as possible, but was eventually escorted across the Border to Berwick on 3 March 1566.[24] Before he left Edinburgh, he had already played his part in the plot to assassinate Mary's secretary, David Riccio.

Riccio was a native of Savoy who had come to Scotland in 1561 in the retinue of the Duke of Savoy's ambassador and had remained there in Mary's service as her lute-player and as a bass singer in her chapel. By the autumn of 1564 he had become her confidential secretary. He was in his early thirties, a Catholic, and apparently small, hunchbacked and ugly. He overdressed, was rather bumptious, and quickly amassed a fortune in Mary's service, probably by taking bribes,[25] which was not in the least unusual among royal officials in the sixteenth century.

By March 1565 Randolph was writing to Cecil that 'David' was a most powerful and nefarious influence in Mary's entourage, and Randolph and the Scottish Protestants became convinced that he was a very dangerous Papist agent and the arch-director of the Catholic counter-reformation in Scotland. But we today, who can read the extensive secret correspondence which Mary carried on with the Pope, the Jesuits, and other foreign Catholics, know that he was nothing more than a secretary, and not responsible for any policy decisions.[26] There is even less reason to believe that he was Mary's lover, though it is not at all surprising that the Protestants spread the rumour, just as the Catholics in England spread rumours that Leicester was Elizabeth's lover. Queens were always being suspected of having love affairs with their lute-players and musicians who sang and played love-songs to them, and a secretary who stayed up late in Mary's rooms at night, writing letters, playing the lute, or engaged in their usual pastime of playing cards, was an obvious target for gossip.

Mary and Henry had fallen out within six months of their marriage. She quickly became disgusted with his drunken orgies. They quarrelled; she refused him his marital rights, and he insulted her in public. He was also very disappointed that she refused to grant him the Crown Matrimonial. Mary was pregnant, and Darnley believed that Riccio was her lover and the father of her child.

Darnley's quarrel with Mary and his suspicions of Riccio gave the Scottish

Protestants and Elizabeth a golden opportunity to produce a split among the Scottish Catholics. A plot was hatched between Darnley, James Douglas Earl of Morton, and Moray and the exiled Lords of the Congregation at Newcastle. Morton was a Protestant, but he had been neutral in 1560 and had supported Mary and Darnley against the rebels in September 1565, and was therefore still at Mary's court; but he and other courtiers who were parties to the plot resented Riccio's influence and arrogance. They agreed with Darnley that they would help him to kill Riccio and would give him the Crown Matrimonial, if in return he would see to it that the exiles in Newcastle were pardoned and restored to their lands in Scotland.

On the evening of 9 March 1566, Darnley, Morton and some thirty others broke into a little room in Holyroodhouse where Mary was having supper with Riccio, the Countess of Argyll and four gentlemen of the court.[27] The intruders intended to take Riccio into another part of the palace, give him a summary trial, and hang him in public in the Canongate; but while Mary indignantly protested, and Riccio clung to her skirts begging her to save him, they were carried away in their excitement and stabbed him to death as they dragged him from her presence into the next room. Mary was held back by force, and one of the murderers pointed a pistol at her breast. It was not only murder, but a monstrous affront to Mary as a Queen; after all, in England anyone who even drew his sword anywhere within the curtilage of the court was sentenced to have his hand cut off. But the more outrageous the circumstances of Riccio's death, the better for the Protestants, for the more irreconcilable became the division between Mary and Darnley.

Randolph in Edinburgh, Bedford in Berwick, and Cecil and Leicester at Greenwich certainly knew about the plot to murder Riccio a month in advance. There is no evidence as to whether they played any active part in organising the murder, or whether they merely knew about it, kept quiet, and hoped for the best; but they certainly welcomed it, and probably encouraged it. Elizabeth, too, may have known, though it is more likely that Cecil and Leicester took care not to tell her, realising that she would prefer not to know. By the time that Randolph had been expelled from Scotland and had joined Bedford in Berwick, he had been informed about all the details.

On 6 March, three days before the murder, Bedford dictated to Randolph a letter in which they told Cecil about the plot, 'knowing how needful it is . . . that Her Majesty should not be ignorant of anything that cometh to our knowledge' and that they thought it 'our duty to utter the same to you, Mr Secretary, to make declaration thereof as shall seem best to your wisdom'.[28] On Friday 8 March they wrote to Leicester and Cecil that Moray was returning to Scotland from Newcastle and would be in Edinburgh by Sunday evening, and that 'that which is intended shall be executed before his coming there, we mean upon him whom you know'.[29]

The murder of Riccio shows the moral degeneration which was developing as the sixteenth century advanced and the wars of religion became more bitter. In 1546 the Protestants had assassinated Cardinal Beaton, and justified their action because he was a persecutor of Protestant martyrs; but Riccio in 1566 was not a persecutor of Protestants. The murderers, and the English diplomats and statesmen who backed them, no doubt persuaded themselves that Riccio was an important Papist agent, as well as an adulterer who had seduced the Queen of Scots; but the real reason for his murder was that it would have the excellent indirect result of causing a rift between Mary and Darnley which would help the Scottish Protestants and Elizabeth's foreign policy.

Mary outwitted and defeated the plotters. Taking advantage of the fact that Darnley was in love with her, she offered him the sexual satisfaction which she had recently refused him, and persuaded him to betray his fellow-conspirators. She escaped with him from Holyroodhouse, gathered an army, and drove Morton and the other murderers across the Border. She now pardoned Moray and the rebels of 1565, but not the murderers of 1566, who changed places with Moray and his colleagues and in their turn went to Newcastle. For the second time in five months, Elizabeth was put in the awkward position of having to consider whether to grant asylum to Mary's defeated rebels. This time it was even more difficult to justify this harbouring of the Scottish traitors.

If Cecil had told Elizabeth that there was a plot to kill Riccio, he probably had not told her, and did not know himself, that it would be done in Mary's presence; and this shocked Elizabeth. When she gave audience to Guzman de Silva on 9 April, wearing a belt with a portrait of Mary hanging from it by a golden chain, she showed genuine indignation at the 'disrespect' shown to Mary and at Darnley's part in the affair. She said that if she had been in Mary's place, she would have snatched her husband's dagger and stabbed him with it; but she added, jokingly, that she did not wish Guzman or King Philip to think that she would do this to Archduke Charles if she married him. She assured Guzman that none of the Scottish refugees to whom she had given asylum after the revolt of 1565 had any knowledge of Riccio's murder.[30] This was of course untrue, but Elizabeth may not have known that they knew.

She refused Mary's request for the extradition of Riccio's murderers, but ordered them to leave England. Morton sailed for Flanders on 14 June. Within a month, he returned secretly to Newcastle. Elizabeth ordered him either to go back to Flanders as soon as possible, or to keep his presence in England very secret. Her officials knew that he was in Northumberland, and there is no doubt that Elizabeth winked at his presence there. Meanwhile his friends in Scotland were working to obtain a pardon for him. Moray, faithful to the alliance that he had made with Morton before Riccio's murder, used his influence with Mary in his favour; and so did Mary's stalwart supporter, Bothwell, who apparently hoped that Morton would help him get rid of Darnley, for he knew that Morton was indignant with Darnley for betraying him and his fellow-murderers to Mary. In January, Morton and all the murderers of Riccio were pardoned and returned to Scotland.[31]

On 19 June 1566 Mary's baby was born. It was a son, the future King James VI of Scotland and I of England. Mary invited Elizabeth to be his godmother, and Elizabeth, who asked Lady Argyll to be her proxy at the christening, sent a magnificent gold font as a gift.[32] It seemed that she had again established friendly relations with Mary, and that the murder of Riccio had had the desired effect, with the Catholic forces in Scotland split, and Mary once more relying on Moray and the Protestant lords, and professing her friendship for Elizabeth. But it was only the lull before a greater storm.

IN DEFENCE OF MONARCHY

ELIZABETH had only prorogued Parliament in 1563, but it had not met for more than three years, which was not unusual in the sixteenth century. In the autumn of 1566 she was again short of money, and ordered Parliament to reassemble so that the MPs could vote new taxes which would give her £250,000. She found them in a dissatisfied mood. The Puritan members, who exercised a powerful influence in the House of Commons, did not like the policy which she had pursued during the last three years, with her refusal to marry, her drive against the opponents of vestments, her continued hostility to Katherine Grey, and her apparent rapprochement with Mary Queen of Scots. 'The Queen is not popular or beloved', wrote Guzman de Silva, 'either by Catholics or heretics; the former do not like her because she is not a Catholic, and the others because she is not so furious and violent a heretic as they wish'.[1]

Her counsellors were as eager as the MPs that she should marry, and she showed signs of weakening in her opposition to marriage. There had been talks about a possible marriage with Charles IX of France, and she had told the French ambassador that the fact that Charles was seventeen years younger than she, was not necessarily a bar to their marriage.[2] Her counsellors thought that the best match for her would be the Archduke Charles. He would be a more powerful ally against France than Eric XIV of Sweden, and though he was a relative and ally of Philip II he was not so directly under Philip's influence as to prevent Elizabeth, if she married him, from pursuing a neutral and switching policy between France and Spain. But the marriage negotiations were advancing very slowly, and Elizabeth made no effort to hurry them up.

When Parliament reassembled in October 1566 the MPs, instead of immediately voting Elizabeth the supplies that she needed, began a debate about her marriage and about who should be appointed to succeed her if she had no issue. Elizabeth was angry. The House of Commons was not only interfering with her royal prerogative by discussing her marriage and the succession, but were refusing to vote her supplies until she had satisfied them about this; and they were supported by the bishops and by many lay peers in the House of Lords. She demanded that they vote the supplies, and shouted abuse at her counsellors when they advised her to give way and allow Parliament to discuss first her marriage and the succession.[3]

She confided her feelings to Guzman de Silva, whom she liked. She complained that the Commons were trying to blackmail her, offering to vote her £250,000 on condition that she satisfied them about her marriage and the succession. She told him that they were encouraged by some peers who had once dared to say that she and her sister were bastards – she must have been referring to the supporters of Lady Jane Grey – and who had tried to persuade her to engage in conspiracies when her sister was Queen. Guzman was sympathetic. He urged her to marry Archduke Charles, and she said that she intended to write to him, accepting his proposal, within a week.

As for her difficulties with the House of Commons, Guzman said that she should have expected nothing else from heretics. 'I told her', he wrote to Philip II, 'to look at the intentions which these people professing the new religion displayed, their only object being to disregard their superiors and order things in their own way, without respect or consideration. I told her it was meet she should take measures in time, and bear in mind the obedience and quietude of the Catholics compared with the turbulence of the Prot-estants. She answered me that she did not know what these devils wanted. I said what they wanted was simply liberty, and if Kings did not look out for themselves, and combine together to check them, it was easy to see how the license that these people had taken, would end'.[4]

After the deadlock had continued for nearly a fortnight, the House of Commons asked permission to present a petition to Elizabeth. She received them in Whitehall on 5 November. She said that, under the pretence of loyalty, they had come near to committing treason by trying to compel her to marry; and if she did marry, they would almost certainly object to the husband whom she was intending to choose. In a rather obscure passage, she referred to the attempts which some of those present had made to persuade her to take part in plots during the reign of her sister, 'who I would to God were alive again'. She said that it was wrong, in a commonwealth, for the feet to try to dictate to the head; it was the duty of the head to stop the feet from running into trouble. She said that she hoped to marry, and also to have children, for otherwise she would never marry. At some future time, it might be beneficial to consider the question of her marriage and the succession; but she ordered Parliament to stop discussing it in the present session.[5]

Then on 25 November, after more than a month of conflict, she gave way. She sent a message to the House that she was prepared to grant their petition, and that they could discuss her marriage and the succession if they wished. A few days later, she agreed to remit one-third of the subsidy of £250,000 for which she had asked Parliament. Her gracious message was received with profound thanks and expressions of loyalty by the MPs, who voted the money and were satisfied with her promise to marry soon. Nothing was said about the succession.[6]

Elizabeth dissolved Parliament on 2 January 1567. In her speech on the occasion, she gently reprimanded the members for the trouble that they had caused during the session. 'As to liberties, who is so simple that doubts whether a Prince that is head of all the body may not command the feet not to stray when they would slip?'[7] It was a face-saving speech to cover her unprecedented defeat. Henry VIII sometimes made graceful concessions to public opinion, but he had never lost a head-on clash with Parliament. Elizabeth had, and no words of hers could hide it.

Elizabeth should have taken comfort from the fact that however difficult her House of Commons might be, she had less turbulent subjects than Mary Queen of Scots. Mary was quite incapable of dealing with them. The Papal Nuncio in Paris, the Cardinal of Lorraine and the Jesuits advised her to arrest all the troublesome Protestant lords by a sudden *coup* and put them to death as traitors;[8] but Mary was not a woman who could act in such a ruthless and Machiavellian way, and she refused point blank to do this. Instead, she fell in love with a Protestant, the Earl of Bothwell, and lost the support of both Protestants and Catholics.

On the night of 9 February 1567, Darnley's house at Kirk-o'-Field, just outside Edinburgh, was blown up by gunpowder, and Darnley was found dead in the garden, having been smothered by unknown men. It was immediately believed on all sides that Bothwell had organised the murder, and many suggested that Mary had been a party to the crime. As soon as Elizabeth heard about the murder, she wrote a personal letter to Mary, commiserating with her on her husband's death and giving her sisterly advice. She warned her how essential it was for her reputation that Darnley's murderers should be found, brought to justice, and punished.[9]

Darnley's father, Lennox, accused Bothwell of the murder. Bothwell agreed to stand trial before the High Court in Edinburgh, but came to the city with an escort of armed retainers, and Lennox, fearing for his life, failed to appear to present his case. Bothwell was acquitted, and a week later, only two months after Darnley's murder, he informed the other Scottish lords that he intended to marry Mary, and asked them for their support. They all promised, in writing, to support him, but afterwards got together behind his back and agreed to oppose him and destroy him. Bothwell organised a genuine or faked abduction of Mary, whom he carried off to his castle at Dunbar, where, according to Mary's statement, he raped her; but she agreed, almost immediately, to marry him, with a Protestant marriage service, after he had obtained a dubious divorce from his first wife. Pope Pius V and the Cardinal of Lorraine, who were disgusted at her marriage to Bothwell, decided to have nothing more to do with her. Nearly all the lords in Scotland united against Mary and Bothwell, and at Carberry Hill, on 15 June, she surrendered to them, while Bothwell fled to Dunbar, to the Shetlands, and ultimately to internment, imprisonment and death in Denmark. Mary was imprisoned in the island castle in Lochleven in Kinross-shire.

Even by the standards of Catholic and Protestant propaganda in the sixteenth century, the campaign of the Protestant lords against Mary and Bothwell in the summer of 1567 was extraordinarily hypocritical. Darnley, the vicious and dissolute young Catholic, whom the Protestants had so recently refused to accept as Mary's husband, was now elevated into a paragon of virtue. He was portrayed as a spotless and innocent victim of his wicked adulterous wife and her paramour. Cecil and Elizabeth followed this propaganda line. Cecil went so far as to make a note that Darnley, whom he and all the English diplomats had insisted so recently on calling 'the Queen's husband', had been constituted King by Mary, 'and so he was a public person and her superior'.[10] Cecil knew that this was nonsense, for though Darnley had the title of King, he was Mary's consort and subject. Even if she had granted him the Crown Matrimonial, which she never did, he would only have been her equal.

On 23 June Elizabeth wrote to Mary. She explained that she was writing to comfort her, because it had always been held in friendship 'that prosperity provideth, but adversity proveth, friends'. She wrote that she would do all in her power to procure the punishment of any of Mary's subjects who was guilty of Darnley's murder, 'how dear soever you should hold him', and to protect Mary's safety and honour and her son Prince James.[11] It is clear from the tone and content of Elizabeth's letters to Mary, and her references to her, that she despised her. Elizabeth herself, when she was deeply in love with Leicester, had made the sacrifice and refrained from marrying him or being his mistress because the interests of state and of her crown demanded it. Mary had not refrained from rushing headlong into marriage with Darnley and Bothwell regardless of the political consequences. In Elizabeth's eyes, she had shown herself unworthy of her position as a Queen. But Elizabeth would not permit Mary's subjects to punish her for her misdeeds, and, out of her regard for the privileges of sovereigns, would intervene to save Mary from the consequences of her own folly.

Elizabeth decided to send Throckmorton to the Scottish lords, and on 30 June she gave him his instructions. He was to tell them that she would not allow a sister Queen to be detained as a prisoner or deprived of her princely state; for though she admitted that Mary had been guilty of faults and oversights, it was 'not to be appertaining to subjects in such manner to reform their Prince, but uprightly to act by advice and counsel, and failing thereof, to recommend the rest to Almighty God'. She herself would not fail to censure Mary for her faults, 'which we think not unlawful or unworthy for us to do, being a Queen as she is, and her next cousin and neighbour'.[12]

Throckmorton found the Scottish lords, especially Morton and

Lethington with whom he chiefly had to do, in a most truculent mood. They refused his request to see Mary at Lochleven, for they were subjecting her to extreme psychological pressure to force her to abdicate, and did not wish her to receive any encouragement from his visit. They refused to agree to Elizabeth's suggestion that Prince James should be sent to England for his safety; and when Throckmorton reminded them of the debt of gratitude which they owed to Elizabeth for her help to the Scottish Protestants in the past, Lethington said that she had given very little help to Morton when he took refuge in England after the murder of Riccio.[13]

Elizabeth's plan was that Mary should agree to divorce Bothwell, and that after he was caught and punished she should be released; but Mary refused to sacrifice Bothwell. According to Lethington, she said that 'she would leave her kingdom and dignity to live as a simple damsel with him, and that she will never consent that he shall fare worse or have more harm than herself'.[14] Throckmorton became increasingly pessimistic about his chances of helping Mary, because the popular feeling against her in Scotland was so strong. 'It is public speech of all estates', he wrote to Elizabeth, 'saving the councillors, that she has no more privilege to commit murder nor adultery than any other private person'.[15] On 21 July he warned Elizabeth that unless Mary agreed to abdicate in favour of her son, the lords would hold a public trial and sentence her to death before the end of the month.[16]

On 24 July some of the lords visited Mary at Lochleven, and forced her to abdicate after threatening her with death if she did not do so; she afterwards stated that Lord Lindsay seized her hand and compelled her by physical force to sign the deed of abdication. Throckmorton had succeeded in smuggling a letter to her, in which he assured her that if she abdicated under duress while she was being held in strict seclusion in her prison, the world would never recognise the abdication as valid.[17] On 29 July her son, at the age of thirteen months, was crowned King James VI at Stirling. Moray, who had been absent in France during the revolution against Mary, and returned to Scotland through England after a meeting with Elizabeth, was appointed Regent for the infant King. Morton acted as his second-in-command, and Lethington as the Secretary of State.

Elizabeth did not know that Mary had abdicated when she wrote to Throckmorton on 27 July that he was to tell the lords that if they deprived Mary of her royal estate, she was sure that the other Princes of Christendom would join with her to revenge the deposition of Mary 'for example to all posterity'. She reminded them that St Paul had exhorted subjects to obey their rulers. 'You may assure them we so detest and abhor the murder committed upon our cousin their King, and mislike as much as any of them the marriage of the Queen our sister with Bothwell. But herein we dissent from them, that we think it is not lawful nor tolerable for them, being by God's ordinance subjects, to call her, whom also by God's ordinance is their superior and Prince, to answer to their accusations by way of force;

for we do not think it consonant in nature the head should be subject to the foot'.[18]

Throckmorton could only report back to her that the Scots had paid no attention to his remonstrances, and had crowned James VI as their King. Elizabeth decided that it was hopeless, and on 7 August wrote to Throckmorton telling him that there was no point in his remaining in Scotland any longer, and recalling him.[19] But four days later, she changed her mind. Cecil believed that it was as a result of her talk with Guzman de Silva, who had fuelled her indignation at the conduct of the Scots towards their Queen; and Guzman's letters to Philip II confirm this. He spoke with her on 9 August at Windsor, where she had gone on her progress during the exceptionally hot weather. She told Guzman that she hesitated to send an army to invade Scotland for fear that the Scots would then invite the French to come and help them; and after Guzman said that her honour obliged her to act against rebels who had deposed their sovereign, she asked him about the possibility of King Philip joining her and the French in a combined military intervention in Scotland.[20]

On 11 August, at about 5 p.m., she summoned Cecil to her apartments at Windsor, and to his dismay declared, in an outburst of indignation, that she had decided to go to war with the Scots to restore Mary to her throne. He tried to dissuade her and to point out the consequences of waging war against the pro-English party in Scotland; but she would not listen. Cecil tried again later that evening, with Leicester and Pembroke to help him; but she was adamant.[21] She wrote on the same day to Throckmorton, ordering him to protest about Mary's abdication. 'And this message we will and charge you to do as roundly and sharply as you can, for sure we be you shall not express it with more vehemency than we mean and intend'.[22] Cecil was almost in despair. He wrote to Throckmorton that if Elizabeth insisted on pursuing her hostility towards the Scottish Protestants, he would have to obey and carry out her policy.[23]

The Scots stood firm. On 21 August Throckmorton had a meeting with Moray and Lethington and delivered Elizabeth's message to them. They said that they had no intention of harming Mary, but hinted that if Elizabeth declared war on Scotland, Mary might be put to death. They said that they were not afraid of war with England, for it would simply mean that the English would burn their Borders and they would burn the English Borders; and they were sure that France would then come to their aid, and be very willing to re-establish the old alliance between France and Scotland.[24]

Elizabeth's intervention may have prevented the Scots from staging a public trial of Mary and executing her; but Throckmorton could do nothing more. On 29 August Elizabeth ordered him to return home without accepting the customary gift which was offered to envoys who came on a diplomatic mission. He therefore refused the silver plate which Moray proposed to give him.[25]

When he reached Windsor on 12 September, he found Elizabeth as vehement as ever against the Scottish lords; but she had realised the drawbacks of military intervention. So she considered that unsatisfactory alternative to war, economic sanctions. On 27 September she ordered Norris, her ambassador in France, to propose to Charles IX that they should agree not to allow any Scottish trader to enter England or France unless he declared that he still recognised Mary as his lawful sovereign.[26]

Charles IX and Catherine de Medici had not replied to the proposal when a new civil war broke out in France. Condé and the Protestants, alarmed at the return of the Cardinal of Lorraine to the King's favour and by rumours that Charles IX would repeal the edict of toleration and arrest the Protestant leaders, took up arms. This time, Elizabeth was careful not to intervene. Philip II, who sent 1,500 horsemen and two regiments of German foot soldiers to help Charles IX and the Catholics, warned Dr Man, the English ambassador in Madrid, that there would be serious consequences if Elizabeth again intervened on the side of the French Huguenots; but Elizabeth, far from responding to the Huguenots' appeal for help, ordered Norris to tell Charles that she would render him any service which she could in his difficulties with his rebellious subjects.[27]

But as usual the reaction of Elizabeth's diplomats and of her people were very different from her own. Norris wrote to Elizabeth urging her to support the Huguenots. Many Englishmen wished to volunteer to fight in France, and so did many of the Protestant refugees from the Netherlands who had come to England to escape persecution. Guzman heard that a Spanish Protestant, Ximenes, who had fought in Condé's army in the first French civil war, was organising the secret transport of English and Flemish volunteers from England to France. Guzman was annoyed when Ximenes was captured by the French Catholics and promptly hanged before he could be interrogated about the route taken by the volunteers.[28]

Elizabeth was very angry when she heard that English gentlemen wished to volunteer, and, according to Guzman, said that if anyone asked her for permission to go, she would cut off his head. She agreed with Guzman when he said that the French Protestants were as much rebels as the Scottish Protestants, and that if the French Protestants won the civil war, the situation in France would be as dangerous as it was in Scotland. But she took no active steps to stop the volunteers from going to Dieppe. She insisted that no harquebuses or pistols should be sent to the Huguenots, and Guzman was satisfied that she was firmly refusing to help them, though he feared that her counsellors might persuade her to do so.[29]

The second civil war did not last long. A battle took place at St Denis near Paris on 10 November, but on 4 January the two sides made peace. The Protestants were to have religious toleration, and, except in Paris, the right to hold prayer-meetings, provided that no more than fifty persons and their families attended.[30]

The fighting in France put an end to Elizabeth's plans for action against the Scottish Protestants. It left Charles IX and Catherine de Medici with no time to think about economic sanctions against Scotland; and after the war was over, Elizabeth did not revive the proposal. This was not the time to quarrel with her Scottish allies, when Philip II and Charles IX were drawing closer together, and Norris was sending reports about talk in France that when they had defeated their own Protestants they would join with Philip II and crush the heretics in England.[31] Elizabeth did nothing more against the Scots, though she refused to recognise James VI as King or Moray as Regent.

Moray did not worry. Hoping that deeds and self-interest would weigh more with Elizabeth than words and principles, he went to the Border districts, where he hanged and drowned a considerable number of cattle thieves, who for many years had robbed both in Scotland and in England.[32] The result was that English farmers suffered less from the thieves of Liddisdale and Teviotdale than at any time within living memory, and Elizabeth's officials at Carlisle were very pleased with Moray's government. Moray continued to carry on a private correspondence with Cecil, who was a personal friend. On 14 October he wrote to Cecil, thanking him for his part in preserving friendship between these nations 'whom God hath thus from the beginning enclosed within one isle and separate from the rest of the world'.[33] On 29 February 1568 he wrote again to Cecil. 'And although the Queen's Majesty your mistress outwardly seem not altogether to allow the present state here, yet doubt I not but Her Highness in heart likes it well enough'.[34] We can be sure that Cecil took good care not to show this letter to Elizabeth.

Elizabeth had never felt so strongly on any matter as she did in her support of Mary in 1567. She never caused her counsellors such anxiety, and was never more determined to disregard their advice. Yet in the end, she again gave way. She was never more conscious of the slippery slope on which she had embarked when she agreed to support Protestant rebels against their Prince, but there was nothing which she could now do to hold them back.

From her point of view, her attitude had an unforeseeable and beneficial result. In May 1568, after Mary had escaped from Lochleven and her army had been defeated at Langside, she decided to take refuge in England, rather than stay in Scotland with her supporters or take ship for France. She took this decision very largely because of the resolute support which Elizabeth had given her in the previous summer. As a result, Elizabeth had the Queen of Scots in her power. This gave her a great advantage over both Mary and the Scottish Protestants, which she ruthlessly exploited for several years. We are tempted to say – though the phrase and the concept would have seemed strange to the people of the sixteenth century – that Elizabeth was lucky.

THE REVOLT IN THE NETHERLANDS

IN April 1565 the Spanish ambassador in France received a letter from his confidential agent describing a conversation which he had had with the Abbé Mina, a close friend of the Cardinal of Lorraine. 'Nowadays', said the Abbé, 'Catholic Princes must change their old ways. In the past, friends and foes were distinguished by the boundaries of provinces and kingdoms; men were called English, Germans, French, Spaniards, Italians. Today one should speak only of Catholics and heretics. A Catholic Prince should reckon as friends all the Catholics of all lands, just as heretics consider all heretics as their friends and their subjects whether they be vassals of their own or of others'. He said that the heretics were a greater menace than ever Mahomet had been, because they had the weapon of the printing press at their disposal; but he had no fear of the outcome of the struggle, for although there were many heretics, there were five times as many Catholics.[1]

The Catholic Kings of Europe were reluctant to agree with Mina, but events were driving them into a religious war against international Protestantism. Philip II was a pious Catholic, but it needed the revolt in the Netherlands to persuade him that the heretics were a greater menace than his family's traditional enemies, the Valois Kings of France. The Netherlands had for forty years been a breeding-ground for heresy and Protestant extremism, producing not only Lutherans and Calvinists, but all kinds of Anabaptist sects. The heretics were savagely suppressed. Under Charles V's decree of 1550, which was reissued by Philip II, anyone who disseminated Protestant books, who argued on the meaning of Scripture, who defaced images, or who attended a Protestant prayer-meeting, was to be put to death. Men who recanted were to be beheaded; women who recanted were to be buried alive. Both men and women who refused to recant were to be burned. The same penalties were to be inflicted on persons who, though not heretics themselves, gave shelter to heretics or failed to denounce them to the authorities.[2] The number of victims far exceeded those in England or any other country, though the Protestant estimate of between 50,000 and 100,000 in the course of fifty years is doubtless exaggerated.

Margaret of Parma, as Philip's Regent in the Netherlands, continued the practice of governing the country through native, and not Spanish, counsellors. By 1566 the most prominent among them were Count Egmont, Count Horn, and William Count of Nassau, who was a German by birth but had been educated and had spent all his adult life at the court in the Netherlands. He was also Prince of the small principality of Orange in the south of France. This was later to prove very convenient for him, as it enabled him to claim that he was fighting against Philip as one independent Prince against another, and not as a rebel against his own Prince. Egmont, Horn and Orange were Catholics, and loyal servants of King Philip, but they wished to modify the severity of the religious persecution.

In April 1566 a group of noblemen led by Count Brederode, the Sieur of Sainte Aldegonde, and William of Orange's brother Count Louis of Nassau, organised a petition, which was signed by many of the local gentry and members of the merchant class, against the increased activity of the Spanish Inquisition in the Netherlands. Three hundred of them came to Brussels and presented the petition to Margaret of Parma. One of her counsellors ridiculed the petitioners as the '*Gueux*', the beggars, and they proudly accepted the name. Philip, in Madrid, regarded the petition as seditious.

Elizabeth took the same attitude. When Guzman de Silva discussed the events in the Netherlands with her on 17 April 1566, she said that the presentation of the petition against the Inquisition was 'a very daring act', and that if they had planned to do such a thing in England, even if they had not carried it out, she would have punished them severely. But she added that she was not surprised that the people of the Netherlands were opposed to the Inquisition, for she thought that it acted with excessive severity.[3]

She returned to the subject in a conversation with Guzman on 24 May. She spoke very angrily, saying that the action of Brederode and the petitioners 'was extremely rash and wicked, and that it was fine Christianity which led subjects to defy their sovereign'. She said that it had begun in Germany and France, and had then spread to Scotland and now to Flanders, 'and perhaps some day will happen here, as things were going now'. She was indignant that some rogues had tried to make out that she had encouraged Brederode and the petitioners. 'Only let me get them into my hands', she said, 'and I will make them understand the interest with which I regard all matters concerning the King my brother'. Then, deploring the disobedience shown everywhere to Princes, she referred to Riccio's murder, which had taken place two months before. 'Do you think the Queen of Scotland has been well treated to have armed men entering her chamber as if it were that of a public woman, for the purpose of killing a man without reason?'[4]

The opposition in the Netherlands came to a head in the great commercial city of Antwerp. There had been strong popular feeling in Antwerp for some time, and the burning of Protestant martyrs had led to riots. In August 1566 the people attacked images and churches. Margaret of Parma sent William of Orange to suppress the riot, and he succeeded in calming the people.

Many Protestants in England were delighted when they heard about the events in Antwerp. A drawing was published and sold in London, showing the people, named the Beggars in the picture, trying to tear down a placard fastened to a tree announcing the establishment of the Inquisition, while the Catholic clergy tried to stop them from doing this. Elizabeth banned the drawing, and gave orders for the copies to be seized.[5] On 31 August she raised the matter again with Guzman de Silva, who had accompanied her on her visit to Oxford. She 'began to speak very angrily about the rioters in the Netherlands, saying that they deserved a heavy punishment, as their cause had neither reason, virtue nor religion, the only aim being liberty against God and Princes'.[6]

Philip decided to send his veteran general and counsellor, the Duke of Alva, with an army to suppress the disorders in the Netherlands. He began to assemble an army in Spain during the winter, and rumours were circulating in the Netherlands and all over Europe that the Spanish army would be coming in the spring. Before Alva left Madrid, he spoke to the English ambassador, Dr Man, and explained that the King would not be sending him with a large force to the Netherlands if it were merely a question of religious disagreements, but that it was necessary to suppress what amounted to a rebellion. Man said that in that case, the Queen his mistress would strongly favour Alva's expedition.[7]

But public opinion in England was becoming increasingly moved by events in the Netherlands; and the people of the Netherlands, feeling the sympathy communicated to them by the English merchants in Antwerp, believed that Elizabeth would come to their aid, as she had helped the French Protestants in 1562. Rumours that the English were coming to save them spread through the Netherlands.[8] In January 1567 Elizabeth discussed the position with Guzman, 'and as usual expatiated on the insolence and disrespect they, the rebels, show'. She said that she had heard that Philip was sending an army to punish them, and she wished that he would send one three times the size to castigate such bad subjects as they deserved. She strongly denied that she was intending to help the rebels, and said that if any of her counsellors dared to suggest such a thing she would hang him as a traitor. She said that she would not repeat the mistake which she had made when she had been persuaded, against her better judgment and to her very great cost, to support the French Protestants in 1562.[9]

Alva, marching with his army from Genoa, arrived in Brussels in August 1567, and took over the government from Margaret of Parma. Philip had ordered him to strike terror into the opposition by executing William of Orange, Egmont and Horn. William had escaped to Germany, but Egmont and Horn were arrested and charged with treason for having encouraged the resistance of the people. Their wives and friends tried to use their influence to save them. Letters appealing for clemency were written to Alva and Philip by Philip's cousin the Emperor Maximilian of Austria, by several of the German Princes, by the Knights of the Order of the Golden Fleece, and by the Estates of Brabant.

The Countess of Egmont wrote to Elizabeth and asked her to write to Philip and intercede for Egmont's life. Elizabeth told Guzman of the countess's request, and that she had decided not to write to Philip, as she did not wish to intervene in the internal affairs of his countries. But some weeks later she changed her mind; perhaps Cecil, Leicester, or the rising indignation in England had influenced her. On 20 March 1568 she spent a day hunting in the country with Guzman, and mentioned to him again that Countess Egmont had asked her to intervene. She said that the countess had written so piteously that she felt unable to refuse her request and wished to write to Philip, but would show her letter to Guzman before sending it. She assured him that she would phrase the letter in the way that friends ask each other for favours.[10]

Her counsellors spoke to Guzman more forcibly. When the news reached England that Egmont and Horn had been sentenced to death by the 'Council of Blood' on 4 June and beheaded next day in the public square in Brussels, Leicester and Sussex strongly protested to Guzman.[11]

When Elizabeth heard that Mary Queen of Scots had escaped from Lochleven, she wrote to her to congratulate her and to express the hope that in future she would have more regard for her own honour than for the fate of a 'wretched rogue'.*[12] Before Mary received the letter, her army had been defeated at Langside near Glasgow, and she had crossed the Border and was in Carlisle Castle. Both Guzman de Silva and the French ambassador reported that Elizabeth's first reaction was to receive Mary as a Queen and to take steps to restore her to her throne; but Cecil and her other counsellors had no wish to support Mary against the Scottish Protestants. 'It is said that this Queen took the part of the Queen of Scotland', wrote Guzman, 'but her views did not prevail, as a majority of the Council was of a different opinion. The Duke of Norfolk and the Earls of Arundel and Leicester were ordered to be summoned, so that a full Council might decide what was to be done'.[13] It is interesting that Guzman, who knew Elizabeth better than many people, should have formed this opinion about how policy decisions were taken in her government.

Cecil realised that Mary's presence in England gave Elizabeth a hold over her and over her Scottish enemies which should be maintained for as long as possible. He thought out a way of doing this. Elizabeth announced that she could not compel the Scots to restore Mary to her throne until Mary had been

*'Un malheureux méchant'. Elizabeth always wrote to Mary in French.

cleared of the suspicion that she had connived at the murder of her husband, and Mary would remain in England until her guilt or innocence had been established. She invited Moray and Mary to submit their evidence to commissioners whom she would appoint to hear the case. But how could she justify her action in appointing commissioners to sit in judgement on the guilt or innocence of a foreign sovereign? Cecil thought of relying on the old argument that the Kings of England had overlordship over Scotland; but the most satisfactory way of surmounting this difficulty would be for Mary to submit voluntarily to the jurisdiction of Elizabeth's commissioners. As Mary's only hope was to win Elizabeth's support, she agreed to do this in the hope of pleasing Elizabeth. Meanwhile Mary was held at Bolton Castle in Wensleydale in Yorkshire.

Within a few weeks of her arrival in England, Mary realised that she was being held as a prisoner, and her envoy asked Elizabeth, if she would not restore Mary to her throne, to allow her to go to France. Charles IX and Catherine de Medici also asked that Mary be allowed to come to France. Elizabeth refused, on the grounds that when Mary had lived in France she had caused trouble by claiming Elizabeth's throne and sending French troops to Scotland.

In the autumn of 1568, Moray and Lethington and Mary's representatives appeared before Elizabeth's commissioners, first at York and afterwards at Westminster. Moray now produced in evidence against Mary the famous Casket Letters, those extraordinary documents which cannot have been written by Mary, but which no forger would have thought of forging in this form. They were probably a random collection of pages put together out of context.[14] Mary asked to be allowed to appear in person and plead her case before Elizabeth and the Council; but Elizabeth refused to meet Mary while she was under suspicion of her husband's murder. Perhaps Cecil persuaded Elizabeth to refuse to meet her because he was afraid that Mary might persuade Elizabeth to change her mind and restore her to her throne.

Eventually Mary's representatives withdrew from the hearings without replying to Moray's charges against her. Elizabeth then declared that the commissioners could not reach a decision until they had heard the case for Mary. This meant that she could continue holding Mary in custody indefinitely.

Among all the many documents drafted by Cecil, Moray and Mary and her representatives about the hearing before the commissioners and the conditions for restoring her to the Scottish throne, there are no surviving records, and probably none ever existed, showing how Cecil persuaded Elizabeth to abandon her original intention of supporting Mary, and instead to accept Moray's government in Scotland. Perhaps she was influenced by the Casket Letters, despite their doubtful authenticity. She may have become alarmed when she discovered that her chief commissioner, Norfolk, had been having secret discussions with Moray and Lethington about the possibility that he might marry Mary after she had obtained a divorce from Bothwell, and that this made Elizabeth suspicious of Mary. Perhaps Lethington and Moray, acting as *agents provocateurs*, suggested the marriage to Norfolk and then leaked the information to Cecil and Elizabeth, in order to turn Elizabeth against Mary.

But evidently, by some argument or other, Cecil persuaded Elizabeth that Mary was a threat to her security. Mary was, in Protestant eyes, the key figure in an international Catholic conspiracy to defeat the Protestant cause in Europe, overthrow Elizabeth, and restore Popery in England and the fires of Smithfield. Norris was sending reports from Paris of Catholic plots to rescue Mary from her English prison and bring her to France, as a first step to launching an expedition to conquer England and extirpate the English, French and Dutch Protestants. He sent a warning from Admiral Coligny, supporting his advice that Mary should be carefully guarded, and that Elizabeth should on no account allow her to go to France.[15]

In 1568 William of Orange and his brother Louis, who had become Calvinists, invaded the Netherlands from Germany in the north and the south with an army of German mercenaries and Dutch Protestant refugees, and the French Huguenots invaded near Mons and Valenciennes. Alva's forces scattered the Huguenots, and he himself annihilated Louis's army in Friesland, and then defeated William in the south. In France, there was only a short lull before the third civil war broke out. Charles IX had promised religious toleration, but the Catholics would not accept it. Nearly every day a Protestant was murdered in some town in France; and every murder in France, and every execution in the Netherlands, helped seal the fate of Mary Queen of Scots.

Many Protestants fled from the Netherlands to England to avoid the persecution. Guzman complained to Elizabeth that money was being raised, not only in the Dutch Protestant church in London but also in the English churches, to pay for arms to be sent to Orange and the rebels in the Netherlands, though he did not tell Elizabeth that he had heard that some of her counsellors had contributed to the fund. Elizabeth said that she could not forbid the raising of money; but she issued a proclamation prohibiting the sending of arms to Orange and the rebels. Although the proclamation was issued on 18 July, it was not published until four days later. Guzman believed that the officials had deliberately held up the publication for four days to allow more arms to be shipped before the proclamation came into force.[16]

On 25 August 1568 Charles IX announced that the complaints of the Protestants leaders that their supporters were being murdered by Catholics were malicious lies. The Protestants answered by once again taking up arms. Charles appointed his brother, the seventeen-year-old Henry Duke of Anjou, as Lieutenant-General of the royal army to crush the heretics. Elizabeth gave no more help to the Huguenots in the third civil war than she had done in 1567, but many young English gentlemen went to France to fight for them. They included young Walter Raleigh, a gentleman of Devon, though he was only sixteen. He had been aged six when Elizabeth became Queen, but he and many other young men of his age, who could barely remember living under Queen Mary, had read Foxe's *Book of Martyrs* and knew what had happened when Popery reigned, and what would happen again if Elizabeth died and was succeeded by another Papist Queen.

In March 1569 Anjou defeated the Protestants at the battle of Jarnac, near Bordeaux. Condé was taken prisoner in the battle, and a few hours later was shot dead in cold blood by one of Anjou's officers. But the Queen of Navarre appointed Admiral Coligny and her fifteen-year-old son, Prince Henry of Navarre, to command the Protestant forces in Condé's place. The Protestants hanged several of their Catholic prisoners. At Orleans, the Catholics put thirty Protestant prisoners into a house and set fire to it, burning all the prisoners. Another fifty were stabbed, and thrown into the river.[17]

On 3 October 1569, Anjou defeated Coligny at Moncontour. Elizabeth sent him a message of congratulation.[18] She had no intention of quarrelling with Charles IX and Catherine de Medici, for her relations with Spain had become very bad.

For nearly two hundred years the alliance with 'Burgundy'* had been the cornerstone of English foreign policy. It was a military alliance against France and a flourishing trade relationship. The English sold their wool in the Netherlands, and imported linen, oils and horses. In the days of Henry VIII and Charles V, the self-interest of the two nations enabled the trade and the alliance to survive all political and religious differences; but the disagreements about religion affected the position of the ambassadors. When the Mass was banned in England under Edward VI, Charles V demanded that his ambassador in London should be permitted to hold Mass in his embassy for himself and his staff; but he refused to allow the English ambassador at his court to hold the Protestant service of the Book of Common Prayer in his embassy. The English government asked for reciprocity; but Charles replied that there was no comparison between the two cases, for his ambassador expected to be allowed to attend Mass, as all ambassadors had done for centuries, while the English ambassador wished to have a new, heretical service. Charles declared that under no circumstances would he permit any ambassador at his court to hold a Protestant service in the embassy, but that if his ambassador was not permitted to have the Mass, he would withdraw him from London.[19] The English government accepted this unequal situation, as they did not wish to sever diplomatic relations with the Emperor.

---

*The independent duchy of Burgundy included modern Belgium and Holland and north-east France to within three miles of Calais. In the sixteenth century, the English ordinarily called the Netherlands 'Flanders' or 'the Low Countries', but continued to refer to 'Burgundy' when they were discussing the traditional alliance.

The problem arose again when England reverted to Protestantism under Elizabeth. Feria, Quadra and Guzman de Silva were allowed to hear the Mass in their embassies, and the service was illegally attended by many English Catholics without interference by the English authorities. Ambassadors in Spain were in a more difficult position. Philip's forebears, Ferdinand and Isabella, had granted wide powers in religious affairs to the Spanish Inquisition, and had agreed not to interfere with it. Whenever the English ambassador complained to Philip about the activities of the Inquisition, Philip replied that he had no power to prevent them, and that as his own counsellors and courtiers were subject to the Inquisition, so too were foreign ambassadors and their staff. He therefore told the ambassadors that they would have to raise the matter themselves with the Inquisition authorities, and the most that he could do was to put in a favourable word with the Inquisition on their behalf.

When relations between Philip and Elizabeth were reasonably friendly, the Inquisition did not inquire too closely into the religious services which were held in the English ambassador's house; but more serious difficulties arose outside the embassy, particularly in connection with the religious processions which were often held through the streets of Spanish towns and villages, with the Host held high for all to worship. All the bystanders were required to doff their hats and genuflect as the Host went by, and failure to do so was punishable as heresy by the Inquisition. The English ambassadors abroad had instructions from their government to refuse to worship the Host, but to do this in as discreet a manner as possible. They usually stayed away from ceremonies at court when they knew that the proceedings would include the Mass, or unobtrusively withdrew before the Mass was celebrated. But there was serious trouble when members of their embassy staff refused to remove their caps or kneel to processions which passed them in the street. They were arrested by the Inquisition, and Philip made it clear that no claim of diplomatic immunity would save them from punishment. There was also trouble with Elizabeth's ambassador Dr Man himself, who sometimes tactlessly became involved in arguments about religion, and on one occasion referred to the Pope as a 'canting little monk'.[20]

On 19 February 1568 Elizabeth asked Guzman de Silva to request Philip to allow Man and his staff the same privilege to worship in his embassy according to the religion of their Queen and country as Guzman had to hold the Mass in his house in London.[21] But Philip was hardening in his attitude to Elizabeth. In February he wrote to Guzman asking whether 'you think there is any hope of the Queen some day coming to her senses and recognising her error . . . because, so far as we can judge here, by her words and actions, she seems so wedded to heresy that it will be difficult for her to free herself from it'.[22]

At the beginning of April, he ordered Man to leave Madrid and remain, virtually under house arrest, in a small town not far away; from there he could carry out his diplomatic duties by communicating when necessary with Philip's counsellors, though Philip himself would refuse to receive him, in view of his disgraceful attacks on religion. If he continued to make such attacks, he would be punished by the Inquisition in the same way as anyone else, for Philip wrote that he felt a little guilty that he had done so much in the past to shield Man from the consequences of his actions.[23]

Elizabeth told Guzman that she regretted that Man had annoyed the authorities in Spain, but if he had uttered some indiscreet words in a private conversation, it was a very insignificant matter. Guzman said that it was not an insignificant matter in Spain to call the Pope a 'canting little monk', and that if anyone except a foreign ambassador had said this, he would have been severely punished.[24] Elizabeth then decided, in view of Philip's attitude, to withdraw Man from Spain and not to replace him with a new ambassador.

Guzman remained at Elizabeth's court for three more months, but in September 1568 he was recalled and replaced by a new ambassador, Guerau de Espés. Elizabeth was sorry that Guzman was leaving, as she had always liked him. Her relationship with Espés was bad from the first. Espés's personality may have been a factor which aggravated a situation which would in any case have become difficult, for his arrival almost coincided with Philip's change of policy. He came with instructions, which he was very eager to carry out, to get into contact with Catholics who were prepared to overthrow Elizabeth, and to encourage them to launch a rebellion, to free Mary Queen of Scots from her prison, and put her on the throne of England in Elizabeth's place.

THE CONTEST WITH ALVA

NINETY years earlier, during the lifetime of a few old people who were still living in 1568, no one in Europe knew of the existence of the American continent, and everyone believed that the Gulf of Guinea was the southernmost point of Africa. Then the Portuguese sailed around the Cape of Good Hope to India, Columbus sailed from Spain to discover the West Indies, and the Spaniards conquered the empires of Mexico and Peru. The Portuguese and the Spaniards agreed to share the newly discovered territories between them, and this was confirmed by the Papal bull of 1494, which gave Portugal the territories east of a line of longitude 370 leagues (1,110 miles) west of the Cape Verde Islands, and Spain the territories west of this line. This gave Asia and Africa to Portugal, and America to Spain.* Elizabeth's Protestant subjects in 1568 did not recognise the right of the Pope to give these new lands to Portugal and Spain and to exclude the English from them.

In the West Indies, the Spaniards found a native population which was used to an easy-going life, and not to the long hours of heavy work which the Spaniards forced them to undergo in the plantations. After twenty years, hardly any of the natives survived. A kindly Spanish priest, Bartolomé de Las Casas, was moved to pity by their sufferings. He went to Spain and persuaded Charles V to authorise the transportation to the West Indies of black slaves from the coast of Guinea, who were physically stronger than the natives of the West Indies and better able to survive the hard labour on the plantations. Thus began the slave trade between Africa and America, the terrible product of the selective pity of a well-meaning priest who lived to bitterly regret what he had done; but even before his intervention, this source of labour had not been overlooked by profit-seeking Spanish *conquistadores*.

---

*Except for Brazil, which was not discovered by Europeans till 1500, six years after the Papal bull of 1494. As the coast of Brazil was east of the Pope's line, Brazil was given to Portugal, and as a result today speaks Portuguese, not Spanish.

The moral aspect of slavery and the slave trade was not ignored by the men of the sixteenth century; but the institution of slavery had never been condemned by the Christian Church. The biblical texts from St Paul's Epistles, exhorting servants to obey their masters, which were so often quoted by English clergymen and gentlemen, had originally referred to slaves, who were the servants in St Paul's time. When the Roman Empire became Christian in the fourth century, slavery continued with the full approval of the Christian theologians, and the Catholic Church continued to support slavery until the nineteenth century. Christian doctrine taught that masters should treat their slaves, like all their servants, with kindness, and that slaves, like all servants, should obey their masters whether their masters were kind or cruel. The observance and non-observance of these precepts by both masters and slaves would be rewarded or punished after death in Heaven or Hell.

Slavery was well known in sixteenty-century Europe. Any Spaniard or other Christian who had the misfortune to be captured by the Turks or by the Moors of North Africa would be held for years as a slave, and Turks and Moors who were captured by the Christian powers were also enslaved. It was a proud achievement of Charles V that after his capture of Tunis in 1535 he took twenty thousand Moslem prisoners and sold them as slaves. Slavery was not completely unknown even in England. A handful of peasants were still slaves in law, and in 1547 Parliament reintroduced slavery on a larger scale as a punishment for vagabonds, though the statute was not enforced and was repealed two years later.[1]

In the case of African slaves from Guinea, there was another factor to be considered. The blacks of Guinea had never been taught the doctrines of Christianity. It was therefore impossible for them to go to Heaven. If they were kidnapped and brought to the West Indies as slaves, they could be taught to become Christians and their immortal souls could be saved. This was the theory, though how much time in practice was spent in teaching Christianity to the slaves was another matter. But the argument was accepted by both Catholics and Protestants in the sixteenth century. It was not until more than two hundred years later, after the Protestant nonconformist sects had won their battles with the Catholic Church and the absolute monarchy, that they played an important part in the movement which ultimately abolished the slave trade and black slavery.

That acute observer of human nature, William Shakespeare, understood the moral problem of negro slavery and the attitude of his contemporaries towards it. When he wrote his *Merchant of Venice* in the last years of Elizabeth's reign, he made his character, the Jew Shylock, when censured by the Christians for his cruel insistence on his legal right to his pound of flesh, defend himself by comparing his critics' attitude towards slavery:

You have among you many a purchased slave,
Which, like your asses and your dogs and mules,
You use in abject and in slavish parts
Because you bought them. Shall I say to you,
Let them be free, marry them to your heirs?
Why sweat they under burdens? Let their beds
Be made as soft as yours, and let their palates
Be seasoned with such viands? You will answer,
The slaves are ours; so do I answer you.[2]

The source of the supply of slaves was theoretically in the Portuguese zone, but the Portuguese government had in practice very little control as far south as the Gulf of Guinea. The demand for slaves came from the West Indies in the Spanish zone, where the authority of the Spanish government was well established. Spain had therefore a much greater control over the slave trade than Portugal, and the Kings of Spain, in return for money, granted monopoly rights in slave trading to the highest bidder. Any French or English sea captain who decided to break the monopoly and assert his right of free trade in negro slaves would find it easy enough to buy or kidnap the blacks in Africa, but much more difficult to sell them in the West Indies without getting into trouble with the Spanish authorities. It could sometimes be done by bribing local officials and avoiding the Spanish warships which could not effectively patrol the long coastline of the whole of the Caribbean.

The first sailors who effectively challenged the Spanish monopoly of the slave trade were the French from Dieppe and La Rochelle, which by the 1550s had become Protestant towns; but the sailors of Devon and Cornwall soon had the same idea. William Hawkins sailed to the coast of Guinea in search of slaves as early as 1538, and other attempts were made even in the reign of Philip and Mary, despite the alliance with Spain. These sailors came from one of the most Catholic districts in England, where the revolt against the abolition of the Mass had broken out in Edward VI's reign and where only one Protestant had been burned under Mary. But the younger generation were being brought up as Protestants, and soon the seamen of the West would be associating their battles against the Spaniards in the Atlantic and the Caribbean with the fight for the Protestant cause against Popery. When they met Spanish merchant ships, they attacked and robbed them if they could. If they were caught by the Spaniards, they were immediately hanged as pirates, and expected nothing less.

By 1560 William Hawkins's son, John Hawkins, had conceived the idea of breaking the Spanish slave-trading monopoly on a larger scale than had been done hitherto. His plan was for the expeditions to be financed by a syndicate of influential courtiers who would put up the money and share the profits with him and the other sea captains. The courtiers would use their influence to obtain letters of marque from Elizabeth, which would make the captains and their crews lawful privateers, not criminal pirates, if they robbed foreign ships at sea; and Elizabeth, too, would take a share of the profits. These letters of marque were unlikely to be of much use if the sailors were caught by foreign warships, but would at least protect them from a prosecution for piracy in England at the insistence of foreign governments or merchants.

Elizabeth took some time to make up her mind, and was reluctant to authorise a venture which might bring her into conflict with foreign governments. But the prospect of obtaining her share of the profits was enough to persuade her to risk a clash with Portugal, provided that it did not embroil her with Spain. She agreed to allow Hawkins to sail with letters of marque. He went on two voyages to Guinea, in 1562 and 1564, and on both occasions managed to sell his slaves in the West Indies with the connivance of local Spanish officials.

Among his crew was his young relative, Francis Drake, who came from a rather different background than Hawkins and the other sailors. He was born at Crowndale near Tavistock in Devon, probably in 1542, the son of a retired sailor, Edmund Drake, who had become a Protestant. When the Catholic revolt broke out in Devon in 1549, Edmund Drake fled to Kent with his family to escape the fate of other Protestants who were murdered by the rebels, and lived for a time in a hulk in the Medway near Chatham. This was the seven-year-old Francis Drake's first experience of the religious conflict; and in Kent, between 1555 and 1558, while he was between the ages of thirteen and sixteen, he heard nearly every week of the arrest of a Protestant in some nearby village, and of burnings of martyrs in Dartford, Rochester, Maidstone or Canterbury. After Elizabeth's accession, Edmund Drake became a clergyman and was appointed vicar of Upchurch in Kent. His son Francis, who had learned to love the sea on the Medway, joined Hawkins on expeditions to Guinea and the West Indies.[3]

In October 1567 Hawkins sailed from Plymouth with seven ships on his third slave-trading voyage. Francis Drake went with him. They reached the coast of Guinea, where they obtained a few slaves by kidnapping some healthy young blacks in night raids on the coastal villages. Hawkins was then asked by a local black chief to take part in an expedition against an enemy tribe and their town of Conga, which had eight thousand inhabitants. After a successful assault on Conga, Hawkins obtained more slaves, though fewer than he would have got if he had been able to restrain his sailors and his black allies from indulging in a wholesale massacre of the inhabitants. He eventually sailed for America with five hundred negroes in his ships.[4]

He succeeded in selling some of his slaves on the coast of Venezuela, but Drake became involved in an exchange of fire with the Spanish batteries. In September 1568 the English ships were driven by storms into the little harbour of San Juan de Ulua near Vera Cruz. While they were there, the Spanish Viceroy of Mexico arrived at the port with his fleet. The Viceroy would have had some difficulty in entering the port if Hawkins had opened fire on him; but Hawkins allowed him to enter after he had promised to do the English no harm. Once he was safely inside the port, he attacked the English ships.

Drake and Hawkins managed to escape with difficulty, and made their way separately to England; but only seventy of the four hundred sailors who had set out on the voyage in October 1567 returned fifteen months later. About a hundred were abandoned on the coast of Mexico because there was not enough food for them on the journey homeward, and they eventually fell into the hands of the Spaniards. Some were kindly treated, but others were handed over to the Inquisition as heretics. Some were burned for heresy in Spain; others were burned in Mexico. Those who recanted their heresies were treated more leniently, and were sentenced to be flogged and to serve for many years as galley-slaves in the Spanish navy. A few reached England twenty-three years later.[5]

The news of Alva's repression in the Netherlands and the third civil war in France was arousing the strongest feelings in England, where nearly every Protestant, except the Queen, enthusiastically supported the struggle of the Huguenots and the Dutch. 'The heretics here are more impassioned than those in the camp of the Prince of Orange itself', wrote Espés to Philip in October 1568.[6]

In November five Spanish ships sailed from Spain to the Netherlands carrying £85,000 in silver which some Genoese bankers had agreed to lend to King Philip for the pay of Alva's troops. The ships were attacked in the Channel by French Huguenot ships from La Rochelle, and took refuge in Plymouth and Southampton. When Eizabeth's counsellors heard that there was £85,000 on board the ships which was intended to pay Alva's troops, they considered whether there was any way in which they could seize the money and prevent it from reaching Alva; and just at this time a rumour reached London of the attack on Hawkins's ships at San Juan de Ulua, though Hawkins and Drake did not arrive in England until a month later. The counsellors discovered that under the terms of the bankers' agreement with Philip, the money was still the property of the bankers; and they persuaded the bankers' agents in London to lend the money to Elizabeth instead of to Philip, which would have the advantage, from the bankers' point of view, that there would be no risk of the money being stolen on the way from England to Antwerp. At first Elizabeth refused to agree to the proposal, and promised Espés that she would send a warship to escort the money safely to the Netherlands; but a fortnight later she changed her mind, and ordered that the money be removed from the ships and brought to London.

Espés was indignant at the seizure of the money, which he knew would seriously inconvenience Alva's plans; apart from other difficulties, it would force Alva to levy new taxes in the Netherlands which would increase his unpopularity there. Espés wrote to Alva advising him to retaliate by seizing all

English property in the Netherlands. Alva was a very competent soldier, but showed on several occasions that he was not an astute politican. He presumably thought that the seizure of the property of the English merchants would frighten Elizabeth into returning the money, and on 29 December he issued a proclamation ordering the confiscation of the property.[7]

Elizabeth immediately retaliated by seizing the property in England of all Philip's subjects in the Netherlands. Philip then seized English property in Spain, and Elizabeth seized all Spanish property in England. She also placed Espés under house arrest in his embassy, and stopped and opened his letters to Philip. When he protested, Cecil told him that Philip had placed stricter restrictions on Man in Spain, and that Elizabeth's action was a reprisal for Philip's treatment of Man and for the fact that Espés had advised Alva to seize the property of her subjects in the Netherlands. The principle of diplomatic immunity had not been finally established in the sixteenth century. Heralds who came to declare war in their herald's uniform were safe from any violence or arrest; but the position of resident ambassadors was more obscure.

Alva soon realised that he had made a blunder in seizing English property in the Netherlands. He discovered that the value of the property of Philip's subjects which Elizabeth had seized in England was about five times the value of English property in the Netherlands and Spain, and that the Spanish property in Elizabeth's hands was increased every time a Spanish ship on the journey from Spain to the Netherlands was forced by weather or Huguenot privateers to put in to an English port. He thought that it was impossible to go to war with England until more money was available, and war would only make the loss of the property in England irrecoverable; so he advised Philip to adopt a conciliatory policy towards Elizabeth. He realised that if Philip made the first overtures to her, she might interpret this as a sign of weakness and stiffen her demands; but he decided to send an envoy to England to propose that the dispute be ended by returning the property which had been seized on both sides, including the money of the Genoese bankers that Elizabeth had taken in the first place.[8]

Elizabeth reacted as Alva had expected. When his envoy reached Rochester he was told that Elizabeth would not receive an envoy from Alva. She said that although she had acted quite lawfully in borrowing the money of the Genoese bankers with their consent, Alva, instead of resorting to the methods laid down in the treaties between England and the Netherlands for settling disputes, had simply seized English property in the Netherlands. She would not negotiate with him, but only with Philip or some other minister whom Philip might appoint to carry on the negotiations.[9]

Meanwhile the Spanish property in England was being sold off by auction. Alva told the Spanish merchants to send secret agents to buy the property at the auctions; he could think of no other way of recovering it. Discontent grew in the Netherlands as the trade embargo hit the Netherlands much harder than England. The English found an alternative market for their woollen cloth in Hamburg and Emden, and ships sailed there regularly from Harwich and the Thames. The English suffered a minor inconvenience from being unable to import oil from the Netherlands, but overcame it by planting oil seed rape in their fields and obtained the oil from this crop.[10]

Espés complained bitterly about the treatment of the crews of the arrested Spanish ships, who were left to starve or beg in the streets. A hundred and fifty of them were interned in the Bridewell prison in London. Espés was incensed that the English authorities sent a Spanish Protestant, who had fled from Spain to escape from the Inquisition, to preach his heresies to the imprisoned Spaniards; but he was delighted when the internees told the preacher to go to Calahara.*[11]

In April 1569 Elizabeth released Espés from house arrest, and allowed him to resume his correspondence with Philip. He had in fact succeeded in smuggling letters to Philip while he was confined in the embassy, sending them to Spain in fishing boats from Cornwall.[12] He was now trying to organise a revolt against Elizabeth. He got in touch with important English Catholics. The Earls of Northumberland and Westmorland were prepared to rise in revolt in the North, release the Queen of Scots from captivity and place her on the throne in Elizabeth's place, and restore the Catholic faith in England, if they were sure that they would receive military aid and money from Philip. Espés urged Philip to give them this promise, but Alva advised against it, and told Espés that an unsuccessful revolt would make things worse for the Queen of Scots and the English Catholics.[13]

In October 1569 Cecil discovered about the plot, and Northumberland and Westmorland were ordered to come to court. They became alarmed that their plans had been discovered, and this precipitated a premature revolt. They refused to come, and called on their tenants in the North to rise. Within a few days they were at the head of an army of five thousand men. They claimed that they were fighting to reform the abuses in religion, but ended their appeals for aid with the words 'God save the Queen and the nobility!'[14] They planned to make a dash for Tutbury Castle in Staffordshire where Mary Queen of Scots was imprisoned; but Mary had been rapidly moved to Coventry, some forty miles to the south. On 14 November the rebels entered Durham. They went to the cathedral, publicly burned the English Bible and the Book of Common Prayer, and celebrated Mass.[15] It was the first time for over ten years that the Mass had been celebrated in a church in England.

The news of the rising heartened the Catholics all over Europe. But Alva was convinced from the start that the rising was bound to fail, and was unenthusiastic about sending them aid, though he sent 10,000 ducats to Mary Queen of Scots. Philip II was equally cautious and dilatory.[16]

---

*'Calahara' was the name given to the district in Spanish towns where bread was distributed to the poor in time of famine, and the expression 'Go to Calahara' meant that the person addressed would do anything if he were bribed by a gift of bread.

Elizabeth received the news from the North quite calmly. She raised an army of 28,000 men in the traditional way by calling on the noblemen and gentlemen to enlist their tenants and servants. She placed the vanguard of the army under the command of the Earl of Sussex, and he marched against the rebels. She ordered him to make it clear to the gentlemen in the northern counties that the rebels' pretence that they were fighting for the cause of religion was a cloak to hide the fact that their real objectives 'in this their traitorous enterprise' was 'the subduing of this realm under the yoke of foreign Princes, to make it the spoil of strangers'.[17] But the Privy Council did not obscure the religious issue, and called on Sussex and his men 'to suppress those Popish traitors, being sworn enemies to God's truth and their country' and 'to confound the wicked and false idolatry of the rebels'.[18]

Within six weeks, Sussex had driven the rebels across the Scottish Border and was pacifying the northern counties by executing rebels under martial law. Rebels who had no property were summarily hanged, and their bodies left hanging, in the villages and on the trees along the roadside. The wealthier rebels were spared for the moment, so that their property could be forfeited to the Queen after their conviction for high treason, and many escaped by bribing influential courtiers. Altogether over six hundred were hanged.

Moray seized the opportunity to show Elizabeth who were her friends and who were her enemies. He assembled an army, and ordered it to march to the assistance of the Queen of England's forces against the English rebels who had 'presumed to erect the Papistical religion in the bounds where they have repaired'.[19] But the Scottish borderers in Liddisdale, who were sympathetic to Mary, gave shelter to the defeated English rebels, and joined with them in raids across the Border into England.

Moray persuaded the local lairds in the Border districts to seize the Earl of Northumberland and hand him over to him; but when Elizabeth asked for Northumberland to be extradited, Moray hedged. He was in no hurry to surrender Northumberland to Elizabeth while she refused to surrender Mary Queen of Scots to him, for Northumberland could be used as a bargaining factor with Elizabeth. He was therefore imprisoned in the castle in the lake of Lochleven where Mary had been held. The Scots refused to extradite him till Elizabeth paid them money, ostensibly to reimburse the Douglases for the expense they had incurred in keeping him at Lochleven. Moray failed to catch the Earl of Westmorland and the Countess of Northumberland, who escaped to the Netherlands. Lady Northumberland offered money to the Scots to let her husband go free; but Elizabeth was prepared to pay more for Northumberland than his wife could afford to give, and after he had been held at Lochleven for more than two years he was handed over to Elizabeth for £2,000 and was beheaded at York in August 1572.[20]

Even if Philip and Alva had been willing to send help to the English Catholic rebels, they would not have had time to do so; but the Pope was determined to give them at least moral support. On 25 February 1570 he issued his bull excommunicating and deposing Elizabeth, and by May a bold English Catholic had ventured to nail a copy of the bull to the door of the Bishop of London's house in St Paul's churchyard. It denounced 'that servant of all iniquity, Elizabeth, pretended Queen of England, with whom, as in a most secure place, all the worst kind of men find a refuge'. She had overthrown the true religion which had been restored by Queen Mary, had appointed 'ignoble and heretical persons' as her counsellors, and had expressly ordered that books be published in her kingdom which taught 'the impious constitutions and atrocious mysteries of Calvin'. He therefore, with the authority with which God had invested him, declared 'that the aforesaid Elizabeth is a heretic and a favourer of heretics . . . and that she is wholly deprived of her pretended right to the aforesaid kingdom'. He absolved her subjects from their oaths of allegiance to her, and ordered them not to obey her laws and commandments under pain of being similarly damned along with her.[21]

On 21 January 1570, a few weeks after the suppression of the rising in the North, Moray was assassinated as he rode through the streets of Linlithgow by James Hamilton of Bothwellhaugh, who shot him from the window of a house. As Bothwellhaugh escaped and reached safety in Paris, he could not be interrogated about who instigated the murder, but Moray's supporters were almost certainly right in suspecting Archbishop Hamilton, the Duke of Châtelherault's brother, who was in Dumbarton Castle. Mary afterwards wrote that she had had no knowledge of Bothwellhaugh's plans, but warmly approved of the assassination, and rewarded him with a pension.[22]

The Protestants had set the Catholics a precedent for assassinating prominent leaders of the opposite party, with the murders of Beaton, Guise and Riccio; but they denounced the assassination of Moray as a horrible example of Papist wickedness. Moray's funeral in Edinburgh was made the occasion for a great popular demonstration against the Hamiltons. All over Scotland men named Hamilton were attacked by their enemies under pretext of avenging the death of the 'good Regent'. The Hamiltons had no alternative except to take up arms in self-defence, and they marched into Edinburgh. They wrote to Elizabeth, assuring her of their friendship, and pointed out that nearly all the Hamiltons, except the archbishop, were Protestants; they wished to punish Bothwell and Darnley's murderers, but they still regarded Mary as their Queen.[23] This was the same line which Elizabeth herself had adopted in 1567; but since then the situation had changed, and Elizabeth's policy in Scotland had changed. She refused to accept the Hamiltons' assurances of friendship, accused them of collaborating with her rebels in the North, and ordered Sussex to invade Scotland and punish the English rebels and the Hamiltons.

Sussex, who told Elizabeth that he had been taught by his grandfather never to trust any Scot or Frenchman,[24] was eager to carry out his orders. 'I trust, before the light of this moon be past, to leave a memory in Scotland whereof they and their children shall be afraid to offer war to England'.[25] He ravaged the lands of Mary's supporters in the Border districts, burned the Hamiltons' castle at Hamilton, and advanced to within a few miles of Edinburgh. The supporters of the party of Moray and Morton – the 'King's lords', as they were called – hoped that his army would complete the job by crushing the resistance of the Hamiltons and the 'Queen's lords'; but Charles IX and Catherine de Medici became alarmed at the prospect of a conquest of Scotland by Elizabeth and the complete destruction of French influence there. They told Elizabeth that unless she withdrew her army from Scotland, they would send French troops to support the Queen's lords.[26] This was no idle threat, for they had made peace again with the Queen of Navarre and the Huguenots, granting them religious toleration; and as the Hamiltons held Dumbarton Castle, which with its guns commanded the entrance to the Clyde, French troops could safely land at Dumbarton.

Elizabeth called a meeting of the Privy Council, which she attended in person. According to the French ambassador in London, La Mothe Fénélon, Cecil tried hard to persuade her to intervene decisively in Scotland against Mary and in favour of the King's lords, but she said to him: 'Mr Secretary, I wish to get out of this business and agree to what the King [Charles IX] asks me, and I will no longer be stopped by you and your brothers in Christ'.*[27] It is impossible to say how far Fénélon's report was accurate; but all we know about Elizabeth, Cecil, and her other councillors confirms Fénélon's belief that Cecil and many of the councillors urged her to use her army in Scotland to support the King's lords, but that she insisted on withdrawing her troops across the Border in order to placate the French. Apart from her usual caution, she was particularly anxious not to quarrel with France at a time when her relations with Spain were so bad, and she and her advisers were seriously discussing with the French the possibility of her marrying the Duke of Anjou.

Sussex withdrew his army across the Border, and Elizabeth congratulated him on his achievement, telling him that no English army had ever done so much damage to the Scots for so little loss.[28] He had, in fact, encountered virtually no armed resistance at all, for the Queen's lords were most anxious to propitiate Elizabeth.

After Moray's death, the King's lords had to choose another Regent, and they wrote to Elizabeth, offering to elect anyone whom she nominated.[29] She chose Lennox, telling the lords that he, as the King's grandfather, was the most suitable Regent. Lennox was still a Catholic, but Elizabeth and her counsellors considered that he was an English subject, because he had sworn allegiance to Henry VIII; and after he left for Scotland, his wife stayed at the English court as an unofficial hostage for his good behaviour.

---

*'Maistre Secretary, dict elle, je veulx sortyr hors de cest affère et entendre à ce que le Roy me mande, et ne m'en arrester plus à vous aultres frères en Christ'.

But many Scots were not happy to see an English army ravaging Scotland, and the office of Regent given to an English subject. Others supported the Queen's lords merely out of fear of Lennox and Morton. When Lethington was accused by his enemies of having been a party to Darnley's murder, he persuaded the captain of Edinburgh Castle, Kirkcaldy of Grange, who had been a mainstay of the Protestant cause ever since he participated in the murder of Beaton, to change sides and hold the castle for Mary.[30]

In October 1570 Elizabeth, chiefly in order to please the French, reopened negotiations with Mary. She offered to restore her to her throne, but under conditions which no independent sovereign could have freely accepted. Mary was not only to confirm the Treaty of Edinburgh of 1560, to undertake to maintain the Protestant religion in Scotland, and to renounce her claim to the English throne during the lifetime of Elizabeth and 'her issue'; she was to be governed by a Council of twelve counsellors, of whom seven were to be appointed by Mary and five by the King's lords, and who could only take decisions which were approved by at least eight of the counsellors. Her son James was to be sent to live in England; she was to extradite Elizabeth's rebels; and English garrisons were to be stationed in three Scottish castles.[31]

Mary tried to argue, and objected particularly to the last two conditions; but she was in no position to bargain, and finally accepted Elizabeth's terms, after Elizabeth had agreed to her request to spare the lives of any of the rebels who were extradited to England. Mary also suggested that the wording of her renunciation of her right to the English throne during the lifetime of Elizabeth and 'her issue' should be changed to the more usual form of 'her lawful issue'. Elizabeth testily replied that although she might have treated Mary's proposed amendment as a slur on her honour, 'yet considering she may peradventure measure other folks' dispositions by her own actions (which we trust in God shall always be far from us), we are content the rather to repress in silence what we think thereof'. She would not agree to 'lawful issue', but would change the wording to 'any issue by any lawful husband'.[32]

The King's lords in Scotland were alarmed at the prospect of Mary's return. They did not wish to annoy Elizabeth by rejecting her terms after Mary had accepted them; but they resorted to every trick to play for time. In the end they said that they could not decide until they had consulted the Scottish Parliament; but after six months the Parliament had still not met, they still had not given their answer, and Mary was still imprisoned.[33]

Then, very early on a misty morning in April 1571, a band of mercenaries in the pay of the King's lords accomplished the daring feat of scaling the high rock of Dumbarton Castle without being observed by the garrison, and captured the castle in a surprise attack. By Lennox's orders, Archbishop Hamilton, who was in the castle, was hanged in his episcopal vestments for his complicity in the murders of Darnley and Moray. The fall of Dumbarton was a heavy blow to Mary, for it would no longer be possible for the French or any foreign army to disembark in the Clyde; and it was not much compensation to the Queen's lords that Lennox was assassinated in a night attack on Stirling Castle. The new Regent was Lord Erskine, now Earl of Mar, a rather colourless figure who had always tended to adopt a neutral attitude in the struggles in Scotland, rather than the far more formidable, and more hated, Morton.

As Elizabeth turned more and more in favour of the King's lords, Mary became convinced that she would never be set free, however far she went in complying with Elizabeth's demands. It is not surprising that she was prepared to co-operate in the schemes of a Florentine banker, Roberto Ridolfi, who was in touch with the Duke of Norfolk, Espés, Philip II and the Pope, to assassinate Elizabeth, free Mary from captivity and proclaim her Queen of England, and to organise a Catholic rebellion and an invasion of England by Alva's armies. The plot was discovered. Norfolk was sent to the Tower; Espés was ordered to leave England; and Mary was more closely guarded in Sheffield Castle.[34] Her cause was lost.

In January 1572 Elizabeth at last took an irrevocable decision about Scotland. She announced that she would recognise James VI as King of Scots, and use all her influence to induce the Queen's lords to submit to the Regent. She applied pressure on Grange and Lethington in Edinburgh Castle, insisting that they acknowledge the authority of James VI and Mar. If they did, she would mediate on their behalf with the Regent; if not, she would regard them as her enemies. But she refused the request of the King's lords that she should send an army to capture Edinburgh Castle, and told them to do the job themselves. In April, Charles IX and Catherine de Medici accepted the position in Scotland, and signed the Treaty of Blois with Elizabeth's ambassador, Francis Walsingham. Negotiations were to be pursued for Elizabeth's marriage to the Duke of Anjou.[35]

When Parliament assembled in May 1572, the MPs urged Elizabeth to take drastic action against the Queen of Scots. In the same month, Norfolk was beheaded for high treason for his part in the Ridolfi plot, and the MPs demanded that Mary should suffer the same fate. The member for New Windsor denounced her as a Clytemnestra, the murderess of her husband and an adulteress. The member for Weymouth compared the two Queens, 'the one our sovereign lady Elizabeth, the other a Scot, an enemy to England, an adulterous woman, a homicide.' The bishops in the House of Lords issued a declaration that Elizabeth would 'offend in conscience before God' if she did not punish Mary. Both Houses then proceeded to pass a bill which, after reciting all the misdeeds of the Queen's 'very unnatural sister, Lady Mary Stuart, late Queen of Scots', enacted that if Mary or any of her supporters should at any time in the future take part in any plot against the Queen, or encourage any foreign ruler to invade the kingdom, Mary should be put to death for high treason, though one MP pointed out the injustice of executing Mary for an act committed by her supporters of which she herself might have had no knowledge.[36]

Elizabeth sent a message to Parliament that she did not wish them to proceed with the bill. They thereupon drafted an alternative bill which provided that Mary was incapable of succeeding to the throne of England, and that if, at any time in the future, she should lay claim to the throne or plot to overthrow Elizabeth or to induce a foreign Prince to invade the realm, she should be deemed to be guilty of high treason and should suffer death. Six years earlier, Elizabeth would have reacted angrily to such an attempt by Parliament to persuade her to execute a foreign sovereign. When confronted with this bill in 1572, she thanked the peers and MPs for their concern for her welfare, but said that she would defer her decision as to whether to give or refuse her royal assent to the bill. She then dissolved Parliament, and did not summon a new one for four years.[37]

The Protestant cause in the Netherlands appeared hopeless after the shattering defeats of William of Orange and his brother in 1568. But William would not give up, and he found hardy Protestant seamen who were prepared to carry on the fight at sea. The opponents of Philip's tyranny had been contemptuously called 'the beggars' and had proudly accepted the name; now the sailors called themselves the *Gueux de mer*, the sea-beggars. William, as Prince of Orange, an independent sovereign, issued letters of marque to the sea-beggars, authorising them to plunder Spanish ships and all ships trading with the Spanish-occupied Netherlands. After Alva seized the English property, Elizabeth was prepared to help the sea-beggars by allowing them to use English ports as a refuge and to obtain supplies, and the English port officials gave them every assistance to continue the struggle against Alva, Spain and Popery.

During the state of tension between England and Spain, the English Protestants were able to bring at least one of the Papist persecutors of Philip and Mary's reign to the justice from which most of his colleagues had escaped. John Story had been one of the counsel for the prosecution at Cranmer's trial for heresy. After Elizabeth came to the throne he had denounced the religious changes in his speech in the House of Commons, boasting of how he had treated the heretic at Uxbridge and regretting that they had not 'chopped at the root' in Mary's reign.[38] He was arrested in his barrister's robes on the Western circuit, but managed to escape with Quadra's assistance to the Netherlands, where Alva employed him as a persecutor of heretics in the office of the Inquisition in Antwerp. He was also entrusted with the duty of ensuring that no heretical books were smuggled into the country.

Some English agents laid a trap for Story. They sent a ship to Bergen-op-

Zoom and told him that there was an English ship in the harbour full of seditious and heretical propaganda tracts which the Protestants were planning to disseminate in the Netherlands. Story went on board the ship to investigate the allegation. He was seized, and the ship made sail for England with Story on board. They landed at Yarmouth, and Story was taken to London and imprisoned in the Tower. He was accused of inciting Alva to invade England and of instigating the rising in the North, and after being interrogated under torture he was put on trial for high treason. He refused to plead on the grounds that he was a Spanish subject, but was found guilty. Espés protested to Cecil and the Council against the kidnapping and conviction, but Story was hanged, drawn and quartered at Tyburn in June 1571.[39] Philip II sent money to his widow in the Netherlands, and wrote to Espés that they should be grateful to God for producing such martyrs as Dr Story, who was 'so firm and faithful in the Catholic religion' in the hour of his death.[40]

Elizabeth was in no hurry to accept Alva's offers to end the dispute over the seizure of the property in England and the Netherlands; but she sent Sir Henry Cobham to Madrid to discuss the matter with Philip, and carried on negotiations in England with some Spanish merchants and unofficial envoys whom Alva sent to her. A settlement was finally agreed at the end of December 1572, four years almost to the day from the seizure of the goods by Alva, though the treaty was not actually signed till April 1573. Both sides agreed to abandon their claims for compensation for any property which had been seized and sold by the other, which meant that Elizabeth retained the proceeds of the sale of property about five times as valuable as that which Philip and Alva had seized in the Netherlands and Spain. Trade between the two countries was to be resumed. The attempt by Elizabeth to obtain immunity for English traders from prosecution by the Inquisition was firmly rejected by Philip and Alva.[41]

During the course of the negotiations, Elizabeth decided that she would no longer tolerate the privateering by William of Orange's sea-beggars. Apart from her wish to improve relations with Spain, she had been urged to take action by the governments of the German Hanse towns, whose ships had often been attacked by the sea-beggars when they were trading with the Netherlands. In March 1572 she issued an order denying the sea-beggars the right to use English ports.[42] It was a heavy blow to William of Orange and the Dutch resistance. The only course open to them, if they were to continue the struggle, was to take the desperate step of seizing a harbour in the Netherlands and operating from there. In April they captured Brill. When the news spread through the Netherlands, the whole country rose against the Spaniards and began the war of independence which eventually ended in victory after thirty-seven years.

So Elizabeth's order expelling the sea-beggars from her ports was the immediate cause of the capture of Brill and the national rising in Holland.

Her Catholic enemies at the time, like many modern historians, believed that it was a cunning ruse on her part, designed to encourage the rebels of the Netherlands, to whom she secretly promised the aid which came to them soon afterwards from English volunteers. But if Elizabeth had wished to help them in this way she would hardly have done so at the very moment when she was seeking a rapprochement with Philip and Alva after three years of hostility. In view of all we know about her dislike for the Dutch rebels, it is much more likely that, intending to injure them, she unintentionally helped their cause. It typified her relationship with the Calvinist revolutionaries in the Netherlands and in Scotland. She hated them, but was driven by circumstances which she could not control into helping them to victory.

---------------------------------- ❧ 17 ❧ ----------------------------------

THE MASSACRE OF ST BARTHOLOMEW

E LIZABETH had won the economic war with Alva, and had secured herself against the Spaniards by her alliance with France; but she was coming increasingly into conflict with the forces of Protestant extremism, with the Puritans in England and with rebels abroad who rose in revolt against their Princes and expected her to help them. Her worst problem was that she was surrounded by counsellors who sympathised with the Puritans and the foreign rebels, and their influence was increasing.

During the first decade of her reign, Cecil had been the driving force in favour of an active pro-Protestant policy, against the half-hearted opposition of Arundel, Bacon and Elizabeth herself, though Elizabeth always trusted Cecil and refused to countenance any attempts by other counsellors to get rid of him. In 1571 she created him a peer and appointed him Lord Treasurer. He took the title of Lord Burghley from the name of his house at Stamford. He was replaced as Secretary of State by Francis Walsingham, and by Thomas Wilson, who had been imprisoned and tortured as a suspected heretic by the Inquisition in Rome before escaping when his prison was stormed by rioters. Walsingham and Wilson, and their assistants Robert Beale and William Davison, were even more zealous than Burghley for the Protestant cause. They had the support of Leicester, who in the past, for whatever reason, had sometimes encouraged the French and Spanish ambassadors to think that he might favour a pro-Catholic, or at least a moderate, policy, but by 1572 was adopting a strong pro-Puritan line. This was perhaps because of his association with Knollys's daughter Lettice, the Countess of Essex, whom he married a few years later after Essex's death. In view of the affection which Elizabeth felt for him, which was not abated by his marriage to Lady Essex, his support was invaluable for the Puritan cause.

Elizabeth came into conflict with these advisers in nearly every field of policy – over Mary Queen of Scots, the King's lords in Scotland, the Protestants in the Netherlands, the French Huguenots, and the Puritans in England. The history of her reign is really a history of these conflicts.

Elizabeth had a great advantage over her counsellors: she was their Queen, and nearly all her subjects, and these counsellors themselves, accepted that they had a duty to obey her. But she could not enforce her orders without their assistance, and she found that they frustrated her at every step. They delayed carrying out her orders, and turned the blind eye to breaches of them. Occasionally they conspired together to prevent her from finding out what was happening by suppressing reports and agreeing to tell her falsehoods. The result of the struggle varied. Sometimes Elizabeth got her way, sometimes she did not.

She would have liked to act as Henry VIII had done, and often said bitterly that her father would never have tolerated the opposition which she had to endure. But times had changed; it was 1570, not 1540. Henry VIII burned or beheaded his Protestant counsellors at the slightest sign of opposition, deliberately appointing a Council which was divided between Catholics and Protestants and playing them off against each other. He could rely on the support of his people, or of those classes who mattered; the lords, the country gentlemen, the JPs, the merchants in the borough corporations, approved when he burned Lutheran troublemakers and sacramentaries. Their sons in Elizabeth's reign were in many cases at least vaguely sympathetic to Puritans, and even if they did not agree with them, they would not have approved of burning them.

It was both a strength and a weakness for Elizabeth that she was under greater threat from Catholic Europe than Henry VIII had ever been. There had been a great outcry abroad when Henry executed Cardinal Fisher and burned St Thomas Becket's bones, but no assassination plots, no Jesuit missionaries travelling through the kingdom, no Spanish soldiers landing in Ireland and threatening to invade England, no clear call from the Pope to English Catholics to rebel and depose the heretic sovereign. However much Elizabeth might disapprove of the Protestant rebels in the Netherlands, Scotland and France, the Catholics were convinced that she was secretly supporting the rebels, and that her apparent disagreements with her Protestant counsellors were play-acting designed to hide the fact that she was granting them military and financial aid. Elizabeth might wish that she could act like her father's daughter, but to the Catholics she was her mother's daughter, the Lutheran she-devil who was responsible for all their troubles.

This had the result of increasing the devotion of the Protestants to Elizabeth, and removing any possibility that her Protestant opponents could come out into open opposition to her. But it also meant that there was no faction to which she could turn for support against the Protestants. The events of Mary's reign, and the opposition of the Catholic bishops in Elizabeth's first Parliament in 1559, had destroyed the possibility of the revival of an Anglo-Catholic party which Elizabeth could use against her Protestant counsellors, as Henry VIII had used Gardiner and Norfolk against Cranmer and Thomas Cromwell.

Like her father, and her sister too, Elizabeth knew how to be gracious and charming towards her subjects when she came into personal contact with them. She also knew, like Henry VIII, the importance of putting on a show of wealth and magnificence to impress her people and foreign ambassadors and visitors. She continued the custom, which was an established part of court life all over Europe, of admitting the public to see her go to her chapel royal for divine service every morning, and receiving petitions on the way from those petitioners who, after bribing the necessary officials, had been allowed to wait for her and to kneel to present their petitions to her as she passed.

Her royal progresses through the country were another opportunity for her people to see her and to marvel at her wealth and dazzling splendour, at the value of the many rings and jewels which she wore, and at the number of lords, ladies, gentlemen and servants who escorted her. It also enabled her to save some money, for when she travelled she stayed at the houses of her nobles and gentlemen at their expense.

When she was in Westminster she lived usually at her palace of Whitehall, though she sometimes stayed at St James's; but, like Henry VIII, she was more often at Greenwich or Richmond. She also resided at Hampton Court and at Nonesuch near Ewell, the largest of all her palaces, which Henry had built in the last years of his life but was not finished in time for him to live there. These palaces were further than Westminster from the bad air of London and the risk of infection. The sweating sickness, the dreaded disease of her childhood days, had passed away, for it never returned after the visitation of 1551; but the plague came repeatedly to London, though not on the scale of the terrible epidemic of 1563, which was not equalled until the outbreak of 1603, a few months after her death.[1] She did not react to the plague with the panic measures which Henry VIII had taken to avoid the slightest risk of catching 'the sweat', but she took sensible precautions.

In general, her health was good. She had a hearty appetite, and took a good deal of exercise, not only riding and hunting, but often walking with her ladies and gentlemen in the gardens or parks of her palaces, and going two or three miles from the palace before turning back. She periodically alarmed her counsellors and courtiers by falling ill. Apart from the smallpox in 1562, she developed a fever on several occasions, but recovered quite soon.

She went further from London on her progresses in the summer, leaving at the end of July or beginning of August and returning early in October. She went not only to Windsor Castle and to her royal manors of Enfield in Middlesex, Oatlands near Weybridge in Surrey, Easthampstead in Berkshire, Woodstock in Oxfordshire, and Grafton in Northamptonshire; more regularly than earlier sovereigns she visited some part of south-east England or the Midlands nearly every year. She travelled slowly at the rate of ten or fifteen miles a day, being slowed down not only by the dreadful state of the sixteenth-century roads and the pace of a long convoy of coaches, litters, carts and horsemen which accompanied her, but by the formal receptions of welcome at the county and parish boundaries, with loyal addresses and her gracious replies, and toasts in wine.

In 1560 she went to Winchester and Basing House, the residence near Basingstoke of the Lord Treasurer, the Marquess of Winchester. In 1561 she went through Essex, by Colchester and Harwich, to Ipswich, and in 1564 to Huntingdonshire and to Cambridge, where she was received with great loyalty by the university. She made a speech to them in her excellent Latin, and won their hearts by her charm.[2]

In 1565 she went to Coventry, and next year, after staying with Cecil at Stamford, to Oxford, where the university gave her as loyal a welcome as Cambridge had done.[3] One of the doctors of the university who greeted her was Laurence Humphrey, who had reluctantly obeyed the order to wear vestments in the university. When he kissed her hand, wearing his scarlet robes, she greeted him with a charming smile, and commented: 'Dr Humphrey, methinks this gown and habit becomes you very well, and I marvel that you are so straitlaced in this point; but I come not now to chide.'[4] At Oxford, as in many of the houses where she stayed on her journeys, she was welcomed by youths and girls who recited verses in Latin in praise of virgin Queens.

In 1569 she visited Southampton, and in 1572 went to Warwickshire and Gloucestershire on the longest progress that she had so far undertaken.[5] The foreign ambassadors in London usually accompanied the Queen and court on a progress, and on 18 August 1572 Elizabeth had a talk with Fénélon at Warwick about the possibility of her marrying Charles IX's youngest brother, Francis, Duke of Alençon. It was unfortunate that he was aged eighteen while Elizabeth was thirty-nine, and that he was considered to be very ugly, with a face scarred by smallpox; but there were great political advantages in the match. He was not prominently associated with the Catholic cause, like his brother, the Duke of Anjou, but on the contrary was thought to be vaguely sympathetic to the Huguenots, who were in favour of his marriage to Elizabeth.

The agreement for the marriage of King Henry of Navarre to Charles IX's sister Margaret of Valois raised hopes that the peace between the King and the Huguenots would not be followed this time by another civil war. Admiral Coligny spent much time at court, and seemed to be high in favour with Charles. They were discussing a plan for Charles's armies and the Huguenots to invade the Netherlands in support of William of Orange, to defeat the Spaniards, and persuade the Protestants of the Netherlands to accept Alençon as their ruler. They knew that this would alarm Elizabeth, in view of the traditional English alliance with Burgundy against France; but if Elizabeth married Alençon, she might well be prepared to accept him as ruler of the Netherlands.

Burghley favoured the marriage with Alençon, and had high hopes of persuading Elizabeth to agree; but as usual she was reluctant to commit herself. When she spoke to Fénélon at Warwick, she said that she could not agree to marry Alençon until she had met him.[6] No one could say that this was unreasonable, though Princes and Princesses often agreed to diplomatic marriages without first seeing their spouses. Burghley was disappointed. On 22 August, when the court had reached Kenilworth, he wrote to Coligny in Paris that the Queen's marriage 'is more important for the good of this realm and of Christendom in general and for the advancement of religion, than I fear our sins will suffer us to receive'.[7] But before Burghley's letter reached Paris, Coligny was dead.

The wedding of Henry of Navarre and Margaret of Valois took place in Notre Dame in Paris on 18 August; but on the morning of 22 August Coligny was shot at when he was walking back from the Louvre to his house after a meeting with the King. The shot was fired by a hired assassin in the pay of the Duke of Guise, who was convinced that Coligny had instigated the murder of his father. The harquebus bullets took off two fingers of Coligny's right hand and shattered his left elbow. When the King was informed, he appeared to be very indignant, and promised that those responsible would be punished. The Protestants in Paris were furious, and throughout the afternoon spoke angrily of taking up arms to avenge the attempt on the Admiral's life.

The Protestants throughout Europe afterwards believed that the Massacre of St Bartholomew had been planned long in advance by Catherine de Medici and the Catholics, who had invited the Huguenots to Paris for the wedding of Henry and Margaret with the intention of murdering them all on the night of St Bartholomew's Eve. But this is almost certainly wrong, for everything indicates that the massacre was a panic decision taken at the last moment, on the evening of 22 August, by Catherine and Anjou, and perhaps also the Duke of Nevers, Marshal Tavannes, the Count of Retz, and Guise's mother, the Duchess of Nemours. They believed that the Huguenots, indignant at the attempt on Coligny, were planning to massacre the Catholics in Paris, and they decided to forestall the Huguenots by killing them first, before they could carry out their plan. They invited Guise to take the opportunity of avenging his father by completing the job which his hired assassin had begun, and finishing off Coligny; and they knew that if the King's guards and Guise's followers began the work, they could rely on the people of Paris to complete it. At eleven o'clock that night Catherine persuaded Charles IX to agree, and the massacre began within twenty-four hours on the evening of 23 August.

Guise went to Coligny's house and watched while one of his Swiss soldiers killed the Admiral as he sat wounded in his bedroom; but he took no further part in the killing, which was largely left to the Parisians. It continued for two days, during which nearly all the Huguenots in Paris were killed, though the King of Navarre and the Prince of Condé were spared on condition that they became Catholics, and they were held virtually as prisoners at court. When the news reached the provinces, more massacres took place there, particularly in Rouen, Orleans, Lyons, Meaux, Bordeaux and Toulouse. In all, about eight thousand Protestants were killed.

The English embassy was just outside Paris, across the river in the suburb of St Germain des Prés. Here Walsingham was protected by the King's guards who surrounded his house, and he offered a refuge there to some Englishmen who had come to Paris for the royal wedding, or were passing through on their foreign travels, including young Walter Raleigh and young Philip Sidney. They did not find out for some time what was happening in Paris, though they could hear the sound of firing and screaming from across the Seine. When Walsingham learned the whole story, the report which he sent to Elizabeth was held up for some days while his courier waited at Calais for a favourable wind. But the desperate Huguenots were more eager than the courier to cross the Channel, and managed to reach safety in England and bring the first news of the massacre before Walsingham's letter arrived on 3 September.[8]

The news of the Massacre of St Bartholomew was greeted with joy in the Catholic states, where official thanksgiving services were held. In Rome, Pope Gregory XIII proclaimed a Jubilee to celebrate the glorious event. But the English Protestants were horrified, and demanded vengeance against the most prominent Papist who was in their power, the unfortunate Mary Queen of Scots, who was certainly not responsible for the Massacre of St Bartholomew and who had rejected the advice of the leading Papist churchmen in Europe when they had urged her to act in a similar way in Scotland. Sandys, the Bishop of London, wrote to Burghley and urged him 'forthwith to cut off the Scottish Queen's head'; and Archbishop Parker, hearing that the Catholics in England, at their meetings, were rejoicing over the news from Paris, agreed that Mary, 'that only desperate person', should be removed. In Scotland, the Protestants went further. The dying Knox, in his last sermon, denounced the massacre and demanded the punishment of the Papists; and the Church of Scotland sent a petition to James VI and his Regent asking that every Catholic in the kingdom should be put to death without trial unless he agreed to become a Protestant.[9]

As Elizabeth travelled south on her progress, past Bristol to Berkeley Castle and east into Oxfordshire, Fénélon became very conscious of the indignation of the courtiers and of everyone whom he encountered;[10] but Elizabeth avoided meeting him until 8 September, when she received him at Woodstock, withdrawing with him into a 'window' – one of the alcoves in the long gallery in the palace where it was customary to sit and hold conversations. The account of their talk which Fénélon wrote to Charles IX differs in some respects from Burghley's report of it to Walsingham; but it is clear that Elizabeth made only a mild protest about the massacre, for she was determined not to allow it to damage her good relations with France. She asked Fénélon for his explanation of the events in Paris, and he followed the official line of the French government: it was not a question of religion, but Coligny and the Huguenots had plotted an insurrection in Paris, and the King had been forced to act to prevent their treason and to punish them summarily, because they were too numerous and well armed for him to arrest them and bring them to trial by ordinary legal process.

Elizabeth made it plain that she was not convinced by Fénélon's arguments, but her chief anxiety was that the French King's change of policy towards the Huguenots would lead him to change his policy towards her and break the alliance. Fénélon assured her that Charles was determined to continue his policy of friendship with her. She then asked him to continue the conversation with her Council. Here Fénélon met with a very different reception, for all the counsellors expressed their indignation about the massacre in the most outspoken terms.[11]

Charles IX and Catherine de Medici logically added insult to injury, and followed up the massacre by denouncing Coligny and the Huguenots as traitors, and ordering the dismissal of all Protestants from judicial and other public offices. The *Parlement* of Paris put Coligny posthumously on trial for treason, and ordered that his corpse be hanged for twenty-four hours in the Place de Grève in Paris and then left hanging indefinitely by the feet on the public gibbet at Montfaucon outside the city. His banner and coat-of-arms were to be dragged through the streets of Paris at the horse's tail, and broken in pieces, on St Bartholomew's Day every year, when prayers of thanksgiving were to be held throughout Paris. His family château at Châtillon was to be burned down, the trees planted for its adornment were to be cut down, his property was to be forfeited to the King, and his sons were to be infamous and debarred from holding any office or dignity in France. But nothing that was done in France, and no amount of public indignation in England, would prevent Elizabeth from pursuing her policy of friendship with Charles IX, and in January 1573 she sent the Earl of Worcester on a special embassy to consolidate the alliance and continue the marriage negotiations. He was received with great ceremony in Paris.[12]

With Coligny dead, and the King of Navarre and Condé prisoners in Catherine de Medici's hands, the Huguenots were still able to resist, for they held La Rochelle. They appealed to Elizabeth to send them arms and money. She refused, but the people of La Rochelle held out, with the help of French and English Protestant privateers, who were able to break the blockade imposed by Anjou's besieging army. After a four-month siege they were granted peace terms by which the Huguenots obtained religious toleration in La Rochelle, Montauban, Sancerre and Nîmes, though it was no longer to be allowed elsewhere in France. Dale, who replaced Walsingham as ambassador to the French court, wrote to Burghley that La Rochelle could never have held out if it had not been for the help which they had received from England.[13] After peace had been made, the people of La Rochelle praised Elizabeth as the Defender of the Christian Faith, and appealed to the English Protestants for financial help in rebuilding the town, for 'we are all one body, and one member cannot be injured without the rest feeling it'.[14]

In the Netherlands, too, the Protestants were hard pressed, and desperately defending themselves against Alva's armies. They received no help from Elizabeth, but a great deal from the English people and from the French and Scottish Protestants. In one fortnight alone in May 1572, 150 volunteers from Dieppe arrived at Flushing, 200 from the French congregation in London, and 120 from Norwich. In the following week, 450 more came from France, and more from Norwich. Sir Humphrey Gilbert led 1,200 Englishmen and many Frenchmen and 100 Walloons in a successful attack which captured Sluys. The 'Rhinegrave', the Protestant Elector of the Rhine Palatinate, sent cavalry, the well-trained professional German *reiters*. On the other hand, 120 English Catholics sailed from Lowestoft to fight for Alva, safeguarding themselves by agreeing to serve him against anyone except the Queen of England.[15]

By July 1572 William of Orange had an army of 13,500 infantry and 7,500 *reiters*, while the sea-beggars, under the command of the ferocious patriot, William de La Marck, Count of Lumey, continued their very successful guerrilla warfare against the Spanish army of occupation. They usually hanged the Spanish soldiers whom they captured, and killed many Catholic priests and monks. The Spaniards slaughtered the soldiers and the civil population on a large scale in the towns which they captured, and burned all the cottages of the peasants in every district where they encountered resistance.[16]

In the pacified areas, the executions of traitors and burning of heretics continued. One of the victims was a Dutchman who had come to England as a refugee and had lived at Rye for twenty-eight years. When the resistance developed, he returned to the Netherlands, leaving his wife and children at Rye. He went into a church in Antwerp during Mass, seized the Host when the priest elevated it, and threw it to the ground, shouting that it was against the word of God to worship strange gods. He was sentenced to death, and executed in Antwerp. They drove a bodkin through his tongue, then cut off his right hand with a chisel and burned it while he watched; then he was fastened to the stake and burned till his bowels fell out, after which he was dragged out of the fire in the hope that he was still alive, and hanged on a gibbet in a field, where his corpse was left hanging for many months.[17]

The Protestants held only the islands of Zeeland and a narrow strip of territory on the west coast of the province of Holland. They failed to capture Amsterdam, but the Calvinists of Haarlem hastened to join them, and in December 1572 Alva sent his son to recapture the town. After two attempts to take it by assault had failed, the Spaniards decided to starve the four thousand defenders into surrender. But Haarlem held out, keeping in contact with the sea-beggars by couriers who crossed the ice during the foggy winter nights, though all attempts by William of Orange and La Marck to relieve Haarlem were thwarted. For seven months the Protestants in England watched anxiously, and applauded the heroism of the soldiers and citizens of Haarlem as well as the defenders of La Rochelle. Philip Sidney, touring Germany, wrote to his uncle, the Earl of Leicester, from Frankfort on 29 March 1573: 'All men's eyes are as bent to the affairs of France and Flanders that there is no talk here of any other country'.[18]

In the end Haarlem was starved out, and surrendered on 11 July 1573. The Spaniards hanged all the surviving 1,600 soldiers of the garrison except the German mercenaries, who were allowed to go free on payment of a ransom. They also hanged four hundred of the most prominent civilians of Haarlem, and imposed a fine of 250,000 guilders on the inhabitants who were spared. The news was sent to England from Delft, which was held by Sir Humphrey Gilbert's Englishmen; they had suffered serious losses in their unsuccessful attempts to relieve Haarlem. They reported that the Spaniards, in hanging the defenders of Haarlem, had violated the terms of surrender.[19]

The capture of towns and fortresses during the wars of religion in the sixteenth century was often followed by executions of the besieged garrison, and by accusations that this had been done in breach of the surrender terms. This allegation was afterwards made against Elizabeth's commanders in Ireland. It was usually not strictly true, and was the result of misunderstandings which were sometimes intentional. There were accepted practices about the terms of which a besieged garrison might surrender. A surrender with full honours of war allowed the defenders to march out with their flags flying and taking their arms, equipment and horses with them. Less favourable terms would only allow the garrison to leave after they had abandoned their arms, equipment, horses and flags to the besiegers. Even less favourably, they might be promised only their lives, which meant that though their lives would be spared, they would remain as prisoners of their captors until their release could be negotiated for a ransom or under an exchange of prisoners. The worst was when the besiegers insisted, and the defenders agreed, that they should surrender 'at mercy'. This was an unconditional surrender which left the victorious commander free to decide, at his absolute discretion, whether to hang them, to keep them as prisoners, or to set them free. The usual practice was for him to hang a few of them, sometimes as many as the number of soldiers that he had lost in capturing the fortress; to keep as prisoners the wealthy officers who would be worth a good ransom; and to let the others go free.

If the defenders did not surrender, the besieging general would order an assault on the fortress after a bombardment with his cannons had made a breach in the walls through which his soldiers could enter. If the defenders did not surrender before the bombardment began – if they decided 'to abide the cannon' – then no quarter would be given, and they would all be put to the sword after the fortress fell. The defenders had therefore a slight incentive, if they could not obtain better terms, to surrender at mercy, because there was then a reasonable chance that only a few of them would be hanged, whereas if they abided the cannon all of them would be slaughtered. They could not complain of a breach of faith by the enemy if they were all hanged, but those who had surrendered at mercy in the hope that they would be spared nearly always accused the enemy of breaking the surrender terms if they were sentenced to be hanged. The besiegers, of course, hoped that they would be spared the necessity of taking the fortress by storm, with the losses which they would suffer in the process; and individual officers were sometimes tempted to offer, or hint, that the defenders' lives would be spared when in fact they were being required to surrender at mercy.

If the Protestants suffered defeats in Holland and France, they were at least masters of the situation in Scotland, and while Charles IX's armies were engaged in the siege of La Rochelle, Elizabeth at last took the necessary steps to end the resistance of the Queen's lords. In October 1572 Mar died, and Morton took office as Regent with Elizabeth's approval. On 1 January 1573 he demanded the surrender of Edinburgh Castle. Grange and Lethington, who did not trust themselves to Morton's mercy once they no longer had the protection of the castle, offered to recognise the authority of James VI and to give four hostages to Elizabeth to ensure that they did not invite any foreign army to enter Scotland, on condition that Grange was allowed to hold Edinburgh Castle. But Morton insisted on the surrender of the castle, and laid siege to it.[20]

Edinburgh Castle had only once been captured in all its long history, and Morton was sure that he could not take it without siege guns. But he had no cannons available, while Grange had the guns of the castle. When Morton's men dug their trenches around the castle and began the siege, Grange fired eighty-seven rounds into the town, though the King's lords claimed that the only damage that they did was to kill one dog who was about to enter Morton's house. Morton then asked Elizabeth to send him English soldiers with siege guns.[21]

Elizabeth sent cannon from the iron-foundries of the Sussex Weald, and Sir William Drury with soldiers from Berwick. Before leaving Berwick, Drury wrote to Burghley about the latest news from Haarlem and La Rochelle.[22] For him and many others, Haarlem, La Rochelle and Edinburgh Castle were all part of the same struggle.

By 25 April the English had reached Edinburgh and taken up their positions around the castle with Morton's troops. It took Drury and Morton a month to take the castle, for the strong walls stood up well to the bombardment. Then the cannon balls knocked down a part of one of the towers which fell into the castle well, nearly blocking it up, and the little trickle of water which could still be drawn from the well was contaminated by the rubble. This made it impossible for the defenders to hold out any longer, and on 27 May Grange offered to surrender if they were granted their lives. Morton offered to spare the lives of all the defenders except for Grange, Lethington, Lord Home, and eight others, whose fate would depend on the decision of the Queen of England. Grange accepted these terms, and the castle surrendered next morning.[23]

Elizabeth was not pleased that Morton had referred to her the decision as to what to do with the leading defenders of the castle. She replied that she considered that it would be improper for a foreign sovereign to decide the fate of the Scottish rebels, and that Morton as Regent must decide.[24] Lethington had meanwhile died while he was being held as a prisoner. It was thought that he had committed suicide by taking poison, though in fact he had fallen ill before the castle surrendered.

The prisoners were rich enough to be able to offer bribes to Morton and his friends in return for their lives; but the ministers of the Church of Scotland demanded their deaths. Knox, who had died six months earlier, had spent the last months of his life denouncing his old comrade Grange as a traitor to the Protestant cause; and the ministers, in their sermons, preached on the divine commandment to punish idolaters and on the sin of Saul in sparing the city of Amalek. Grange was hanged at the Market Cross of Edinburgh on 3 August, with his brother and two of his officers.[25] The other prisoners were set free after a short imprisonment. The Spaniards had hanged many more than four at Haarlem three weeks earlier.

PURITANS AND ANABAPTISTS

P HILIP II recalled Alva to Spain and appointed the Comendador Mayor
Don Luis de Requesens to succeed him in the Netherlands. In the
spring of 1574 Requesens's troops besieged Leyden, which prepared
for a defence as heroic as Haarlem's, and the Spaniards gained a decisive
victory over Louis of Nassau, in which Louis and another of William's
brothers were killed. At this most critical moment for the Protestant cause in
the Netherlands, William became involved in a dispute with Elizabeth about
the activities of the sea-beggars. They raised money to finance their operations from native and foreign merchants who paid for licences permitting
them to trade with the Spanish-occupied provinces of the Netherlands. If
merchants tried to trade there without the licence, their ships were seized and
pillaged by the sea-beggars.

A London merchant whose ships and goods were seized unless he paid
money for a licence from the sea-beggars had to be a very zealous Protestant
to agree willingly to pay this contribution to the cause, and not to see it as a
scandalous case of extortion by pirates. Some of the merchants complained to
Elizabeth, who asked William to order the sea-beggars not to interfere with
her subjects' trade. As her protests had no effect, she ordered the seizure of
some ships in English ports owned by merchants of Dordrecht, which was
held by William's forces. On 2 January 1574 William wrote and asked her to
release the ships and not to punish innocent Dordrecht merchants for acts of
piracy committed by men who used his name without his authority. But at the
moment when all the Protestants of Europe were applauding the heroic
defenders of Alkmaar and Leyden, and Elizabeth's Protestant subjects were
fighting valiantly for William and the Protestant cause in Holland, their
Queen stabbed them in the back by seizing the ships of the Protestant
merchants of the liberated territory.[1]

On 22 April 1574 William wrote to Elizabeth explaining how harmful it
would be to the common cause of religion which she and he upheld if he were
to permit free trade with the Spanish-occupied Netherlands; and he asked

her to forgive him if he refused to comply with her request. Elizabeth sent Rogers to William to tell him that he was making a good cause odious in the eyes of the world by the methods which he was using to advance it, and to warn him that if he did not stop the seizures she would 'revenge' the injuries done to her subjects.[2]

In view of Elizabeth's unfriendly attitude and her failure to give any help to the Protestants of the Netherlands, William decided to turn to France for support and to invite Alençon to come to their aid and become ruler of the Netherlands instead of Philip. When Elizabeth heard about this, she became alarmed at the prospect of the Netherlands falling under the control of France. She instructed Rogers to warn William that if he invited Alençon to take over the Netherlands, she would ally herself with Philip to prevent this, and would urge the Emperor and the German Princes to join with England and Spain against France and William.[3]

The seizures by the Flushing privateers continued, and Elizabeth became more indignant. In the summer of 1576 she seized four of William's ships which had put in to Falmouth, and sent Sir William Winter to tell William that the sea-beggars had seized thirty English ships in a month, and were holding English goods worth £200,000 at Flushing. She said that she would release his four ships when this £200,000 was returned to the English merchants. William insisted that without the privateering the Protestant cause would be defeated in the Netherlands, and that Philip would then turn his weapons against England. Elizabeth was not impressed. She told Winter to inform William that she was strong enough to defend herself without his aid. 'By the way, you may let fall that in the judgement of the world the aptest mean for Her Majesty to withstand or prevent the peril that he conceives might grow to her by his overthrow were to join the King of Spain against him'. If these arguments did not move William, Winter was to contact the English officers who were fighting for William and tell them either to join the Spaniards or to seize one of William's towns and hold it for Elizabeth against him.[4]

But Walsingham had been exerting all his efforts to appease Elizabeth and to help William. He persuaded Elizabeth to release William's ships at Falmouth, and he urged William to restrain the activities of the men of Flushing, which were being used by pro-Spanish elements in England to anger the Queen against the Dutch Protestants. William told Elizabeth how distressed he was to have offended her, and the dispute was settled after William had returned a ship which had been seized in particularly flagrant circumstances; but the men of Flushing retained nearly all the English goods which they had taken.[5]

Elizabeth quarrelled with Morton and the Scottish Protestants as well as with William of Orange and the Dutch. Morton had completely established his authority in Scotland after the fall of Edinburgh Castle. He was a late and insincere adherent to the Protestant cause, but he was the strongest and most ruthless leader in Scotland, and was now firmly linked to Protestantism and the English alliance. He proposed that a new treaty of alliance should be made between England and Scotland for the defence of the Protestant religion, which the German Lutheran Princes and the Protestant Kings of Denmark and Sweden should be invited to join. Walsingham strongly favoured this proposal, but Elizabeth would not agree.[6]

She had still not made up her mind about Morton's proposal when an unfortunate incident endangered Anglo-Scottish friendship and the Protestant cause. It had for many years been the practice for the English and Scottish Border officials to meet regularly four times a year to discuss the problems created by the thieves on both sides of the Border and their raids into the other country. These meetings, which took place alternately on the English and Scottish side of the frontier, were normally friendly, though they were not very effective in suppressing the robberies of the Scots of Liddisdale and the English of Tynedale.

On 7 July 1575 the quarterly meeting took place at Reedswire in Scotland between Sir John Forster, the English Warden of the Middle Marches, and Sir James Carmichael, the Scottish Keeper of Liddisdale, who was a kinsman of Morton's. There is a conflict of evidence as to what happened at the meeting. According to the English, a band of horsemen from Jedburgh, who had escorted Carmichael to the meeting, suddenly attacked the English, shouting 'A Jedworth, a Jedworth!' The Scots said that the men of Tynedale escorting Forster suddenly attacked them, shouting 'A Tynedale, a Tynedale!' The Scots got the better of it, and chased the Tynedale men over the Border into England, where they encountered an English troop under Forster's brother-in-law, Sir Giles Heron. In the ensuing clash, Heron and five other Englishmen were killed and others wounded before the Scots returned to Scotland taking some English prisoners with them. Meanwhile at Reedswire Carmichael had seized Forster and his escort and taken them as prisoners to Morton at Dalkeith.[7]

Morton released Forster and his officers next day, and sent them back to England. He wrote to Elizabeth expressing his regret at the incident, and suggested that she should send an envoy to meet him near Eyemouth, four miles north of the Border, to discuss how such occurrences could be avoided in future. Elizabeth reacted with a furious letter to Killigrew, her agent at Berwick. She wrote that Morton's action in detaining her Warden had so greatly wounded her honour and was so foul a fact that it was inexcusable. If she were to prosecute her just revenge, he would learn what it was for one of his base calling to offend one of her quality. But as she did not wish the whole realm of Scotland to smart for the folly of one man, she agreed to send the Earl of Huntingdon, the President of the Council of the North, to meet Morton, though she thought it was very insolent of Morton to suggest that the meeting should take place four miles inside Scotland. Huntingdon would meet him at the Bound Rock on the frontier just north of Berwick.[8]

Walsingham had not only persuaded Elizabeth to refrain from immediately taking reprisals against the Scots, but had arranged for her to send the stalwart Protestant, Huntingdon, as her representative in the negotiations with Morton. Huntingdon and Morton met on the Border in August, and agreed that it was essential that the incident should be settled peaceably. Huntingdon tried to appease Elizabeth's anger against the Scots, and at the same time he persuaded Morton to offer to send Carmichael as a prisoner to Elizabeth.[9] But Elizabeth was far from appeased. She reprimanded Huntingdon and Killigrew for not being sufficiently zealous against the Scots, and told Huntingdon to remind Morton 'that another King in my seat would have revenged with deeds and left with him his words'.[10]

Morton sent Carmichael as a prisoner to Huntingdon; but Huntingdon kept him at York and did not send him up to London. After he had been held there for six weeks he was sent back to Scotland, and Morton was informed that Elizabeth regarded the incident as closed. The veteran Scottish Protestant, Captain Cockburn, wrote to Burghley from Edinburgh on 4 November that all their enemies who looked for war between England and Scotland had been disappointed.[11]

Elizabeth was also frustrated in her policies towards the Protestant extremists in her own kingdom. After the vestments controversy of 1566 had subsided, a group of Puritans in London and Northamptonshire and elsewhere began a campaign for the abolition of bishops and the foundation of a Presbyterian Church of England. They advocated their doctrines in sermons and in what they called 'prophecyings'. These were discussion groups at which the participants gave their own interpretations of a given text of Scripture, and compared their different views. They were often attended not only by the clergy but also by local gentlemen and other laymen who participated in the discussions.

Elizabeth was very hostile to the Puritans and the prophecyings. Archbishop Parker did his best to suppress them; but several bishops, Privy Councillors and influential courtiers were sympathetic, and encouraged the prophecyings. These included Grindal, who had been appointed Archbishop of York in 1569, Leicester, Huntingdon, Bedford, Knollys, Walsingham, Wilson, Beale and Davison. In the Privy Council, only the Earl of Sussex and Sir Christopher Hatton were hostile, while Burghley took a more neutral position.[12] 'The comfort that these Puritans have, and their countenance, is marvellous', wrote Parker to Burghley in March 1573, '. . . and but that we have our whole trust in God, in Her Majesty, and in two or three of her Council, I see it will be no dwelling for us in England'.[13]

On Easter Day 1575 twenty-seven Dutch Anabaptists – twelve men, fourteen women, and one boy – were discovered by a constable of the watch at a prayer meeting in a house near Aldgate in London. Two of the men succeeded in escaping, but the other twenty-five were arrested and examined by Sandys, the Bishop of London. He discovered that they denied that Christ was man as well as God, denied that a Christian could be a 'magistrate' – that is to say, a government official – and denounced infant baptism and the taking of oaths. He informed Elizabeth, who appointed Sandys and five other commissioners to try the Anabaptists on a charge of heresy. One of the commissioners was Mr Justice Monson of the Court of Common Pleas, who was sympathetic to the Puritans.

Five of the Anabaptists recanted, and after publicly confessing their error at Paul's Cross were ordered to join the Dutch Protestant Church in London. The others were tried in St Paul's Cathedral on 15 May and condemned as heretics. This meant that they could be burned,* though no one had been burned for heresy since Elizabeth came to the throne.

There was a surprising amount of opposition in many quarters to the idea of burning them, for since Mary's reign and the publication of Foxe's *Book of Martyrs* the burning of heretics had become so closely associated with Papist tyranny. One of the condemned women recanted. The other women and the boy were banished to Holland after the boy had been whipped at the cart tail through London. This left five men who were still liable to be burned. The authorities decided to spare three of them and burn the other two. They were Henry Terwoort, a goldsmith aged thirty-five, and a poor man aged over fifty, John Pieters, whose first wife had been burned as a heretic in Ghent, as had the first husband of his present wife.[14]

Elizabeth received several petitions for mercy, asking her not to burn the two men. One was from the Dutch Protestant Church in London, and another from Sir Thomas Bodley, who had been Elizabeth's agent in the Netherlands. A powerful plea came from John Foxe. He wrote to Elizabeth that though he hated the Anabaptists' doctrine, he believed that they should be punished by banishment, imprisonment or flogging, but not by burning, which 'belongs more to the example of Rome than to the spirit of the Gospel'. He explained that one of his weaknesses was that he could not bear the idea of killing any human being, or even animals, for he was distressed whenever he passed a butcher's slaughteryard.[15]

Elizabeth informed Foxe that she had referred the decision as to whether to burn or spare the men to the commissioners who had tried the case. Foxe interceded with them in vain, and was equally unsuccessful in his attempts to persuade the Anabaptists to recant. On 15 July Elizabeth signed the warrant for their execution, and they were burned at Smithfield on 22 July, dying 'in great horror, with roaring and crying'.[16] We do not know what Elizabeth herself felt about the burning of Terwoort and Pieters, and whether there is any truth in the story told by a Dutch Protestant author of the seventeenth century that she became very angry with her maids of honour when they presented a petition for mercy to her.

* The Act of Parliament of 1401, which authorised the burning of heretics, had been repealed in 1547, re-enacted in 1555, and again repealed in 1559. But the Judges had ruled in Joan Bocher's case in 1550 that the King had power to order heretics to be burned under the common law, independently of statute.

The Puritans, with their influential sympathisers in the Church and at court, were a much greater danger than the Anabaptists, and Elizabeth became increasingly irked at her inability to induce her officers to root them out. In May 1575 Parker died. Elizabeth reluctantly agreed to appoint Grindal to succeed him as Archbishop of Canterbury, although she feared that he would be too tolerant towards the Puritans.[17]

Her worst fears were soon realised. When she ordered Grindal to suppress the prophecyings, he refused to obey, and in December 1576 wrote his famous letter to her. 'I am forced, with all humility and yet plainly, to profess that I cannot with safe conscience and without the offence of the Majesty of God, give my assent to the suppressing of the said exercises ... Bear with me, I beseech you, Madam, if I choose rather to offend your earthly Majesty than to offend the heavenly Majesty of God'. He reminded her of St Ambrose's resistance, in the fourth century, to the Emperor Theodosius's attempt to coerce him in his exercise of his spiritual authority as Bishop of Milan, and urged her: 'Remember, Madam, that you are a mortal creature'.[18]

The Puritan sympathisers at court were annoyed that Grindal had been so tactless as to confront Elizabeth with his conscientious objections, instead of carrying on the tactic of compliance in theory and obstruction in practice which they had employed so successfully to check, if not completely to thwart, her anti-Puritan policy. Even so, they succeeded in saving Grindal from the worst consequences of his boldness. Elizabeth took no action against him for six months. Then she placed him in effect under house arrest in Lambeth Palace, and suspended him from exercising his archiepiscopal duties; but she did not deprive him of his office as she wished to do, for she was advised that there would be legal difficulties about this.[19]

Elizabeth's counsellors did not like her attempts to deprive Grindal, and were not afraid to write this in their letters to each other. Walsingham wrote to Burghley that he regretted that 'we proceed still in making war against God'. Burghley agreed that 'these proceedings cannot but irritate our merciful God'.[20] But Elizabeth wrote directly to the bishops and ordered them to suppress the prophecying, which caused the people, 'especially the vulgar sort' who should be engaged in honest labour, to attend disputations 'upon points of divinity far and unmeet of unlearned people'.[21]

Grindal was eventually permitted to carry out some of his functions, and had still not been deprived when he died in July 1583. Elizabeth appointed Whitgift to succeed him. She had found an Archbishop of Canterbury who shared her hatred of the Puritans.

As usual there was trouble when Parliament, after having been prorogued for nearly four years, reassembled in February 1576. On the first day of the new session, Peter Wentworth, the MP for Barnstaple, made a speech in which he criticised Elizabeth for refusing to give her assent to the bills which had been passed against Mary Queen of Scots when Parliament had last met in 1572. 'Certain it is, Mr Speaker, that none is without fault; no, not our noble Queen. Since, then, Her Majesty hath committed great faults – yea, dangerous faults to herself and the State – love, even perfect love, void of dissimulation, will not suffer me to hide them to Her Majesty's peril, but to utter them to Her Majesty's safety'.[22]

The House of Commons condemned his speech, and ordered that he be sent to the Tower. After he had been imprisoned for a month, Elizabeth sent a message to the House, thanking them for the action which they had taken about Wentworth, but stating that she was releasing him from the Tower, as she realised that he had spoken as he did because of his zeal for her interests. The motion to commit him to the Tower had been moved in the House of Commons by Knollys.[23] He and his faction realised that there must be no public criticism of Elizabeth by Puritans which might drive her into the arms of the Catholics, just as the opposition of the Catholic bishops and the Papal bull had forced her to rely on the support of the Protestants. It was far wiser to make a public display of indignation with Wentworth, and then work behind the scenes at court to persuade Elizabeth to pardon him. The Puritan sympathisers at court were experienced politicians, and they knew how to handle Elizabeth.

THE RIFT WITH SPAIN

E LIZABETH'S attitude to the struggle of the people of the Netherlands
against Philip II was a mass of contradictions. She sympathised with
them in so far as they were Protestants, but hated them as rebels
against their Prince. Many of her subjects strongly supported their fight for
the Protestant cause, and some of them had gone to take part in it; but her
merchants resented the depredations of the sea-beggars and being forced to
pay them for licences to trade with the Spanish-occupied territories. She was
becoming increasingly aware of the danger which threatened her from Spain,
and was being continually warned by her Protestant counsellors that if Philip
succeeded in suppressing the revolt in the Netherlands he would use the
ports of Flanders and Zeeland as bases from which to invade England; but the
whole tradition of English foreign policy and the old alliance with Burgundy
made her fear the prospect that the French would conquer the Netherlands
under the pretence of liberating the country from Spain.

On one point she was quite clear: she strongly resented the fact that
Philip's government in the Netherlands was giving shelter and financial aid
to her Catholic rebels. The Earl of Westmorland and the Countess of
Northumberland were there, and so were a number of English Catholics who
had gone to Douai and other towns in the Netherlands as refugees, and were
receiving pensions from Philip. In December 1574 she sent Sir Thomas
Wilson to Brussels to protest to Requesens that the granting of asylum to her
rebels was a breach of the Treaty of 1495 between England and Burgundy.
The English refugees knew all about Wilson, and he heard that they were
saying in Lady Northumberland's house in Brussels that it was a pity that
Pope Paul IV did not burn him when he was a prisoner of the Inquisition in
Rome.[1]

Wilson had several unfriendly meetings with Requesens, who told him that
he could not trust the English government because they were of the same
religion as his master's rebels. When Wilson asked him if he would trust
Elizabeth, Requesens said that he would trust her because he hoped that she

would one day become a Catholic when she realised how she was being misled by the heretics in her Council. 'Here began a hot dispute betwixt us', wrote Wilson to Burghley, 'which religion was better, he condemning mine and I condemning his; and I told him that this advantage I had of him, that I had read the writers of his religion, and he had read none of mine'. But when Wilson offered to show him a Latin translation of the communion service of the Church of England, he said that he would not read it. 'I told him it was strange for him to condemn the religion of England before he did know it. Nay, quoth he, it is enough that the Church doth condemn England . . . I have sent to Rome for absolution from His Holiness for talking with such as you are'.[2]

On Philip's instructions, Requesens offered an amnesty to all the rebels in the Netherlands, including William of Orange, and promised to grant their chief demand and withdraw all Spanish troops and advisers and to govern the Netherlands solely through native counsellors. But he absolutely refused to grant religious toleration, for Philip insisted that all his subjects must accept the Catholic faith. The only concession that he was prepared to make in this respect was to allow the Protestants to emigrate.[3]

William of Orange was worried about this new conciliatory policy of the Spaniards, for he feared that it would win over the Catholics in the south who had only joined the struggle against Spain because they objected to the presence of the Spanish troops and counsellors. He became even more anxious when Requesens died of a fever, and was succeeded by Philip's illegitimate half-brother, Don John of Austria. Don John, the son of Charles V by his mistress Barabara Blomberg, the Regensburg merchant's daughter, was the hero of the Spanish naval victory over the Turks at Lepanto. He was also a very charming man; a Dutch Protestant wrote that he surpassed Circe as a seducer, and won over everyone who met him. He displayed his charm on Wilson, and ordered all Elizabeth's rebels to leave the Netherlands; but they remained secretly at Cambrai, where they continued to receive pensions from Philip. Don John wrote a very friendly letter to William of Orange, offering to meet him anywhere and to withdraw all Spanish troops and civil servants from the Netherlands; but on Philip's orders he insisted that there would be no toleration for any religion except the Catholic faith, and issued a proclamation ordering magistrates to inflict the severest punishment on heretics and to suppress all heretical books.[4]

In January 1576 Elizabeth, after her customary hesitation, categorically refused the request of the Protestants of the Netherlands that she should send aid to the rebels, on the grounds that this would probably involve her in war with Spain and the loss of all the property of her merchants in Spain and the Netherlands. She would therefore try to help them in another way, by mediating with Philip on their behalf.[5]

She duly sent Edward Horsey to Don John of Austria and Sir John Smith to Philip II. They told Don John and Philip that she had warned the States-

General of the Netherlands, who had joined William of Orange and the struggle against Spain, that if they repudiated their natural allegiance to Philip and rebelled against their Prince, she would join with Philip to suppress them. But she had discovered that they had no such intention, and merely wished to free their country from Spanish oppression and to see it once again governed for King Philip by native counsellors, as it had been in the time of Charles V. She advised Philip that it would be in his interests to withdraw the Spaniards and grant religious toleration in the Netherlands. She justified her intervention in his internal affairs as the well-meant advice of a loving sister, and also because she feared that if he did not grant these terms to his subjects, they would repudiate their allegiance to him and invite the French to come to their aid. This would be a dangerous threat to English interests, and she was therefore urging Philip to take the necessary steps to avert it.[6]

In her message to Philip she added a personal note. She said that she would never forget the great kindness which he had shown her during her sister's reign, and that this gave her an additional reason for advising him to adopt a course which would be in his best interests as well as hers, and could lead to an improvement in Anglo-Spanish relations.[7]

Both Philip and Don John courteously thanked Elizabeth for her well-meant attempt at mediation, but assured her that it was quite unnecessary, as they were perfectly capable of dealing with the revolt in the Netherlands without her assistance. They said that they had already offered to withdraw all Spaniards from the Netherlands, but that under no circumstances would Philip ever agree to grant religious toleration there. They pointed out that Elizabeth herself did not grant toleration to the English Catholics. Elizabeth and her envoys said that Catholics were not persecuted in England, as Protestants were in the Netherlands, unless they were rebels or had committed other acts of high treason or sedition; and in any case, the situation was different in England.[8]

Elizabeth's attitude about religious toleration was not as illogical as it may appear to people in the twentieth century. She fully recognised that Philip, like herself and all other sovereigns, had the right to decide whether to enforce religious uniformity on his subjects or to grant them toleration. She was merely suggesting to him that although it was feasible to enforce uniformity in England and in Spain, it was politically impracticable to try to do so in the Netherlands, owing to the strength of the Protestant movement there. Philip, of course, knowing that she was herself a Protestant, did not believe that she was giving him disinterested sisterly advice when she recommended that he should grant toleration to the Protestants in the Netherlands.

The situation in France was a little different, for there the Huguenot rebels were at least led by Princes of the Blood like the King of Navarre and the Prince of Condé, and the most active popular element, the artisans and lower classes of Paris, were on the Catholic side. After her disastrous intervention in 1562, Elizabeth was determined not to repeat the error; but she repeatedly suggested to Charles IX and Catherine de Medici that they should grant religious toleration to the Huguenots, who asked for nothing more, and were not rebels but loyal subjects forced to defend themselves against the persecution and the murderous attacks of the agents of those ambitious and overbearing subjects, the Guises.

In March 1574 Henry of Navarre and Alençon were arrested, accused of complicity in a plot to murder Charles IX, and held prisoners in the Louvre. Alençon managed to get into contact with the English ambassador, and asked to be supplied with money with which he could bribe his guards to allow him to escape. Burghley advised Elizabeth to send him the money, but before she had made up her mind, Alençon had succeeded in escaping without her help. He made an alliance with the Huguenots and began another civil war against his brother King Henry III, who, after a short spell as King of Poland, had become King of France when Charles IX died in May 1574. The young Prince of Condé also escaped from the Louvre, and placed himself at the head of the Huguenot forces in alliance with Alençon. He went to Germany to raise an army of *reiters*, and asked Elizabeth for money to hire them. Burghley with difficulty persuaded Elizabeth to lend Condé £3,000.[9]

The forces of Condé and Alençon were stronger than the King's, and were joined by Henry of Navarre, who also succeeded in escaping from Paris, and immediately reconverted to Protestantism. In May 1576 Henry III agreed to a peace treaty by which he granted religious toleration to the Huguenots everywhere in France and posthumously rehabilitated Coligny and the victims of the Massacre of St Bartholomew, who were now declared to have been not guilty of treason.[10] He also conferred his old title of Duke of Anjou on Alençon, who was heir to the throne of France until Henry III had children. Henry of Navarre was given the province of Guienne, and established his capital at Nérac.

The Catholics again refused to agree to religious toleration, and formed a new organisation, the Holy League, under the leadership of the Duke of Guise, to fight for the Catholic faith against the heretics. There were attacks on the Protestants in Paris and elsewhere in France, and in February 1577 Henry of Navarre began the sixth civil war.

The English ambassador in Paris, Sir Amyas Paulet, urged Elizabeth to help the Huguenots. He wrote to Burghley on 4 March that there would never be a better opportunity to limit French power.[11] But Elizabeth would not help the Huguenots, and pursued her policy of mediating with Henry III on their behalf, urging them to submit to him, and advising him to grant them religious toleration. She refused Henry of Navarre's request for money to hire German *reiters*, and pressed Condé to repay the £3,000 which she had lent him in the last war. As a result, Henry of Navarre, having no funds to carry on the war, was forced to agree to a peace which was less advantageous to the Huguenots than the peace treaty of the previous year. They were no longer to have religious toleration in Paris or in any of the provincial capitals, and on the lands of the higher nobility could enjoy it only with the consent of the lord. This meant that they could worship only in the smaller towns and in the territories of the Protestant nobles, who were entitled to, and did, suppress the Mass on their lands.[12]

Elizabeth's Protestant counsellors confided to each other how disappointed they were with her policy. On 10 August 1577 Leicester wrote to Walsingham that he wished 'that she was both willing (as she is able) to defend not only so good a cause, being the general cause now of Christendom, but to provide like a wise Princess for her own safety and surety'; for if the Protestants were defeated in France and the Netherlands, 'it is not possible for Her Majesty long to stand without God's miraculous assistance, for then hath she all the mighty Princes of the world against her, and not one friend left to trust to as able to relieve her. God Almighty direct her heart the best way for her preservation every way'.[13] Five days later, he wrote at midnight to Walsingham that he had spent the evening with Elizabeth trying to convince her of the dangers involved in 'this slack dealing with her friends'.[14]

William of Orange decided that before committing his cause irrevocably to the alliance with Anjou, he would make a last attempt to obtain financial aid from Elizabeth, and asked her to lend the States-General £100,000. Elizabeth sent Davison to explain to William that she could not do this, because if she gave them this help, Philip II would seize the goods of English merchants in Spain, which were worth twice as much. Leicester was distressed, and wrote to Davison that he personally regretted Elizabeth's decision.[15]

Leicester and Walsingham at last won over Elizabeth. On 14 December 1577 she wrote to the States-General that as Don John of Austria had rejected her offer of mediation, and as she knew that they were not rebels against the King of Spain but were merely fighting to expel the Spanish troops and counsellors and for religious toleration, she was willing to grant them the aid for which they asked.[16] But three months later, she had not made the arrangements for sending the money, and in March 1578 Davison was shocked to receive instructions to tell the States-General that she had changed her mind and would not be sending them the money. He wrote to Leicester that he much regretted that Elizabeth had not sent the money to save the Netherlands and 'the whole commonwealth of Christendom', which is 'like to participate in the fire already kindled here. And therefore . . . I am in this public respect for this alteration'.[17]

Davison was so disgusted that he expressed his feelings not only to Leicester and Walsingham but also to the States. Reports about this reached Elizabeth's court, and Walsingham had to write to remind him that it was his duty in Antwerp to defend Elizabeth's policy and not to criticise it.[18]

In view of Elizabeth's decision, the States on 19 April 1578 sent envoys to invite Anjou to invade the Netherlands, make war on Don John, and become their ruler. Elizabeth became seriously alarmed at the States' negotiations with Anjou. Her first reaction had been to threaten William of Orange that she would join with Philip II to make war against him and the French; then, when the States persisted in their negotiations with Anjou, she warned William that it was risky to trust the French. William assured her that he had no love at all for the French, and was only turning to them as a last resort, like a dying man was forced to enlist the help of any available physician. But Elizabeth now began to listen to those counsellors who advised her that the only way to stop the States from turning to the French for help was to help them herself. She sent Walsingham and Lord Cobham to join Davison in the Netherlands on a mission to persuade Don John to accept her mediation and the States to break off their negotiations with Anjou.[19]

It was time for Elizabeth to go on her summer progress. She continued to go on progresses nearly every year. In 1573 she went through Kent, by Knole, Eridge and Benenden to Rye, and by Sissinghurst to Dover Castle and Sandwich before staying with Archbishop Parker for a fortnight at Canterbury, and returning to Greenwich by Faversham, Sittingbourne, Rochester and Dartford. In 1574 she went to Bristol and Salisbury, and in 1575 to Kenilworth, Lichfield, Stafford and Worcester and to Sudeley Castle in Gloucestershire. In 1576 and 1577 she went only into Surrey, Hertfordshire and Berkshire.[20]

At the end of July 1578 she set off for Suffolk and Norfolk,[21] accompanied by Leicester, Wilson and even by Burghley, who at the age of fifty-eight and suffering from gout ordinarily avoided long journeys. They urged her continually, on the progress, to help the States. She could not decide what to do, and changed her mind from one day to another. Having promised financial help to the States in December 1577 and changed her mind in March 1578, she decided in May to order Davison to raise the money on the Bourse in Antwerp and pay it over to the States; but on 18 July she wrote to Davison, telling him to hold on to the money and not to pay any of it to the States till he received further orders from her.[22]

On 29 July Burghley wrote to Walsingham from Audley End that he had tried to persuade Elizabeth to allow Davison to pay over the money to the States, 'but no argument can yet prevail ... It is strange to see God's goodness, so abundantly offered for Her Majesty's safety, so daintily hearkened unto'.[23] Wilson wrote to Walsingham on the same day that they would only have themselves to blame if Anjou took advantage of the situation, 'because of our careless dealing hitherto'.[24]

Sussex, too, was all in favour of action. On 6 August, when the progress had reached Bury St Edmunds, he wrote to Walsingham: 'You have done all you could ... It rests with God to dispose her heart as shall please Him ... To delay, so that either Spanish or French shall have their will of the Low

Countries is the dangerest matter for the Queen and England, in my opinion, that may be'.[25] But next day Leicester wrote to Walsingham that Elizabeth had quite changed her mind about helping the States since they were at Oatlands and Windsor. 'I am sorry to see both our travails fall out to no better effect, good Mr Secretary . . . How loath she is to come to any manner of dealing that way, specially to be at any charges, it is very strange'.[26]

The court was still at Bury on 9 August when Burghley, Leicester and Knollys discussed the situation in the Netherlands with Elizabeth and persuaded her to agree that if Walsingham and Cobham confirmed that it was really necessary, she would send Leicester to the Netherlands with an expeditionary force to help the States. But Burghley thought that it was still possible that she would change her mind again. 'Her Majesty is greatly perplexed to think that the Low Countries may become French, and whilst she is in fear hereof, she seemeth ready to hazard any expense . . . Nevertheless though this be for the present earnestly meant, I can assure nothing, but this only, that I am here uncertain of much'.[27]

It was too late. On 18 August the States signed their treaty with Anjou. Walsingham wrote sadly to Burghley that he did not know who had persuaded Elizabeth to treat her friends in the Netherlands so badly, but he was sure that the day would come when she would curse those who gave her this advice. When he returned from the Netherlands to Richmond in October, he was able to persuade her, 'after long conference and persuasion used with Her Majesty', to allow Davison to give £8,000 of the money in his hands to the States.[28]

After the settlement of the dispute with Philip and Alva over the property-seizures, Elizabeth tried to improve her relations with Spain. She sent Sir Henry Cobham to Madrid in the autumn of 1575, and Sir John Smith fifteen months later, to tell Philip of her gratitude and friendly feelings towards him. Alva, who had returned to Madrid, told Cobham that Philip too wished to improve Anglo-Spanish relations, and that this would be facilitated if Elizabeth sent an ambassador to Spain who was a Catholic. Elizabeth did not respond to this suggestion, and did not appoint any resident ambassador in Madrid because of Philip's refusal to allow him to hold a Protestant service in his embassy.[29] After Espés's expulsion from England, he was replaced by Antonio de Guaras, a Spanish merchant who had for some time been an influential figure in the mercantile community in London. Philip appointed Guaras to represent his interests in England, though Guaras was not officially accredited as an ambassador. He established good relations with Burghley and had several friendly conversations with Elizabeth.

But the activities of the Spanish Inquisition were causing more friction between Elizabeth and Philip. The Inquisition claimed jurisdiction over all foreign ships in Spanish waters, and from time to time sent agents to board English merchant ships in the ports of Cadiz, Ferrol and Corunna. If they found copies of the English Book of Common Prayer in the ships, they arrested the captain and crew for possessing heretical literature. There were also cases where the agents of the Inquisition, finding nothing incriminating in the ships, arrested the crew as heretics because they admitted that they had attended Protestant Church services in the ships on the high seas or in the churches in England. Occasionally an Englishman was burned for heresy in Spain; but more often the Inquisition adopted a more merciful attitude, and took into consideration, as a mitigating factor, that the English heretics had been brought up in a heretical country and corrupted by their heretical parents and teachers. They were therefore sentenced, not to be burned, but to serve for some years as galley-slaves in the Spanish navy. By the law of Spain, all the goods of a condemned heretic were forfeited to the Inquisition, and when an English seaman was condemned as a heretic, the Inquisition sometimes seized all the goods on his ships and the ship herself.[30]

In March 1575 Guaras met Elizabeth when she was walking, surrounded by all her courtiers, quite a long way from the palace at Richmond. She asked him to walk with her, and they walked as the courtiers fell back and followed a little way behind. The conversation began with trivialities. She said that she wished she could speak to Guaras in Spanish, but though she could read it and understand it without difficulty, she did not feel competent to speak in Spanish. Guaras said that this surprised him, as everyone knew that her Spanish was as perfect as her French, Italian and Latin. After this, she began to deal with more controversial subjects, and while discussing the persecution of Englishmen in Spain by the Inquisition, she became rather excited. 'I promise you', she said, 'that my father would not have put up with it, and if the matter is not put right I shall be obliged to order the arrest of some of the King of Spain's subjects and treat them in the same way'. She afterwards became very friendly again, and said: 'You understand very well, old wine, old bread and old friends should be valued, and if only for the sake of showing these Frenchmen, who are weighing up whether our friendship is firm or not'.[31]

Philip continued to insist that he had no power to interfere with the Inquisition's jurisdiction; but in October 1576 Alva and the Inquisitor-General agreed on new guidelines for dealing with foreign heretics who came on a visit to Spain. The Inquisition would not inquire into any heresies commited by the foreigners before they came to Spain, but would punish them as heretics if, while they were in Spain, they expressed any opinion which was 'contrary to the Catholic faith, as it is believed, confessed and taught by the Church of Rome', or if they brought any heretical book into Spain. Non-resident foreigners in Spain need not go to church, but if they did, they must honour the Sacrament. If they encountered a procession in the street, they could try to avoid it by entering a house or a side-street, but if they were there when the procession passed by, they must kneel to the Host. If any of them were convicted of heresy, only his personal goods would be confiscated, and not the goods of the merchants or shipowners which he had in his possession. These concessions only applied to non-resident foreigners; all aliens who lived in Spain must conform to the law to the same extent as Spanish subjects.[32] This was no hardship for the Duchess of Feria, for Queen Mary's old counsellor Sir Francis Englefield and the other English refugees, or for the adventurer Sir Thomas Stucley, who was living in Madrid in very luxurious style as he waited to command a Spanish expedition to invade Ireland.

The new directive was undoubtedly an improvement, but it did not end the trouble. English seamen who went ashore in the Spanish ports were often taunted with being heretics by Spaniards in inns and elsewhere, and were provoked into defending the doctrines of the Church of England, which was heresy. They then found themselves in the prisons of the Inquisition. Whenever Sir John Smith complained, Philip and his counsellors referred him to the Inquisition, and on 19 May 1577 Smith called on the Inquisitor-General, the Archbishop of Toledo, to ask him to release the English subjects. The conversation was not friendly, and ended with the Archbishop telling the ambassador that were it not for certain special considerations, he would have him arrested and punished as an example to all men of his nation. He ordered Smith to leave his house. Smith said that he would complain to King Philip about the way that the Archbishop had spoken to the Queen's ambassador. The Archbishop said that he could complain to anyone he liked provided that he left his house.[33]

On 20 October 1577 Elizabeth's officers entered Guaras's house at midnight, searched it, and after holding him for some days as a prisoner in the house, removed him to the Tower. He was accused of plotting with the Earl of Westmorland, who was at Maestricht, to launch a new Catholic insurrection in England, and of being in touch with Mary Queen of Scots. When he protested against this treatment of the King of Spain's ambassador, he was told that he was not a properly accredited ambassador but in the position of an ordinary foreigner resident in England. He managed to smuggle a letter to Philip, in which he insisted that he had never plotted with Westmorland or the Queen of Scots, and believed that the English intended to hold him as a hostage who could be exchanged for Hawkins's seamen who were in the prisons of the Inquisition in Spain.[34]

Philip sent a new ambassador, Don Bernardino de Mendoza, to replace Guaras. Mendoza was a Spanish nobleman who had had a distinguished career in the army. He had recently served in the Netherlands. His rank, and the fact that he was a fully accredited ambassador, placed him in a stronger position than Guaras, but as Elizabeth had arrested Philip's last two envoys, he knew the risks that he was running in England. He was no coward, and believed that both the interests of his King and his own safety were best served by taking a tough line with Elizabeth and her counsellors. They therefore thought him arrogant and offensive, and he has been remembered in English history books as a proud and stiffnecked Spanish aristocrat who tried unsuccessfully to bully Elizabeth. But he was more intelligent and tactful that Guerau de Espés, and unlike Espés he did not overestimate the strength of the English Catholics.

His conversations with Elizabeth were sometimes friendly, and sometimes very unfriendly. Sometimes they threatened each other; sometimes she was charming, and said that she was requesting him to take some course of action not as a Queen addressing an ambassador, but as a lady asking a Spanish gentleman for a favour.[35] On these occasions, Mendoza usually managed to reply with a flattering compliment without giving anything away.

His instructions from Philip were to do his best to secure the release of Guaras, to dissuade Elizabeth from helping the Protestants in the Netherlands, and to obtain compensation for the Spanish merchants whose ships and goods had been pillaged by Drake and Hawkins and other English 'pirates' on the Spanish Main in the Atlantic and the Caribbean.[36] Three months before Mendoza arrived in England in March 1578, Drake had sailed with five ships and 164 men from Plymouth on 13 December on a voyage round the world. The voyage had been planned by Walsingham, and he, Leicester and Hatton were members of the consortium who financed it. Elizabeth knew about it, and that the object of the expedition was to obtain gold and riches by plundering Spanish and Portuguese ships, and perhaps also Spanish towns in America.[37]

Steps were taken to make the Spaniards believe that the ships were sailing to the Mediterranean. Guaras reported that they were heading for the Caribbean.[38] In fact they sailed to Brazil, through the Straits of Magellan and up the west coast of America, looting Callao on the way, to some place which is today on the coast of Canada; then across the Pacific Ocean, sailing for sixty-eight days without sighting land, to the Philippines, the Molucca Islands, and round the Cape of Good Hope. The fifty-seven survivors reached Plymouth on 26 September 1580, after a voyage of 1,013 days.

The cost of the expedition had been £5,000. Drake brought back bullion and jewels worth £600,000, which is £150,000,000 in terms of today's prices. The members of the consortium received £47 for every £1 which they had invested; but Elizabeth was entitled to half of the total takings. Burghley, Sussex and Wilson advised her to disown Drake and return the money in order to avoid the risk of war with Spain; but Leicester, Hatton and Walsingham urged that Mendoza's protests should be ignored, and that the treasure should be retained for Elizabeth and themselves.

For once, Elizabeth was on the side of the anti-Spanish party in the Council, and hesitated for a shorter time than usual before deciding to defy Mendoza and Philip, and accept her share of Drake's loot. At the festivities at court on New Year's Day, she wore some of the jewels which Drake had given her; and when in April 1581 he brought his ship, the *Golden Hind*, to Deptford, she went on board and knighted him and dined with him.[39]

THE VIRGIN QUEEN

WHILE Anjou was alarming Elizabeth by his preparations to go to the help of the Protestants of the Netherlands, he was a suitor for her hand in marriage. Her relationship with him is the strangest of all the stories in the long-protracted negotiations about her marriage.

Elizabeth's contemporaries, and students of history ever since, have speculated as to why she never married and always remained the Virgin Queen. It has sometimes been suggested that she had some physical deformity which made it impossible for her to have sexual intercourse or at least to have children. Others have thought that she had an insurmountable psychological aversion to sex and marriage. Others again believe that personal and psychological motives played no part at all in her attitude to the marriage negotiations, and that it was entirely a question of foreign policy. Others suggest that, having been unable to marry Leicester – or, according to Clapham, Edward Courtenay[1] – she refused to marry anyone else.

It is very unlikely that she had any physical malformation which prevented marriage. When she was a child under Henry VIII and a young girl under Edward VI, negotiations were opened for her marriage to a number of foreign Princes. During royal marriage negotiations it was the custom for ambassadors to emphasise not only the beauty, virtue and religious piety of the Princess who was being offered as a bride, but also that her physicians reported that she was capable of bearing healthy children and that they agreed with the astrologers that she was more likely to have sons than daughters. These assurances were almost certainly given by the ambassadors of Henry VIII and Edward VI in Elizabeth's case, and it is very unlikely that they would have ventured to say this if she had been physically incapable of intercourse or child-bearing. A strong psychological aversion to marriage is much more likely, because it is difficult to explain her consistent refusal to marry on grounds of political expediency alone.

She was only thirteen when Henry VIII died, but by the time of Edward VI's death she was nearly twenty, and it was surprising that she was not already married. In Mary's reign, her imprisonment and disgrace held up for a time the negotiations for her marriage, but during the last three years of the reign she was offered as a bride to the Duke of Savoy and other suitors. She knew that this was an attempt to banish her from England, and perhaps to prevent her from succeeding to the crown, so she had good reason to object to marrying under these circumstances. The reason which she gave, that she wished to live and die a virgin, was the best excuse which she could have put forward to Mary. After she became Queen she gave the same excuse for refusing to marry Philip II and the young Earl of Arran, and again it was the least offensive reason which she could give for refusing their offers of marriage.

There were good political reasons for not wishing to tie herself too closely, by a matrimonial alliance, to the Papist Philip or the Scottish Protestant Arran. When Eric XIV of Sweden proposed to her in the first years of her reign, he had not yet indulged in the violent outbursts of cruelty which eventually caused his nobles to depose him on the grounds that he was insane; but an alliance with Sweden would have been of only minor use to her, and she wanted to be free to offer herself to more important sovereigns. The same applied to the Duke of Holstein; but Archduke Charles was a very satisfactory match. She encouraged his suit for several years, and on one occasion actually told Guzman de Silva that she had decided to accept his proposal;[2] but at the last moment she changed her mind, and refused him.

In 1571 there were strong diplomatic arguments in favour of a marriage to Henry, Duke of Anjou, but there were some drawbacks. His Catholic zeal would certainly have created difficulties in England. Elizabeth did not wish to offend the Protestants, and encourage the Catholics, by marrying a husband who would insist on going to Mass, not only in his private chapel, but publicly with a band of priests and monks in attendance. There was also the obstacle that Henry was passionately in love with his enemy's sister, the Protestant Princess of Condé, and was very unwilling to marry Elizabeth; and she herself was, as usual, reluctant. Burghley was in favour of the marriage, but in view of the difficulties and Elizabeth's feelings, he felt obliged in the end to tell her that if she wished to break off the marriage negotiations, the best way would be to inform Henry that she could not permit him to have his Mass if he married her.[3] She did so, and Henry broke off the negotiations.

Henry duly became first King of Poland and then King of France, and, overcoming his love for the Princess of Condé, married Louise of Lorraine, a relation of the Guises; but he suggested that Elizabeth should marry his brother Francis, Duke of Alençon, who succeeded him as Duke of Anjou. Despite the strong political arguments in favour of the marriage, Elizabeth toyed with the idea for seven years, but could not make up her mind to accept Francis. At last in 1579 she agreed to his suggestion that he should come to England and visit her. He arrived at Greenwich on 14 August and spent thirteen days with her.

The seventh of September 1579 was Elizabeth's forty-sixth birthday. The day was celebrated every year throughout the kingdom by her loyal subjects, though in previous reigns the English people had never been aware of the date in the year on which their sovereign was born. The idea of celebrating the Queen's birthday seems to have started spontaneously, without any official order or prompting, and it was followed two months later by the even greater celebrations on 17 November, her accession day. Anjou was aged twenty-four. Elizabeth had been warned that he was small, ugly and pock-marked, but she was delighted with him, and he with her. He addressed her in devoted and passionate language, and she seemed to enjoy it, and showed every sign of falling in love with him. Her Protestant subjects strongly objected to his visit, for as a Frenchman and a Catholic he aroused their nationalist and religious hatred. It was particularly unfortunate that his stay at Greenwich coincided with the Feast of St Bartholomew.

The storm of criticism continued after his departure. In the Council, Burghley and Sussex favoured the marriage, but Leicester strongly opposed it. The Puritan preachers denounced the marriage in their sermons as the first step towards the establishment of Popery in England; they compared it to Queen Mary's marriage to Philip of Spain twenty-five years before.

A barrister of Lincoln's Inn, John Stubbs, who was the brother-in-law of the prominent Puritan, Thomas Cartwright, criticised the proposed marriage in his book *The Discovery of a Gaping Gulf whereinto England is like to be swallowed in another French Marriage if the Lord forbid not the banns by letting Her Majesty see the sin and punishment thereof.* He expressed his devotion to the Queen and praised her virtues, but denounced Anjou as the serpent who had come in the form of a man 'to seduce our Eve that she and we may lose this English paradise'; he would bring the Mass with him to England, and his wedding to the Queen would be a 'Parisian marriage', like the wedding of Henry of Navarre and Margaret of Valois in Paris, to be followed by another Massacre of St Bartholomew. It was true that Parliament had always wanted the Queen to marry in order that she should give birth to an heir; but Stubbs pointed out that this benefit was unlikely to result from her marriage to Anjou, for she was now too old to have children. If any children were born to her and Anjou, they would suffer from syphilis which Anjou had acquired by his dissolute life and with which he would infect the Queen.[4]

Philip Sidney risked losing Elizabeth's favour by writing to her to urge her not to marry Anjou. He told her that Anjou was 'a Frenchman and a Papist . . . the son of a Jezebel of our age', and that the marriage was strongly opposed by the English Protestants, 'your chief, if not your sole, strength'.[5] But his language was more moderate than Stubbs's, and he did not publish his letter.

Elizabeth was very angry with Sidney, but he escaped with nothing worse than the loss of her favour. She considered Stubbs's offence to be much more serious, for his book had been published, and many copies sold by William Page at his bookshop in the city of London were circulating throughout the south of England from Wiltshire to Lincolnshire and Staffordshire. She was indignant at Stubbs's attack on Anjou, the brother of a King with whom she was at amity, for it was the recognised custom of sovereigns to forbid publications and sermons which criticised foreign Princes, even those with whom their relations were unfriendly, and she had recently persuaded Philip II to suppress a Spanish Catholic book about the Reformation in England in which she was denounced as a heretic and a bastard. She was also personally affronted by the abuse of Anjou, with whom she was at least a little in love, and by Stubbs's reference to her age and inability to have children. But what she most resented was that it was, in her view, a seditious attempt by the Puritans to interfere in matters which did not concern them, and to influence her decision about her marriage and her foreign policy. Stubbs had professed his devotion to her, but according to Camden she would not 'be persuaded that the author of this book had any other purpose than to bring her into hatred with her subjects and to open a gap to some prodigious innovation'.[6]

She ordered the arrest of Stubbs, his publisher Singleton, and Page the bookseller, and decided to make them the victims of a terrible showdown with the Puritans. After the lawyers had advised her that they could not be charged with high treason, they were prosecuted under the Act against Seditious Words and Rumours of 1555,[7] which had been passed to suppress the criticisms of Mary and of Philip II when he was King of England. It enacted that anyone who should 'write, print or set forth' anything in writing 'containing any false matter, clause or sentence of slander, reproach and dishonour of the King and Queen's Majesties or of either of them' should have his right hand cut off. Froude, surprisingly, misunderstood the statute,[8] and he and other writers who followed him have stated that the Act, which punished libels on 'the Queen's husband', was strained in Stubbs's case to include denunciations of 'the Queen's suitor', Anjou. But there was no reference to 'the Queen's husband' in the Act of 1555, which was passed after Philip had become King of England, and referred to attacks on the sovereigns. Stubbs and his colleagues were prosecuted not for libelling Anjou, but on the grounds that the book libelled the Queen by suggesting that her plans to marry Anjou were foolish and that, if she married him, she would allow him to subvert the Protestant religion which she had established in her realm.

Elizabeth issued a long proclamation, which she ordered the Lord Mayor of London and the bishops to read out to the city livery companies and in the churches throughout the south of England. It denounced Stubbs's book as a 'trump of sedition', which, 'under a pretence of dissuading her away from marriage with the Duke of Anjou, the French King's brother', had told 'a heap of slanders and reproaches of the said Prince, bolstered up with manifest lies', and had thereby stirred up the people to fear 'the alteration of Christian religion by Her Majesty's marriage' and 'to move a general murmuring and disliking in her loving people concerning Her Majesty's actions in this behalf'. The proclamation denied that Anjou had ever attempted to subvert the Protestant religion in England, and mentioned that he had helped the Protestants in France, who owed most of what they had gained to him. This was true enough, because Anjou's intervention on their side in the fifth civil war had won them better peace terms than they had obtained after any war before or since. The proclamation ended by ordering that all the copies of Stubbs's book were to be seized and destroyed.[9]

On 27 September the Privy Council wrote to the Lord Mayor of London ordering him to implement the proclamation, and repeating that Anjou had never attempted to subvert the Protestant religion which the Queen had done more than any other Prince to uphold. The letter was signed by Leicester, Walsingham, and Philip Sidney's father Sir Henry Sidney, as well as by Burghley, Hatton, Lord Chancellor Bromley, and Hunsdon.[10] If there was any truth in the current rumour that Leicester and his faction had instigated the publication of Stubbs's book, they took care to dissociate themselves from it; but according to a report which reached the Venetian ambassador in Paris, Elizabeth believed that Walsingham was responsible for the publication.[11]

When Stubbs, Singleton and Page were tried in the Court of Queen's Bench, the jury, under the firm direction of the Lord Chief Justice, Sir Christopher Wray, returned a verdict of guilty, and they were sentenced to lose their right hands. Some lawyers thought that the conviction was illegal, as the Act of 1555, with its reference to 'the King and Queen's Majesties or of either of them' applied only to Philip and Mary and had lapsed at Mary's death. Wray had no difficulty in demolishing this argument, for not only did the principle that 'the King never dies' extend the Act of Parliament for the benefit of his successor, but the Act of 1555 had been expressly re-enacted by Elizabeth's first Parliament in 1559. A barrister named Dalton, who criticised the verdict in what Camden called 'clamourous speeches',* was sent to the Tower;[12] and Mr Justice Monson of the Court of Common Pleas, who also said that the conviction was illegal, was severely reprimanded and ordered to resign his seat on the bench and return to his estates in Lincolnshire.

Elizabeth pardoned Singleton the publisher, but insisted that the sentence should be carried out on Stubbs and the bookseller Page, though the French ambassador and Anjou himself asked her to show mercy to them. On 3 November they were taken to Palace Yard at Westminster. Before the sentence was carried out, Stubbs spoke to the crowd of onlookers. 'I pray you all to pray with me that God will strengthen me to endure and abide the pain that I am to suffer, and grant me this grace, that the loss of my hand do not withdraw any part of my duty and affection toward Her Majesty ... My masters, if there be any among you that do love me, if your love be not in God and Her Majesty, I utterly deny your love'. After the executioner had struck

---

*These are the words used in the 1625 English edition. It is 'Dalton, who often spake it openly' in the 1635 English edition, and '*Daltonus qui hoc clamitabat*' in Camden's Latin.

off his hand, Stubbs took off his hat with his left hand, and cried 'God save the Queen!' before he fainted.

Then it was Page's turn. In his speech, he said that as he had always earned his living with his right hand, it would have been kinder of the Queen to have taken his left hand or his life; but he was confident that if he could not earn his living, God would provide for him. After his hand was cut off, he said: 'I have left there a true Englishman's hand'.[13]

Many of the contemporaries do not seem to have shared the opinion expressed by Sir John Neale in the twentieth century that the sentence was not severe by the standards of the age.[14] Both Stow and Camden, who were present at the punishment, stated that the crowd was shocked. According to Camden, when Stubbs cried 'God save the Queen!', the people were 'altogether silent, either out of horror at this new unusual punishment, or else out of pity for a man of unblemished reputation . . . or else out of hatred of the marriage, which most men feared would lead to the overthrow of religion'.[15] The significance of Camden's words has sometimes been overlooked; it was not at the striking off of the hand, but at the words 'God save the Queen', that the crowd stood silent.

From the Tower, Stubbs wrote to Elizabeth and the Privy Council expressing his regret at having offended her, and asking her to show mercy and release him from his prison.[16] He wrote to the Council that when he had cried 'God save the Queen!' after his hand had been struck off, 'this was no more than every man should do which maketh conscience to give none evil example to others of the least repining thought against the Lord's sacred magistrate or due execution of justice'.[17] He was released after just over a year in prison. The Puritan sympathisers had been unable to save him, but they persuaded Elizabeth to employ him in future years as an anti-Catholic propagandist and send him as an agent to the Dutch Protestants. He retained the confidence of the people of his town of Great Yarmouth, who elected him as their MP. He often signed his letters '*Scaeva*' (left-handed), or ended the letter: 'Written with his left hand, John Stubbs'.

Faced with this widespread opposition to her marriage to Anjou, Elizabeth asked her Council for their opinion. They discussed it at several meetings, culminating in a session on 7 October, when they sent away all the clerks of the Council and sat continuously in the Council chamber from eight o'clock in the morning to seven in the evening, with Burghley himself taking the minutes in the absence of the clerks. Burghley, Sussex, Wilson and Hunsdon favoured the marriage. Walsingham did not attend the meeting, probably because Elizabeth had ordered him to stay away, or because he thought it wise to do so in view of her indignation with him. But Leicester and Sir Henry Sidney were strongly against the marriage, and the majority of the Council supported them, and advised Elizabeth that she should refuse Anjou's proposal, as there was strong opposition among her subjects to her marriage to any Catholic.[18]

Elizabeth very reluctantly accepted their advice. She agreed not to marry Anjou, though she did not send him a definite refusal, for neither she nor her Council wished to damage her friendship with France at a time when her relations with Spain were worsening. She did not reply to the proposal, hoping that it would lapse. Mendoza reported that she was very sad, and had told her ladies and her intimate associates that she had very much wanted to marry Anjou and to have children; she was very angry with everyone who opposed the marriage, and spoke bitterly to them, telling Walsingham that he was good for nothing except to act as a protector of heretics.[19] Mendoza gave so many details of her conversations and feelings that he must have received his information from someone very close to her, and his information was usually reliable. She gave one tangible sign of her love for Anjou. A fortnight after she had decided not to marry him, she gave his envoy a gift for him of jewels worth 8,000 crowns.[20]

But the proposal for a marriage with Anjou was revived again eighteen months later, in the summer of 1581, when relations between England and Spain had become a good deal worse, and it was more essential than ever for Elizabeth to protect herself against Philip by an alliance with France. All Elizabeth's counsellors were in favour of the French alliance, which they thought was especially necessary after Anjou had accepted the offer of the rebels in the Netherlands to make him their ruler; for if a French Prince was to control the Netherlands, it was essential that he should be England's ally. In view of the strong opposition in England to the marriage with Anjou, they wished to see England and France enter into a military alliance without the marriage taking place.

In June 1581 Walsingham told Cobham to explain to Henry III and Catherine de Medici that although Elizabeth was very eager for an alliance, she had never wished to marry, and had always hoped to remain a virgin. She had only agreed to consider proposals of marriage because her people had formerly urged her to marry; but now that her people were no longer in favour of her marrying, it would be better if Henry III and Elizabeth made an alliance without a marriage. Catherine de Medici rejected this proposal. Apart from the fact that she was eager to find a bride for her son, and that Elizabeth would be a splendid match for Anjou, she felt that only a marriage could ensure that the alliance would be permanent and that Elizabeth would not repudiate it at some future date and resume the traditional alliance with Burgundy and Spain against France.[21]

This presented Elizabeth and her counsellors with a difficult problem. In June 1581 Anjou visited Elizabeth secretly, and he came again on an official visit in October. Once again they exchanged passionate declarations of love, which culminated in a scene at Whitehall on 22 November. Elizabeth, in the presence of the French ambassador, Mauvissière, took off one of her rings and placed it on Anjou's finger and told Mauvissière that she and Anjou were to be married. Catherine de Medici was delighted. She and Henry III treated it as being in effect an official engagement, and announced the news at court, and celebrated it at a ball in the Louvre. But a few days later, Elizabeth changed her mind, and assured Burghley and her counsellors that she had said nothing to Anjou which definitely committed her to marrying him.[22]

At the end of November, only a few days after the gift of the ring at Whitehall, she ordered Cobham to tell Henry III that if he refused to make a treaty of alliance with her unless she married Anjou, she was ready to marry him on condition that if she became involved in war with Spain as a result of Anjou's intervention in the Netherlands and her connection with him, Henry III would declare war on Spain and that he and the States-General of the Netherlands would reimburse her for the whole of her costs in fighting the war, and agree to bear all the expenses of their joint military operations without calling on her to contribute. Henry III rejected these conditions, and in February 1582 Elizabeth wrote to him, saying how sad she was that the marriage would not take place, and how she hoped that this would not impair their friendship. As Henry III would not agree to an alliance without the marriage, no treaty was signed, and Anjou left England to join his army in the Netherlands. Elizabeth escorted him on his journey as far as Canterbury, and had a most loving parting from him. She also agreed to give him £60,000 towards the cost of his campaign in the Netherlands, and gave him £10,000 at once.[23]

Elizabeth's behaviour towards Anjou in November 1581 is the supreme example of her waywardness with her suitors, and of her changeability on the subject of her marriage. As so often with her actions, they have been interpreted in different ways – as indecision, as coquetry, and as calculated policy. But her love-making with Anjou and the scene at Whitehall on 22 November did nothing to help her foreign policy. The best solution, from her point of view, was certainly an alliance with France without the marriage; but if she had definitely decided that on no account would she marry Anjou, and Henry III had made up his mind not to make the alliance until the marriage had taken place, there could be no agreement, no marriage and no alliance, and there was no advantage in misleading Anjou, Henry III and everyone else for a few weeks. To go as far as she did on 22 November and then in effect break off the engagement by imposing impossible conditions, was bound to irritate the French and worsen Anglo-French relations at a time when Elizabeth was eager to improve them. It is much more likely that she was carried away by the stimulation of her love affair with Anjou, and acted impetuously on 22 November; then, of course, she changed her mind, decided not to marry him, and put forward the wholly unreasonable proposal that the French should pay all the costs of a possible war against Spain, knowing that Henry III would refuse them and give her an excuse for breaking the engagement.

One man, who had once known her very well, was not surprised at the outcome of the marriage negotiations. Philip II wrote to Mendoza that he had always been convinced that, in the last resort, she would refuse to marry Anjou.[24]

This was the last occasion on which Elizabeth, who was now aged forty-eight, considered the possibility of marriage; after this, she and everyone else accepted that she would always be the Virgin Queen. She never came nearer to agreeing to marry than she did on 22 November 1581. She had fallen a little in love with her frog, as she called Anjou, not in the passionate way in which she had fallen for Leicester in 1560, but enough to land herself in difficulties. She wanted to marry him, but could not definitely make up her mind to do so.

Marriage was not, of course, the only thing about which Elizabeth could not make up her mind. Her reluctance to take decisions and her irresolution in adhering to them became worse and worse as she grew older, and was the most dominant factor in her character and in her domestic and foreign policy. This is surely the simple and real explanation of why she never married. When it was a question of invading Scotland or helping the Dutch, she could take a decision one day and reverse it the next; but once she married, there was no going back, for she did not wish to become involved, like her father, in a series of divorces with the long and embarrassing theological arguments and nullity proceedings which they entailed.

There is no better explanation of Elizabeth's failure to marry, unless we are prepared to accept the suggestion put forward by Clapham in the little book which he wrote within four months of her death. He wrote that the reason why she never married was perhaps because 'God Himself had so ordained it, to the end, her posterity being buried in her own body, the two kingdoms of England and Scotland might in these our days be united in the person of the present King'.[25]

IRELAND

F OR four hundred years the Kings of England had been Lords of Ireland – a title which had been changed to 'King of Ireland' by Henry VIII in 1541. But they had never controlled more than a small part of the country, the English Pale, a semicircle about sixty miles deep around Dublin, and a small area around Wexford, Waterford and Cork. The rest of the country was ruled by native Irish chiefs. Ireland had been nominally Christian for more than a thousand years, and the Catholic Church was duly established there, as elsewhere in Europe; but the Church in Ireland was lax, and the English complained that paganism still survived in the more remote areas. Irish bishoprics and benefices were normally given to lazy and unambitious priests who were content to opt out of the rat-race for wealth and power in which more greedy and ambitious churchmen engaged in England.

The situation did not change when Henry VIII repudiated Papal supremacy. The Archbishops of Dublin and Armagh and their bishops and vicars duly conformed to the new religious policy, and made some effort to enforce it in the Pale; but nothing changed in the rest of Ireland. In Mary's reign, a few English Protestants took refuge in Ireland, knowing that any persecution of heretics would be carried through in a most lackadaisical manner over there. After Mary's death, Roman Catholicism did not again become the state religion in Ireland until 1922, with the result that Ireland is the only country in Western Europe, apart from Scandinavia, in which no one has ever been burned for heresy.

Henry VIII made no attempt to extend his authority beyond the Pale, being content to receive the formal homage of some Irish chiefs whom he invited to Hampton Court; but in Mary's reign, the English embarked on a new policy of colonising Munster and other parts of Ireland. The King and Queen of Ireland, Philip and Mary, as theoretical overlords of all the country, granted uncultivated tracts of territory to English gentlemen and other adventurers to cultivate at their own expense and risk. At first the new landlords employed

Irish labour, but they soon began importing English tenants and agricultural labourers, who were less resentful than the natives and more skilled in English methods of husbandry.

This led to an increase in bitterness between English and Irish. Most of the English colonists despised the Irish as primitive barbarians with strange customs and clothes, as sub-humans to whom the ordinary rules of morality and fair dealing did not apply. The Irish bitterly hated the foreigners who had invaded their territory, stolen their lands, and uprooted their native way of life. In view of the long history of religious hatreds in Ireland, which still continues today, it is an irony that this colonial system, which later became so closely connected with religion, was inaugurated by those most Catholic sovereigns, Philip and Mary; but it only reached its full development under Elizabeth.

By this time, the religious question had intervened in Anglo-Irish relations. After Elizabeth's accession and the reversion to Protestantism in England, the Catholics succeeded in exploiting the religious void in Ireland as effectively as the Calvinists ten years earlier had exploited the religious void in Scotland. Within a few years of Elizabeth's accession, her Protestant bishops and officials in Ireland were complaining of the illegal proselytising activity of Catholic missionaries and of their extraordinary success in influencing the Irish population. The more zealous Protestants attributed this to the slackness of the government, for the laws punishing Catholics for attending Mass and absenting themselves from the Protestant Church services were not enforced in Ireland.[1]

William Walsh, who had been appointed Bishop of Meath by Mary and deprived by Elizabeth for refusing the oath of supremacy, continued to be recognised as bishop by the Pope, and despite being imprisoned in Dublin for a time, succeeded in directing the Catholic propaganda in Ireland, at first from within the country, and later in exile in Spain. The 'Irish bishop', as Elizabeth's officials called him, was regarded by them as a dangerous enemy.

Soon after she came to the throne, Elizabeth was confronted with a more traditional danger from Shane O'Neill, a native Irish chief in Ulster. He claimed the title of 'The O'Neill' and suzerainty over all the neighbouring chiefs, and soon had established his authority over the province from his strong castle at Benburb near Armagh. Some of his neighbours complained to the Lord Deputy, the Earl of Sussex, who thought that Shane's growing strength threatened the security of Elizabeth's government in Ireland; and Shane sometimes raided the English Pale and stole cattle. Shane's principal opponents in Ulster were the M'Donnells, who were related to the M'Donnells in Scotland. Raiders and immigrants often crossed the twenty miles of water between Scotland and Ulster. They were not Lowland Scottish Protestants, like the Scottish immigrants of the next century, but Catholics, chiefly from the Western Isles and the territory of the Earl of Argyll. When Mary Queen of Scots was still reigning in Scotland, Elizabeth complained to her on several occasions about the inroads into Ireland by Argyll's Scots, but Mary was unable to do anything to prevent it.

The chief of the M'Donnells in Ireland was Sorley Boy M'Donnell, and in 1561 Sussex made an alliance with Sorley Boy against Shane O'Neill. Elizabeth rather reluctantly agreed to Sussex's suggestion that she should allow him to invade Ulster with an army to crush Shane O'Neill, while Sorley Boy simultaneously attacked him on his flank. But Sussex's army was unable to follow Shane into the forests. Sussex then suggested to Elizabeth that he should send an agent to Benburb to assassinate Shane; but Elizabeth decided instead to invite Shane to visit her and do homage to her in return for being confirmed as chief of his territories.[2]

Sussex and most of his officials in Dublin had misgivings about Elizabeth's conciliatory policy; but Elizabeth insisted on granting Shane a safe-conduct to come to her court. He arrived in London in December 1561. The Londoners were surprised and amused at the strange Irish dress worn by Shane and his retinue; but Elizabeth received him very graciously on Twelfth Day.[3] He could not speak English and she could not speak Gaelic, but they could talk very easily in Latin.

As soon as Shane got back to Ulster, Sussex began complaining to Elizabeth about his activities. On 27 August 1562 he wrote to her that in the course of a few months Shane had stolen twenty thousand head of cattle from his neighbours and in the Pale. After Elizabeth had received complaints from many quarters about Shane's depredations, she authorised Sussex to raise an army and march against him in alliance with Sorley Boy M'Donnell. But Shane defeated Sussex and Sorley Boy, and in September 1563, after Sussex had sent an envoy to Shane at Benburb to ask for peace, Elizabeth agreed to pardon Shane and confirm him as ruler of Ulster. Next month she wrote to Sussex how horrified she was to hear that one of Shane's enemies had tried to murder him by giving him a cup of poisoned wine.[4]

Sussex continued to complain about Shane's depredations. To make matters worse, Shane asked the Cardinal of Lorraine to send 6,000 French troops to help him, as he was fighting for the Catholic faith.[5] In May 1565 Shane attacked a force of Scots who had come to help the M'Donnells against him, and killed seven hundred of them. This started a new war in Ulster, despite Elizabeth's attempts to persuade Shane and Sorley Boy to settle their differences by peaceful means in her courts of law. She recalled Sussex and appointed Sir Henry Sidney to be Lord Deputy in his place, and authorised Sidney to begin another campaign against Shane; but Sidney was worried at the numbers of Scots who were coming from the Isles of Scotland to help the M'Donnells, and Elizabeth told him to discourage the influx of Scots as far as possible.[6]

The M'Donnells eventually defeated Shane O'Neill, and in June 1567 he visited them to discuss surrender terms. The English had offered a reward to anyone who killed Shane, so the M'Donnells hacked him to pieces and sent his head to Captain Piers, the governor of Carrickfergus, who cheated the M'Donnells and claimed the reward for himself.[7] The government's chief concern now was to get rid of the surplus M'Donnells who had arrived from Scotland with their wives and children to fight against Shane, and on 10 December 1567 Elizabeth wrote to the Council in Dublin that the Scots should be speedily expelled from Ireland.[8] But this could not be done without incurring the cost of raising an army and waging war against the M'Donnells; so Elizabeth negotiated with them for nearly seven years, recognising many of Sorley Boy's claims to lands and overlordships in Ulster, and alternately threatening and cajoling him. Sorley Boy's confidence increased as he saw that Elizabeth took no action against him, and he often raided Carrickfergus and the northern parts of the Pale as well as the lands of his neighbours in Ulster.

The English government in Ireland had for many years had trouble from native chieftains like Shane O'Neill and Sorley Boy; but there was now the new danger which had been created by the English colonists and the remarkably successful proselytising by the Catholic missionaries. In the spring of 1569 a widespread revolt broke out in Munster against the English colonists under the leadership of the Earl of Desmond's nephew, James FitzMaurice FitzGerald. Elizabeth sent Lord Desmond to the Tower, and when he was released he remained at her court, half-prisoner and half-collaborator, issuing appeals to his tenants in Munster to remain loyal to the Queen; but nearly all of them followed his nephew, and drove out the English settlers, who abandoned their properties and fled to the Pale, telling stories about the murder of Englishmen by the rebels, though these seem to have been very rare. There were also risings in County Leix and other parts of Leinster, and the handful of English colonists who had settled in Connaught were also attacked, and fled.

Six months earlier, Alva had seized the English property in the Netherlands, and relations between Philip and Elizabeth were very bad. The outbreak of the insurrection in Ireland came at a very convenient time for Philip, and James FitzMaurice and the Bishop of Meath asked him for aid. The spies whom the English government had planted among the English merchants at Ferrol and other Spanish ports sent reports of naval and military preparations, and the government in London and Dublin believed that Stucley was preparing to sail with a Spanish army to help the rebels in Munster. Stucley, who was popularly believed to be an illegitimate son of Henry VIII, had all his life been an adventurer, a spy and double agent for both England and France, a privateer and a pirate with no strong religious principles; but after he quarrelled with some of Elizabeth's officials in Ireland, he went to Spain with a sense of grievance, became a Catholic, and was granted the title of Duke of Ireland by Philip, as well as a luxury villa near Madrid and the very large pension of 2,000 ducats a month.

But Philip, as usual, was cautious, and reluctant to become involved in a military expedition to either Ireland or England; and he had other enemies besides Elizabeth. He decided to send a large naval force, under the command of Don John of Austria, against the Turks in the Eastern Mediterranean; and Stucley, who had become friendly with Don John in Madrid, was as happy to fight the Turks as anyone else. He and his men, instead of sailing to Munster, took part in the Battle of Lepanto in October 1571, when Don John annihilated the Turkish fleet. Elizabeth, even at the height of her dispute with Spain about the property seizures, congratulated the Venetian ambassador on the great victory of Philip and the Venetians over the Turkish infidels.[9]

The English in Ireland fought ruthlessly against the rebels, whom they now regarded not only as savages but also as Papists, who in both capacities deserved no pity but could quite properly be massacred. They were disgusted to find that within a very short time nearly everyone in Ireland had heard about the Massacre of St Bartholomew, for the priests had spread the good news throughout the country.[10] That zealous Protestant, Sir Humphrey Gilbert, commanded a detachment of troops which he led against the rebels in Munster before he left with his volunteers to fight for the Protestant cause in the Netherlands. He wrote to Sir Henry Sidney from Limerick on 6 December 1569 that he refused to parley with any rebels, put many to the sword, and spared none that fell into his hands.[11] He and the other English commanders hanged many rebels.

The revolt in Munster finally subsided in 1573. It was clear by this time that there was no immediate prospect of Spanish help, because Philip and Elizabeth had reached agreement about the property seizures and had resumed trade between England and the Netherlands and Spain. James FitzMaurice escaped to Spain, and Elizabeth granted an amnesty to nearly all the surviving rebels. The officials in Ireland did not approve of the amnesty. The Council in Dublin were more vindictive towards the Irish than Elizabeth, and the local commanders and colonists were more vindictive than the Council in Dublin.[12]

The suppression of the revolt in Munster made it possible for Elizabeth to deal with the M'Donnells in Ulster, and in the summer of 1573 she sent the Earl of Essex, whose son was later to play so important a part in her life, to take charge of the operation. Essex fought some successful skirmishes against the M'Donnells, but could not achieve very much, with the small number of troops available, before the winter set in. It was obviously necessary to send him reinforcements for next year's campaign. But Elizabeth could not make up her mind what to do. In April 1574 she was insisting that the expedition against Ulster should go forward, and telling Essex and the Lord Deputy, Fitzwilliam, to be sure not to grant the rebels too favourable terms. By July she was urging Essex to allure the rude Irish to civility by his discretion rather than by the shedding of blood. Because of Elizabeth's indecision, nothing was done in the summer of 1574; but the M'Donnells continued to raid their neighbours in Ulster and the Pale. Essex was annoyed that people in Ireland were saying that the planned campaign against Ulster was his war, not the Queen's.[13]

When the question arose as to whether the long-awaited invasion of Ulster should take place in the summer of 1575, Elizabeth decided to pass the buck to the Lord Deputy. On 24 February 1575 she wrote to Fitzwilliam that she left it to him to decide whether or not to undertake the Ulster expedition. Burghley thought that this was not good enough. He was too ill with his gout to go to court, but he sent his secretary Edward Tremayne to Richmond to give Elizabeth his written advice to send the necessary reinforcements to Essex for a campaign in the summer. On 13 March Tremayne wrote to Burghley that Elizabeth could not make up her mind; but two days later she wrote to Fitzwilliam that she was very doubtful about the prospects for an expedition into Ulster and was reluctant to authorise it, but said again that she left the final decision to him.[14] In these circumstances Fitzwilliam did not venture to take the responsibility of authorising the campaign, and ordered that it should be called off. Essex, who had been waiting in Dublin for twenty months for the campaign to begin, was told that his services were no longer required. He received a warm letter from Elizabeth thanking him for his achievements,[15] but he wrote to Burghley: 'My service is extinguished in utter disgrace. If I still had but ten days' warning!'[16]

Essex was not beaten, and with the full support of his army officers and the English colonists used all his efforts to persuade Elizabeth and Fitzwilliam to allow him to march against the M'Donnells. At first he had no success. On 22 May Elizabeth wrote to Essex that despite her high opinion of him, she had decided not to authorise the Ulster campaign. But he and the men on the spot set out to force Elizabeth's hand, and confront her with a *fait accompli*. There were clashes with the Ulster rebels as their raids into the Pale continued, and on 22 July Essex wrote to Elizabeth that on 6 July he had set out in pursuit of the raiders and had inflicted so much damage on them that Sorley Boy had sued for peace.[17]

Sorley Boy had sent all the M'Donnell women and children for safety to Rathlin Island off the north coast of Ulster, the furthest point in his territories from the English forces at Drogheda, while he and his men prepared to attack Carrickfergus. The island contained nothing but the M'Donnell castle and a few farms, and could be approached only through a channel which was difficult to find, leading to the only bay from which it was possible to land. Essex decided to send a naval force to capture Rathlin, deep in Sorley Boy's rear, while he and his forces were occupied at Carrickfergus. Drake, who had returned from a privateering voyage to the Caribbean and was doing a spell of duty in home waters before setting off on his voyage round the world, was put in command of three frigates and ordered to take three hundred soldiers with two cannon to Rathlin Island.[18] The soldiers were under the command of Sir

John Norris, an able and experienced professional soldier who was an ardent Protestant and hated Papists. He was the grandson of Anne Boleyn's friend.

Drake managed to find the way into the cove from which debarkation was possible, and landed Norris and the soldiers. They marched to the castle, where all the M'Donnell women and children were herded for safety, guarded by a garrison of two hundred men. After Norris had bombarded the castle with his cannon and had made an unsuccessful attempt to take it by storm, he persuaded the constable of the castle to surrender the castle on the sole condition that his own life would be spared, though the others were to surrender at mercy. Sorley Boy had meanwhile heard about the English attack on Rathlin, and quickly returned from Carrickfergus to the north coast; but as the English had burned his ships, he could not go to the rescue of his people, and could only watch from the shore what was happening across the seven miles of water.

Norris spared the life of the constable and of the family of a leading Ulster chieftain for whom he thought that a ransom would be paid. All the rest of the two hundred soldiers of the garrison were killed, as were all the women and children. Some of the women managed to escape with their babies and hid in the caves on the shore; but Norris's men found them, smoked them out, and killed them as they emerged from the caves.

Norris undoubtedly knew that God required His Elect to punish all idolaters, and remembered that Moses had expressly commanded the Israelites not to spare the women and children of Midian; but Essex wrote three rather different accounts of the events at Rathlin in his letters of 31 July to Elizabeth, to the Privy Council, and to Walsingham. He told Elizabeth only that all the people in the castle, and those hiding in the caves, were slain, of whom there were two hundred 'of all sorts'; he did not expressly state that the women and children were killed. He added no further details in his letter to the Council. He wrote to Walsingham that 'Sorley Boy and his gentlemen sent their wives and children to the Rathlins, which be all taken and executed to the number of six hundred', and that Sorley Boy 'stood upon the mainland of the Glynnes and saw the taking of the island, and was likely to have run mad for sorrow, tearing and tormenting himself and saying that he there had lost all that ever he had'. Elizabeth, in her reply to Essex, complimented him on the success of the operation, and asked him to convey her thanks to Norris.[19]

Whatever Sorley Boy's feelings may have been, he concealed them in later years. He made peace with Elizabeth, and, after she had allowed him to retain his lands, collaborated with the English authorities on several occasions during the next twenty-five years.

For two years Ireland was reasonably quiet, but in 1577 Elizabeth and her counsellors became very alarmed at the reports from their spies of a renewed threat of Spanish intervention. Her relations with Philip had worsened again as her subjects continued to fight for his rebels in the Netherlands, and

Stucley returned to Madrid and prepared a new naval expedition. James FitzMaurice and Walsh found that the Pope was prepared to do more for them than Philip. He offered to supply the money which they needed to raise an army of Spanish and Italian volunteers and mercenaries for an expedition to liberate Ireland from the heretics. Philip agreed to allow recruiting for volunteers to take place in Spain and for the expedition to be equipped and victualled in Spain and to sail from Spanish ports, on condition that the soldiers were officially the army of the Pope, displaying the Papal banner. The expedition was to be commanded by Stucley.

Walsingham's intelligence service was efficient. His most important spy was Roger Bodenham, posing as an English merchant at San Lucar; but he had several other agents in the Spanish ports and throughout Spain and Italy, where the soldiers for the Papal force were being recruited. The spies sent reports to Walsingham that a powerful fleet and army were being prepared to sail to Ireland in the spring of 1578. But again the expedition intended for Ireland was diverted elsewhere. The Pope told Stucley to sail with his ships to Lisbon and join the forces which King Sebastian of Portugal was preparing to lead against the Moors in North Africa. Stucley was again ready to serve anywhere, and happily complied with the Pope's wishes; but the Moors annihilated the Portuguese army at the Battle of Al Kasr el Kebir on 4 August 1578, where both King Sebastian and Stucley were killed.

A third expedition to Ireland was prepared, though this time without any commander who could equal Stucley in daring. Again Walsingham's spies sent their reports, and by March 1579 the garrisons and ports of Munster were waiting every day for the invasion. It did not come, but as the news spread through the country that the Spanish liberators were on their way, another formidable revolt broke out in Munster, though this time Connaught remained quiet.[20]

James FitzMaurice hurried through preparations in Spain so that at least a small force could be sent to Ireland as soon as possible, and he sailed from Ferrol with two ships and fifty men. They landed at Dingle on the Kerry Peninsula on 17 July 1579. FitzMaurice's spiritual and political adviser on the expedition was Nicholas Sanders, the English refugee priest and author. He had left England for the Netherlands when Elizabeth became Queen, and wrote his book *The Anglican Schism*, which still today is one of the main Catholic histories of the Reformation in England. The soldiers were Italians and Spaniards in approximately equal numbers. They were all volunteers; some were gentlemen or men of lower rank who had enlisted out of devotion to the Catholic faith, and others were mercenaries. They marched west from Dingle to the extreme point of the peninsula and built a fort on the sea at Smerwick, which they named the Fort del Oro. It was the best place in which to hold out until more reinforcements came from Spain, for the troops could conveniently land in the harbour at Smerwick, some three miles from the fort.[21]

A few days after they landed, James FitzMaurice left the main force to go to worship at the Holy Cross in Tipperary, where he hoped to contact the Munster rebels; but he was attacked and killed by the English forces. This loss for the Catholics had one compensating advantage; his uncle the Earl of Desmond, who had opposed the previous rising out of his hatred for James FitzMaurice, now placed himself at the head of the rebels.

Soon the rebels were in control of nearly the whole of Munster. On 3 August Waterhouse, who was with the army at Limerick, wrote to Walsingham that the rebellion was the most dangerous that had ever broken out in Ireland.[22] Sanders carried a copy of the Papal bull excommunicating Elizabeth and absolving her subjects from their allegiance. He called on the people to fight 'in this holy enterprise for maintenance of the Catholic faith and the liberty of their country'. He announced that everyone who served in Elizabeth's army against the rebels would be excommunicated and his followers threatened to behead any priest who refused to celebrate Mass. The rebels burned Youghal, Kinsale, Dingle and Tralee. Cork held out, but no Englishman dared to venture more than 'half a quarter of a mile' outside the town.[23] In November, Sir Warham St Leger wrote to Burghley that all Munster was bent to the Papist religion.[24]

The English troops fought back energetically and mercilessly. There were only 1,211 English soldiers in Munster in March 1579, though reinforcements were being sent from England, and in every engagement the rebels outnumbered the government forces by five to one. But the English won nearly every fight because of their superior discipline and training, and soon they had forced the rebels to take refuge in the woods.[25] In March 1580 an English officer wrote to Walsingham that the traitors were like savage beasts lurking in wild desert places and woods.[26]

The government had called up a number of Irishmen to serve in the army. Many of them deserted to the rebels, taking their arms and ammunition with them. Some of the English soldiers from Lancashire, where many of the people were Catholics, were reluctant to fight against the Irish rebels, and were hurriedly sent home to England.[27] But most of the English were loyal and pitiless. 'If Her Majesty do not use her sword more sharply, she will lose both sword and realm', wrote Malby to Walsingham,[28] who was also informed that the Irish were such 'as Satan himself doth not exceed them in subtlety, treachery and cruelty'.[29] Whenever the English found an Irishman in the woods, they hanged him without more ado.[30] The government troops under the Earl of Ormond, marching from Cork to Limerick, captured the house of Carrigafoyle, which was defended by sixteen Spanish soldiers and was full of women and children. 'Some sought to swim away', wrote Captain Zouche to Walsingham, 'but they scaped not one, neither of man, woman nor child'.[31] The rebels did not often capture English soldiers, but when they did, they killed them.[32]

In September 1580 three Spanish ships arrived at Smerwick with reinforcements for the garrison of Fort del Oro, bringing their total strength to 600 men. Some of the original garrison in the fort had left to take part in the fighting elsewhere in Munster, and Sanders had gone with them. The English were also sending reinforcements to Ireland; by October they had 6,437 men there, and another 1,344 in the ships off the Irish coast.[33] The government decided to reduce Fort del Oro. They sent 600 foot and 200 horse to Smerwick under the command of Lord Grey of Wilton, while Winter sailed there with his fleet to cut off the invaders' escape. Although Grey's forces barely outnumbered the defenders, he did not wait for reinforcements but began the siege of the fort on 7 November 1580.

For two days there was an exchange of fire, and skirmishes, between the besiegers and the fort, but on the evening of 9 November the garrison asked for a parley. Grey described what happened in a long letter which he wrote to Elizabeth three days later. An Italian and a Spanish officer came out of the fort to speak with him. Grey said to the Spaniard that he could not understand what he and his men were doing there, as the King of Spain was an absolute Prince who was in league and amity with the Queen his mistress, and would surely not send a force to invade her realm. The Spanish officer admitted that they had not been sent by King Philip, but that the Governor of Bilbao had ordered him to go with his men to Santander and place themselves under the orders of Colonel Don Sebastian de San Giuseppe, who was now their commanding officer at Smerwick. The Italian officer said that they had been sent by the Pope to fight for the Catholic faith.

Grey replied that he could understand that men might do a wrongful act at the command of their natural and absolute Prince, but not that men of good family, as they appeared to be, 'should be carried into unjust, desperate and wicked actions by one that neither from God nor man could claim any princely power or empire, but indeed a detestable shaveling, the right Antichrist and general ambitious tyrant over all right principalities, and patron of the diabolic *fede*'. He told them that the only terms which he would offer them was that 'they should render me the fort, and yield their selves to my will for life or death'.

The two officers then returned to the fort, and after a further exchange of fire between the two armies, Colonel Don Sebastian agreed to surrender at mercy next day. Next morning, Grey drew up his army in battle array in front of the fort, and Don Sebastian came out with his chief officers, who laid down their flags and weapons at Grey's feet. 'Then put I in certain bands', wrote Grey to Elizabeth, 'who straight fell to execution. There were six hundred slain . . . Those that I gave life unto I have bestowed upon the captains and gentlemen whose service hath well deserved', for ransom. Grey thanked God for having given the Queen this great victory, for his only loss during the two-day siege had been one officer killed.[34]

Grey's report was supplemented by letters which two officers in his army wrote to Walsingham on 11 and 14 November. They stated that all the Irish men and women in the fort were hanged, and over four hundred Italians, Spaniards and Basques put to the sword. Twenty or thirty captains and other men were spared and set free, so that they could report in Spain and Italy the poverty and infidelity of their Irish associates.[35] There was an Irish Catholic priest, and an English and an Irish layman, in the fort who had come from Spain with Sanders. They were saved from the initial slaughter on 9 November to be dealt with as traitors. They were taken to a nearby blacksmith, who was ordered to break their arms and legs with his hammer as a form of torture. Two days later, after a summary court martial, they were executed.[36]

The twenty or thirty captains who were set free told a different story in Spain and Italy from what the English officers had hoped. Soon it was being reported in all the Catholic countries in Europe that the garrison at Smerwick had surrendered after being promised their lives, and that the English heretics had shamefully broken the surrender terms and massacred their prisoners.[37] It was the same allegation that the Protestants had made when the Spaniards killed the defenders of Haarlem after their surrender. If the defenders of Fort del Oro were promised their lives, the detailed report which Grey wrote to Elizabeth of his conversation with Don Sebastian and the other two officers was a complete fabrication, which is unlikely, but not impossible.

Edmund Spenser was already a well-known poet at the age of thirty-two; but as his poetry did not bring in a great deal of money, he had obtained the post of secretary to Lord Grey through the influence of his great friend, Philip Sidney. Spenser went with Grey to Smerwick, and when he wrote his *View of the present state of Ireland* in 1596, he refuted the charge against Grey of having broken his word to the defenders of Fort del Oro, and gave what is basically the same version which Grey wrote to Elizabeth, though it differs in some details. According to Spenser, Grey asked Don Sebastian if he could show him his commission from either the Pope or the King of Spain; and when Don Sebastian said that he had no commission, Grey said that it would dishonour the Queen if he were to negotiate with such 'rascals', and he would only accept their surrender at mercy.

It is perhaps significant that Spenser not only denied that Grey was guilty of a deliberate breach of faith, but, as an alternative possibility, that 'at the least he did put them in hope' of life.[38] If neither Grey nor any subordinate officer held out any hope at all to Don Sebastian, it is difficult to see why six hundred men in a fortress should have surrendered to eight hundred besiegers, who would certainly have lost more than one officer killed if they had been compelled to take the fort by storm; unless the explanation is that Don Sebastian, realising that he himself as a wealthy gentleman would be reserved for ransom, was prepared to run the risk that his soldiers would be massacred in the hope of saving his own life; but, though Sanders and other Catholics accused him of cowardice and treachery, there is no real evidence to support the view of some eminent modern historians that he arranged with Grey that his men should be slaughtered so that none of them would survive to reveal his treachery.[39]

Elizabeth wrote to Grey, congratulating him on his success at Smerwick. Although her letter as usual, was written by a secretary, she added a passage in her own hand, saying that she was glad that Grey had been the instrument of God's glory when the Almighty had shown His strength by giving victory to one of her weak sex. But she criticised Grey for having spared the lives of the Spanish commander and the wealthy prisoners, instead of leaving her to decide if any of them should be saved; for it would have been a greater deterrent to any other men who might think of engaging in 'so wicked an enterprise' if the leaders as well as the rank-and-file had been put to death.[40] There seems at first sight to be a contradiction between this letter and Camden's statement that while Elizabeth realised that the slaughter of the prisoners was necessary, she wished that it had not been done;[41] but it is perfectly possible that in later years she changed her mind and regretted that the prisoners had been killed, in view of the criticism which it had aroused abroad.

One man who did not protest about the killing of the prisoners at Smerwick was Don Bernardino de Mendoza, for the ambassador persisted in maintaining that if there were any Spaniards in Ireland, King Philip knew nothing about it and that it was nothing to do with him. On several occasions Elizabeth complained to Mendoza about the Spanish intervention in Ireland. Mendoza denied this, and referred to the Englishmen who were fighting with King Philip's rebels in the Netherlands; he told her that he knew this, because he had fought against them himself.[42]

Sometimes their discussions became heated. When they spoke together at Whitehall on 6 April 1580, before reinforcements were sent to Smerwick, Elizabeth told Mendoza that she had heard that fifteen Spaniards had joined the Irish rebels in a fort in Ireland. Mendoza replied that if her subjects continued to intervene in the Netherlands, she would soon see not fifteen Spaniards but many thousands of them, and so near too that she would not have time to repent of what she had done.[43]

The government in Ireland adopted a policy which became recognised as the only way in which a revolt by the Irish could be defeated: the crops throughout the whole district were destroyed in order to starve the rebels into surrender. The rebels themselves had already done a great deal of damage, for they had burned the houses and farms of the English colonists in Munster; and the English soldiers now completed the work. From Cashel to Dingle, a distance of nearly a hundred miles, every cottage and all the corn was burned.[44] This defeated the rebellion, and started a famine which continued for some years after the rebels had submitted. Spenser wrote about the terrible effects of the famine in a province which had previously been a rich country full of corn and cattle, though he believed that the Irish had brought this well-deserved punishment on themselves. 'Out of every corner of the wood and glens they came creeping forth upon their hands, for their legs could not bear them', to eat the corpses of the animals lying dead in the fields; after this source of food had gone, they opened the graves in the churchyards to eat the corpses of the dead human beings. 'In all that war there perished not many by the sword, but all by the extremity of famine, which they themselves had wrought'.[45]

In April 1581 Elizabeth decided to offer an amnesty to nearly every rebel who submitted, including the Earl of Desmond, with only a handful of exceptions for those who had committed particularly atrocious murders.[46] Her officials in Ireland did not like this. 'If the proclamation and general pardon come over, it will do great hurt', wrote Grey to Walsingham, and he wrote nearly as forcibly to Elizabeth herself.[47] Andrew Trollope wrote to Walsingham that 'every chief rebel's pardon is a hundred men's deaths'. He thought that the Irish had been too much trusted, favoured and preferred. 'The Irishmen, except the walled towns, are not Christians, ay well or human creatures, but heathen, or rather savage, and brute beasts'[48] Sir William Gerard, the Lord Chancellor of Ireland, had suggested to Walsingham already in 1577 that the only satisfactory solution of the Irish problem was to 'subject the whole Irishry to the sword', so that the potentially fertile soil could be cultivated by Englishmen, whose skills and hard work could make Ireland a profitable land after all the Irish had been exterminated.[49]

Sir Warham St Leger, a tough soldier, had disapproved as much as anyone of Elizabeth's offer of amnesty to the rebels;[50] but he was worried at the consequences of the famine in Munster, for in March 1582 he estimated that at least thirty thousand people had died of hunger during the last six months. He wrote to Elizabeth that this would cause 'four great inconveniences': many poor innocent people would die; it would lead to the decay of the towns; Elizabeth would lose revenue; and it would cause a new revolt throughout the whole country.[51]

The scattered remnants of the rebels were hunted down. Sanders was pursued through the woods, but though his chalice and vestments were found and his servant captured and executed, he himself always escaped. In the spring of 1581 he died of dysentery in the woods. The government troops, and the Irish who now joined them in hope of pardon, came even closer to catching the Earl of Desmond; but he too always managed to escape until November 1583, when five Irishmen, who hated him and were collaborating with the English, found him sleeping in a wood, and murdered him.

---- ✦⧽ 22 ⧼✦ ----

THE JESUITS

OR the Irish, the Spanish units which landed in the Kerry Peninsula
were the vanguard of an army which was coming to liberate them from
foreign oppression; for the English, they were the spearhead of the
international Catholic attempt, using Ireland as a springboard, to reconquer
England for Popery. The English Protestants were also aware that the blow
might be struck through Scotland as well as through Ireland. This made
Burghley, Walsingham and all Elizabeth's counsellors determined not to
weaken the hold which Elizabeth had exercised over Scotland since 1560.
'Scotland is the postern gate to any mischief or peril that may befall this
realm', wrote Walsingham. 'It will therefore behove Her Majesty to look well
to it'.[1]

But Elizabeth was lukewarm about the Scottish alliance. She did not like
Puritans and Presbyterians, and she did not like rebels who revolted against
their sovereign. After she had been persuaded to recognise James VI as the
lawful King of Scots, she had conscientious scruples as to how far she might
properly go in interfering in the internal affairs of his realm; and she did not
wish to quarrel with France, or to bear the expense of sending an army into
Scotland. Walsingham and Leicester had succeeded in dissuading her from a
violent rupture with Morton after the Reedswire incident; but they could not
persuade her to agree to Morton's proposal that England and Scotland
should sign a new treaty for an anti-Catholic alliance.[2]

Henry III and Catherine de Medici had virtually written off Scotland, just
as Elizabeth had given up hope of ever recovering Calais; but Mary Queen of
Scots's cousins the Guises were still very interested in Scottish affairs, for
they were as conscious as Walsingham that Scotland was the back door to
England, and was the place where they could best advance Mary's interests
and the Catholic faith. The old Cardinal of Lorraine had died in 1574, but
the younger generation of Guises, the children of Francis Duke of Guise,
were there in strength – Henry Duke of Guise and his three brothers, Charles
Duke of Mayenne, Louis the new Cardinal of Lorraine, and Francis of

Lorraine. There was also a sister, the formidable Catherine Duchess of Montpensier, who had married Louis of Bourbon, Duke of Montpensier. Although her husband was related to Henry of Navarre and the Prince of Condé, and was sympathetic to the Huguenots, Catherine was a ferocious Catholic and a devoted partisan of her brothers.

Guise had close links with the Scottish Catholic refugees in Paris, and they laid their plans for winning Scotland as a prelude to winning England. They realised that they must act with great caution, and that it would be premature even to work for the grant of religious toleration to the Catholics in Scotland. But they encouraged and helped Jesuits and other Catholic priests to go secretly to Scotland, at the risk of their lives, to proselytise among potential converts to Catholicism, and they entered into secret contacts with the Earl of Huntly and other Scottish Catholic lords, and with Protestants who did not like Morton, including some of the former 'Queen's lords' who had accepted James VI as King.

In March 1578 the Earl of Atholl denounced Morton as an over-ambitious subject, and convened a council of notables who removed him from the office of Regent and decided that the King, who would be aged twelve in June, was old enough to rule himself. They placed him in the custody of Lord Erskine, and excluded Morton and his supporters from power. Elizabeth was angry when she heard the news, and sent an envoy to protest to James VI's new counsellors against the exclusion of Morton. She ordered Lord Hunsdon to prepare an army at Berwick to go to Morton's assistance; but before she had decided what action to take, the young Earl of Mar carried out a new *coup d'état* in Scotland on 26 April which brought Morton back to power. He did not resume the title of Regent, but in practice he exercised all his previous authority.[3]

Guise and the refugees in Paris tried again. Their most hopeful course was to attempt to influence the young King as he grew up. James's cousin, Esmé Stuart, the Sieur of Aubigny, was a charming man in his late thirties who had spent most of his life in France. He had always been a Catholic. The Guises now sent him to Scotland, where he became a Protestant, probably at the instigation of the Guises as a political trick. He became very intimate with James VI, and soon developed a homosexual relationship with him. This was probably something which the Guises had not foreseen, and an unexpected bonus for them. D'Aubigny became friendly with Lord Ochiltre's son, Captain James Stewart, whose half-sister had married John Knox. Although James Stewart had fought for the Protestants in the Netherlands, he now worked closely with D'Aubigny. He too became the homosexual partner of James VI, who created D'Aubigny Earl of Lennox and James Stewart Earl of Arran, and appointed Lennox to be Lord Chancellor of Scotland.

On 31 December 1580 Lennox accused Morton in the Council chamber of having been an accessory to the murder of the King's father fourteen years before. During these fourteen years nearly every prominent Scotsman who had fallen foul of the government of the day had been accused of having participated in Darnley's murder, and now it was Morton's turn to be brought to justice for the crime for which he had executed several of his rivals. He was imprisoned in Edinburgh Castle while he awaited his trial.[4]

Elizabeth and her Council interpreted Morton's arrest as a blow struck at the English party in Scotland, and as the first step by the Papists to implement their plans to conquer Scotland and England; and they wanted to save Morton in order to show that Elizabeth could protect her supporters. The messengers riding 'in post' had hardly brought the news of his arrest to Whitehall before Elizabeth on 6 January ordered Randolph to set out at once for Edinburgh to demand his release and reinstatement, and the banishment of Lennox from Scotland. She ordered Hunsdon to prepare an army of 2,500 men at Berwick to be ready to cross the Border into Scotland if the Scots did not accede to Randolph's demands. She also sent ships to patrol the Scottish coast to intercept any communications between Lennox and Guise and the refugees in France.

The Scottish Privy Council firmly rejected Randolph's demands, and moved Morton to Dumbarton Castle, where it would be more difficult for Randolph to engineer his escape. Randolph discovered that the situation was more serious than he had realised. He was sure that if an English army invaded Scotland, not only would Morton be immediately put to death, but the great majority of the nation would rally to resist the invaders, though the ministers of the Church of Scotland were still loyal to Morton and strongly opposed to Lennox. Randolph therefore turned to the Douglases, who were Morton's kinsmen and for the last sixty years had been the agents of Henry VIII and Elizabeth. The head of the family, the Earl of Angus, agreed with Randolph to organise a plot to assassinate Lennox and the Earls of Argyll and Montrose, who had always been sympathetic to Mary Queen of Scots. Then they would get hold of the King, and release Morton and reinstate him and the English party in power. Randolph advised Elizabeth to refrain from military intervention and to leave it to Angus and his fellow-conspirators, though Hunsdon believed that the only hope was to send in the English army.

Randolph and Walsingham did not find it easy to persuade Elizabeth to authorise Angus's plot. She eventually agreed that the plotters might 'surprise' Lennox, but only on condition that it was not done in the King's presence, so as to avoid any risk that he might be harmed. She had been genuinely shocked when Riccio was murdered in the presence of Mary Queen of Scots, and would have no repetition of this flagrant affront to a sovereign. If she knew that when the plotters spoke of 'surprising' Lennox, they meant assassinating him, she and her counsellors preferred not to talk about it; and she does not appear to have been told that Argyll and Montrose were to be killed as well as Lennox.[5]

On 20 March Randolph heard that one of the plotters had betrayed their plans to the Scottish government, and that 'whatsoever we intended by my Lord of Angus is discovered'.[6] The plotter's confession incriminated Randolph, who escaped with Angus to Berwick. Randolph now agreed that military intervention was the only way of saving Morton, and joined with Walsingham and all Elizabeth's counsellors in urging her to assemble an army of nine or ten thousand men and to invade Scotland as soon as possible. Elizabeth agreed, and on 31 March ordered Hunsdon to muster the army and cross the Border; but four days later she changed her mind, after the French ambassador Mauvissière had protested to her about the reports which he had received that she was planning to invade Scotland. On 4 April she told Hunsdon not to enlist more men, but to discharge all except 500 of the force of 2,500 which had been waiting at Berwick since January. Walsingham wrote to Hunsdon that though all the Council advised Elizabeth to invade, 'she liked not of it, by reason of the charges that the necessity must needs ensue'.[7] On 9 April Mauvissière wrote to Henry III that he had persuaded Elizabeth to leave Morton to his fate.

On 1 June Morton was brought to trial in Edinburgh. He denied that he had been a party to Darnley's death, though he admitted that he had known that Bothwell intended to murder him. He was found guilty, and beheaded next day by a mechanical instrument operated by pulleys which was called 'the maiden' and which closely resembled the instrument invented two hundred years later in France by Dr Guillotin, known ever since as the guillotine.

After Morton's death, Walsingham and Elizabeth's agents in Scotland continued to work for the overthrow of Lennox and his faction. Angus got into contact with other lords and hatched another plot. He offered to obtain the support of every lord in Scotland for Elizabeth if she would undertake to pay 4,000 crowns to every earl and 2,000 crowns to every baron who joined an insurrection against Lennox. Elizabeth said that she might pay them the money, but could not definitely promise to do so; she eventually gave Angus £1,000, but no more. In view of her grudging attitude, only a few of the Scottish lords joined the plot which Walsingham organised with the Earls of Gowrie and Mar and others whom Elizabeth's ambassador in Scotland, Robert Bowes, called 'persons well affected to Her Majesty and the cause'.[8] In August 1582 James VI was kidnapped and taken to Ruthven Castle, and Lennox was overthrown, in the operation which became known as the Raid of Ruthven.

Elizabeth sent an envoy to James VI to advise him to trust the lords who had taken him to Ruthven Castle and to have Lennox and Arran tried and executed as traitors; but she would not act on the advice of Walsingham and Bowes to pay large pensions to the Scottish lords to win them over to her party. When Walsingham urged her to allow £10,000 for this purpose, she agreed to give £100, and followed this with another grant of £100 some time later. Walsingham feared the worst. 'I fear Her Majesty shall learn by dangerous effects to see the error of her own judgement', he wrote to Bowes in February 1583.[9]

Lennox left Scotland and returned to France, but in August 1583 James VI, who was now aged seventeen, escaped from the lords of the English party, and Arran overthrew them by a *coup d'état*. In October Gowrie was executed for high treason for organising the Raid of Ruthven. Elizabeth took no action, and decided to abandon her attempt to maintain an English party in Scotland. This did not turn out as badly for her as her counsellors expected, for James VI did not wish to do anything to offend her and impair his chances of becoming King of England after her death. She had solved the Scottish problem by muddling through.

Catholic activity threatened Elizabeth and the Protestant cause in England itself as well as in Ireland and Scotland. The English Catholic refugees, with their colleges at Douai and Rome and their contacts in Paris and Madrid, trained missionaries to go to England to maintain the morale of the Catholics there and secretly to win converts for the Catholic faith. The leaders of the English Catholics abroad after Sanders's death were William Allen and Robert Parsons, two priests who had studied at Oxford in the Protestant university during the first decade of Elizabeth's reign but had never sincerely conformed, and went abroad to carry on their fight for the Catholic Church. They directed the Catholic resistance movement in England and abroad from their headquarters in Rheims. Most of the priests whom they sent to England were Jesuits, the members of the Society of Jesus which Ignatius of Loyola had founded forty years before.[10]

After the rift between Elizabeth and Philip II over the property-seizures in 1568, Allen and Parsons and their followers based their hopes on a Spanish invasion of England, when Philip's navy and army would come as liberators to restore the true faith in their homeland. Like so many other opposition groups during the whole of recorded history, from the days of ancient Rome to the Second World War, they hoped to see the government of their country overthrown by the armies of the national enemy. Their government called them traitors; they themselves believed that they were better patriots than the government supporters.

Elizabeth continued to treat the Catholics in her kingdom comparatively mildly. The punishment of six months' imprisonment for celebrating Mass, and a fine of 100 marks (£66.13s.4d.) for attending Mass, for the first offence, rising to life imprisonment for both celebrant and participant for the third offence, was no light matter; but the law was not rigorously enforced in practice,[11] and was in any case less severe than the punishment of burning alive which the Catholics, when they were in power, inflicted on the Protestants, and which the Protestants inflicted on Anabaptists. Elizabeth drew a clear distinction, at least in theory, between Catholics who merely went illegally to Mass and those who published the Pope's bull which excommunicated and deposed her and absolved her subjects from their duty of obedience. This was high treason, and those found guilty were hanged, drawn and quartered; suspects were arrested and tortured to force them to disclose information about their treasonable activities or to admit their guilt.

In 1574 Allen sent three priests to England. They were the first of over a hundred missionaries who travelled secretly through the country contacting the Catholics in London, Northamptonshire, Lancashire and elsewhere. They were sheltered by the members of their secret congregations, especially by the aristocratic families who had remained true to the old religion, who hid them in their houses, sometimes in the secret 'priest holes' which can still be seen today. A few were never caught, but most were eventually tracked down and arrested by the very efficient security service which Walsingham directed, with his agents, informers and *agents provocateurs* who infiltrated the illegal Catholic organisations in England and at their headquarters in France, the Netherlands and Italy.

In 1580 two Jesuits, Edmund Campion and Parsons himself, arrived, and from then on the missionaries were mostly Jesuits. Parsons, after spending more than a year in England, escaped to France. Campion was arrested in Berkshire, and taken to the Tower. He was repeatedly examined by Leicester, Bedford and other counsellors, and once by Elizabeth herself; and after he had been held for nearly five months in the Tower, and tortured three times on the rack, he was hanged, drawn and quartered on 1 December 1581. His activities, arrest and execution were widely publicised by the government.[12]

When the Jesuits and the other missionary priests were examined, they denied that they were traitors and maintained that the English Catholics were loyal subjects and would never support any foreign Prince against their Queen and country, whatever some English Catholic refugees abroad might say. On the other side, Elizabeth and her government always denied that they persecuted Catholics because of their religion, and claimed that the only Catholics who were imprisoned, tortured and executed were those who had committed high treason against their Queen. Francis Bacon wrote that Elizabeth, 'not liking to make windows into men's hearts and secret thoughts', punished them only if they challenged 'Her Majesty's supreme power' and for 'maintaining and extolling a foreign jurisdiction'.[13]

But in practice, it became more and more difficult to maintain this distinction. There were some Catholics who wished only to exercise their religion and were loyal to their Protestant Queen; but many of them, at least in sympathy, were on the Catholic against the Protestant side in the international religious struggle, were saddened when they heard of a Protestant victory in Scotland, France and the Netherlands, and rejoiced at the news that the Catholics in Paris, by their timely action on St Bartholomew's Eve, had forestalled the plans of the heretics to massacre the Catholics. It is not surprising that the Protestants believed that the Catholics supported the policy of their spiritual father the Pope, and only denied it when they were in prison in England in order to avoid incurring the penalty for their treason.

The interrogators therefore asked the imprisoned priests and the laymen who had sheltered them whether they believed that the Queen should be obeyed as Queen despite the Papal bull of 1570, and whether, if the Pope sent an army to invade the realm, they would support the Pope or the Queen. The Catholics called this 'the Bloody Question', and denounced it as a trick to trap them into either confessing to treason or repudiating God's Vicar; but for Elizabeth and her government it was a very pertinent question.

After several Catholic martyrs had died for giving the wrong answer to the Bloody Question, the Jesuits in Rome, with the Pope's consent, devised an answer to it. They said that the bull of 1570 had been issued at the time of the rising in the North and was no longer in operation, and that they would therefore obey the Queen until the Pope renewed the bull.[14] Elizabeth's government did not consider that this was a satisfactory position for the English Catholics to adopt.

The Jesuits and their flock were justified in claiming that the missionary priests had not come to England with the intention of committing high treason, and that their only purpose was to minister to the English Catholics and make converts to the Catholic faith. But this maintained the Catholic Church in England as an organisation which could act against Elizabeth and overthrow her when the right time came. In 1581 the Puritans in Parliament introduced a bill which made it high treason to convert any of the Queen's subjects to the Romish religion in order to withdraw them from their allegiance to the Queen. Elizabeth reluctantly gave her royal assent to the bill in a modified form, and to other provisions which increased the penalties for attending Mass and for failure to attend the lawful church services.[15]

The Catholics who were convicted of high treason in Elizabeth's reign, and sentenced to be hanged, drawn and quartered, all endured the terrible punishment with great courage. Campion, in one of the last letters that he wrote before he was captured, claimed that the sufferings of the Catholics had eclipsed those of the Protestants in Mary's reign. 'Of their martyrs they brag no more now. For it is now come to pass that, for a few apostates and cobblers of theirs burned, we have bishops, lords, knights, the old nobility . . . and of the inferior sort innumerable, either martyred at once or by consuming prisonment dying daily'.[16] The Protestant readers of Foxe's *Book of Martyrs* did not see it in this light; but when Philip II read Mendoza's report about the execution of the Catholics in England, he replied that he both grieved over their sufferings and rejoiced at the constancy with which they had borne them, and that it proved how right he was to refuse to grant religious toleration to the Protestants in the Netherlands.[17]

Relations between Philip and Elizabeth grew worse and worse. Mendoza at last succeeded in persuading Elizabeth to release Guaras from the Tower and to allow him to leave England in May 1579 after he had been held in prison for nineteen months;[18] but there was more trouble when Philip found himself in a position to do a tit-for-tat to Elizabeth. In September 1580 she sent Daniel Rogers, who had been on several diplomatic missions to the Protestants in the Netherlands, to contact the German Lutheran Princes and to discuss with them the possibility of their joining in a general alliance of the Protestant powers. Rogers was seized on his way through Cleves by Captain Schenck, a commander of mercenaries who was in Philip II's pay. Schenck refused to release him until he had paid a large ransom, accused him of being a spy, and threatened him with torture. Elizabeth sent an envoy to the Regent of the Netherlands, Alexander Farnese, Duke of Parma, the son of Margaret of Parma, who had succeeded Don John of Austria after Don John's death in 1578. She protested at Rogers's detention and demanded his release; but Parma referred the matter to Philip, who ordered him not to release Rogers, but to retain him as a prisoner in Schenck's custody until further notice.

Elizabeth became increasingly indignant, and warned Parma that if Rogers were not released she might take reprisals against Mendoza. Parma wrote her a most courteous letter, in which, after paying her a number of compliments, he said that Rogers was being held while certain suspicious matters concerning him were being investigated, and that he was sure that she would not inflict any inconvenience on an entirely innocent man like Mendoza, who was an official ambassador from King Philip at her court, whereas Rogers, a person of lower rank than Mendoza, was only her envoy on his way to visit a third party, the German Princes. At last, Parma ordered Schenck to reduce the ransom for which he was asking; but Rogers was not finally set free until the summer of 1584, after more than three years' imprisonment.[19]

One of the excuses which Schenck and Parma made for detaining Rogers for so long was that he had in his possession a family tree of the Portuguese royal family, and that they therefore suspected that he was being sent as an English agent to Portugal;[20] for Portugal had now become another arena of conflict between Philip and Elizabeth. When King Sebastian was killed at the Battle of Al Kasr el Kebir, his nearest surviving relatives and heirs were the children and descendants of his great-grandfather King Emanuel I. The next heir to the throne was King Emanuel's seventh child Prince Henry, who had entered the Church and become a cardinal, and he duly succeeded to the throne at the age of sixty-seven, but everyone realised that the 'Cardinal-King' had not long to live, and intrigues began at once as to who should become King after his death.

King Emanuel's daughter Isabel had married Charles V and was Philip II's mother, and Philip claimed the throne. So did Don Antonio; his father Luiz, Duke of Beja, was Emanuel's son, and his mother was a Jewish girl who was Luiz's mistress. She afterwards converted to Christianity and became a nun; but did she secretly marry Luiz before she became a nun? If she did, her illegitimate son Don Antonio would have been legitimised by the subsequent marriage of his parents and would be entitled to succeed to the throne. There were a number of other claimants, including King Emanuel's granddaughter Catherine Duchess of Braganza. A more far-fetched claim was put forward by Catherine de Medici as the descendant of the thirteenth-century King Alfonso III.

Philip set to work to win over the Portuguese nobles by large bribes and propaganda; but the majority of the notables favoured the Duchess of Braganza. Don Antonio had very little support among the nobility or the ecclesiastical hierarchy, but was very popular with the artisans and the peasants; and Catherine de Medici put forward her remoter claim with great determination, as she did not wish to see Spain acquire Portugal and its territories in Asia, Africa and America.

The Cardinal-King died in January 1580, and Philip began assembling a navy and army ready to invade Portugal. He persuaded the Portuguese Council of Notables to acknowledge him as their King, after he had promised to preserve Portugal with its overseas territories as an independent kingdom governed by Portuguese counsellors and joined to Spain only by the unity of the crowns in his own person; but Don Antonio was proclaimed King in Lisbon, and he called on his supporters to resist Philip. He appealed to Elizabeth for help. She sent him a message of support for his struggle to maintain the independence of Portugal from Spanish domination, and urged his followers to unite behind one King in opposition to Philip and not to split their forces by supporting several of the rival claimants. She also sent an envoy to tell Don Antonio that she was grateful for his friendship, but that if his claim to the throne was unjustified, about which she could not comment, she would be unable to support him and hoped that he would not pursue it.[21]

Philip ordered Alva, at the age of seventy-two, to invade Portugal, and he quickly overran the whole kingdom. Antonio escaped to France, and appealed for help to both Elizabeth and Catherine de Medici. Elizabeth replied that she sympathised with him, but could not risk war with Philip by giving him military or financial assistance; but Catherine de Medici was prepared to help him, and agreed to support his claim to Portugal in return for his undertaking to cede Brazil to her.[22]

It did not take Philip long to dash Antonio's hopes of gaining control of Ceuta, Tangier, Majorca and the Molucca Islands in the East Indies; but Antonio persuaded the island of Terceira in the Azores to declare for him, though the garrison in St Michael's Island held out for Philip. Both Philip and Catherine de Medici prepared a naval expedition to take possession of the islands 850 miles from the Portuguese coast. Catherine asked Elizabeth to send warships to join the expedition. Elizabeth was reluctant to become involved. In view of her bad relations with Philip and his intervention in Ireland, she was ready to do him an ill turn, and it would be useful for Drake and her seamen on their Atlantic voyages if the Azores were in friendly hands; but she did not wish to become involved in open war with Spain, and knew that Don Antonio and Catherine de Medici, and not she, would be the chief beneficiaries if the expedition were successful. She instructed Cobham, her ambassador in France, to offer to send some ships if Henry III would give an undertaking that if her intervention led to war with Spain and the seizure of the English merchants' goods in Philip's territories, he would compensate her for the loss of the goods out of the proceeds of the Spanish property which he would seize in France. She explained to Cobham that she felt obliged to insist on this safeguard, because as Spain and France were both Catholic states, the Pope might induce them to come to an agreement and leave her to take the brunt of Philip's revenge.[23]

Henry III and Catherine de Medici did not accept Elizabeth's offer, and no English warships took part in the expedition which sailed from Belle-Île-en-Mer on 16 June 1582. It consisted of 55 ships carrying 5,000 soldiers, of whom 1,200 were Portuguese led by Don Antonio, and most of the rest French, including many Huguenots from La Rochelle; but there were seven English transport ships carrying French soldiers. They reached the Azores after a four-weeks' voyage; but two days later, a Spanish fleet of 98 ships and 15,765 men arrived from Lisbon and defeated the French fleet. The Spaniards beheaded the nobles whom they captured and hanged all the other prisoners over the age of seventeen.[24] When Cobham expressed his sympathies to Catherine de Medici, she bitterly reproached Elizabeth, and attributed the defeat to Elizabeth's failure to send warships to take part in the expedition.[25]

Don Antonio spent the next few years alternately in France and England, trying to persuade Catherine de Medici and Elizabeth to give him financial aid. Elizabeth refused Philip's demand for his extradition, and gave him enough to maintain himself and a small staff, but would not finance him on a large scale. His intelligence service was useful to the English government, for his agents in Portugal, Spain and France often sent him information about Philip's military and diplomatic plans which he passed on to Walsingham. Philip's agents occasionally tried to murder him, but were unsuccessful.[26]

❧ 23 ❧

INTERVENTION IN THE NETHERLANDS

ON 15 March 1580 Philip II issued a proclamation. It stated that William of Nassau, Prince of Orange, was the chief disturber of the state of Christendom, and particularly of the Netherlands, and that consequently the King authorised all men to fall on him and put him out of the world as a public pest; and the King would pay a reward to anyone who did so. In June, the Duke of Parma ordered the governors of all the provinces of the Netherlands to publish the proclamation.[1] It shocked the Protestants everywhere; here was the King of Spain openly inciting the murder of a prominent Protestant leader. In England it was cited as a proof that the Catholics would try to assassinate the Queen, and a reason for suppressing them more ruthlessly.

On 18 March 1582 William was shot at in Antwerp and wounded in the cheek by a Biscayan who was employed as a cashier by a Spanish merchant in the city. His surgeons found it difficult to stop the bleeding, and it was not until six weeks later that William was out of danger. The Biscayan's employer was implicated in the plot, and other conspirators were arrested. One of them confessed that he had been ordered to carry out the assassination by Philip's secretary, who had promised the murderers a reward of 80,000 crowns.

William asked the authorities in Antwerp to spare the life of the Biscayan, but the councillors insisted that both he and his employer should be executed by being torn apart by four horses. At William's insistence, they agreed that the men should suffer the more merciful death of strangulation, which was carried out in the public square in Antwerp.[2]

Parma was informed that William had died, and he issued a proclamation calling on all the people of the Netherlands to submit now that God had been pleased to open the way for this by the death of the Prince of Orange.[3] When Mary Queen of Scots heard about the assassination attempt, she smuggled out a letter from her prison to Mendoza. 'Pray God', she wrote on 6 April, 'that He may grant just vengeance against the Prince of Orange and all his fellows, the enemies of religion and public peace'. On 22 April she wrote again to Mendoza: 'I have received intelligence of the danger in which the

Prince of Orange recently was in because of the great loss of blood from a wound under the eye. I praise God for this, seeing the advantage which may accrue to His Church and to the King my brother, who is now its principal protector'.[4]

Her cousin the Duke of Guise was planning a private expedition to release her and restore the Catholic faith in the British Isles. At the beginning of May 1582 a very secret meeting was held at the house of the Papal Nuncio in Paris, which was attended by the Nuncio, Guise, Dr Allen, and the three leading Scottish Catholic refugees in France – James Beaton, Archbishop of Glasgow and the Jesuits Creighton and Hay. Guise proposed that the Pope should raise an army of 6,000 Italian and 4,000 German mercenaries and volunteers who would sail from Spanish ports to Scotland; they would be provided with every assistance by King Philip, but, like the expedition to Smerwick, would march under the Papal banner as the Pope's army, not Philip's. After landing in Scotland they would gain control of the castles of Edinburgh and Dumbarton by collusion with James VI's officials. Meanwhile Guise himself would lead a force of 4,000 volunteers and mercenaries who would land in Sussex and distract Elizabeth's attention to prevent her from sending her armies against the invading force in Scotland. A few days later, Guise, the Nuncio, Allen and the Scots had another secret meeting at the house of Tassis, the Spanish ambassador in Paris, and put their proposals to him.[5] Neither the English ambassador, Cobham, nor any of Walsingham's agents in France discovered about these secret meetings and Guise's plans.

Tassis reported to Philip, but as usual the King was cautious. He consulted Cardinal Granvelle, who since his resignation as Margaret of Parma's minister in Brussels had been living in semi-retirement and was now in Madrid. Granvelle had no enthusiasm for the plans of the younger Catholic zealots. He advised Philip that if the planned invasion of England and Scotland were to fail, it would 'cause the utter ruin of the Scottish and English Catholics without any hope of resuscitation'; and there was no guarantee that if Guise conquered England and Scotland he would not hand them over to the King of France.[6] Spanish statesmen of the older generation like Granvelle still believed that the House of Valois was a greater enemy than the heretical Queen of England. Philip persuaded the Pope to reject Guise's proposal.

Elizabeth, on the other hand, realised that the situation had changed since the days when Granvelle was in his prime, and that Spain, not France, was now the enemy. The new element in the situation was the 'Spanish Main' – the waters of the Caribbean and the Western Atlantic – where Drake and other English privateers could attack the Spanish treasure-ships and return with booty which Elizabeth would not give up, even if this meant war with Spain, which she was very eager to avoid.

Mendoza, in his talks with Elizabeth, reminded her that she owed her crown and her life to Philip, who had saved her in Mary's reign, and accused her of ingratitude. Elizabeth said that she would always be grateful to Philip for having protected her in her sister's reign, but that after she became Queen he had abandoned her by making a peace with France which allowed the French to retain Calais; and he had left her alone to deal with the French in Scotland. Afterwards, he had allowed Alva to seize English property in the Netherlands, and he had assisted her rebels in Ireland. It was he, not she, who was responsible for the deterioration in their relations.[7]

If Spain was a potential enemy, it was essential to have France as an ally. This made Elizabeth more reluctant than ever to help the French Huguenots. In February 1580 Henry of Navarre discovered that a Catholic nobleman had planned to murder or kidnap him when he was out hunting, and Henry made this the excuse to begin the seventh civil war. In May he captured the town of Cahors in the south by a daring attack, but then found that he had no money to carry on the war. Elizabeth refused to lend him money with which he could hire German mercenaries, and urged him to make peace at once, and not to appear to be rebelling against his Prince. At the same time she assured Henry III that Henry of Navarre and the Huguenots were not rebels but were only defending themselves against the attacks of the Catholics.[8] Henry of Navarre was therefore compelled, after a few months, to make a peace by which he retained Cahors but won no better terms than before for the Huguenots.

Elizabeth's new policy led to a complete change in her attitude towards the Netherlands. She now urged Henry III to send troops to help his brother and to contribute to the cost of the operations. But Henry III refused to take any action against Philip II until Elizabeth married Anjou.[9] So Elizabeth found herself in the position, which would have been unthinkable a few years earlier, of financing by herself a French Prince's attempt to conquer the Netherlands. She could do this with a clear conscience, because though it was a sin for a people to revolt against their Prince, it was quite acceptable that a Prince should try to conquer another Prince's territory.

Elizabeth remained as hostile as ever to the Protestants of the Netherlands. 'Of late having some speech with Her Majesty of Low Country matters', wrote Wilson to Davison on 2 January 1579, 'I did find that Her Highness disliked the States greatly';[10] and this emotional antagonism grew stronger. She made no attempt to conciliate the States, and treated them throughout as troublesome inferiors whom she could order to adopt first one course and then the opposite one. Having threatened them with war in 1576 if they invited Anjou to become their ruler, she wrote to William of Orange on 6 February 1582, when Anjou was at last about to sail from England to the Netherlands, and warned him, in almost threatening language, to treat 'our dearest cousin the Duke of Anjou' with all honour, because she would regard any dishonour done to Anjou as being done to herself.[11]

William was in fact the strongest supporter of the alliance with Anjou; but many of his followers were far less enthusiastic. Anjou promised to uphold the Protestant religion in the Netherlands, and to grant religious toleration to both Protestants and Catholics; but though William succeeded with difficulty in persuading the States-General to agree to this, the local authorities in many of the Protestant provinces, particularly in Ghent, refused to grant toleration to the Catholics. The chief trouble was in Antwerp, where Anjou established his headquarters. The authorities agreed that Anjou himself and the members of his immediate entourage could attend Mass in private, but would not permit the Catholic officers of his army to do so.[12]

William had barely recovered from his wound, and from the death of his wife which immediately followed it, when Elizabeth began pressing him and the States-General to pay the interest due on the loan that she had made to them. She also protested about the difficulties which they were causing for Anjou. On 9 August 1582 she wrote to William that she was surprised that the people of the Netherlands should be so ungrateful to Anjou, a Prince to whom they owed so much, and that if Anjou, disgusted by their attitude, decided to leave and abandon the States to Philip's mercy, they would get no help from her. But she realised that William himself was the last person who could be blamed for the people's hostility to Anjou, and at the end of the formal letter, which her secretary had written, with its reproachful tone, she added a friendly note in her own hand about Anjou: 'Do not torment him too much'.[13] William assured her that he was doing all he could to persuade the States to accept and placate Anjou.[14]

In the Netherlands, the heroic mood of 1573 and 1574 was giving way to cynicism and selfishness. The leaders of the seventeen provinces were quarrelling with each other, with the States-General, and with the Council of State – the supreme executive body of the United Provinces – whose members were also engaged in personal feuds and intrigues. The soldiers in the army had not been paid their wages, and were threatening to mutiny. While the sea-beggars of Flushing continued to seize the ships and goods of foreign merchants who traded with the Spanish-occupied territories, many of the local Dutch and Flemish merchants were trading with the enemy. Fortunately for the States, the Spaniards, too, were in difficulties. They were short of money, and Parma's Spanish and Italian soldiers were threatening to mutiny unless they received their arrears of pay. The military operations were limited to periodic attempts to besiege towns. The States captured Eindhoven and Alost, but Parma took Tournai, where the defenders surrendered on honourable terms after a two-month siege.

The English volunteers in Norris's regiment complained bitterly that their wages were five months in arrears and that they were short of food and inadequately clothed during the cold winter weather. When they appealed to the local inhabitants, for whose freedom they were fighting, to help them in their distress, they found that many of them were reluctant to help. The English nearly mutinied in October 1582, when they heard that their colonel, Norris, had given a banquet at the English merchants' house in Antwerp, to which he had invited Anjou, William of Orange, the leading citizens of

Antwerp, and twenty-four of the most expensive courtesans of the city. When the English soldiers begged the people of Antwerp to provide them with food and shelter, the people told them to ask their colonel, who could afford to entertain Anjou, William, and the harlots so lavishly.[15]

Anjou became exasperated with the bickerings among the authorities at Antwerp, and with their refusal to allow his Catholic officers to go to Mass. In the end, he was persuaded by his officers to solve the problem by a military *coup*. He had an escort of 600 French soldiers in Antwerp, but he assembled a force of 4,000 French soldiers and Swiss mercenaries outside the town. On 17 January* 1583 he informed the authorities of Antwerp that he wished to ride out of the city with two hundred of his horsemen; but when the Kipdorf Gate was opened to allow him to go out, his troops outside the town rushed in, shouting 'The town is won!' and 'Long live the Mass!' The Burgomaster and City Council called on the people of Antwerp to resist, and the local militia took up arms. After seven or eight hundred men had been killed on both sides, the French were driven out of Antwerp, leaving some fourteen or fifteen hundred prisoners behind, including several lords and gentlemen. On the same day, a French force tried to seize Bruges, but the citizens refused to admit them, and the French withdrew when news arrived of their defeat at Antwerp. The people of Bruges celebrated, crying: 'Help, good Queen of England, help!'[16]

Anjou withdrew with his army to Düffel, some fifteen miles south of Antwerp. He tried to explain away the events at Antwerp as a regrettable incident for which one of his colonels was to blame; but the authorities at Antwerp issued a declaration denouncing Anjou and the French, referring to the Massacre of St Bartholomew, and announcing that in view of this new treachery they would no longer accept Anjou as their ruler. William of Orange, who was alarmed at the prospect of the people of the Netherlands finding themselves at war simultaneously with Spain and France, worked hard for a reconciliation; but the local inhabitants spontaneously took up arms against the French, prevented food supplies from being sent to Anjou's army, and cut the dikes in the country south of Antwerp to drown or drive out the French.[17]

Norris's English regiment was stationed near Antwerp, and Anjou ordered Norris to confine his men to camp and to take no part in any operations. But the English soldiers, hating Frenchmen and Papists, were very ready to believe that Anjou and his French Catholic officers had intended to carry out another St Bartholomew's massacre of the Protestants in Antwerp, and they at once joined the popular resistance. They manned the banks of the Scheldt

---

*Thanks to Anjou, Pope Gregory XIII's New Style calendar was introduced in the liberated territories of the Netherlands at Christmas 1582, where, as a correspondent wrote to Walsingham from Antwerp, they celebrated Christmas Day on 15 December. The 17 January 1583 in Antwerp was 7 January in England (see Preface, p. 11).

to prevent Anjou's forces from crossing the river and marching on Antwerp. This was a serious blow to Anjou, for his army was short of food on the south bank of the Scheldt, and could not reach the food supplies on the northern bank without fighting Norris's men. Anjou bitterly denounced Norris for having betrayed him, and declared that he was his greatest enemy.[18]

When Elizabeth heard about the events in the Netherlands, she immediately came down on Anjou's side. She sent an envoy to Anjou at Termonde to express her sympathy, and wrote indignant letters to the States-General, to William, and to Norris. She was particularly incensed with Norris for having joined the States against Anjou.[19] Norris barely troubled to apologise. 'Here are bruits cast out', he wrote to Walsingham, 'that grieve me not a little, that Her Majesty should be displeased with me, and misliked the course I had taken. I will not presume upon my own judgement, but when I understood that His Highness had attempted to make himself absolute master of ten or twelve of the chief towns in the country, that he had cried *Vive la messe!*, that our English troops were commanded to keep their houses and afterwards divers of them disarmed and slain, I thought it not for Her Majesty's service that I should have seconded any such enterprises'.[20] Another English official explained to Walsingham that it needed all Norris's efforts to prevent the English soldiers from attacking the French.[21]

Elizabeth ordered Norris to withdraw his troops from the Scheldt and to allow Anjou's forces to cross it to obtain victuals. Norris thereupon wrote to Walsingham that the Queen was misinformed if she thought that Anjou's troops across the river were starving, for in fact they had more provisions than he and his men had; and that as it would be harmful to the Queen's interests if he obeyed her orders, he intended to disregard them until he received confirmation that it was really her wish that he should withdraw from the Scheldt.[22] By this time, the authorities at Antwerp had written to Elizabeth giving her their side of the story, and William had also written to assure her that he would do his best to reconcile the States and Anjou. Before Elizabeth could send any further orders to Norris, the States had agreed to open negotiations for a settlement with Anjou, and in the meantime to send him food supplies and withdraw Norris's troops from the Scheldt.[23]

When Elizabeth sent an envoy to the States in March 1583, she had calmed down, and was adopting a more balanced attitude. She stated that if the French at Antwerp had committed mistakes, they had suffered the consequences, and that the States should remember that they could not resist the tyranny of the King of Spain without the support of some powerful foreign sovereign; they had accepted Anjou as their Prince, and should not now reject his well-meant efforts to reach a friendly settlement with them and to remedy their just grievances.[24] Eventually the States were reconciled to Anjou, after he had dismissed some of his French officers, who were made the scapegoats for the trouble at Antwerp, and had agreed to limit the number of troops who should be stationed in the towns of the Netherlands.

Parma tried to take advantage of the quarrel between the States and Anjou by urging the people of the Netherlands to accept King Philip's offer of amnesty and free themselves from the hated French.[25] The Protestants would not consider this offer as long as Philip refused to grant them religious toleration; but the Catholics in the south were increasingly tempted to accept, after the trouble with the French. In the summer of 1583 Parma captured Dunkirk, Nieuport, Eindhoven and Zutphen. The threat to the Protestant cause in the Netherlands was greater than it had been at any time since the dark days of 1574.

In the summer of 1583 another English expedition sailed to the Spanish Main. As reports reached Europe of the seizures of Spanish ships and treasure, Mendoza protested to Elizabeth's counsellors and asked for an audience with the Queen. Elizabeth made one excuse after another for refusing him an audience, and when he insisted and protested, the Council told him that she would not receive him until Philip gave her satisfaction for his intervention in Ireland.[26]

On 9 January 1584 Mendoza was summoned to attend a meeting with Lord Chancellor Bromley, Leicester, Walsingham, Lord Howard of Effingham, and Hunsdon. Walsingham said that as he spoke Italian better than the others, he would be their spokesman, and he then told him that they had discovered that he had been secretly corresponding with Mary Queen of Scots and plotting with Guise to arrange for her escape from England; the Queen was therefore ordering him to leave England within fifteen days. Mendoza replied by accusing Elizabeth and her counsellors of supporting Philip's rebels in the Netherlands and Don Antonio in Portugal. The conversation became heated. They 'spoke so impertinently', wrote Mendoza to Philip, 'that I dare not repeat it to Your Majesty'. They said that he should be grateful that Elizabeth was expelling him and not punishing him for what he had done. Mendoza was not frightened by this warning, or by the recollection of the way in which Elizabeth had treated Guaras. He said that as she was a lady, there was nothing strange in her being ungrateful to those who wished to serve her, as he had done, but as he had apparently failed to please her as a minister of peace, he would in future try to satisfy her in war.[27]

Philip sent him to Paris as his ambassador at the French court. He continued his secret contacts with the Catholics in England, and directed their plots against Elizabeth; and, despite his rapidly failing eyesight, he carried out his various duties with devotion and skill.

Anjou, after patching up his quarrel with the States, went on a protracted visit to France. He fell ill at Château-Thierry, where he died of consumption after a long illness on 10 June 1584 (N.S.). He was aged only thirty, and as no satisfactory explanation of his illness could be given, it was widely suspected that he had been poisoned by the Guises, who had been implicated in a plot to murder him two years before.[28] Elizabeth was sad, for she had been very fond of him.

His death caused grave political problems in both the Netherlands and in France. The States in the Netherlands had to find a new ruler. In France, Henry III was still childless, and though he had once been in love with women, he now devoted himself to religious exercises and flagellations with a series of male favourites, and it seemed unlikely that he and his Queen would produce an heir. He was the last surviving son of Henry II, and as the Salic Law excluded women and their descendants from succeeding to the crown, the heir to the throne was the descendant of the sixth son of St Louis, who had reigned three hundred years before. This was none other than Henry of Navarre. But the Holy League, at the instigation of the Guises, announced that they would never accept a heretic as their King, and the Pope ruled that a heretic was incapable of succeeding to the throne. Henry of Navarre's cousin, the Cardinal of Bourbon, was the nearest Catholic in line of succession.

Henry III, who was suspicious of Guise, offered to recognise Henry of Navarre as his heir if he became a Catholic. Henry of Navarre was no religious bigot; he had already once converted to Catholicism after the Massacre of St Bartholomew, and no one would have been surprised if he had done so again in order to win the crown. But he was faced with a difficult political decision. If he became a Catholic, the League, the Pope, and many Catholics would probably refuse to accept his conversion as sincere, and would continue to oppose him, while he would forfeit the support of the French Huguenots and of Elizabeth and the German Lutheran Princes, who would switch their support to his cousin Condé, and he would be left with no supporters at all. After considering the matter for some days, he told Henry III that his conscience would not allow him to abandon the Protestant religion.[29]

Henry III then approached Elizabeth, and asked her to persuade Henry of Navarre to become a Catholic, so that he could recognise him as his heir and make an alliance with him against the Guises. Elizabeth replied that she had always used her influence with Henry of Navarre to persuade him to be loyal to his King and had always found him eager to do so, but that it would offend her conscience to try to persuade him to abandon the Protestant religion in which she herself devoutly believed. She was sure that even if she urged him to do so, he would refuse; and it would not be in Henry III's interest if Henry of Navarre became a Catholic, for then he would lose the support of the French Huguenots, and would no longer be able to persuade them to defend their King against the Guises.[30]

A month after Anjou died, William of Orange, who had taken up residence at Delft, received a report about Anjou's last hours from a young man aged twenty-seven whom William had sent to France to learn the full facts. William and his household believed that the young man was Francis Guion, the son of a Protestant of Besançon who had been put to death for his religion by the

Catholics; but in fact he was Balthasar Gérard, whose Catholic father and mother were still living at Villefons in Burgundy. He had been waiting for seven years for the opportunity to kill William, and had been assured by two eminent Jesuit theologians and an equally eminent Franciscan that he would be doing a great service to the Church if he did so. He had had an interview with Parma's secretary, who had promised him that King Philip would pay the reward to him if he survived, and to his heirs if he did not.

When Gérard spoke to William on 8 July (N.S.), he was unable to kill him because he had no weapon; but he asked William to give him some money to relieve his poverty, and with this he bought a pistol. On 10 July (N.S.) he slipped into William's house, and as William walked from the dining room to the staircase leading to his study, Gérard shot him. William died within the hour.

Gérard ran up the garden path, intending to jump over the wall into the town moat and swim across to a place where he had left a horse on which he could escape; but he stumbled on a pile of refuse, and was seized by William's pages. That evening his infuriated guards whipped him and cut out pieces of his flesh with the points of quill pens; then they immersed him in a bath of salt water, and dressed him in a shirt which they had soaked in vinegar and brandy. Next day he was tortured more officially on the rack by the judicial authorities; but though he made a detailed statement about his preparations to kill William, he did not mention his contacts with Parma's secretary.

The authorities wished to deny him the satisfaction of knowing that he had succeeded in killing William, and he was therefore put on trial on the charge of having attempted to murder the Prince of Orange. He was sentenced to be put to death by having his right hand burned off, then to have the flesh of his body burned with red-hot pincers in six different places, and then to be disembowelled, and to have his heart cut out and thrown in his face before being beheaded and quartered. The sentence was carried out in public in the market square at Delft on 14 July (N.S.). He endured his torments in silence with a happy smile on his face.[31]

Parma asked Philip to pay to Gérard's father and mother the reward which his 'laudable and generous deed had so well deserved', and Philip complied with the request.[32] In the Catholic countries, Gérard was hailed as a noble martyr for the Church; in Protestant countries, his deed aroused the greatest horror and was seen as a warning of the danger which threatened all Protestant rulers, and above all Elizabeth. A pamphlet entitled *The Punishment of the wicked traitor who villainously killed the noble Prince of Orange and of his obstinacy after committing this abominable deed*, which contained a detailed and inaccurate account of the torture and execution of Gérard, was published in London and sold in the bookshops and in the streets. In Paris, the Catholics published a very similar book extolling the bravery of Gérard.[33]

Parma timed his new offensive at the right psychological moment. Within ten days of William's murder his armies were at the gates of Antwerp, and in

October he captured the great Protestant city of Ghent. These were serious blows, but the loss of Antwerp would be even more serious, for Antwerp, where the States-General had established their capital, was one of the great commercial centres of Europe and handled seventy per cent of the total trade of the Netherlands. The city prepared to resist Parma under the leadership of the Sieur of Sainte Aldegonde, who from the earliest days had been one of the chiefs of the national movement, and was probably the author of the great battle-hymn *Wilhelmus van Nassouwe*.

Throughout the autumn of 1584, while Parma built a boom across the mouth of the Scheldt to cut off Antwerp from the sea, the politicians in the Council of State, the States-General and the provincial States assemblies argued about whom they should invite to be their ruler. Some of them wished to ask Henry III to succeed his brother as their sovereign; others would have preferred the Protestant Queen Elizabeth to a Catholic King who had been one of the authors of the Massacre of St Bartholomew, though Elizabeth had been a very half-hearted and changeable champion of their cause.[34] Elizabeth herself was very reluctant to become involved in the Netherlands to any greater extent than she was already, as this would cost money and might mean war with Spain; but her counsellors were convinced that every effort must be made to prevent Philip from reconquering the Netherlands, for he would then be able to use the ports for an invasion of England. On 10 October 1584 the Privy Council discussed the situation. It was decided to wait and see whether Henry III would help the Netherlands, but that if he did not, Elizabeth might be compelled to intervene to save them.[35]

In January 1585 the States-General sent envoys to Paris to invite Henry III to become their ruler; but he was under strong pressure from Mendoza and Guise to refuse to help the rebels in the Netherlands, and instead to join with Philip II in a united Catholic drive against the heretics.[36] In March 1585 Guise seized the town of Châlons, and he and the League issued a 'manifesto', which, as Sir Edward Stafford, the ambassador in Paris, explained to Walsingham, was a new Italian word meaning a document in which a political faction declares its policy. They announced that they were taking up arms against Henry of Navarre and the heretics. Henry III refused the States-General's offer, and sent Catherine de Medici to negotiate with Guise.[37]

At the beginning of March the defenders of Brussels and Malines opened negotiations with Parma about the surrender of the two cities, while at Antwerp the Spaniards succeeded in closing the last route into the city. The States-General, seeing that Henry III refused to help them, turned to Elizabeth; and on 7 March Elizabeth informed the States that although she was not prepared to accept the sovereignty of the Netherlands, she would take them under her protection and send an army to help defend them against Philip on condition that they granted her, as a pledge, the towns of Flushing, Brill and Enkhuisen, which Elizabeth would hold for as long as her armies remained in the Netherlands and until the States had repaid the money that she had lent them. The States did not like these conditions; but Davison explained to them that Elizabeth had not forgotten how she had been betrayed by the French Protestants in 1563, and therefore insisted on being given the three ports.[38]

Walsingham's agents in the Netherlands had very little doubt that the States would accept Elizabeth's conditions; but Davison was worried about the danger to Antwerp, and feared that Elizabeth's lukewarm attitude to the States would weaken their will to resist.[39] Walsingham feared that Elizabeth might indeed abandon them, and wrote to Davison on 22 April that he found those whose judgment she most trusted were so coldly affected to the cause that he had no great hope of success; but as the hearts of Princes were in the hands of God, it might be possible to reach agreement if the States sent envoys to England.[40]

By the beginning of May the Catholics in Antwerp were suggesting that the city had better surrender to Parma, but the Protestants insisted on continuing their resistance. The States made two attemps to relieve them by landing a force on the dike; but both attempts failed, though on the second occasion the English soldiers in the relieving army gained possession of the dike at 3 a.m. and held it for seven hours before they were driven off by the Spaniards. Meanwhile the negotiations between Elizabeth and the States were proceeding very slowly. On 27 May (N.S.), the day on which the second attempt to relieve Antwerp was repulsed, the envoys of the States-General at last embarked for England; but by the beginning of June, with food supplies in Antwerp running very low, the people were demonstrating before the town hall in favour of surrender. Sainte Aldegonde refused to agree, and said that help would soon be coming from England; but most of the people refused to believe this, and on 12 July (N.S.) he agreed to send envoys to discuss surrender terms with Parma.[41]

The envoys of the States had reached London three weeks earlier, and began negotiations with Elizabeth's counsellors. They asked, as a matter of urgency, that help should be sent to Antwerp. Elizabeth was reluctant to agree to this until an agreement had been reached with the States about the conditions on which she would aid them. She issued orders for a force to be raised to help Antwerp; but on 20 July, three weeks after the envoys of the States arrived, Walsingham was still uncertain as to whether or not she would agree to the men being sent.[42] News was smuggled into Antwerp that Elizabeth was sending Norris with an army to save the city; but by this time even Sainte Aldegonde was in favour of accepting the honourable terms which Parma offered, and he told the people of Antwerp that it was foolish to rely on a promise of help from a lady, especially from the most inconstant lady in the world.[43]

Antwerp surrendered on 17 August (N.S.). Parma promised that no punishment would be inflicted on the inhabitants, and though he rejected all demands for religious toleration, he agreed that the Protestants in Antwerp should be allowed four years in which either to become Catholics or to sell their property and leave the Netherlands.[44]

The treaty between Elizabeth and the States was signed at the palace of Nonesuch on 10 August (20 August N.S.). She did not accept the sovereignty of the Netherlands, but agreed, as their protector, to supply them with 4,000 foot, 400 horse, and 700 men for garrison duty. She was to appoint three Englishmen to sit on the Council of State. She and the States were to pay their agreed share of the cost of operations. She waived her demand for Enkhuisen, but Flushing and Brill were granted to her as a pledge, and she agreed to allow the citizens of the two ports the same trading privileges as her English subjects.[45]

Six days later, Norris sailed from Queenborough in the Isle of Sheppey with the advance-guard of the army. They were at least three weeks too late to save Antwerp; but the news that Elizabeth was sending an army to the Netherlands heartened the Protestants there and throughout Europe, for it would yet be in time to prevent Zeeland, Holland and the northern provinces from falling again under Spanish Catholic tyranny.[46] Unfortunately, Elizabeth began almost immediately to regret the decision which she had taken, and to look for ways of extricating herself from the Netherlands.

There was a clause in the treaty between Elizabeth and the States which provided that neither party would enter into peace negotiations with Philip without informing the other and joining them as a party to the negotiations. But twelve days after making the treaty, and six days after Norris sailed, Elizabeth sent Sir John Smith on a secret mission to Calais to attempt to make contact with Parma. If Parma agreed to receive him, he was to tell Parma that if Philip would promise to govern the Netherlands through native administrators and to grant religious toleration, she would use her influence to persuade the States to accept Philip as their sovereign and to return to their obedience.[47]

Parma, who knew that Philip would never agree to grant religious toleration, did not respond to Elizabeth's proposals; but he and Philip, and Elizabeth and Burghley, all wanted peace. Neither side wished to take the first step in proposing that they should hold peace talks for fear that this would be interpreted as a sign of weakness. So the negotiations were conducted through four Italian bankers, all acting unofficially. Andrea De Loo in London talked to Burghley, and sometimes to Elizabeth herself, while Carlo Lanfranchi in Antwerp talked to Parma and his secretary; and De Loo and Lanfranchi wrote to each other about the progress of their negotiations. Their efforts were supplemented by those of Elizabeth's financial agent, Horatio Pallavicino, in Frankfort-on-Main and Lorenzo Grimaldo in Genoa, for Grimaldo sometimes visited Madrid and spoke to Philip and his ministers.[48] Elizabeth justified her failure to inform the States on the grounds that these were not peace negotiations, but only preliminary negotiations about the possibility of entering into peace negotiations.[49]

Elizabeth appointed Leicester to be the commander of her army in the Netherlands. He chose his nephew Sir Philip Sidney to be Governor of Flushing, and Burghley's son, Sir Thomas Cecil, to be Governor of Brill. Sidney, who had been on the point of enlisting to join Drake's new expedition to the Spanish Main, accepted the post at Flushing as an alternative way of serving the Queen and the Protestant cause.

The enthusiasm in the Netherlands changed to anxiety as Leicester, Sidney and Cecil had still not arrived in November 1585, three months after the treaty between Elizabeth and the States had been signed. When Davison wrote from The Hague to Leicester to tell him this, Leicester assured him that he was not responsible for the delay.[50] It was in fact caused by Elizabeth's refusal to authorise the necessary expenditure for the expedition. Walsingham wrote to Davison that all the difficulties in the Netherlands 'would be easily redressed if we could take a thorough resolute course here, a matter that men may rather pray than hope for'.[51]

Norris's troops captured a fort from the Spaniards in the Netherlands. Elizabeth congratulated Norris, but wrote that she would have preferred it if he had not taken the offensive but had stood on the defensive until he was attacked by the enemy. This was because of her care for her subjects' lives, 'which the offensive cannot but put into overgreat hazard', and because she had announced to the world that she had sent her forces to the Netherlands to defend the country and not to pursue offensive operations. She added that Norris was to take special care that the lives of 'the young gentlemen of best birth' should not be risked in hazardous attempts, so that they could be reserved for her service in England.[52] Norris replied, in a letter to Walsingham, that he regretted that the Queen was displeased with his offensive operations, but 'I know not what war that might be called, to suffer the enemy to carry away four or five towns from us, when so easily they might be saved'. As for Elizabeth's reluctance to risk her soldiers' lives, he had lost more men from lack of provisions than in his attack on the Spaniards.[53]

Sidney had reached Flushing before the end of November, and he immediately won the goodwill of the inhabitants by his tact and by his firmness in punishing any looting or misconduct by his soldiers.[54] But Elizabeth was becoming increasingly resentful that she had been persuaded to help the Dutch. She made difficulties about sending the necessary money to Leicester, though he had paid £2,000 more from his own pocket than all the money which he had received from her. She was also angry because she had heard an untrue rumour that he was taking his wife with him to the Netherlands; and she blamed Walsingham for urging her to send money to Leicester.[55]

Leicester embarked at last at Harwich on 8 December.[56] He was received with great enthusiasm in the Netherlands, and found the people basing all their hopes on aid from Elizabeth; but the bickerings continued. The English garrison at Ostend was in difficulties because their wages were in arrears and they had not enough money to buy food and proper clothing. Elizabeth refused to send them any money, for she said that under the terms of her agreement with the States-General, it was the States' obligation to pay for the garrison at Ostend.[57] The States disputed this interpretation of the treaty, and while Elizabeth and the States argued the point, the soldiers at Ostend became more destitute.

Many people in Holland and Zeeland, disgusted with the quarrelling among the politicians of the States, wished that Leicester would assume dictatorial powers. On 11 January 1586 (N.S.), the States-General invited him to assume the government of the Netherlands on Elizabeth's behalf. He replied that there was no provision in the treaty between Elizabeth and the States which would allow him to take office as Governor, and that he could not accept their offer or make any further reply at present. When Elizabeth heard about this, she ordered the Privy Council to write to Leicester reprimanding him sharply; he ought to have rejected the States-General's offer out of hand, and to have told them that under no circumstances would Elizabeth allow him to become Governor.[58] But before Leicester received this letter, he had decided to confront Elizabeth with a *fait accompli.*

On 4 February (N.S.) he was inaugurated at The Hague as Governor of the Netherlands and Captain-General of all the armies of the States, and after the President of the Council of State had expressed their gratitude to Elizabeth for her help, and the members of the Council took an oath of obedience to Leicester, and he took his oath to serve the States. A proclamation announcing Leicester's appointment was published throughout all the liberated parts of the Netherlands.[59]

Elizabeth was furious when she heard what Leicester had done. She sent her trusted official, Sir Thomas Heneage, to The Hague with letters to Leicester and to the States,[60] stating that they had treated her with contempt by making and accepting the appointment in defiance of her express orders, which 'giveth the world just cause to think that there is not that reverent respect carried towards us by our subjects as in duty appertaineth, especially seeing so notorious a contempt committed against us by one whom we have raised up and yielded in the eye of the world, even from the beginning of our reign, as great a portion of our favour as ever subject enjoyed at any Prince's hands'.[61]

Burghley and Walsingham tried to make excuses for Leicester, but Elizabeth became so angry with them that Burghley retired to bed, stating that he was ill with gout, and Walsingham thought it best to keep quiet on the subject. She blamed Davison and Sir Philip Sidney, whom she believed had egged on Leicester to take this step, for she knew that both Davison and Sidney were ardent supporters of the cause of the Netherlands and were eager to tie England and the States more closely together.

Leicester sent Davison to England with a letter to Elizabeth. Davison found her in a fury against him and Leicester. At his first audience she would hardly allow him to say a word in Leicester's defence, and when he handed her Leicester's letter she refused to take it. Davison tried again at a second audience next day, and this time she accepted and read the letter and seemed a little appeased.[62] But three weeks later, Leicester's brother, the Earl of Warwick, wrote to him: 'Our mistress's extreme rage doth increase rather than diminish, and she giveth out great threatening words against you'.[63]

Neither Davison, Burghley, Walsingham, nor Leicester's own apologetic letters, could dissuade Elizabeth from sending Heneage to the States, insisting that Leicester should be immediately dismissed from his office of Governor and Captain-General, although this was bound to disgrace and discredit him in the eyes of all the people of the Netherlands, and to make them doubt Elizabeth's determination to help them against the Spaniards. But the Privy Council persuaded her to add a passage in her instructions to Heneage, allowing him to exercise his discretion as to the time at which he should present her demand for Leicester's dismissal.[64] This was enough, for Heneage, like nearly all Elizabeth's officers and diplomats, was far more eager than Elizabeth herself to help the Netherlands and to avoid exacerbating the divisions between England and the States. When Heneage reached Middelburg, he met Philip Sidney, who was so encouraged by Heneage's attitude that he wrote to his father-in-law, Walsingham, that he was sure that Heneage would minimise the damage caused by the incident 'if it be not pursued from thence with some new violence, but that all things will proceed well, Her Majesty obeyed in her will and I hope satisfied in her opinion'. He thought that the position was satisfactory, provided 'only that the poor soldiers meanwhile famish not for want of money'.[65]

After discussing the situation with Leicester, Heneage decided to exercise the discretionary powers which he had been given in his instructions and to suppress the message which Elizabeth had sent to the States insisting on Leicester's immediate dismissal. Elizabeth had meanwhile been somewhat placated by a series of letters from Leicester expressing the devotion and affection which he felt for her and his deep regret at having offended her;[66] and Burghley, Walsingham, Hatton and other counsellors had ventured again to use their influence on his behalf. On 30 March she wrote to the States that although she had been justly displeased with Leicester's action in accepting the office of Governor of the Netherlands, she had decided not to insist on his immediate dismissal, but to allow him to continue to hold the office for the time being until it was convenient to make other arrangements.[67]

Leicester had relied on the old affection which Elizabeth had always felt for him, and had gone further than anyone else would have dared to go in defying her wishes and her authority. He had very nearly gone too far, but he had just got away with it.

EXECUTION OF A QUEEN

WHEN Grindal died in July 1583, and Elizabeth at last got rid of her troublesome Archbishop of Canterbury, she found a successor to him, John Whitgift, who was just what she wanted. In his younger days, Whitgift had been regarded as something of a radical; but he had changed, and as Master of Trinity College, Vice-Chancellor of Cambridge University, and Bishop of Worcester he had adopted a firm stand against the Puritans. He still hated Papists as strongly as he had done when, as a divinity student, he wrote his doctoral thesis proving that the Pope was Antichrist; but he considered that the Puritans were the main enemy.

In 1582 the Puritan leaders decided, at a conference in Cambridge, to begin an active campaign to convert the Church of England to Presbyterianism. They held meetings in various parts of the country, especially at the great international fairs in London and Cambridgeshire; they preached sermons and published pamphlets; and when Parliament was in session they sent their supporters to the Palace of Westminster to lobby MPs, which was an idea which had never occurred to anyone before.

Whitgift struck back by requiring all the clergy to sign a declaration that they supported Elizabeth's supremacy over the church, that they believed in the Thirty-nine Articles of Religion of 1562, and that they accepted everything in the Book of Common Prayer of 1559 and would use the Prayer Book and no other form of worship. The Puritans strongly supported the royal supremacy, and could with a little difficulty accept the Thirty-nine Articles; but they believed that the Prayer Book contained dregs of Popery and that some of the ceremonies which it prescribed were sinful. Whitgift ordered that any clergyman who refused to sign the declaration was to be deprived of his benefice and all his offices in the Church.

He followed this with a measure which shocked the lawyers as well as the Puritans and their sympathisers. Any clergyman could be required to appear before a commissioner appointed by Whitgift and to reply on oath to the questions which were put to him. If he refused to take the oath, he was imprisoned for contempt of court. If he agreed to be duly sworn, he was forced to reply on oath to questions about his religious beliefs which could lead to his dismissal if he gave a truthful answer. The common lawyers denounced the procedure as a violation of the principles of the common law which smacked of the Romish Inquisition. Whitgift dismissed their opinion contemptuously as legalistic hair-splitting.

The Puritans' friends in high places rallied to their support. Leicester, Walsingham, Knollys and Burghley protested to Whitgift against his persecution of the Puritans. Whitgift paid no attention to their protests. He relied on those perennial conservative supporters, the silent majority, against the Puritan activists and their supporters in the Privy Council. He told Burghley and his other critics that in his own diocese of Canterbury only ten of his parish priests opposed his action against the Puritans, while over a hundred of them enthusiastically supported him.[1]

Most important of all, he had the support of Elizabeth. She thought that Puritans were seditious revolutionaries and troublemakers; and just as she hated the Protestant rebels in the Netherlands more than Philip II, Parma and the Spaniards, she hated and feared her ardent Puritan supporters more than the Papists who were planning to depose and assassinate her. For years she had felt isolated, surrounded by Puritan-lovers, and almost powerless in their hands; now she had a strong conservative Archbishop of Canterbury who was prepared to defy the Puritans, confident in his power because of her support. She announced that she would not allow the House of Commons to 'meddle with matters above their capacity' and attack Whitgift and the bishops; and if some members of her Council continued to support the MPs in these attacks, she would 'uncouncil some of them'.[2]

Her hatred for the Puritans did not lessen their devotion to her when they heard that the foreign Papists and their friends, the Catholic traitors in England, were planning to assassinate her as they had assassinated the Prince of Orange. In the autumn of 1584, many Protestants throughout the country formed the Bond of Association, and took an oath that if anyone assassinated, or tried to assassinate, the Queen in order to place some other person on the throne, they would kill all those who were involved in the murder plot, and the person whom the murderers intended to place on the throne, and anyone claiming the throne through such a person. This meant that if the Catholics attempted to murder Elizabeth in order to make Mary Queen of Scots the Queen of England, the members of the Bond of Association would kill the murderers and Mary Queen of Scots, and James VI of Scotland too if he claimed to succeed to the throne of England through his descent from his mother. When Parliament met in November, the MPs introduced a bill to give statutory authority to the Oath of Association.[3]

The Bond of Association was apparently organised by Walsingham and other Privy Councillors without Elizabeth's knowledge, for she told a deputation of MPs that it was 'done (I protest to God) before I ever heard it', and that the first she knew of it was when she was shown the oath at Hampton Court after it had been signed by thousands of people.[4] When the bill to legalise the oath was introduced in Parliament, she refused to agree to it. She finally accepted it in a greatly modified form by which her loyal subjects would be entitled to kill only those persons who had been proclaimed by the Privy Council as having been parties to a plot to assassinate her.[5]

This was not enough to counter the greatest danger which threatened the Protestant cause in England and in all Europe. If Elizabeth were assassinated, Mary Queen of Scots would succeed to the throne. Many Englishmen who were loyal to Elizabeth as long as she lived would then accept Mary as their lawful Queen by hereditary succession, and would obey her when she made England a Catholic realm once again. But Elizabeth would not allow any steps to be taken to prevent this. She refused to give her royal assent to bills excluding Mary from the succession, or to accept Burghley's proposal that when Elizabeth died, the Privy Council and Parliament should proclaim a new sovereign whom they would select.[6] Did Elizabeth's conscience prevent her from excluding a future Catholic Queen, remembering that the Catholics in her sister's reign had not excluded her from the succession? Or did the idea of Parliament exercising sovereign authority, even temporarily, shock her so greatly that she preferred to allow a Catholic Queen to succeed to the throne and overturn the Protestant religion? If she had agreed to Burghley's plan, the Protestants might have been a little less eager to find any excuse to have Mary put to death.

In the spring of 1585 Dr William Parry, MP, plotted with Mary Queen of Scots's agents in Paris to assassinate Elizabeth, and was hanged, drawn and quartered; but next year a group of young Catholic gentlemen, led by Anthony Babington, tried again. They were in touch with Mendoza in Paris and with Mary Queen of Scots in her prison at Chartley Hall in Staffordshire. One of the conspirators, Gilbert Gifford, devised an ingenious method by which letters could be smuggled to and from Mary hidden in a beer barrel. Unfortunately for Mary, Gifford was an agent of Walsingham, and he handed over all the letters in the beer barrel to Mary's jailer, Sir Amyas Paulet, and to Walsingham. At least two other members of Babington's group were Walsingham's spies, and he may have had as many as seven agents working with the plotters*.[7]

Walsingham was eager to find evidence which would incriminate Mary and persuade Elizabeth to take action against her; and he obtained it when he read the intercepted correspondence between Babington and Mary. Babington wrote to her that he planned to liberate her from prison, after which six gentlemen would assassinate Elizabeth and a Spanish army would invade England. On 17 July 1586 Mary wrote to Babington that before any attempt

*Certainly William and Gilbert Gifford, and Nicholas Berden; possibly also Robert Poley, Thomas Bowes, Barnard Maude and Captain Jacques.

was made to set her free, 'the affairs being thus prepared, and forces in readiness both without and within the realm, then shall it be time to set the six gentlemen to work, taking order upon the accomplishing of their design I may be suddenly transported out of this place'.[8] Walsingham ordered his agent to forge a postscript to Mary's letter before forwarding it to Babington, in order to lure Babington into revealing the names of the six gentlemen; but it is very unlikely that he forged the passage in the letter which contained the fatal words: 'Then shall it be time to set the six gentlemen to work'.*

Walsingham told Elizabeth about the plot, showed her a copy of Mary's letter, and obtained her consent to his plan that Mary should be invited to go hunting, and then suddenly charged with high treason during the hunt and detained while her room at Chartley was searched and her papers seized. Babington and most of the other plotters were arrested, and in September 1586 were convicted of high treason at their trial in Westminster Hall for attempting to murder the Queen.

The news of the plot aroused the greatest indignation in the country, and no one was more indignant than Elizabeth herself. Her sister Mary had always been more severe towards heretics than towards traitors, being sometimes prepared to pardon offences against herself but never offences against God. Elizabeth was exactly the opposite. She was lenient towards Catholics who did nothing except practise their religion, but considered that treason, and particularly attempted regicide, was an unpardonable crime. It would be unfair to think that this was merely because of a selfish fear for her own safety or a desire for personal revenge. She believed that treason against the Prince, God's representative on earth, was the supreme offence, and if she, though unworthy, had been placed by God in this position, it was her duty to punish crimes against herself with the greatest severity.

During the trial of Babington and his accomplices, she wrote to Burghley that she thought the prisoners should be subjected to some slow and painful death as an additional punishment to mark the gravity of their offence. She thought that hanging, drawing and quartering was too merciful. She suggested to Burghley that after the Lord Chief Justice had passed the sentence required by law, and sentenced Babington and the others to be hanged, cut down while still alive, castrated, disembowelled, and then beheaded and quartered, he should add that in view of the wickedness of their offence he was referring the case to the Privy Council to decide the method of their execution. It would then be possible for the Council to devise a more cruel form of death. Burghley replied that this would be illegal; and he assured her

---

*See Conyers Read, (*Walsingham*, iii, 33–44), for the authenticity of Mary's letter, and his conclusion that only the postscript of the letter was forged by Walsingham's agents. Both Father Pollen (in *Mary Queen of Scots and the Babington Plot*, 32) and Antonia Fraser (in *Mary Queen of Scots*, 488–92) accept the authenticity of the incriminating passage in the letter, though they believe that it indicates nothing more than a passive acquiescence by Mary in the plot to assassinate Elizabeth.

that if the executioner took care to perform the execution properly, hanging, drawing and quartering could be extremely painful, and that life could be prolonged throughout the disembowelling. In practice, this was not always the case, for often the executioner was bribed by the victim or his friends to finish him off as quickly as possible, or even to allow him to hang until he was dead, contrary to the sentence imposed by the court.

Elizabeth refused to accept Burghley's arguments, and insisted that the judges should be consulted about the possibility of inflicting a more painful death on the prisoners. They all agreed that this would be illegal, and she reluctantly accepted their decision. On 20 September Babington and three of his accomplices were hanged, drawn and quartered, and the execution was prolonged for as long as possible. When their sufferings were described to Elizabeth, she suddenly experienced a feeling of revulsion. Next day seven more conspirators were executed, but at Elizabeth's orders they were allowed to hang until they were dead.[9]

It was another matter with Mary, for Elizabeth was still very reluctant to put a Queen on trial and execute her. She was fully aware of the legal, diplomatic and political difficulties. There were various arguments which could be used to rebut any plea by Mary that no English court had jurisdiction to try her. It could be said that, having abdicated, she was no longer a sovereign; that she was in the same position as any other alien resident in England, and therefore liable to be tried and punished if she broke the law of the land; and there was even the old argument that the Kings of Scotland were vassals of the Kings of England, having done homage to them in the twelfth and thirteenth centuries.

But the diplomatic objections were more serious. Henry III warned Elizabeth that he would deeply resent it if his sister-in-law, a former Queen Consort of France, was put on trial and executed; and James VI also protested. The Scots, who a few years earlier had been urging Elizabeth to allow them to put their Queen to death, now resented the idea that Elizabeth would execute her.[10] More fundamental than any of these objections was Elizabeth's high view of monarchy, and her feeling that no Queen, or former Queen, should be put on trial and executed, even by order of another Queen. Did some instinct tell her that if Mary were tried and executed, her case would be cited as a precedent sixty-two years later by John Milton to justify the trial and execution of a King of England by his subjects?

It would be less objectionable if Mary were surreptitiously murdered, like Edward II, Richard II and Henry VI, for then the crime could at least be denied and not brazenly justified. According to Camden, Leicester suggested that Mary should be poisoned.[11] But Walsingham and Burghley wished to put her on trial, and persuaded all the other counsellors to agree. The idea of a public trial of Mary was as attractive to the Puritans as it was shocking to Elizabeth.

The Council persuaded Elizabeth to summon her prorogued Parliament in order to give the proceedings against Mary the force of statutory authority. The summoning of Parliament increased the pressure on Elizabeth, for the Puritan MPs reinforced the demands of the Council for Mary's trial and execution. Under this pressure and the dictates of her conscience, Elizabeth wavered and repeatedly changed her mind.

When Babington and his accomplices were put on trial, she insisted that there should be no reference to Mary in their indictments or in the evidence given or the speeches made at their trial. A fortnight later, at the end of September, she agreed to appoint forty-two commissioners to sit in judgement on Mary; but she would not agree that Mary should be imprisoned in the Tower, or that her trial should take place in London. Nor would she agree to it being held at Hertford Castle, which she thought was too near London; she insisted that it be held at Fotheringhay Castle in Northamptonshire, where she thought it would attract less public notice.[12]

Thirty-six of the commissioners, including Burghley and Walsingham, travelled to Fotheringhay, where the trial was held over two days on 14 and 15 October. Mary denied her guilt, but a copy of her letter to Babington and the confession of her two secretaries were given in evidence against her, and she was found guilty by the court, who brushed aside her objection to their jurisdiction.[13]

On the day before the trial began, Elizabeth changed her mind. She ordered Davison, who had recently been appointed Secretary of State on his return from the Netherlands, to send instructions to the commissioners that although they should proceed with the trial, they were not to pronounce sentence against Mary, but must announce that they would give their verdict and sentence at a later date. Davison, with his Puritan sympathies, was as eager as Walsingham and Burghley that Mary should be executed. He sent off Elizabeth's order to the commissioners, but privately wrote to Walsingham that he hoped and believed that the courier would arrive at Fotheringhay too late to stop the commissioners from pronouncing sentence. The courier reached Fotheringhay in time, and at the end of the second day's proceedings the presiding judge, Lord Chancellor Bromley, announced that judgement and sentence would be reserved.[14]

Parliament had been summoned to meet on 15 October. Elizabeth postponed the date of the meeting to 27 October, for she did not wish to have Parliament in session, with the MPs in the House of Commons clamouring for Mary's death, while the trial at Fotheringhay was in progress. Then she postponed the meeting again to 29 October.[15] Meanwhile the Privy Council was urging Elizabeth to allow the commissioners to pass sentence on Mary. On 23 October she received the French ambassador, Mauvissière, who conveyed to her the feelings of his master. 'There is no special law in England', wrote Henry III, 'which can make my sister-in-law criminally liable and subject to any jurisdiction for this accusation, or for any other which could be brought, having been born a sovereign Princess, and who, by the privilege common to all other Kings, is exempt from human jurisdiction, and subject only to the judgement of God.'[16] He added that Mary's execution would outrage all the Kings of Christendom.

Mauvissière seems to have annoyed Elizabeth, for his intervention had the opposite effect from what he intended. She told him that it was impossible to stop the proceedings now, and that any further intervention by Henry III on Mary's behalf would endanger their friendship. She ordered the commissioners to pronounce sentence, and on 25 October they met in the Star Chamber in Whitehall and declared that Mary was guilty of attempting to assassinate the Queen.[17] Their sentence had no force of law, for an *ad hoc* tribunal had no power to impose the death penalty. But the Council had decided to proceed against her under the Act of 1585, which authorised anyone to put to death a person who had been proclaimed as guilty of an attempt to assassinate the Queen. Before this could be done, it was necessary for Elizabeth to issue the proclamation naming Mary.

When Parliament at last reassembled on 29 October, both the backbench MPs and the government spokesmen in the House of Lords and the House of Commons demanded that Mary should be put to death. Sir Ralph Sadler, who had been Henry VIII's leading expert on Scottish affairs and now, at the age of seventy-nine, was Chancellor of the Duchy of Lancaster, urged Elizabeth 'to take away this most wicked and filthy woman' who had murdered her husband and was 'a most detestable traitor to our sovereign and enemy to us all'.[18]

Elizabeth normally stayed at Whitehall or at her other houses in Westminster when Parliament was in session; but on this occasion she remained at Richmond in order to dissociate herself as far as possible from the outcry in Parliament against the Queen of Scots. So Parliament sent a deputation of twenty peers and forty members of the House of Commons to visit Elizabeth at Richmond to ask her to put Mary to death. She received them on 12 November and made a speech which was afterwards put into writing and approved by her with many minor corrections. She thanked them for their loyalty in spontaneously forming the Bond of Association, and ended by saying that she would think about their petition and let them know her decision later. They returned to Westminster and waited for her answer; but it did not come. On 21 November Mauvissière made another attempt to save Mary. This time Elizabeth reacted more favourably, and promised Mauvissière that she would not issue the proclamation naming Mary during the next ten days.[19]

On 24 November the Parliamentary delegation went to Richmond to hear Elizabeth's reply. She made another speech which was a rather rambling apologia and was obviously intended to be published in due course as a justification to foreign rulers and to show her reluctance to proceed against Mary. 'Since now it is resolved that my surety cannot be established without a Princess's head, I have just cause to complain that I, who have in my time

[259]

pardoned so many rebels . . . should now be forced to this proceeding against such a person'. It was a typical Elizabeth speech, rather difficult to follow, with a reference to Alcibiades in classical history and flattering to her listeners. She ended by neither granting nor rejecting their petition. 'If I should say I would not do what you request, it might peradventure be more than I thought, and to say I would do it might perhaps breed peril of that you labour to preserve, being more than in your own wisdoms and discretions would seem convenient, circumstances of place and time being duly considered'.[20]

That evening, after the Parliamentary delegation had left, she decided to prorogue Parliament next day. Burghley and her other counsellors were dismayed, for they knew how the MPs would resent it if Parliament were prorogued without the proclamation against Mary having been issued. Next morning Elizabeth announced that she had changed her mind, and would adjourn Parliament for a week's recess instead of proroguing it. The Council sent a courier in great haste from Richmond to Westminster, and he arrived just in time to stop Bromley from announcing the prorogation to the two Houses.

The counsellors kept up their pressure on Elizabeth to issue the proclamation, but for six days she refused to do so. Eventually on 1 December, the day before Parliament was due to reassemble after the week's recess, she signed Burghley's draft of the proclamation naming Mary as a traitor who had plotted her death. Next day, Burghley announced in the House of Lords that the Queen had decided to issue the proclamation, and it was officially published on 4 December. The people celebrated in the usual way by lighting bonfires in London and in many other parts of the country.[21]

It was now lawful for anyone to kill Mary, but no one intended to do so without authority from the Queen, and the counsellors waited for her to sign the warrant for Mary's execution. She did not do so. She broke out in bitter recriminations against Walsingham, who wrote to Burghley about his anxiety that she would not agree to Mary's death.[22] But though she was reluctant to execute Mary, she resented the efforts of the French and Scottish ambassadors to save her, for she felt that they were asking her to risk her own life, which was in danger as long as Mary lived. At the beginning of January, she wrote in her own hand to Henry III: 'My brother . . . how can you be so mad as to think that it is honourable or good friendship to prevent the oppressed from escaping and to cause the death of an innocent woman by making her the prey of a murderess?'*[23]

A few days later, Walsingham told Elizabeth that William Stafford, the brother of the ambassador in France, Sir Edward Stafford, had confessed that he and another man had plotted with the Sieur Des Trappes, an attaché at the

*'Monsieur mon frère . . . Comment estes vous forcené a croire que se soit honneur ou bonne amitié a resprendre l'opprimé et recherchir la mort d'une innocent pour la faire proye d'une meurtrière'.

French embassy in London, to assassinate Elizabeth, and that Mauvissière knew about the plot. Des Trappes was arrested at Rochester on his way to Dover to return to France, and he and William Stafford were examined by the Privy Council. The counsellors also questioned Mauvissière, who denied that Des Trappes was involved in any plot, but admitted that he himself had been approached by Babington, who had told him about his plan to murder Elizabeth, which Mauvissière had refused to support. When Burghley said that Mauvissière ought to have informed the English authorities about Babington's plot, Mauvissière said that his only duty was to report information to his King and not to the English government. Mauvissière was then placed under house arrest in his embassy, and Des Trappes was imprisoned in the Tower.[24]

Elizabeth sent Waad to Paris to tell Henry III about Des Trappes and Mauvissière. She wrote a sympathetic letter to Sir Edward Stafford, explaining that she was entrusting this duty to Waad and not to him in order to save him from the embarrassment of having to act in a case which involved his brother. She added that she much regretted the distress which William Stafford's action must be causing to Sir Edward and his mother, who was one of Elizabeth's ladies-in-waiting. Sir Edward Stafford had been very successful in infiltrating his agents into the organisations of the English Catholic refugees in France and in causing disunity and personal feuds among them, and he was continually supplying Walsingham with information about Jesuits and other Catholics in England. He wrote to express his embarrassment at his brother's treasonable activities.[25] It caused him more embarrassment than Elizabeth and Walsingham realised, because Sir Edward Stafford was himself an agent in the pay of Mendoza, to whom he regularly betrayed important diplomatic and military secrets. Elizabeth and Walsingham never found out about his treason. Historians have disagreed as to whether he was a traitor or a double agent who gave the Spaniards misleading information, perhaps with Burghley's knowledge, in order to win their trust so as to be able to betray them to the English government.[26]

Elizabeth was angry and alarmed when she heard about this new assassination plot, and this may have persuaded her to take action at last against Mary. On 1 February 1587 she signed the warrant for Mary's execution, and gave it to Davison, commenting sarcastically that he should tell Walsingham, who was ill at his house, because the news would kill him outright. Then, as Davison was leaving the room with the warrant, she called him back and asked him whether it would not be possible to arrange for someone to murder Mary on his own responsibility without her having to issue the warrant.[27]

Her suggestion was discussed in the Privy Council. Walsingham and Burghley were strongly opposed to it, and most of the other counsellors agreed with them, though Whitgift favoured the idea of assassination by a private individual. With his conservative and authoritarian views, he believed that it was better to murder than to execute a Queen; but the pro-Puritan members of the Council wished, in the words of the regicides who condemned Charles I sixty years later, that the deed should be done openly in the light and not surreptitiously in a corner.

Elizabeth ordered Walsingham to write to Sir Amyas Paulet, Mary's Puritan jailer at Fotheringhay, and ask him to murder Mary. Paulet firmly refused, and said that he would never agree to commit a shameful murder. Elizabeth was angry; she complained that neither Paulet nor any of the other members of the Bond of Association were prepared to perform their oath to kill any person who was proclaimed under the Act for having plotted to murder her.[28] Davison had meanwhile sent the warrant for Mary's execution, which Elizabeth had given him, to the Lord Chancellor, in the usual way, for him to affix the Great Seal to it. The Lord Chancellor returned the sealed warrant to Davison, who informed the Privy Council. At Burghley's suggestion, the Council decided to send the warrant to Fotheringhay without consulting Elizabeth. On 8 February (18 February N.S.) Mary was beheaded.

Elizabeth was not informed about the execution for four days. When she was told, she burst out in grief and anger, and said that it had been done without her authority, and that those responsible would be punished. Her first reaction was apparently to blame Walsingham; but he had been ill at his home for some weeks, and was not present at the Council meeting on 5 February when it was decided to send the warrant to Fotheringhay. She knew that Burghley was chiefly responsible, but he was in bad health from his gout, and she had not forgotten his many years of loyal service and their long personal friendship. She said that she feared that it would kill him if she were to send him to the Tower. So she turned on Davison, who was certainly as pro-Puritan and anti-Mary as any of the counsellors, and as secretary could easily be held responsible for what had happened. She ordered that he was to be imprisoned in the Tower.

During the next few days her rage against Davison increased, and she decided that he should be executed. She would then inform all the members of the Privy Council that they were also liable to be executed, but would pardon all or most of them. She summoned Sir Edmund Anderson, the Chief Justice of the Court of Common Pleas, to Greenwich on 24 February, and asked him if she could lawfully order Davison to be hanged. Anderson seems to have hesitated about his reply, but when she pressed him and asked if her prerogative was not absolute, he said that it was. Although Anderson hated Puritans, and always tried to uphold the royal prerogative in all its forms, it is surprising that he should have gone so far as to tell Elizabeth that she was entitled to hang any of her subjects at her will without statutory authority or due process of law. But this was the impression which he gave her, and it was the answer which she wished to receive.[29]

Her counsellor and cousin, Lord Buckhurst was more resolute than Anderson. He told Elizabeth that she was not entitled to put her subjects to death without trial. She became very angry, and shouted abuse at him; but she decided to consult the other judges. Burghley hastily got in touch with them, and wrote: 'I would be loth to live to see a woman of such wisdom, as she is, to be wrongly advised, for fear or other infirmity . . . with an opinion gotten from her judges that her prerogative is above the law'.[30]

The judges evidently advised Elizabeth that she could not order Davison to be hanged, for he was prosecuted in the Court of Star Chamber for misprision and contempt of the royal authority, which were punishable only by fine and imprisonment. Anderson, who presided at the trial, said that Davison had acted out of negligence, not out of malice, and sentenced him to pay a fine of 10,000 marks and to be imprisoned during the Queen's pleasure. As the months passed by, a few courtiers, including Elizabeth's new favourite, Robert Devereux, Earl of Essex, ventured to intercede with Elizabeth on Davison's behalf; but she would not listen to any pleas or receive any petition for clemency from him. He remained in the Tower for twenty months, but in October 1588 he was released and placed under house arrest, from which he was freed in the summer of 1589. His fine was remitted, as were the fees that he owed for his food, drink and fuel while he was in the Tower. Elizabeth refused all suggestions that she should employ him again in her service, and he retired into private life at his house at Stepney, where he lived for nearly twenty years till he died, five years after Elizabeth, in 1608.[31]

For some months, the French had been complaining about acts of piracy committed by English seamen against French merchants. Complaints and counter-complaints about piracy were common, and were usually settled peaceably; but the arrest of Des Trappes and the detention of Mauvissière under house arrest in his embassy put a new strain on Anglo-French relations. On 5 February (N.S.) Henry III wrote to Elizabeth, repudiating the allegations that Des Trappes had been involved in a plot to assassinate her, and demanding that he be released at once and allowed to return to France. Four days later, the goods of English merchants were seized in Rouen and St Jean de Luz as a reprisal for the piracies committed against French merchants.[32]

On 3 March (N.S.), thirteen days after Mary's execution, the news of it at last reached Henry III, and soon it was generally known in Paris. It caused the greatest indignation. Henry refused to receive Stafford or Waad, who had requested an audience. He placed Waad under house arrest at the embassy, and made it clear to him that he would be held as a hostage and not released till Mauvissière and Des Trappes had returned to France. Waad was happy enough to stay in the embassy, for he had been spat at in the street when the news of Mary's execution arrived.[33] Stafford was worried, or pretended to be, at the violence of the reaction. 'Today I find all men here in a fury', he wrote to Walsingham on 22 Februry (4 March N.S.), 'and all that love not Her Majesty in a great hope to build some great harm to her upon it . . . God is a good God, and I hope, as He hath ever done, will still preserve Her Majesty, but I see if things be not very calmly wrought with this fury that is here, they will fall out into greater extremities'.[34] What did Stafford say to his Spanish paymaster Mendoza? And what did he really think?

In France, too, people would have been less shocked if Mary had been murdered instead of officially executed. Stafford emphasised, in his reports, that it was the manner of her death which particularly outraged them. When he said to Henry III's counsellor, Bellièvre, that he hoped that Anglo-French relations would improve, Bellièvre replied that this would have been possible if 'a hangman* had not touched the head of a Queen of France (so that the manner is it that doth trouble them most).'[35]

On 13 March (N.S.) a requiem Mass for the Queen of Scots was held at Notre Dame, when the sermon was preached by the Archbishop of Bourges, who had attended her wedding to the Dauphin nearly thirty years before. Although it was not customary for a King or Queen of France to attend a requiem Mass for a foreign sovereign, Henry III and Catherine de Medici broke all precedent by being present incognito in Notre Dame. The fury in France grew stronger. Even the Huguenots, whose first reaction had been to rejoice at Mary's death, soon changed their attitude, perhaps for tactical reasons, and went along with public opinion in condemning the execution.[36]

In Scotland, the indignation was nearly as great as in France. James VI and his ambassador in London hinted at war. Philip II expressed his horror. Allen wrote to him from Rome, urging him to crown his 'glorious efforts in the holy cause of Christ by punishing this woman, hated of God and man, and restoring the country to its ancient glory and liberty'.[37] Charles Arundel – a Catholic who had formerly been employed in Elizabeth's service but had joined the refugees in Paris – wrote to Philip's minister, Idiaquez, that the King should 'revenge the wrongs committed against him by the most monstrous and barbarous creature of her sex that ever bore crown or sceptre'.[38]

Burghley and Walsingham were anxious as to how Elizabeth would react to the protests abroad. They urged Stafford to tone down his reports to Elizabeth about the indignation in France, or to send his letters to the Council, not to the Queen; and they told him that they had not shown his letters to Elizabeth for fear that this would enrage her still more against the unfortunate Davison and the other members of the Privy Council.[39] Stafford wrote that he was sorry if his reports had made things worse for Davison, but wrote to Burghley: 'I must needs write unto your lordship the truth, that I never saw a thing more hated by little, great, old, young, and of all religions, than the Queen of Scots' death, and especially the manner of it'.[40]

Burghley, Leicester and Walsingham were anxious to patch up Elizabeth's quarrel with Henry III, for they were convinced that Spain, not France, was the real enemy. They tried to persuade her to release Des Trappes and

---

*'Hangman' was Stafford's word. Bellièvre doubtless said '*bourreau*', which would equally apply to an executioner who had beheaded his victim.

receive Mauvissière in audience; but Elizabeth, feeling that her honour had been affected by Des Trappes' plot, was very difficult to convince, and obstinately refused to give way. Her counsellors hoped that the indignation in France and Scotland would pass away, as self-interest prevailed over emotional sympathy and monarchical principles; that James VI would decide to remain on good terms with Elizabeth so that she would choose him to be her heir to the throne of England; and that Henry III's fear of Philip II, the Guises and the League would drive him to renew the Anglo-French alliance. Their hopes were justified. James VI took no further action. Burghley and Walsingham persuaded Elizabeth, after two months of argument, to release Des Trappes and send him back to France, and to give Mauvissière a most gracious audience; the French merchants were compensated for the seizures by the pirates, and the English ships in France were released; and very slowly relations with Henry III improved.[41]

Elizabeth told James VI and Henry III that she was not responsible for Mary's death, as Davison had sent the death warrant to Fotheringhay without her authority. But the Privy Council did not succumb to the temptation of making Davison the scapegoat without doing what they could to help him. In their instructions to Stafford, they wrote that it was all a most unfortunate mistake. When the Queen had signed the warrant and handed it to Davison, she had told him that he was not to send it to Fotheringhay until he received further orders from her; but he had understood her to say that she wanted to hear nothing more about the matter.[42] The fact that Davison and the Council gave this explanation shows how greatly things had changed during the last forty years. In the days of Henry VIII, Davison would have confessed in grovelling tones that he had been solely to blame, and his fellow-counsellors would have heaped the vilest abuse upon him.

The foreign rulers and the Catholics did not, of course, believe Elizabeth's story; they were sure that she had ordered Mary's execution and had invented the story of Davison's disobedience in order to exculpate herself. This explanation has been generally accepted by later generations, but overlooks too many relevant facts. It overlooks her outburst of rage against Davison and Burghley when she heard about Mary's death, and her wish to have Davison hanged. It also overlooks the point which was at the root of the disagreement between Elizabeth and her counsellors, and which she could not emphasise to foreign sovereigns or to the world – was Mary to be executed or murdered?

Burghley and Walsingham were determined that she should be executed; Elizabeth much preferred that she should be murdered. On 1 February, after she had signed the death warrant, she still hoped that Paulet or someone else would murder Mary. She may not have told Davison to be sure that the warrant was not sent off without further reference to her, but Davison and all the counsellors knew that she might very probably decide to hold back the sending of the warrant while she tried again to find a murderer, and that, if none were found, she might change her mind again and decide to preserve

Mary's life. They had in their possession a warrant for Mary's execution which had passed the Great Seal, and they decided to take the risk of sending it to Fotheringhay without Elizabeth's authority, knowing that she did not wish them to do so.

The Puritans succeeded in killing a Queen, but they paid dearly for their success. Elizabeth never forgave them. When Parliament reassembled in February 1587, the Puritans introduced a bill to abolish the Book of Common Prayer and replace it with a Book of Discipline which closely resembled the Book of Common Order which Knox had drafted in Geneva and which was the prayer book of the Presbyterian Church of Scotland. Elizabeth ordered that the sponsors of the bill should be sent to the Tower for violating her royal prerogative by meddling without her consent in the government of the Church of England; and they were not released at the end of the Parliamentary session.[43] She sent a message to Parliament rejecting the proposal to abolish the Prayer Book. 'Her Majesty is fully resolved, by her own reading and princely judgement, upon the truth of the reformation which we have already ... Her Majesty taketh your petition herein to be against the prerogative of her crown'.[44]

Within a few years, death sentences were being passed and inflicted on Puritan pamphleteers. It was Mary Queen of Scots' posthumous revenge on the enemies of absolute monarchy.

CADIZ

THE Protestant cause in Europe had never been in greater danger. In the summer of 1585, while Parma was winning success after success in the Netherlands, Catherine de Medici persuaded Henry III to ratify the agreement which she had reached with Guise at Lagny and join with the League against Henry of Navarre and the Protestants. In June, the King revoked all the edicts of toleration which had been granted to the Huguenots. All Protestant pastors were ordered to leave France within a month. Other Protestants were given a month in which to become Catholics or to leave France; after this period any who remained would be proceeded against as heretics. Henry of Navarre was to surrender all the towns which he held to the King, or the royal army would join with Guise's troops to take them from him by force.[1]

Henry of Navarre sent his envoy, Ségur Pardeilhan, to London to ask Elizabeth to lend him money to pay for an army of German mercenaries whom Duke John Casimir of the Rhine Palatinate would lead into France to help him defeat the Catholic armies. Ségur impressed on Elizabeth the great urgency of the situation, but Elizabeth took three weeks to make up her mind what to do. She then agreed to lend Henry 100,000 crowns on condition that it was repaid within six months of the end of the war. Ségur hurriedly departed for Heidelberg, but when he arrived there, he found that Elizabeth had not made any arrangements to send the money. On 21 October 1585 Duke Casimir wrote to Walsingham that if Elizabeth had sent the money which she had promised, he would already have raised an army to help the King of Navarre, for if Navarre were abandoned he would drag down all Protestants with him to ruin and perdition.

After Ségur had waited for three months in Germany, Elizabeth had still not sent the money, and on 27 January 1586 he wrote bitterly to Davison that he regretted that the Queen of England, who had promised them help, should be the last to do her duty. But three weeks later, some money came at last from

Elizabeth, though it was only £15,468.15s.0d., half the sum which she had promised Ségur.[2]

The negotiations went on for months, while Elizabeth tried to persuade the King of Denmark and the Protestant German Princes to contribute to the cost of raising an army to help the King of Navarre, and she and the Germans haggled over the conditions of the repayment of the loan, the arrangements for giving security, and the liability of the guarantors. As a result, a whole year was lost, and it was not possible to raise an army to help the French Huguenots for the summer campaign of 1586. Fortunately for the Protestants, Henry of Navarre succeeded in holding his own by playing for time and entering into peace talks with Catherine de Medici and with envoys from the Swiss cantons who tried to mediate between him and Henry III.

Elizabeth, Casimir and the Germans eventually reached an agreement in November 1586, and steps were taken to prepare an army for next year. With an advance of 39,000 florins which he received from Elizabeth, Casimir raised an army of 25,000 infantry and 8,000 *reiters*, half of them Swiss and the rest German, and he led them into France in July 1587. But after they had aroused the hatred of the local population by looting and otherwise misbehaving themselves in Lorraine, a Catholic army led by Guise and his brother, the Duke of Mayenne, fell upon them and annihilated them. Most of them were killed, and the scattered remnants made their way home to Germany and Switzerland as best they could. The disaster was partly offset by a brilliant victory won by Henry of Navarre and his own French Protestant soldiers over Henry III's army at Coutras near Bordeaux.[3]

Elizabeth was angry that her money had been wasted as a result of the defeat of Casimir's army. She was also dissatisfied when she heard that Henry of Navarre, instead of following up his victory by marching on Paris or trying to link up with Casimir, had gone off to Pau to take the captured enemy flags to his latest mistress, Corisande de Gramont, and to hold discussions on politics and philosophy on the way with the famous philosopher Montaigne.[4] But Henry of Navarre had not acted irresponsibly. For political reasons, he did not wish to take the offensive against the King, and hoped, by merely defending himself against the attacks of the royalist armies, to convince Henry III and the moderate Catholics that he was a loyal subject who wanted only to unite with them to defend the King against his rebellious subjects, the Guises and the League. But he would not take the only step which would have won them over to his side: he would not become a Catholic.

The war in the Netherlands was not going well, though it aroused great enthusiasm in England, where the people were reading stirring but largely fictitious ballads about the fighting at Zutphen and Ghent, and the deeds of valour of Norris, 'the brave Lord Willoughby', and the woman soldier, Mary Ambree.[5] In October 1586 the whole nation suffered a deep sense of loss with the death of Sir Philip Sidney, who was wounded in the thigh in a minor skirmish at the siege of Zutphen, and died a month later when the wound became gangrenous. His funeral in St Paul's in February 1587 was attended by thousands of mourners.

The rift between Elizabeth and the people of the Netherlands became worse during 1586. At the beginning of the year she was scolding the States for having invited Leicester to be their Governor and was telling them that he was a disobedient subject; by the end of the year she had completely forgiven him, and was periodically sending abusive letters to the States, denouncing them for not treating Lord Leicester, her dearly beloved cousin and representative in the Netherlands, with proper respect.[6] Leicester became involved in the quarrels between the leading Dutch politicians. Some of them turned to him for help against their rivals, and others conspired against him because he favoured their opponents.

Elizabeth sent the Irish colonel, Sir William Stanley, to hold the town of Deventer with a garrison of Irish soldiers. The Dutch Protestants became worried when they realised that Stanley and many of his soldiers were Catholics; but Elizabeth was always prepared to overlook the religious faith of her Catholic subjects, and to use them in her service if she was convinced that they were loyal to her. Stanley had served her loyally in Ireland for nearly twenty years. He had particularly distinguished himself in suppressing the rebellion in Munster in 1579–81, and had carried out wholesale executions of rebels in Arklow.[7]

Elizabeth and Leicester disregarded the protests of the Dutch Protestants against the employment of Stanley at Deventer; but on 29 January 1587 (N.S.) Stanley surrendered Deventer to Parma, with whom he had been in secret correspondence for some weeks. On the same day, Rowland Yorke surrendered the important Venloe fort before Zutphen to Parma. The news of the fall of Deventer and the fort at Zutphen was a consolation to Mendoza in Paris, who was informed about it when he was hourly expecting to hear of the execution of the Queen of Scots.[8]

Three weeks before Stanley surrendered Deventer, he had written to Walsingham to complain that his men were in great want, and that he had had to pawn his own clothes to raise the money to buy them food and drink. But he did not commit his act of treason because of his anger at Elizabeth's neglect of his troops, nor for the reward of £50,000 which Parma was said to have paid him for his treachery. He had been for many years a secret sympathiser with the Catholic cause and in touch with the English Catholic opponents of Elizabeth. On 26 December 1586 (N.S.) Mendoza wrote to Parma that some of the Babington plotters had informed the authorities, during their interrogation, that they were in touch with Stanley, and Mendoza urged Parma to warn Stanley that the authorities were intending to arrest him when he returned to England, and that he had better take refuge with Parma by surrendering Deventer to him. Stanley and all his Irish soldiers entered

Parma's service, and fought in the Spanish army against their former comrades-in-arms.[9]

There was great indignation in the Netherlands at the loss of their important town of Deventer through the treason of an officer in the army of their English allies, thanks to Elizabeth's refusal to heed their warnings about the dangers of placing her trust in a Catholic. A German visitor wrote from Arnhem in February 1587 that the betrayal of Deventer had stirred up as much hatred against the English as had been felt against the French after Anjou's attempt to seize Antwerp, though so far it was expressed only with the tongue. He was distressed to see it directed against the poor English soldiers who were enduring great misery and poverty for the cause of an ungrateful people.[10]

Elizabeth reacted by blaming the States for all the disasters and difficulties and for their unwillingness to pay their share of the costs of the war. She firmly refused their requests for more money; but a week later she changed her mind, and on 21 February sent £600 to the English garrison in Ostend and £3,000 to Leicester.[11]

While Elizabeth's negotiations with Parma, through De Loo and Lanfranchi, continued very slowly, Walsingham was again receiving reports from his agents in the Spanish ports, in Italy and in France of the Spanish naval and military preparations to invade either England, Ireland or Scotland. The Spaniards were equally alarmed at the reports that Drake was preparing to sail with a fleet of twenty-one ships to be manned by two thousand men.[12] They wondered where Drake was intending to go, for so large a fleet and force, which was ten times the size of the expedition with which he had sailed round the world, would not have been needed for a raid on the Spanish Main.

Drake sailed from Plymouth in his flagship *The Elizabeth Bonaventure* on 14 September 1585, and twelve days later reached Vigo in northern Spain and the neighbouring islands. According to the horrified Spaniards, his men stripped the rich garments off the image of Our Lady of the Bongo on the Isle of Bongo in the bay, and bombarded the Great Cross of Vigo from the sea with their guns. Before he returned to Portsmouth ten months later, he had raided the Cape Verde Islands; destroyed St Augustine, the capital of the Spanish colony in Florida; captured and sacked Cartagena, the greatest and richest city in the New World; and returned to England with booty valued at £60,000.[13] None of his previous expeditions had excited so much attention throughout Europe; it made him the hero of the international Protestant cause, a devilish pirate in Spanish and Catholic eyes, and a romantic adventurer to less committed people who admired a brave man.

Reports of his progress, and the extent of the damage which he had inflicted on the Spaniards, reached Walsingham and Elizabeth from Paris, Lyons, Antwerp, Bordeaux and Frankfort; and Mary Queen of Scots wrote repeatedly from her prison to express her indignation at his activities. In

Spain, the people remembered how Charles V in 1541 had been forced by public opinion to undertake his disastrous expedition to Algiers to avenge far less serious depredations by the Algerian pirates than those which Drake was committing by his interception of the treasure ships from the Levant, Mexico and Peru. They demanded that King Philip should withdraw troops from the Netherlands, and from the fleet which was preparing to invade England, in order to send them to the West Indies to protect the Spanish cities there and to find, catch and punish Drake. A few days later, twenty-four Spanish ships with six thousand men sailed from the Spanish ports for the West Indies; but they missed Drake, who was already well on his way to Portsmouth.[14]

De Loo and Lanfranchi found that Elizabeth and Parma were not so far apart. They agreed that Philip's plans for the Armada, and Drake's naval preparations, should be abandoned; that Elizabeth would withdraw all English troops from the Netherlands and stop all aid to the States, who would be required to return to their allegiance to Philip, while Philip would desist from giving any aid to the Irish or to any of Elizabeth's rebels. Parma agreed to pardon all the rebels in the Netherlands, to withdraw all Spanish troops and advisers, and to govern the country solely through native ministers as Charles V had done. But there was deadlock on the one issue which had always prevented peace in the Netherlands: Parma, on Philip's instructions, refused Elizabeth's demand that he should grant religious toleration there.

Lanfranchi assured De Loo that this was not negotiable. Parma's counsellors asked how Elizabeth could expect Philip, as a sovereign Prince, to agree to fetter his right either to enforce uniformity or grant toleration to his subjects, at his absolute discretion. They were sure that Elizabeth would never agree to do any such thing, and they had not demanded it of her. This was the argument most likely to influence Elizabeth, and as the long negotiations dragged on, and Parma stood absolutely firm on this point, she began to weaken. She suggested that there were degrees of toleration. She would not insist that Philip should grant the Protestants in the Netherlands equality with the Catholics, and the right to hold Protestant prayer-meetings. She asked merely that Philip, whose merciful disposition was so well known, should promise not to persecute the Protestants so long as they obeyed the law, respected the Catholic religion, and worshipped quietly in their homes. Parma agreed to refer this proposal to Philip, but in due course the reply came from Lanfranchi, and from Grimaldo in Genoa, that Philip had rejected it; if Elizabeth realised that he had a merciful disposition, she must leave it to him to exercise his usual mercy at his absolute discretion, without seeking in any way to restrict his sovereign power by treaty.[15]

After the sacking of Cartagena and the enormous losses inflicted on Spanish trade by Drake, Philip at last decided to invade England; and the execution of

Mary Queen of Scots placed him under a moral obligation to punish Elizabeth. It also removed the old Spanish fear that if Elizabeth were overthrown she would be succeeded by Mary, and that this would place a pro-French Queen on the throne of England. Before Mary died, she had bequeathed her title to the English crown to Philip if James VI was still a heretic at the time of her death.[16] Philip intended to claim the throne for himself, and then present it as a gift to his daughter, the Infanta, in order to disarm any English suspicion that he was intending to make England a subject territory of Spain.

Reports reached Walsingham that the preparations for the Armada were being hurried forward at Lisbon and Cadiz, and that the Spanish fleet would be ready to sail to invade England in the summer of 1587. He urged Elizabeth to send Drake to attack Cadiz and sink the Spanish transport ships before they could sail. Elizabeth was very reluctant to agree, for she thought it would wreck the negotiations with Parma and make war inevitable; but her counsellors, as well as Drake and her seamen, warned her that Parma was spinning out the negotiations until the Armada was ready to sail, and that her only chance to defeat it was to allow Drake to sink it in Cadiz. She at last agreed, and at the beginning of March 1587 gave orders for the expedition to prepare to sail as soon as possible.

Walsingham and Drake, who between them planned the details of the expedition, decided to enforce the strictest security. They did not even tell the English ambassadors abroad, and it was only on 21 April, two days after Drake entered the harbour at Cadiz, that Walsingham wrote to tell Stafford that Drake was going to attack Cadiz. This was a wiser precaution than Walsingham realised.[17]

Mendoza had gone to great lengths to conceal the fact that Stafford was a secret agent in his pay, and Walsingham and Elizabeth never knew, though Walsingham suspected him and set agents to spy on him. Mendoza worded his reports to Philip about Stafford with great cunning, for he feared that his letters might be intercepted by Huguenots on the roads of south-west France, or, if they went by sea, off the coast of La Rochelle. The Huguenots would then send the letters to Walsingham, whose clerks might decipher the code in which they were written. So he wrote in a way which he hoped would confuse everyone except Philip. Sometimes he sent Philip information about letters from Walsingham to the English ambassador in Paris which he said had been intercepted by an agent whom he would refer to by the code name of Julio. In fact, the information had been given to Mendoza by Stafford himself. Mendoza often sent reports about the plans of the English government which he stated had been sent to him by Julio from London. Sometimes he would write in the same letter about some diplomatic action taken by the English ambassador in Paris, or about a conversation which he had had with the ambassador, and then go on to report information which he had been given by Julio, as well as other information which he had obtained from another agent, whom he called 'the new confidant'. He gave no indication that the English ambassador, Julio and the new confidant were all one and the same person.[18] When Philip read Mendoza's letters, he realised how Mendoza had really obtained his information.

Mendoza told Philip that he had paid the new confidant 2,000 crowns for his services. Stafford, like Elizabeth's other ambassadors, wrote regularly to Burghley and Walsingham complaining that he was short of money. This helped to conceal the fact that he had received the 2,000 crowns from Mendoza.[19]

But thanks to Walsingham's precautions in not informing the English ambassadors, Stafford knew nothing about the Cadiz expedition, and could only guess where Drake was going. On 13 March (N.S.) one of Mendoza's agents in England wrote to him that twenty-four ships were preparing to sail from Gravesend with 2,500 men, but that it would need at least eighteen days to salt the 2,500 bullocks which would be needed for the usual ration of one bullock per man for a four-month voyage. Another agent told Mendoza that the expedition would not sail till Lord Buckhurst had returned from Holland with news of the situation there, and that though he had no idea where Drake was going, he assumed it was the Spanish Main. In fact, Drake was intending to sail from Plymouth, and there was no intention of waiting for Buckhurst.[20]

Drake sailed on 2 April. On the same day, Elizabeth received a report from Spain that the preparations for the sailing of the Armada had been halted. She decided that Drake should not attack Cadiz, and sent a courier in post to Plymouth ordering Drake to cruise off the coast of Spain but on no account to enter a Spanish port and attack the Armada. Drake sailed a few hours before the courier arrived at Plymouth; so Elizabeth ordered a pinnace to set out at once to catch Drake and give him his new orders.[21] Walsingham was worried, and wrote to Leicester on 11 April: 'This resolution proceedeth altogether upon a hope of peace which I fear will draw a dangerous war upon Her Majesty by the alienation of the hearts of the well-affected people in the Low Countries'.[22]

Mendoza still had no definite information about Drake's plans. On 12 and 19 April (N.S.) he wrote from Paris to Philip that Drake had sailed on 27 March (N.S.) from Gravesend to Plymouth, from whence he was about to sail, and that his destination was almost certainly to intercept the Spanish fleet which was on its way to Spain from the West Indies; but that 'the new friend' – he meant Stafford – had told him that Drake might be planning to attack the Armada in Cadiz or in some other Spanish port, though the destination of the expedition was being kept so secret that Drake was the only man in the fleet who knew where they were going.[23]

Elizabeth changed her mind again. She decided to recall Drake to England to make sure that he did not attack the Armada. Then she reverted to her second decision, that the fleet should cruise off the coast of Spain, but not attack. But the pinnace carrying the dispatch was held up by contrary winds, and could not overtake Drake, who on 29 April (N.S.) arrived outside Cadiz and learned that thirty ships of the Armada were in the harbour. He decided to attack them at once. He entered the harbour with twenty-seven ships and began to bombard the Armada and the defences of the town, and sent in fireships to burn the Spanish ships. After carrying out a difficult operation against well-prepared defences, and remaining in the bay for thirty-six hours, he sailed away to the south-east on 1 May (N.S.).

He did more damage to the Spanish ships in the Algarve and off Cape St Vincent, taking several prisoners. When the Spanish admiral, the Marquis of Santa Cruz, refused his offer of an exchange of prisoners, Drake told him that he would sell his Spanish prisoners as slaves to the Moors and use the money to redeem the English seamen whom the Moors held as slaves. He then returned to England, after plundering the East Indies fleet off the Azores, and reached Plymouth with £57,000 in Spanish loot. He paid £40,000 of it to Elizabeth, and kept £17,000 for himself.[24]

On 13 May (N.S.) Philip wrote to Mendoza that his report that Drake might be intending to attack Cadiz was correct, but that unfortunately Mendoza's letter had reached him at Aranjuez a few hours after Drake entered the harbour at Cadiz, so the warning which Philip had forwarded to the authorities at Cadiz had arrived too late. Mendoza explained that he had sent the information to Philip as soon as he received it, but that it had been held up for four days thanks to the delay by the French bureaucracy in giving his courier a passport.[25]

The losses at Cadiz prevented the Armada from sailing that summer, and put back the expedition for at least six months. The earliest possible date for the invasion of England was now January 1588. It was also a heavy blow to Philip's prestige. The Venetian ambassador in Spain reported that 'the Spaniards say that the King thinks and plans while the Queen of England acts'.[26] The people of England boasted that Drake had singed the King of Spain's beard; and in Ferrera Drake's portrait, which had been brought from France, was repainted as the colours had faded and exhibited in a shop window, under the caption '*Il Draco, quel gran corsaro inglese*', to the large crowds who gathered in the street to look at it.[27]

As Elizabeth's counsellors had expected, the attack on Cadiz did not prevent Parma from continuing with the peace negotiations, though Lanfranchi told De Loo of Parma's pained surprise that Elizabeth should have sanctioned the attack while the negotiations were in progress. Burghley assured De Loo that Elizabeth had sent a courier to tell Drake not to attack Cadiz, but that unfortunately he had arrived too late. Parma himself was prepared to combine war and peace, and while continuing the negotiations he besieged Sluys and forced the garrison to surrender in August 1587. This was a serious setback for the Dutch, but an even more serious one for Elizabeth, for Sluys was an important port which Parma could use for the invasion of England. Elizabeth angrily blamed the Dutch for their failure to send help to the English garrison there. The Dutch blamed the English, and Leicester blamed his subordinate commanders.[28]

The peace negotiations had reached a stage at which Elizabeth decided to tell the States that Parma had invited her to send commissioners to discuss peace terms, and that in accordance with her treaty obligations she was informing them of this and inviting them to send their own commissioners to take part in the peace talks. But the news caused great indignation in the Netherlands, where the leaders of the States and most of the people believed that Elizabeth was about to betray them and make a settlement with the Spaniards at their expense.[29] The Dutch in the northern provinces were particularly alarmed; after fifteen years of *de facto* independence, they did not wish to be ruled once again by Philip, even if Elizabeth could persuade him to grant them religious toleration; for as Leicester wrote to Burghley, 'they are bent. . . upon a popular government for ever'.[30] Sir Thomas Sherley wrote to Walsingham: 'The proposition of peace hath wonderfully offended these people, and made our nation odious unto them. They are ready to shut us out of all their towns and fall into plain suspicion of us'.[31] Some Dutchmen even believed that Elizabeth had been in collusion with Philip from the beginning, and had made her treaty with the States in order to gain possession of Flushing and Brill so that she could hand them over to the Spaniards. But the French Huguenots urged the States not to offend Elizabeth, and to remember that, however exasperating she might be, she had come to their aid when they were in a desperate situation, and that they would be lost if she were to abandon them.[32]

Nearly every English Protestant, except Elizabeth and Burghley, agreed with the Dutch in opposing the peace talks, and thought that Parma was tricking Elizabeth into participating in them while the Armada was being prepared for the invasion of England. 'I am not a little sorry', wrote Sir William Russell to Walsingham from Flushing, 'to see Her Majesty run so violent a course for peace, which can no way be good for her nor these countries'.[33] Sir William Pelham agreed with him,[34] and Stephen Powle in Venice thought that 'a Spanish peace is more dangerous than manifest hatred'.[35] Leicester himself urged Elizabeth to consider that 'not only the cause of God and of these countries, but your own honour and security' were involved, for 'Your Majesty must look for a most dangerous and most troublesome time whensoever the King of Spain shall again possess these countries absolutely'.[36] He thought that Parma's motive in entering into the peace talks was to cause ill-feeling between Elizabeth and the Dutch, and that he had achieved his objective.[37]

In June 1587, as the preparations for the Armada continued, a Spanish ship patrolling the coast off San Sebastian intercepted a boat which was sailing from San Sebastian to France. On board they found a young Englishman aged about twenty-five, who told them that he was a Catholic and had been in Spain to fulfil a vow to go to the shrine of Our Lady of Monserrat and now wished to go to France. They suspected that he was an English spy, and imprisoned him at San Sebastian; but after a few days he asked to see Sir Francis Englefield, and he was taken to Englefield's house in Madrid. He told Englefield a long story, which Englefield asked him to put into writing, and after he had done so, Englefield immediately sent it to the King.[38]

He said that his name was Arthur Dudley. His earliest recollection was being brought up as a small child in a village some sixty miles from London with several other children whom he thought were his brothers and sisters, by Robert Southern, whom he assumed was his father. Southern was a servant of Katherine Ashley, Queen Elizabeth's former governess. One day, when Arthur was about five, Southern put him on his horse, took him to London, and placed him in the care of Katherine Ashley's husband, John Ashley, though Southern's other children remained in the village. Arthur was given a gentleman's education, and was taught Latin, French, Italian, fencing, music and dancing, and the principles of English law. Then John Ashley appointed Southern to be his deputy in supervising the Queen's house at Enfield. Arthur spent the winters in London, but in summer was taken to Enfield to avoid the danger of plague.

When Arthur was about fourteen or fifteen, he told Ashley and Southern that he would like to travel abroad, like many other young gentlemen of his age. He was told that this was impossible; so he ran away to Milford Haven, intending to embark on a ship bound for Spain. There he was arrested and sent back to London by the local justices of the peace, who showed him an order which had come from the Privy Council, commanding that he be prevented at all costs from leaving the kingdom. He was eventually allowed to enlist as a volunteer to fight in the Netherlands, and in 1580 he travelled to Ostend in the care of a servant of the Earl of Leicester.

Towards the end of 1583 he received a message asking him to return to England at once, as his father was very ill and wished to tell him something important before he died. He found Southern dying at Evesham. Southern told him that he was not his father, but that one day he had been ordered by Kate Ashley to go to Hampton Court, where Lady Harington, who was one of the Queen's ladies-in-waiting, had delivered to him a new-born baby. She told him that the baby was the illegitimate son of one of the ladies of the court, who would be ruined if the Queen got to hear of her misconduct, and was therefore giving the child to Southern to bring him up in his village as his own son. Afterwards Ashley had ordered him to bring the child to him. Southern told Arthur that he was this child, and that it was Ashley, not Southern, who had paid for his education. Arthur asked the dying Southern who his father was. At first, Southern said that he knew but dared not say; but in the end he told Arthur that he was the illegitimate child of Leicester and the Queen.

At this point, Arthur Dudley's story to Englefield became very long and complicated. It involved Arthur's travels in the Netherlands, France and Germany, his attempt to betray a town in Holland to the Spaniards, how his act was discovered and he was arrested but protected by Leicester, and his meetings with Leicester, Walsingham and Mauvissière. It ended with his decision, having become a devout Catholic, to go on a pilgrimage to the shrine of Our Lady of Monserrat near Barcelona, and how he had then tried to go to France when he heard of the indignation there at the Queen of Scots' death. He told Englefield that he was afraid that Elizabeth's agents would try to murder him in order to hush up the scandal of his birth, but offered, if King Philip would guarantee him protection, to write a book disclosing the truth.[39]

Englefield was very suspicious. After consulting Philip, he set a number of trick questions for Arthur Dudley, in order to test the truth of his statement that he had had a good education and his knowledge of Elizabeth's household and the people whom he claimed to have known in England. Englefield had to admit that Arthur passed all these tests satisfactorily, but was nevertheless convinced that he was an English spy and was only pretending to be a Catholic. The explanation which Englefield put forward to Philip was nearly as involved as Arthur's narrative. Englefield believed that Elizabeth had invented the story about Arthur being her illegitimate son so that she could, as a last resort, acknowledge him and have him nominated as heir to the throne by Act of Parliament. This would defeat the claim of the King of Scots, with whom she had quarrelled as a result of the execution of his mother; and above all, it would obstruct King Philip's claim to the throne. But Elizabeth hoped to make use of the lie that Arthur Dudley was her son without openly acknowledging her misconduct with Leicester: by merely telling the tale, Arthur would divide the Catholics, for some of them would support him as a Catholic candidate to the throne of England instead of Philip;[40] or 'perhaps they may be making use of him in some other way for their iniquitous ends'.[41]

Philip told Englefield that, as there was obviously some doubt about Arthur Dudley, and as it was not easy to foretell what the effect would be if his story were made public, it would be best to have him incarcerated for the time being in some Spanish monastery.[42] There is no further reference to him in the surviving Spanish state papers. Perhaps he was detained in the monastery for the rest of his life.

THE ARMADA

O N 4 September 1587 (N.S.) Philip wrote to Parma that he had decided to invade England as soon as possible. The Armada would sail from the Spanish and Portuguese ports to Margate, where they would establish a bridgehead; and Parma, who was to begin at once assembling an invasion army, would then sail from the ports of the Netherlands to Margate, and join the soldiers of the Armada in the conquest of England. Philip knew the risks involved in sending a fleet to northern waters in mid-winter, but would trust to God to send the Armada favourable weather, as it would be fighting in His cause.[1]

Parma believed that the operation would be feasible, for the English had no fleet stationed in the Channel or the North Sea to impede the invasion. He borrowed the necessary money from the bankers at Antwerp, enlisted Spanish, Walloon and Italian mercenaries, and assembled a fleet of transport ships at Dunkirk, Nieuport and Sluys; but he had no galleys or warships in the Netherlands which were capable of encountering the English fleet, and he was relying on the fact that it was not there. It was partly in order to lull the English into a false sense of security that on 9 November (N.S.) he wrote for the first time directly to Elizabeth herself and invited her to send commissioners to Ostend to discuss peace terms with his commissioners. Elizabeth accepted on condition that Parma would allow commissioners from the States to attend the talks, and when Parma agreed, she used all her efforts to persuade the States to send commissioners; but Friesland was the only northern province that wished to do so, and the Council of State played for time by refusing to appoint commissioners until a meeting of the States-General had been convened. Elizabeth lost patience, and on 16 December informed the States that in view of their delay, she would send her commissioners to meet Parma's without them. She also told them that as they had shown such disrespect to her Lieutenant-General, Leicester, she was recalling him to England and appointing Lord Willoughby to succeed him.[2]

The prospect of peace talks did not prevent Elizabeth's government from taking the necessary steps to resist the Armada when it came, and at the same time as Elizabeth sent this angry message to the States, she asked them to comply with their treaty obligations by sending ships to assist her against the Armada. Some of the people in the Netherlands were so angry with Elizabeth that they wished to refuse; but the more responsible leaders, including the Assembly of the Protestant Churches in the Netherlands, urged the States to remember that if the Spaniards overthrew Elizabeth in England, it would be the ultimate disaster for the Protestant cause in the Netherlands and everywhere in Europe. On 1 January 1588 (N.S.) the States informed Elizabeth that they were sending thirty ships under William of Orange's illegitimate son, Count Justin of Nassau, to patrol the coast of Zeeland and engage Parma's ships if they came out of Nieuport and Sluys and tried to cross to England.[3]

Elizabeth showed very little gratitude for the help of the Dutch ships, and was soon complaining about their quality to the States;[4] but Parma was aware of their importance. He was waiting in Bruges for the arrival of both the English peace commissioners and of the Armada; but to his dismay the Armada did not come. On 31 January (N.S.) he wrote to Philip that although he had been ready in November and December to invade England, the situation had now changed, for in the last few weeks the English fleet had been made ready for action in the Channel and the North Sea, and Philip's rebels had thirty ships patrolling the coast of Zeeland. He would not venture out of port with his transport ships, for if he did, they would be destroyed by the enemy warships; the Armada would have to come to Nieuport and Sluys to escort his army to Margate. He had other worries. His treasure was being frittered away in paying the costs of the army which was waiting inactive in the ports, and he was finding it difficult to persuade the Antwerp bankers to lend him more money. The invasion force was suffering from plague; whereas in November he had had 28,000 fit fighting men, he wrote on 22 February (N.S.) that the number had now fallen to 18,000.[5]

Because of this, Parma was probably more seriously in favour of making peace when Elizabeth's commissioners arrived at Ostend on 8 March (N.S.) than he had been four months earlier when he invited Elizabeth to send them. But Elizabeth now showed the great importance which she attached to anything which she thought might affront her honour as Queen of England. She might be prepared, for the sake of peace, to give way on the question of religious toleration for the Protestants in the Netherlands, but she would not lower her prestige in the eyes of the world by agreeing to hold peace talks in Philip's territory. She told her commissioners to insist that the talks be held in Ostend. Parma refused to hold the talks in a town which was occupied by English troops, and suggested Antwerp in Spanish-occupied territory; but Elizabeth would not agree to Antwerp, and on 26 March sent instructions to her commissioners that if Parma refused to agree to Ostend, they must break off negotiations and retire to Flushing to await further developments.

Burghley did not wish to see the hope of peace disappear, after nearly three years of preliminary negotiations, because of a disagreement over venue, and he persuaded Elizabeth to send them new instructions: if Parma persisted in refusing to send his commissioners to Ostend, they were to propose that they should meet in tents outside Ostend on the road to Oldenburg, which was held by the Spaniards.[6]

Burghley and Walsingham then realised that there were difficulties about holding the talks in the tents, owing to a lack of transport facilities at Ostend, and on 8 April Burghley persuaded Elizabeth to authorise the commissioners to agree, in the last resort, to go to Antwerp. But a few hours later she changed her mind, brushed aside the objections to holding the talks in the tents, and sent another message to the commissioners ordering them on no account to agree to go to Antwerp.[7]

The first meeting of the English and Spanish commissioners was held in the tents on 21 April (N.S.); but Parma's commissioners would not discuss anything except where the next meeting was to be held, for they refused to hold any further talks in the tents. The English rejected Parma's suggestion that they should meet in Ghent. They offered to go to Sluys, where they and their servants might be able to discover useful information about Parma's naval and military preparations; but Parma guessed that this was their object, and refused to agree to Sluys. The English said that they would agree to Bruges on condition that Parma himself and the English Catholic refugees withdrew from the town while the talks were in progress, to which Parma would not agree. In the end, both sides agreed to Bourbourg in Spanish territory near Dunkirk, where the church of the little town was a landmark visible for many miles across the great plain of Flanders, and where several international peace conferences had been held during the last fifty years.[8]

The commissioners met at Bourbourg on 30 May (N.S.). The English proposed that both sides should agree to a truce while the talks were in progress, but Parma rejected this, and after another month of argument about the truce, Elizabeth sent orders to her commissioners to give way, and the talks on the substantive issues began at last on 24 June (N.S.). The question of religious toleration was again a stumbling block. Elizabeth's commissioners now proposed that Philip should agree to grant religious toleration to the Protestants in the northern provinces for ten years, after which time the question would be discussed again between the King of Spain and the States-General of the Netherlands. One of the reasons why Elizabeth and Burghley put forward this modified proposal was that they thought that Philip, who was so obstinately opposed to religious toleration, would die within ten years, for he was aged sixty-one and one of the oldest sovereigns in Europe.[9]

Parma rejected the proposal, but for the first time made a slight concession about religious toleration. He offered, subject to Philip's agreement, to refrain from enforcing the heresy laws in the Netherlands for two years after the peace treaty was signed, in order to give the Protestants time to decide whether to become Catholics or to sell their property and emigrate, taking all their goods with them. Any Protestant who remained in the Netherlands after the two-year period of grace would be proceeded against as a heretic, and burned. The English commissioners would not agree.[10]

Elizabeth instructed her commissioners to put forward a new demand. She was worried that if she made peace with Philip, the infuriated Dutch would refuse to pay back the loans which she had made to them and for which they had given her Flushing and Brill in pledge; and she asked Parma to guarantee the repayment of the loans by the Dutch, and to agree that she should continue to hold Flushing and Brill till the debt was repaid by the States or by Philip. Parma rejected as outrageous the suggestion that Philip should pay for the expenses which Elizabeth had incurred in helping his subjects to rebel against him; but she argued that as the people of the Netherlands had always been Philip's subjects, he was liable to her for their debts.[11]

The Armada sailed from Lisbon on 30 May (N.S.) under the command of the Duke of Medina Sidonia. It consisted of 130 ships carrying 16,973 Spanish and 2,000 Portuguese soldiers, 8,052 seamen and 167 gunners, giving a grand total, including the gentlemen's servants, the priests, the hospital staff, the officers of justice, and the clerks of the finance department, of 30,693 men. There were 2,431 guns, with 123,790 cannon balls.* The fleet encountered storms soon after leaving Lisbon, which scattered the ships and forced Sidonia to put in to Corunna, where he waited for a month until all his ships had been reunited there. The Governor of Corunna had to surround the port with soldiers to prevent the men on the Armada from deserting.[12]

The Armada was helped by developments in France. On 8 May (N.S.) Guise arrived in Paris, and four days later, on the 'Day of the Barricades', the people rose in his support, and seized control of the city, which passed under the authority of a revolutionary Committee of Sixteen, all ardent supporters of Guise, the Holy League and the Catholic Church. Henry III escaped from Paris, and prepared for war against Guise; but though Elizabeth sent him messages of sympathy and support, and urged him to take firm action to suppress Guise and his rebels in Paris, with the help of his loyal Huguenot subjects, he was persuaded by Catherine de Medici to make peace with the League and to appoint Guise as his Lieutenant-General.[13] The worst aspect from Elizabeth's point of view was that Normandy and most of the Channel coast passed under Guise's control, though the Governor of Calais, who held the town for Henry III, remained neutral, and refused to join Guise's side.

The English Catholic refugees believed that at last the hour of liberation was at hand. Some of them confidently expected that the Catholics in England would rise to support the invading army; but one of them, who gave

*Other reports give slightly different figures of the number of men in the Armada.

the Spanish government a list of the names of Catholic gentlemen in England who could be trusted, feared that the Armada would only be welcomed by the English people if it landed in Westmorland or Northumberland, though there would be some support from Catholics in Lancashire and Norfolk. After mentioning the name of Sir Henry Bedingfield, who had been Elizabeth's guardian when she was a prisoner in Mary's reign, he added: 'I wish to God they had burned her then, as she deserved, with the rest of the heretics who were justly executed. If this had been done, we should be living now in peace and quietness'.[14] Allen, who had recently been made a Cardinal, thought that many Protestants might become Catholics if the soldiers of the Armada established themselves in England, particularly if the Spanish generals were to announce that the lands of all Protestants would be confiscated and given to Catholics.[15]

Elizabeth heard that Allen had written a book, *An Admonition to the Nobility and People of England and Ireland concerning the present Wars*, which had been published in Antwerp in English, for it was intended that copies of the book should be sent to England when the Armada had landed. It denounced Elizabeth, the issue of the 'incestuous copulation' of her 'supposed father', Henry VIII, with 'an infamous courtesan, Anne Boleyn'; she had suppressed the Catholic Church, abolished the Feast of the Virgin on 8 September and replaced it with the celebration of 'her own impure birthday' on the previous day, had made England 'a place of refuge and sanctuary of all Atheists, Anabaptists, heretics, and rebellious of all nations', and had murdered Mary Queen of Scots. He called on all Englishmen to refuse to fight for 'an infamous, deprived, accursed, excommunicate heretic, the very shame of her sex and princely name', and to join the Spanish army when it arrived and fight to depose her and restore the Catholic faith to 'our dear country' in obedience to the orders of 'the general of this holy war'.[16]

On 29 June Elizabeth sent orders to the commissioners at Bourbourg that Dr Dale was to go to Parma at Bruges and demand that he suppress Allen's book and punish the publisher and printer, and that he should also repudiate the new Papal bull which appointed him commander of the army which was to invade England and depose her. If Parma refused, she would break off the negotiations and recall her commissioners. Parma blandly denied all knowledge of Allen's book or of the bull. When Dale reported this to Elizabeth, she wrote to the commissioners on 17 July recalling them to England, but instructing them to tell Parma's commissioners that when Philip's warlike preparations ceased and Allen's book and the bull were withdrawn, she would be very happy to resume the peace talks, which this time should be held in England.[17] Two days after Elizabeth wrote this letter, the Armada was sighted off the Lizard. The commissioners did not return to England until after the battle was over.

Sidonia's orders were to sail to Margate and not to divert from his route in order to capture any English port or to engage the English fleet unless they impeded his progress. He carried sealed orders to Parma, which he was to give him when they landed in England, authorising Parma, if he was unable to gain an outright victory, to negotiate peace with the English on three conditions – that religious toleration was granted to the English Catholics, that Elizabeth withdrew her troops from the Netherlands, and that the English paid compensation for all the damage inflicted on Philip and his merchants by Drake and other pirates.[18]

But there was an ambiguity in Philip's instructions to Sidonia and Parma which was to have unfortunate results for the Spaniards. The careful and conscientious King, who spent the greater part of every day in the Escorial writing and annotating state papers dealing with the most detailed questions of government administration throughout his empire from the Netherlands to Peru, had never clearly told Sidonia about Parma's objection to crossing over to Margate without the protection of the Armada, and that Parma did not intend to leave the ports of the Netherlands until the Armada came to fetch him.[19]

In England the news that the Armada was coming aroused the patriotism of the people, which expressed itself in devotion to the Queen. Elizabeth had never been so popular as in the summer of 1588, when her loyal subjects determined to defeat the wicked practices of the Pope and the King of Spain, who, having failed to contrive the assassination of the Queen by the Jesuits, the English Catholic traitors and the Jezebel Queen of Scots, now hoped to succeed by invading the realm with cruel Spanish troops who would perpetrate in London the acts of murder, rape and pillage in which they had indulged in Antwerp during the 'Spanish fury' of 1576.[20]

The hour of danger brought out the best qualities in Elizabeth. It was not a time for bickering with the Dutch or with the Puritans, but for the whole nation, from Whitgift's authoritarian Anglicans to Cartwright, Wentworth and the Puritans, to unite against the foreign Papist invaders under the leadership of their English Protestant Queen. There were also many Catholics in England who were preparing to fight loyally for Elizabeth instead of following Allen's instructions to offer their services to the Spanish general; but the Privy Council took the precaution of arresting the more prominent Catholic gentlemen throughout England and interning them in Wisbech Castle in Cambridgeshire. They might otherwise have been the target for attacks by patriotic Protestant mobs.[21]

Elizabeth was at her best because she no longer had to take important decisions. The issue of peace or war had been decided, and she had handed over the daily conduct of operations to a Council of War composed of her admirals and generals. The Lord Admiral, Lord Howard of Effingham, was in supreme command of the navy, with Drake as his second-in-command. Drake had become a national hero, but only a nobleman could be given the supreme command without offending the sense of propriety of Elizabeth and of nearly all her subjects, and arousing the resentment and jealousy of the other naval officers. Leicester was appointed to be the Queen's Lieutenant and Captain-General of the land forces in England which were being rapidly enlisted to resist the invaders if they landed.

The Council of War realised that the Armada was planning to sail up the Channel to link up with Parma's forces, for Parma had made no attempt to conceal his preparations for the invasion. But they had not discovered that Margate was the invaders' first objective, and expected that the Spaniards would land in Essex and march on London. They therefore decided to assemble 22,000 men in a camp near Tilbury to bar Parma's road to London, and to build a bridge of boats between Tilbury and Gravesend by which the soldiers could cross the Thames if Parma landed in Kent. The rest of the land forces were to remain for the moment in readiness in their counties until they received orders where to go.[22] Elizabeth remained at Richmond, unafraid, and confident that God would grant her victory over her enemies.

Preparations had been made to light beacons on the hilltops to give warning of the approach of the Armada. It was the only way in which news could be sent from the Channel to the Scottish Border in a few hours.

The Armada left Corunna at last in perfect weather on 22 July (N.S.), and was sighted off the Lizard on 19 July (29 July N.S.). The beacons were lit, and Lord Howard and Drake in Plymouth prepared to attack the enemy. Their aim was to prevent or impede the Armada from linking up with Parma's army. The Spanish ships sailed very slowly eastwards up the Channel, their speed reduced by the lack of wind to less than two knots and forty miles a day. Drake attacked them off Eddystone Point on 21 July, and off Portland Bill on 23 July, fighting four engagements with them in the course of five days. The English ships had the best of these sea-battles, for the superior manoeuvrability of their ships and the longer range of their guns prevented the Spaniards from successfully carrying out their usual tactic of grappling with the enemy ships and boarding them; but, for the English, their success was not good enough, for though Drake captured one enemy warship, another blew up, and a third took refuge in Le Havre, this still left 127 Spanish ships sailing east on 25 July past the Isle of Wight towards the link-up with Parma.[23]

At the 'camp royal' at Tilbury, there was more enthusiasm than efficiency. When Leicester arrived at the camp on 24 July, he found that the food supplies for the soldiers had not arrived, and he had to ride next day to Chelmsford to make hurried arrangements for an emergency supply of victuals to be sent to Tilbury.[24] The bridge of boats across the Thames to Gravesend had still not been erected. But the people of London were confident of victory as they enrolled in their trainbands to defend the city against Parma. Elizabeth decided to come closer to them, and on 25 July she moved from Richmond to St James's.[25]

Sidonia did not know what to do, for he had heard nothing from Parma as to where their fleets were to meet off Margate, while Parma, who thought that Sidonia knew that his army would not leave port except under the protection of the Armada, was waiting for Sidonia to arrive with his fleet at Dunkirk, Nieuport and Sluys. As the winds in the Channel began to rise, Sidonia decided to anchor in Calais Roads outside the harbour while he waited for news from Parma. He reached Calais in the late afternoon of 27 July (6 August N.S.) and waited there for thirty hours while Howard and Drake assembled 150 ships and hastily prepared for the action which was to settle the outcome of the campaign and win one of the greatest victories in English history.

Drake had used fireships, not altogether successfully, against the Spanish fleet at Cadiz; but he realised that in the conditions which existed off Calais they could do far greater damage. He found eight suitable ships and set them on fire to be blown by the gale into the Armada in Calais Roads. The only way to counter fireships was to sink them with gunfire, or change their course with a broadside, before they approached; but the strong winds which blew them forward at high speed made this difficult, and the Spaniards, though they might have expected fireships after their experience at Cadiz, had made no preparations to deal with them. They panicked as they saw the burning ships approach, and hurriedly cut their cables and made out to sea; and Sidonia, seeing many of his ships were leaving, gave orders for the whole fleet to put to sea.[26]

They were attacked by the English and scattered by the winds, which blew them northwards – in Drake's words, 'driven like a flock of sheep' – past Nieuport and Sluys, where Parma was waiting with 16,000 men who were already embarked, and on into the North Sea. Several ships went down off the coast of Zeeland, and during the next few weeks the bodies of the Spanish soldiers and sailors were washed up off the coasts of Friesland and Emden. The English ships pursued the Spaniards, but most of them turned back at Newcastle on 2 August, as they had used up all their ammunition.[27]

The English people soon knew that they had won a victory at Calais, but they did not immediately realise that the Armada was decisively beaten. In Paris, Mendoza continued for some time to claim that the Armada was on its way to conquer England;[28] but Parma knew that all was lost. 'God knows how grieved I am at this news', he wrote to Philip from Dunkirk on 31 July (10 August N.S.), 'at a time when I hoped to send Your Majesty my congratulations on having successfully carried through your intentions . . . I will only say that this must come from the hand of the Lord, who knows well what He does and can redress it all by rewarding Your Majesty with many victories and the full fruition of your desires in His good time'.[29]

Elizabeth still believed that it was possible that the Armada might regroup, turn south, and invade when she accepted Leicester's invitation to visit her army at the camp royal. On 8 August she came from Westminster by barge, and, landing at Tilbury, rode two miles to the camp at the top of the hill where West Tilbury parish church now stands.* She spent the night at Arderne Hall,

---

*The church was closed for worship in 1981, and is now (June 1987) being converted into a private house.

and returned to the camp next day to review her army and address them. There are several contemporary accounts of her words in prose and verse, but the well-known version which has survived is almost certainly the correct one, for it was apparently put into writing and approved by Elizabeth with a view to publication.[30] When it was a question, not of taking the right decision but of saying the right thing, Elizabeth usually succeeded in enthralling her audience, and she struck just the right note at Tilbury, as she had so often done in Parliament, at Oxford and Cambridge, and wherever she went on her progresses.

> My loving people, we have been persuaded by some that are careful of our safety, to take heed how we commit ourselves to armed multitudes, for fear of treachery. But I assure you, I do not desire to live to distrust my faithful and loving people. Let tyrants fear.

She did not mention that it was Leicester who had urged her to come to the camp and had assured her that she would be safe there,[31] though he advised her to keep clear of the coast in case she was captured by a Spanish raiding party from the Armada.

> I have always so behaved myself that, under God, I have placed my chiefest strength and safeguard in the loyal hearts and good will of my subjects, and therefore I am come amongst you as you see, at this time, not for my recreation and disport, but being resolved, in the midst and heat of the battle, to live or die amongst you all, to lay down for my God, and for my kingdom, and for my people, my honour and my blood, even in the dust. I know I have the body of a weak and feeble woman, but I have the heart and stomach of a King, and of a King of England too, and think foul scorn that Parma or Spain or any Prince of Europe should dare to invade the borders of my realm, to which, rather than any dishonour shall grow by me, I myself will take up arms, I myself will be your general, judge and rewarder of every one of your virtues in the field. I know already for your forwardness you have deserved rewards and crowns, and we do assure you, in the word of a Prince, they shall be duly paid you.[32]

She was slow in performing this last promise, for the men who defeated the Armada, like her soldiers in the Netherlands, waited for many weeks, half-starved, before they received their wages.[33]

While she was at the camp, a courier arrived with the news that the Armada had last been seen in full flight sailing north from Newcastle; and when Elizabeth left the camp in the late afternoon on 9 August to spend the night at Belhus before returning to St James's, she knew that the danger of invasion was past and that the Armada had been defeated.[34]

Sidonia decided to take the Armada back to Spain by sailing to the north of

Scotland and west of Ireland. He reduced the rations of everyone on board, even the officers and gentlemen, to half a pound of bread, one pint of water and half a pint of wine a day and nothing more; but sickness spread in the fleet, and 180 men had died in his flagship alone when, after encountering more gales near Cape Wrath and in the Bay of Biscay, he arrived at Santander on 23 September (N.S.). Eventually 67 of the 130 ships of the Armada returned to Spain.[35]

Sidonia had ordered his captains to stay well clear of the treacherous Irish coast by sailing north-west till they reached 61½°N. and then south-west to 58°N. before turning south; but seventeen of his ships, which became separated from the fleet in the gale near Cape Wrath, arrived off the west coast of Ireland. One of them put in to Tralee, where the crew found the local 'savages' unfriendly, and after staying there for a week for repairs sailed safely to Spain; but fifteen or sixteen ships carrying six or seven thousand men were wrecked off Mayo and Galway. Eleven hundred survivors came ashore at Sligo and a shipload in Donegal; and 3,500, most of whom were King Philip's Neapolitan subjects, landed on the north-east coast of Ulster.[36]

The Lord Deputy, Sir William Fitzwilliam, became alarmed when he heard that some five thousand Spanish soldiers had landed in Ireland, for he feared that if they were able to entrench themselves, the Irish would join them and launch a new insurrection. He ordered all his officers, and the English gentlemen and loyal Irish chiefs, to kill all the survivors of the Armada whom they encountered in their districts, and announced that anyone who found one of the invaders was to bring him to a justice of the peace within four hours, on pain of death. But despite this order, many survivors of the Armada were sheltered by the Irish, though others complained that the 'savages' had robbed them and murdered their companions, or betrayed them to the authorities.[37]

Five hundred Spanish and Italian soldiers from the Armada, who were in a Venetian ship, were landed on the east coast some twenty miles north of Drogheda. They met a company of two hundred English soldiers, whose captain asked them why they had invaded the Queen's realm. They replied that they had not come as invaders, but as shipwrecked travellers, and asked only for a boat to take them back to Spain. According to the Spaniards, the English captain told them that this was impossible, but, if they surrendered their arms, their lives would be spared and he would take them to Dublin as prisoners-of-war. After some delay they surrendered, and were marched off towards Dublin. They encamped for the night in a field, and next morning the English captain separated forty-one officers and well-dressed gentlemen from the ordinary soldiers, and the rest of the prisoners were massacred. Some of them ran for it, and escaped into the woods, and were found and rescued by Sorley Boy's vassals. They were fed, nursed back to health, and invited as fellow-Catholics to join their hosts at Mass. Sorley Boy arranged for them to be taken in his boats to Scotland, where James VI gave them alms and arranged for them to be sent back to Spain.[38]

Elizabeth granted all the Spaniards in Scotland a safe conduct if they put in to English ports on the way home. Some of them were attacked at sea off Dunkirk by the Dutch, who captured three hundred prisoners and threw them into the sea. The Spaniards believed that Elizabeth had warned the Dutch that they were coming, and had incited the attack.[39]

The forty-one officers and gentlemen had been separated from the others because their captors thought that they would be worth a ransom. They were taken to Drogheda and handed over to the higher military authorities, who resisted the temptation to try to obtain a ransom, and killed all the prisoners, including the commander, Don Diego de Cordoba.[40]

In England, a number of Spanish prisoners-of-war had been captured in the first battles with the Armada. Drake treated their commander with the greatest courtesy. The Privy Council ordered that the common soldiers were to be imprisoned in Bridewell in London and given the same food and allowance which were granted to the English seamen who were imprisoned in Spain, and that all the Flemings and Dutchmen who had been conscripted against their will into the Armada were to be set free.[41]

Elizabeth immediately opened negotiations with Parma about ransoming the prisoners. She agreed to release all except the most high-ranking officers, who were retained until large ransoms were paid. She handed over the other prisoners to English merchants whose servants were prisoners in Spain or whose property had been confiscated there, to enable them to make their private arrangements with the Spaniards for an exchange of prisoners or to release the Spanish prisoners if they obtained compensation for their property. Most of them had returned home before the end of the winter.[42]

On 14 September Elizabeth wrote to Fitzwilliam and the Council in Dublin that she had heard that the Armada was heading for Ireland and that it was possible that they might land and establish a bridgehead there till reinforcements arrived from Spain. She ordered Fitzwilliam to march against them and defeat them. The Privy Council asked Fitzwilliam to inform them about all the prisoners-of-war whom he captured, and told him that they were sending to Ireland an official, who knew the chief men among the Spaniards, to deal with the prisoners-of-war. The Earl of Ormond, who was with Elizabeth at St James's, wrote to Fitzwilliam that if Sidonia was captured, he was to be treated with great honour; he must not be placed in irons, and must be allowed to retain his horse. The other prisoners were to be held at Galway, Clonmel, Kilkenny and Waterford.[43]

Fitzwilliam wrote to Elizabeth that he was marching against the three thousand Spaniards in Ulster, that he had issued a proclamation offering their lives to all who surrendered, and that he thought it wise to refrain from punishing those Irish who had given shelter to the invaders. Elizabeth and the Privy Council approved of his action.[44] But when Fitzwilliam asked what he should do with the Spaniards 'who doubtless would gladly be prisoners',[45] the Council apparently did not reply. A number of Spaniards who surrendered were spared and sent as prisoners to England; but Fitzwilliam told the Council that he had put most of the Spaniards to death before he issued his offer of mercy.[46]

Sir Richard Bingham, who had once fought in the Spanish army but more recently had served against the Spaniards in the Netherlands, explained what had happened. He reported to Fitzwilliam that his brother George had put to the sword, or 'executed one way or another', about seven or eight hundred in Mayo, Thormond and Galway. He wrote to Elizabeth that he himself had rounded up the eleven hundred survivors at Sligo and put them all to the sword except for thirty officers and gentlemen of quality for whom he thought a good ransom might be paid, and that he had also spared five or six young Dutchmen, all of them boys or very young men, because they said that they had been conscripted into the fleet against their will by the Spaniards. He gave them into the custody of several English gentlemen, after they had promised to surrender when he called on them to do so; but a few weeks later, Fitzwilliam arrived at Athlone and ordered that the thirty surviving officers and all the young Dutchmen should be executed.[47]

But Elizabeth had a greater cause for grief, at this time of national rejoicing which culminated in the thanksgiving service which she attended at St Paul's on 24 November.[48] On 4 September Leicester died at his house in Oxfordshire at the age of fifty-six, less than a month after she had been with him at Tilbury. There were rumours that he had been poisoned by Sir Christopher Blunt, who afterwards married his widow, but his death was undoubtedly due to natural causes. On 27 August he had written to Elizabeth asking her for a favour for an old servant. She wrote at the foot of the letter 'His last letter', and kept it in a chest by her bedside until she died. But she had never liked his widow Lettice, and forced her to sell most of his property to repay the debts which he owed to the crown, without taking into account the jewels which he had bequeathed to Elizabeth in his will.[49]

MUTINIES AND FAILURES

WHILE the English seamen were defeating the Armada, Elizabeth's forces in the Netherlands were involved in a less glorious episode. It is not surprising that the name 'Geertruidenberg' has not been remembered like the 'Spanish Armada' in the annals of English history.

In August 1588 there were officially 7,400 English soldiers in the Netherlands; but the States complained that in fact were only 5,741, because the English companies were not at full strength. The soldiers' wages were paid to their captains, and it became a common practice for captains to reduce the number of soldiers in their companies, while receiving the wages of their full compliment of men, and pocketing the difference. Elizabeth, on her side, continually complained that the States were not paying their share of the cost of operations. The Council of State found it impossible to do this, because although the people of the Netherlands were resolutely determined to defend their freedom, their merchants were very reluctant to pay their contributions to the cost of the struggle.[1]

One of the chief sources of revenue of the Council of State was the sums paid by merchants for licences to trade with the Spanish-occupied territory. It seems strange to the twentieth-century mind that a government should finance a war from the licence fees paid by its citizens for permission to trade with the enemy, and Elizabeth did not like the system, though for the opposite reason that she had objected to it in 1572. Having for many years protested that the sea-beggars interfered with her subjects' trade with the Spanish-occupied Netherlands, she had now placed an embargo on trade with all Philip's kingdoms, and she demanded that the States make it punishable by death for any of their citizens to trade with the enemy. English warships and privateers in the Channel and the North Sea intercepted English, Dutch, Danish, Swedish and Hanseatic ships, and seized any goods which were destined for Spain or the Spanish Netherlands, even if the shippers had obtained a licence from the States. But commodities were sent by the inland waterways from Holland and Zeeland to Antwerp and other towns under Spanish occupation; and some of the merchants of Amsterdam shipped goods to Spain, sending them round the north of Scotland to avoid the English warships.[2]

The money paid for the licences did not enable the Council of State to balance their budget; in May 1588 their income amounted to £20,000 a month and their expenditure to £23,000.[3] The shortage of revenue made it difficult for them to pay their mercenaries.

A company of mercenaries in the pay of the States was stationed in Geertruidenberg, the little town on the Rhine, near the borders of Holland and Zeeland, which was a hereditary possession of William of Orange's son, Count Maurice of Nassau; for if Parma captured Geertruidenberg the road into Holland would be opened to him. The garrison's wages were many months in arrears, and in April 1588 they mutinied. They disarmed the civilian population and imprisoned the leading members of the town council. They refused to serve in the army of the States, but were prepared to enlist as soldiers of the Queen of England, under any commander whom Elizabeth might appoint, on condition that they were immediately paid twenty-three months' pay at the rate of one shilling a day, though the English soldiers in the Netherlands received only eightpence a day. This amounted to a sum of 210,000 florins. They made it clear that if their offer was not accepted, they would get in touch with Parma to find out how much he would pay them to surrender the town to him.

Elizabeth, as she was shortly to inform the English garrison at Ostend, distinguished between mutinies by her English soldiers and by foreign mercenaries.[4] The English were under a duty to serve their natural Queen and country; but foreign mercenaries were only bound to serve under the terms of their contract of hire, and had some justification for mutinying if the hirers broke the contract by defaulting in paying their wages. In any case, she did not wish to use men and resources in suppressing a mutiny at Geertruidenberg when the Armada was expected at any time, and she was therefore prepared to accept the mutineers' terms. She agreed to take the garrison of Geertruidenberg into her service under a captain whom she would select, to hold the town for the States and to ensure that Maurice of Nassau received his rents, on condition that the States would pay the cost and at once deliver the 210,000 florins to the mercenaries.

The States were indignant. They said that they were unable to raise the money, and that there was no term in their treaty with Elizabeth which required them to pay the wages of mercenaries in her service. But Lord Willoughby persuaded them that they had no other choice if Geertruidenberg was to be saved from Parma. Maurice promised to pay them the money as soon as possible; but when, on 21 July (N.S.), Willoughby went to Geertruidenberg and explained that there would be a slight delay in raising the 210,000 florins, the mutineers' leaders became angry, and said that if the money were not paid within forty-eight hours they would open negotiations with Parma.

Willoughby persuaded the mutineers to give the States a little more time to raise the money. On 26 July (N.S.) Maurice and Willoughby came to Geertruidenberg, and handed over 210,000 florins in gold. It was three days before the Armada was sighted off the Lizard.[5]

Elizabeth chose Captain Schenck to command the garrison at Geertruidenberg. He had formerly served in Don John of Austria's army in the Netherlands, and had seized her envoy Rogers on his way to Germany; but Schenck's contract with the Spaniards had expired, and he was looking for new employment. The men at Geertruidenberg refused to accept Schenck, who was a savage disciplinarian; and to Schenck's indignation, Willoughby persuaded Elizabeth to rescind his appointment and to leave Willoughby a free hand to arrange with the mercenaries who should be appointed as their captain. He agreed with them to choose his brother-in-law, Sir John Wingfield.[6]

In August the English garrison at Ostend mutinied. They were angry that their pay was in arrears,[7] and that they were being overcharged for their food by Mr Cox, the victualler who had secured a contract from Elizabeth to supply them with victuals. At a time when wheat could be bought in any market in England for 12d. a bushel, Cox was charging the soldiers £14 for a last of 70 barrels, or four times the price which he must have paid for it in England. He sold them salted butter, which in England cost 13s. for a firkin of 52 lb., at 18s. a firkin, 'and the butter so stinking and loathsome as not fit for men to eat'; and he supplied 'rotten, stinking and unwholesome cheese' for 3d. a pound, though in England the best Suffolk cheese was obtainable at 1½d. per pound.[8] But Cox assured Elizabeth that after he had paid the costs of carriage to Ostend he had only a small profit margin; and as for the quality of the food, Sir John Conway, the garrison commander, reported that except for one consignment of cheese and butter, the victuals had been satisfactory.[9]

On 28 August one of Cox's servants brought a new consignment of corn to Ostend. The soldiers threw him into the river, and rioted; and when Conway seized a pike and tried to restore order, they imprisoned him and their officers in the fortress. They then sent a deputation of the men to Elizabeth at St James's to assure her that they were loyal subjects and true Englishmen who would always serve her loyally and never go over to the enemy.[10]

Elizabeth told them that she had heard of the complaints against Cox, and had already ordered an investigation into his profiteering; but this did not justify their action in mutinying and imprisoning their commanding officer.[11] They should submit unconditionally, as it was unfit for 'subjects of their quality to capitulate or stand upon terms with their natural Prince and sovereign',[12] and if they submitted, they could send four soldiers from each company to Flushing to give evidence against Cox at the inquiry, and could be sure that they would not be punished.

On Conway's advice, Elizabeth granted a pardon to all the mutineers, who released Conway and the officers, and returned to duty. But a few weeks later, another mutiny broke out at Ostend at the instigation of a few trouble-makers. They seized Conway and did not release him until he had promised to give them an increase in wages and to guarantee that he would be personally liable to pay them the money if the government did not do so. About the same time, the garrison at Bergen-op-Zoom mutinied because of the arrears of pay. These two events convinced Conway and Willoughby that sterner methods must be adopted.

Conway was able to take advantage of the mutineers' loyalty to their Queen and country. He told them, untruthfully, that the Spaniards were about to attack Ostend, and the men at once returned to duty and manned the defences. He arranged with Willoughby that another company of three hundred English troops should be sent to Ostend to deal with the two hundred soldiers of the garrison. At first the mutineers declared that they would not admit them into the town; but they agreed to do so when Conway told them that the men were coming as reinforcements against the expected enemy attack. The Privy Council wrote to Willoughby on 28 October that it was necessary, for the Queen's honour, to make an example of a few of the ringleaders at Ostend and Bergen-op-Zoom, and ordered him to see that the executions were carried out on the same day in both towns, so that neither garrison would be warned what to expect.[13]

On 16 November Captain Thomas Wilson and three hundred men entered Ostend without meeting any resistance from the mutineers, though some 'murmured at it'. That night a number of the ringleaders were arrested, and during the next few days thirteen of them were hanged. Some more offenders were banished from Ostend and discharged from the army. The rest returned to duty.[14] The executions at Bergen-op-Zoom were also carried out without resistance.

But the lack of any patriotism among the mercenaries at Geertruidenberg made it more difficult for the authorities to deal with them. Within a month of receiving their 210,000 florins, they were asking for more money, and looting the neighbouring farms and villages. They stopped the boats which sailed down the Rhine carrying goods, under licence from the States, from Holland to Spanish territory, and detained the goods until the owners paid them money to release them. The mercenaries' letters and demands were always signed by Sir John Wingfield, their commander, which made the States and the people of the Netherlands believe that Elizabeth was encouraging the mutineers; but Sir Thomas Bodley, whom Elizabeth had appointed as her representative in The Hague, explained that though Wingfield was nominally the governor of Geertruidenberg, the town was in fact controlled by a committee of the mutineers who used Wingfield's name. At Elizabeth's orders, Willoughby wrote to Maurice, assuring him that he would do everything possible to help recover Geertruidenberg from the mutineers.

In February 1589 Maurice heard that the mutineers had entered into secret negotiations with Parma. Without consulting the Council of State,

Willoughby or Elizabeth, he decided to regain control of Geertruidenberg by force. On 14 March (N.S.) he arrived there with two hundred ships and four thousand men, and bombarded the town; but after less than a week he abandoned his attempts to take it by storm, apparently because of the bad weather. The States then asked Willoughby to make another attempt to negotiate with the mutineers. But Maurice had sent them a copy of Willoughby's letter promising to help him recover the town, hoping that this would encourage them to surrender. The result was that the mutineers refused to have anything more to do with Willoughby.

Elizabeth wrote to Maurice, deploring his unwise attempt to capture Geertruidenberg. She also wrote to the mutineers, assuring them that she condemned the attack upon them, and that if the States refused to satisfy their demands, she would regard it as an injury to herself.* But the mutineers had already surrendered Geertruidenberg to Parma, after he had agreed to pay them fifteen months' wages, to entrol in his army any mercenary who wished to join, and to allow the civilian population to choose either to stay in Geertruidenberg or to go to territory held by the States. Wingfield was sent as a prisoner to Breda.

The loss of Geertruidenberg caused the greatest degree of ill-feeling which had yet arisen between Elizabeth and the States, which was increased when the Council of State issued a proclamation denouncing all the garrison of Geertruidenberg, including Wingfield, as traitors, and offering a reward to anyone who killed any of them. The States blamed Elizabeth for having induced them to pay the 210,000 florins to the mutineers which had not saved Geertruidenberg, and for doing nothing to help suppress the mutiny; and Elizabeth blamed Maurice and the States for the rash and blundering attack on Geertruidenberg.[15] But the disaster ultimately led to a beneficial result for both Elizabeth and the States. Elizabeth agreed to accept Maurice as commander-in-chief of all the forces in the Netherlands, and that none of her soldiers or diplomats would play any part in influencing the military or political actions of the States. This led to a revival in the Netherlands of the old spirit of heroism and self-sacrifice which had been eroded during the years of their resentful dependence on Elizabeth. Within a short time the people were willingly contributing not only to their own defence but, far more enthusiastically than Elizabeth, to a fund to raise money for Henry of Navarre to hire mercenaries to defend the Protestant cause in France.[16]

In the spring of 1589, Elizabeth withdrew some of her troops from the Netherlands to take part in an expedition to Portugal. Drake was to command the fleet and Norris the land forces. Don Antonio and his refugees were to

---

*Elizabeth amended Burghley's draft of this letter so as to modify slightly the extent of her support for the mutineers' demands (see For. Cal. Eliz., xxiii.213.)

accompany them and call on the people of Portugal to rise in their support and drive out the Spanish invader. After their victory over the Armada, the English were confident of success, for an agent in Spain had reported that there 'the name of Drake did kill them alone'.[17] But on this expedition, everything was to go wrong.

Mendoza was given useful information about Drake's plans by Stafford, but more important reports came to him from another agent, Antonio de Veico, a member of Don Antonio's staff in London, who as early as 24 October 1588 sent him the plans for the expedition. Drake sailed from Plymouth on 18 April 1589 with 85 English and 60 Dutch ships, carrying 3,000 English and 900 Dutch sailors and an army of 11,000 men.[18]

They reached Corunna in six days, attacked the Spanish ships in the harbour and bombarded the town. They stayed there for a fortnight, landing, fighting the Spaniards, and suffering some losses, including several men killed when a tower which they were attempting to capture, and which their engineers had mined, fell down ton top of them. They then sailed south to Peniche, some forty miles north of Lisbon. The soldiers landed, and marched towards Lisbon, while the fleet sailed to Lisbon harbour.

Two thousand Portuguese rose in support of Don Antonio, and the town of Torres Vedras surrendered to him; but Philip's nephew, the Cardinal-Archduke Albert, Archbishop of Toledo, who was Viceroy of Portugal, had made careful defensive preparations; and Don Antonio realised, as he advanced, that he would be unable to break through to Lisbon. He therefore withdrew with his forces to Cascaes, seized the town, and persuaded the captain of the castle to surrender it on honourable terms which allowed the garrison to march out. When the garrison reached Lisbon, the Cardinal-Archduke executed the captain as a traitor.

Drake had meanwhile decided that he could not attack Lisbon from the sea, as he had not enough artillery to carry out an effective preliminary bombardment, and the additional cannon which Elizabeth had promised him had not arrived. He therefore sailed to Cascaes, and linked up with Norris and Don Antonio. After remaining on Portuguese soil for three weeks, Don Antonio decided that he could do no more good there, as too few of the inhabitants had joined him. On 13 June (N.S.) the evacuation began, and five days later the fleet and the army sailed away, leaving behind them the two thousand Portuguese who had risen in their support. Many of the Portuguese were executed as traitors, and a few of the English soldiers who were taken prisoners were also executed; but some were spared, after Drake had informed the Cardinal-Archduke that if they were hanged, or burned as heretics by the Inquisition, he would in reprisal capture some Spaniards, and hang or burn them.

On the way back to England, Drake attacked Vigo and burned the ships in the harbour and part of the town; but he did not go to Santander, where fifty-five of the ships that had returned with the Armada were in the harbour, for he had been led to believe that the defences of the port were too strong. An English agent across the French frontier at St Jean de Luz afterwards reported that there were no adequate defences to the harbour at Santander, that nearly all the cannon of the ships were being refitted on land, and that if Drake had gone to Santander, he could have destroyed the Spanish fleet.

Many of the English soldiers and sailors died of plague during the expedition. This was apparently the posthumous revenge of the crews of the Armada, for it was thought that Drake's men had caught the plague from the infected garments of the dead Spanish sailors, which were still lying rotting in the harbour at Corunna when the English arrived there. When Drake and his men reached Plymouth, the inquiries and the recriminations began. Sir Roger Williams, who had been on the expedition, stated that if they had had enough artillery they could have taken and held Lisbon. Others blamed Drake for not destroying the Spanish fleet at Santander.[19] After his unbroken list of successes over seventeen years, his countrymen might have forgiven him for this one comparative failure; but he was not sent to sea again for six years. He retained the confidence of the citizens of Plymouth, who continued to elect him as their Mayor and MP; and he greatly improved the water supply of the town.[20]

On 23 December 1588 (N.S.) Henry III had Guise assassinated at Blois, where the court was in residence. Henry had given no indication that he had turned against Guise, who for the last five months had been his ally and chief minister; but on that morning Guise, who was attending a meeting of the King's Council, was asked to go from the Council chamber to the King's apartments for an audience with the King, and on the way was attacked by some members of Henry III's trusted bodyguard, 'the Forty-five'. Some of them held his arms to prevent him from drawing his sword, while the others stabbed him to death with their daggers.[21]

Guise's brother, the Cardinal of Lorraine, who was also staying in the castle at Blois, was arrested, and strangled next day by Henry III's orders. Henry had also intended to kill the third brother, the Duke of Mayenne, who was at Lyons; but Mayenne was warned that the murderers were on their way, and escaped before they arrived.[22] He went to Paris, and he and his sister, the Duchess of Montpensier, summoned all faithful Catholics to avenge Guise, who had been foully murdered by the treacherous King because of his devotion to the Catholic Church.

The people of Paris, under the leadership of the revolutionary Committee of Sixteen, rallied to the call. The priests denounced Henry III in their sermons. A moving poem was printed and distributed, *The Grief and Lament of Madame de Guise on the death of her husband the late Duke of Guise*, in which the bereaved widow lamented the death of 'him whom I have seen master the heretic', and prayed to God not to permit the 'bloody crown' to exult over his murder.*[23] The divinity faculty of Paris University, the Sorbonne, declared that Henry III had forfeited the crown, and the Council of the French Church excommunicated him. The Pope was more cautious, and did not commit himself when Henry III asked him for absolution for having murdered a cardinal; but it was reported from the Spanish court that Philip II was more distressed by Guise's death than by the loss of the twenty thousand soldiers of the Armada, and Parma advised him to make preparations to send an army to help the League in France. Catherine de Medici, who died a fortnight after Guise was killed, said on her deathbed that her son had made an error which would cost him his throne.[24]

The Protestants everywhere were jubilant. Henry of Navarrre's counsellor, Du Pin, wrote to Walsingham about 'God's marvellous doings in this kingdom',[25] and his representative in London, Buzenval, assured Burghley that 'the event at Blois will settle this quarrel'.**[26] But Henry III hoped to win the support of the Catholics who did not like the Guises and the League. He issued a statement explaining that since 1585 Guise had plotted to deprive him of his crown and life, and he had therefore ordered him to be executed as a traitor. He pointed out that he had proved his hatred of heresy by sending his armies to fight against the Huguenots, though he could have done more to stamp it out if his attention had not been distracted from this task by Guise's treasonable activities. He called on all his subjects to unite in following him, their King, in a new campaign against the Huguenots.[27]

When Elizabeth heard of Guise's death, she wrote to Henry III to congratulate him, and urged him, as she had so often done, to rely on the aid of his loyal subjects, the Huguenots, in suppressing the treasonable activities of the League and his Catholic rebels. When Catherine de Medici died soon afterwards, Elizabeth decided to send Wotton to Henry III to express her sympathies. In Wotton's instructions, which were drafted by Walsingham, she ordered him to advise the French King 'that it will behove him now to take a resolute course, seeing that by his temporising so long, in bearing with the indignities offered by the Duke of Guise, he was forced for his own safety to resort to a violent remedy in taking away his life'.[28]

But before Wotton left, Elizabeth heard from Stafford at Vendôme. When Henry III read Elizabeth's letter, he had told Stafford that he was 'half discontented' that she had written it, as it would compromise his position with the Catholics if he were seen to be her ally. He therefore asked her to excuse him if he did not reply to her letter for the time being.[29] She understood his position, and decided not to send Wotton.

She was right to wait for events to develop. Henry III soon realised that although he had the support of many loyal Catholics, he could not defeat the

* 'A toi, mon Dieu, j'adresse ma prière dolante,
  Et justice je requiens de la vertu criante,
  Ne permets se moquer la couronne sanglante'.
** 'Le faict de Blois desmelera cette querrelle.'

League without the help of the Huguenots. He entered into secret negotiations with Henry of Navarre, and on 30 April 1589 they met at Plessis-les-Tours and announced that they would wage war against the rebels of the League. Henry III asked Elizabeth to lend him money to enable him to hire 8,000 *reiters* and 14,000 foot soldiers in Germany. He sent an envoy to London, who in the course of two months of negotiations increased his demands from £27,000 to £60,000. Meanwhile Henry III and Henry of Navarre, with an army of 30,000 men, defeated the forces of the League in several engagements, and by the middle of July they were in the suburbs of Paris. Inside the city, Mayenne and the League had only 5,000 soldiers and a few weeks' food supplies.[30] It seemed as if Paris was about to fall, and that, as a French refugee in London wrote to Walsingham, the punishment of the Parisians astonish other towns and terrify them into surrendering to the King.[31]

Elizabeth's reaction to Henry III's request for a loan shows how little her foreign policy was influenced by religious sympathies and how much by hard-headed calculations of national advantage; and it also shows how she was prepared to abandon her usual parsimony when she believed that there were real benefits to be obtained by spending money. It was clear that the decisive battles in the struggle with Spain would shortly be waged in France, with Philip II and Parma preparing to send forces to help the League; and it would be a serious threat to England if the League continued to hold Normandy and the Channel ports as allies of the King of Spain. It would be a great advantage if the leader of the fight against Spain in France were not only a lawful King but a Catholic King, who would command the loyalty of many of the French Catholics as well as having the support of the Protestants. To spend money supporting Henry III seemed to Elizabeth to be a much better investment than to subsidise quarrelling Protestant rebels in the Netherlands, an unpopular Huguenot minority in France, or even pro-English lords in Scotland. So she listened far more favourably to a request for a loan from the Papist Henry III, who had been one of the chief authors of the Massacre of St Bartholomew, than to the piteous appeals for help from her co-religionists whose fight against odds for the Protestant cause aroused so much enthusiasm among Protestant Englishmen.

Although Elizabeth needed money to pay for her own operations at sea against Spain, and was already negotiating to borrow 100,000 crowns at 10 per cent interest from bankers at Frankfort and Augsburg, she offered, apparently on her own initiative, to borrow another 327,000 crowns (£60,000) to pay over to Henry III.[32] This was very different from the attitude which she had adopted whenever the Protestants of the Netherlands had asked her for money during the previous twenty years. On 23 July the Privy Council asked the Lord Mayor of London to give the Queen the city's bond for £60,000 which she wished to raise in Germany 'for some special purpose'.[33] She did not know that on the previous day – 1 August (N.S.) – a

Jacobin monk, Jacques Clément, had come from Paris to St Cloud, gained access to Henry III's presence by pretending that he could show him a secret way of entering Paris with his army, and stabbed the King with a dagger. Henry died seven hours later.[34]

This act of regicide aroused the greatest indignation among the Protestants, though as Henry III had stabbed and killed the assassin as they struggled together, Clément was saved from the tortures which would otherwise have been inflicted upon him. It was seen as yet another example of the murderous projects of the Papists. A year or so later, Christopher Marlowe's play, *The Massacre at Paris*, was performed in London. Although the play begins with the Massacre of St Bartholomew, the assassination of Henry III in the last scene is condemned by Marlowe's characters in even stronger language than the massacre itself. The dying King addresses Henry of Navarre:

> Navarre, give me thy hand; I here do swear
> To ruinate that wicked Church of Rome
> That hatcheth up such bloody practices;
> And here protest eternal love to thee,
> And to the Queen of England specially,
> Whom God hath bless'd for hating Papistry.[35]

But once again, in the France of 1588 and 1589, assassination paid. Just as the murder of Guise had dealt a heavy blow to the Catholic cause, the murder of Henry III saved it from imminent defeat. Henry of Navarre was immediately proclaimed as King Henry IV in the camp at St Cloud, and some of the Catholics in the royal army were prepared to accept him as their King and to continue serving under him; but many of them refused to fight for a heretic King, even though he promised to uphold the Catholic faith as the state religion, to maintain Henry III's edicts against the Protestants, and to take instruction from priests with a view to converting to Catholicism. With his army dwindling away, he was unable to continue operations against Paris, and decided to march into Normandy and occupy Dieppe in order to have a Channel port from where he could maintain contact with England. It was clear that his survival would depend on aid from Elizabeth.[36]

ESSEX

TWO months after the great victory over the Armada, a general election was held, and the new Parliament met on 4 February 1589. The Lord Chancellor, Sir Christopher Hatton, opened the proceedings with a powerful speech in which he castigated the present Pope, Sixtus V, 'exceeding all other that went before him in tyranny and cruelty', and especially 'that wicked priest, that shameless atheist and bloody Cardinal Allen'. But he then passed on to deal with the enemy which now caused Elizabeth the greatest anxiety – the Puritans and their supporters in the House of Commons. He informed the MPs that the Queen commanded them that 'you do not in this assembly so much as once meddle with any such matters or causes of religion, except it be to bridle all those, whether Papists or Puritans, which are therewithal discontented'.[1]

The struggle with the Puritans had taken a more savage form. In the autumn of 1588 a small group of Presbyterians began to publish the series of sarcastic and coarse polemics against the bishops which were signed with the pseudonym 'Martin Mar-prelate'. They were probably written by a Welsh clergyman, John Penry, and a Warwickshire gentleman, Job Throckmorton. As no book could be published without the licence of a bishop, they were printed illegally on a secret press in a private house at East Molesey in Surrey. When the authorities got on their track, they went to Warwickshire, moving their printing press from one town and village to another to avoid detection. Whitgift stationed secret agents at the London bookshops to catch the distributors and seize the copies of the books;[2] but the copies circulated secretly, and were read by many readers.

The printing press was moved from Warwickshire to Lancashire, and there, after searching unsuccessfully for nearly a year, the authorities found it in Manchester and destroyed it. In the spring of 1590, Throckmorton was arrested with a number of other Puritan pamphleteers, but Penry escaped to Scotland. Elizabeth demanded that he be extradited; but the ministers of the Church of Scotland would not allow James VI to comply with her request, and

Penry preached in Edinburgh, where for the first time he denounced Elizabeth herself for having turned against Christ and allowed Whitgift to oppress the Puritans.

After a time, James VI ordered Penry to leave Scotland, and he returned to London, where he was recognised and arrested. He was tried for high treason for having denounced the Queen in his sermon in Edinburgh, and sentenced to be hanged, drawn and quartered; but he was allowed to hang until he was dead. Two of his colleagues, Barrow and Greenwood, were convicted under the Act which had been passed in 1581 against the Papists, making it felony to publish seditious writings, and were also executed. Throckmorton, who denied that he had written the Martin Mar-prelate letters, was in due course released from prison.

A new Parliament met in February 1593 at the height of the campaign against the Puritans. Elizabeth made it clear from the start that she would tolerate no criticism from the MPs. This was explained to the House of Commons by Sir John Puckering, who after Hatton's death had been appointed Lord Keeper of the Great Seal, in his reply to the Speaker's traditional request to the Queen to uphold the privileges of the House of Commons. 'For liberty of speech, Her Majesty commandeth me to tell you that to say yea or no to bills, God forbid that any man should be restrained, or afraid to answer according to his best liking, with some short declaration of his reason therein, and therein to have a free voice, which is the very true liberty of the House; not, as some suppose, to speak there of all causes as him listeth, and to frame a form of religion or a state of government, as to their idle brains shall seem meetest. She saith, no King fit for his state will suffer such absurdities . . . She hopeth no man here longeth so much for his ruin as that he mindeth to make such a peril to his own safety'.[3]

Religion was not the only subject which was barred to the MPs. Peter Wentworth, who had spent a few weeks in prison in 1576 because of his utterances in the House of Commons, raised the question of the succession to the crown. He favoured the claim of James VI of Scotland. He asked Parliament to support his petition to the Queen to make provision for the succession, and invited a small group of other MPs to meet him for discussions about the question at his rooms. It was probably these private meetings of MPs which most alarmed Elizabeth. She ordered that Wentworth and several of his colleagues should be arrested for meddling in matters above their station. The others were soon released, but Wentworth was kept in the Tower for four years until he died.[4]

The Puritan MP, James Morice, firmly refused Wentworth's invitation to attend these meetings. He said that he would 'neither in this case or any Parliament matter confer with any man'.[5] But Morice introduced a bill in the House of Commons against the oath *ex officio* which Whitgift and his commissioners compelled the Puritan clergy to take when they were summoned before the ecclesiastical courts. Whitgift was alarmed. He wrote to

Elizabeth that Morice's object was to protect the Puritans 'who seek to bring in a new kind of ecclesiastical government, like unto that in Scotland, and do, as far as they dare, impugn Your Majesty's authority in causes ecclesiastical ... In the end, Your Majesty will find that those which now impugn the ecclesiastical jurisdiction endeavour also to impair the temporal and to bring even Kings and Princes under their censure'.[6] Elizabeth was well aware of this. Even before she received Whitgift's letter, she had ordered that Morice should be arrested; but he was released after only fifty-eight days in prison.

Parliament passed a new statute against seditious activities by Papists and Puritans. The Papists were to be punished by fines, the Puritans by banishment from the realm. Elizabeth now considered that the Puritans were a greater threat than the Papists, and they were being persecuted more severely than any Protestant sects – apart from the Dutch Anabaptists of 1575 – had been persecuted in England since Mary's reign. The Puritans actually complained that in Lancashire, where Catholic sympathies had always been strong, they were tried at Assizes before Mr Justice Walmesley, who they claimed was a secret Catholic sympathiser and whose wife had been prosecuted as a Catholic recusant for illegally attending Mass.[7]

On 10 April 1593 Elizabeth came to the House of Lords and dissolved Parliament. As usual she made them an impressive, if slightly rambling, speech. 'Many wiser Princes than myself you have had, but, one only excepted – whom in the duty of a child I must regard, and to whom I must acknowledge myself far shallow – I may truly say, none whose love and care can be greater, or whose desire can be more to fathom deeper the prevention of danger to come, or resisting of dangers, if attempted towards you, shall ever be found to exceed myself. In love, I say, towards you, and care over you'.[8] It is not surprising that in the spring of 1593, a few weeks before Penry and the other Puritans were executed, Elizabeth should have thought of Henry VIII and referred to him as the only English sovereign whose love and care for his people exceeded hers; for by love and care, she meant a ruthless determination to prevent the people from being seduced by trouble-makers who would disturb religious uniformity, challenge the established order, and set England on the road to revolution and civil war.

Would it have been different if Leicester had still been living? He and most of the other Puritan sympathisers in the Council had died – Bedford in 1585, Mildmay in 1589, and Walsingham in 1590. Burghley was old and ill. He had been lucky to escape trouble for his part in the execution of Mary Queen of Scots, and would take no risks to help the Puritans, especially as he was chiefly concerned with ensuring that his son, Robert Cecil, succeeded him as Elizabeth's chief minister.

Knollys was nearly eighty, but still resolute. 'I do marvel', he wrote to Burghley, 'how Her Majesty can be persuaded that she is in as much danger of such as are called Puritans as she is of the Papists'.[9] He offered to resign from the Privy Council in protest against the anti-Puritan policy of the government, and spoke in support of Morice in the House of Commons; but though he was protected by his age and past association with Elizabeth from the consequences which befell the other Puritans, he was powerless. Perhaps even Leicester could not have deterred Elizabeth from her support of Whitgift, her 'little black husband' as she called him. She had for once firmly made up her mind, and was determined to crush the Puritans who were always causing trouble in the House of Commons, who were closer to the rebels in the Netherlands than to the loyal subjects of her father and herself, who wished to see the feet rule the head, and who had induced her to acquiesce, or half-acquiesce, in the execution of a Queen.

The persecuted Puritans hoped for, and obtained, a little support from Elizabeth's new favourite, Robert Devereux, Earl of Essex. He had succeeded to his father's title at the age of seven, after the death of the first Earl in 1573, when Burghley had been appointed his guardian. He was linked by family ties to the influential Puritan sympathisers. His mother was Knollys's daughter, and after his father's death she had married Leicester; and he himself had married Walsingham's daughter, the widow of Sir Philip Sidney. With Knollys as a grandfather, Leicester as a stepfather, Burghley as a guardian, and Walsingham as a father-in-law, he was presented to the Queen, to whom he was related through the Knollyses and the Boleyns, when he was aged nine. She tried to kiss him, but he was frightened, and shrank from her. On another occasion, the little boy forgot to remove his bonnet in her presence; but neither of these very youthful peccadilloes prejudiced her against him when he came to court in 1587 as a handsome young man of twenty. Elizabeth was fifty-three.[10]

Elizabeth became so attached to Essex that she impeded his natural desire, as a young nobleman, to win glory on the battlefield. Against her wishes, he joined the expedition to Portugal in 1589. When Elizabeth sent instructions to Drake and Norris during the campaign, she included an order that they were to send the Earl of Essex home; and when Essex disregarded the order, she wrote again more insistently, warning Drake and Norris to send Essex back at once, for 'if ye do not, ye shall look to answer at your smart'.[11] Essex then returned to face the angry Queen, and found her very dissatisfied with the progress of the campaign in Portugal.

Essex occasionally intervened on behalf of a persecuted Puritan. The story was told that on one occasion when Elizabeth was telling him that she would take steps to punish anyone who was caught reading the Martin Mar-prelate pamphlets, Essex produced one of the pamphlets from his pocket and said that in that case she would have to punish him.[12] But he took care to avoid coming into any serious conflict with Whitgift. He was too occupied in carrying on his personal competition for Elizabeth's favour with Robert Cecil, who after 1591 increasingly acted as Secretary of State, and with Sir Walter Raleigh, a gentleman of Devon who had come to court and won Elizabeth's favour.

Raleigh was in part an unscrupulous adventurer and in part a Puritan intellectual. His contemporaries were very suspicious of his integrity, and on at least one occasion he offered his services as a spy to Philip II, perhaps in order to double-cross him and supply him with false information. It was not until after Elizabeth's death, as a prisoner in the Tower under James I, that he had time to develop his political ideas which went some way towards modern doctrines of liberal democracy. At Elizabeth's court, he engaged in intrigues to acquire gifts of land and to equip ships to plunder on the Spanish Main, and colonised the territory on the mainland of North America which he named 'Virginia' in honour of the Virgin Queen.

Elizabeth liked him. She took a bite at the potato and a puff at the tobacco which he brought back from America. She appointed him captain of her guard, and gave him valuable gifts. But he was never a serious rival to Essex, with whom she was becoming more and more intimate, going riding and hunting with him during the day, and playing cards with him in her chamber late into the night.[13]

Henry IV of France was in grave danger. Within a month of succeeding to the throne, he was cooped up near Dieppe with a small army, while the forces of the League were preparing to march against him. He asked Elizabeth to send him 400 horsemen and 4,000 foot soldiers immediately, and to lend him money to pay his Swiss mercenaries, who were threatening to go home unless they received their wages.[14] But Elizabeth was much more reluctant to help him with men or money than she had been a month before to lend £60,000 to Henry III, for he was much less likely to succeed now that so many Catholics were refusing to fight for a Protestant King.

A few English gentlemen, including Sir Roger Williams and Essex's brother Walter Devereux, had joined Henry's army, and they and Elizabeth's diplomatic representatives at Dieppe urged her to send men and money to him at once. But she hesitated, and argued with Henry's envoys at Oatlands while Mayenne's army approached Dieppe. On 21 September 1589 (N.S.) they attacked Henry at Arques. Although Henry was outnumbered by three to one, he won a brilliant victory in which he gained the admiration of the English observers by his personal courage and dash.

Elizabeth was still arguing with Henry's ambassador, but on 20 September (30 September N.S.) – nine days after Henry's victory at Arques – she ordered Lord Willoughby to go to Dieppe with the 400 horsemen and 4,000 foot soldiers for whom Henry had asked, to serve in his army at her expense for one month. This did not give Henry much time to make use of their services, especially as Elizabeth insisted on reckoning the beginning of the month from the time when they sailed from Dover. She ordered Willoughby to explain to Henry that she would have sent him more men for a longer time if her subjects had not been exhausted from fighting against the Spaniards in England, Ireland and the Netherlands without receiving help from anyone, though as she was fighting for the Protestant cause, all Protestants should have helped her to bear the burden. She ordered Willoughby to come home with his men after a month if Henry did not pay them to stay with him for a longer period.[15]

Before Willoughby had sailed, Elizabeth heard that Henry had won a victory at Arques, and she therefore countermanded her order and told Willoughby not to go; but her agents at Dieppe persuaded her to change her mind, and Willoughby and his men landed at Dieppe on 28 September – seventeen days too late to take part in the critical battle at Arques. Henry had sold his gold chains to raise money to pay his Swiss to stay for a few more days; but on 30 October Elizabeth agreed to lend him £15,000 if he promised to repay it, with £750 interest, within six months.[16]

Mayenne's defeated army fell back towards Paris, and Henry followed them. He did not wish to capture Paris by storm, for he knew that this would entail the sack of his capital city by foreign mercenaries, whose killing and looting would make him very unpopular with his subjects. He preferred to induce the city to surrender by negotiation, or to starve it into submission; but this took time, and Willoughby's term of service would have expired before then. The English soldiers marched with him into the suburbs of Paris, and were greatly praised by Henry for their skill and valour; but though Elizabeth reluctantly agreed to allow them to stay for a further two months, she insisted on recalling them in December; and as many of the Swiss mercenaries also went home, Henry was forced to abandon his attempt to take Paris, and to concentrate on capturing smaller towns and castles. A few English gentlemen stayed with him out of devotion to the Protestant cause and to him personally. On 14 March 1590 (N.S.) he won another victory over Mayenne at Ivry, near Dreux (today Ivry-la-Bataille). The admiring English gentlemen in his army reported that he had killed thirty of the enemy with his own hand during the battle.[17]

By the summer of 1590, Henry was once more in the suburbs of Paris, and seemed on the point of taking the city, as food supplies were very low. Then Philip ordered Parma to save Paris. Parma marched from Brussels with 12,000 men, and was joined in eastern France by Mayenne with 7,000 men. Henry IV had assembled from all sources a force of 27,000, but 8,000 of these were Swiss and German mercenaries who would leave if he did not pay them in September. So in June he asked Elizabeth for money. Beauvoir explained to Burghley Henry's devotion to the Protestant cause; if, after the assassination of Henry III, he had gone to Mass at St Cloud on 2 August 1589, he would have been joined by 40,000 Catholics who had fought against him for many years.[18]

Elizabeth was sympathetic to his request, for he was the lawful King of France, not a rebel like the Protestants in the Netherlands; but she did not want to waste her money. She promised Beauvoir that within three days she would send Palavicino to Germany to discuss with the German Protestant

Princes how she and they together could help Henry IV. Beauvoir became worried when Palavicino had not left after seventeen days, but soon afterwards he did leave. On the evening of 12 August, when Elizabeth returned to Oatlands after a day's hunting, she wrote to Beauvoir that she hoped that he would soon bring her news of the capture of Paris, and she sent him an emerald as a gift for Henry.[19]

Three weeks after leaving Brussels, Parma reached Bondy, eight miles from Paris, where Henry blocked his road and offered him battle; but Parma slipped away to the south, and on 1 September (N.S.) captured Lagny, where his troops massacred fifteen hundred of the local inhabitants. From Lagny he could send food supplies into Paris by water. Henry again had to abandon his plans to capture Paris, and had to content himself with harrying Parma's army as it marched back to the Netherlands.[20]

Henry's mercenaries now had to be paid, and no money had come from Elizabeth; but on 25 September she agreed to send him £10,000 at once, and the money left Dover ten days later. The negotiations in Germany for a larger loan were a slower business. Elizabeth and the German Lutherans vied with each other in expressing their admiration for Henry and the importance of helping him, as his defeat would be the ruin of the Protestant cause in Europe; but they all urged the others to provide the money.

It was estimated that the total sum required would be 360,000 florins, which was £72,000. Elizabeth, though she insisted that she had already done enough and had other commitments in the Netherlands and in the naval war against Spain, gave Palavicino authority to offer up to £10,000 as her share, if the Germans would provide the rest. Burghley persuaded her to add a secret clause in her instructions to Palavicino, telling him that in the last resort, if the Germans would not provide the necessary money, he could say that she would be willing to pay £13,000. Elizabeth struck out this clause from Burghley's draft, then changed her mind and allowed it to stand.[21]

On 30 November 1590 Elizabeth sent another secret order to Palavicino, in which, after stressing that she ought to be excused from paying anything at all, she wrote that she was prepared, if necessary, to contribute £15,000. This finally persuaded the Germans to agree to raise the rest of the money, and Palavicino signed a contract on Elizabeth's behalf to pay the £15,000. When Elizabeth heard this she was angry, and said that Palavicino had misunderstood her, and had exceeded his instructions. To Palavicino's dismay, she did not send her bonds for the money. By 1 April 1591 she had agreed that he should pay 50,000 florins (£9,760) to Viscount Turenne, Henry's representative at Frankfort; but he wrote to Burghley on 25 April that as the bonds for the remaining £5,000 had not come, he had paid the money himself to save Elizabeth's reputation in Germany, which had already suffered enough from the delay. She eventually paid him back the £5,000.[22]

During the winter of 1590–91, Henry captured a number of towns, of which Chartres was the most important; but in Brittany the Duke of

Mercoeur, the most powerful local magnate, held most of the province for the League and carried on the war against Henry's general, Viscount Dombes. In November 1590 Dombes informed Elizabeth that at Mercoeur's invitation the Spaniards had sent a force to seize the port of Blavet (opposite the modern port of Lorient), and he appealed to her for help against the Spaniards. Beauvoir hoped that there would be no haggling about expense when so much was at stake, as they should not 'lose our week for a Saturday' and 'abandon this province to the ambition of an enemy whom three worlds would not satisfy'.[23] Elizabeth wrote to Dombes that she regretted that she was unable to send him any help; but she changed her mind after Norris had pointed out to her that if the Spaniards conquered Brittany they would be able to prevent English ships from sailing up the Channel, and might use the ports of Brittany to launch an invasion of England. On 31 December Sir Roger Williams urged her to send two thousand soldiers to Brittany as soon as possible.[24]

But a few weeks later, Henry IV made another suggestion. If she would send him four thousand men, he would add them to his ten thousand French soldiers and five thousand Swiss mercenaries and capture Rouen. He would then be able to raise money from the wealthy merchants of Rouen which would enable him to pay all his Swiss mercenaries and repay the money that he had borrowed from Elizabeth. The Rouen project did not greatly appeal to Elizabeth, who was more concerned with the threat to Brittany; but she was with difficulty persuaded by Essex to send four thousand men for two months to Normandy for the Rouen operation and to allow him to lead them.[25] His instructions were to aid the French King against his rebels and the Spaniards;[26] but Elizabeth's enthusiasm for the Protestant cause, as usual, was limited. Before Essex and his captains left Greenwich, she ordered them 'not to adventure their lives in these actions, being but as auxiliaries to another King, as they would do if it were for an action of their own natural country or Prince'.[27] She also sent Norris with nine hundred men to fight the Spaniards in Brittany.

Norris's force landed at Paimpol at the beginning of May, and joined Henry's army under Dombes, who was besieging Guingamp, the headquarters of the armies of the League. After a fortnight, Guingamp surrendered on honourable terms, but disagreement broke out between Dombes and Norris. Dombes wished to march south into High Brittany and take part in the attack on the town of Bloin as a preliminary to capturing Rennes; Norris wished to stay near the coast to prevent the Spaniards from capturing the Channel ports, and if possible to drive them out of Blavet. He refused to take part in the siege of Bloin, and Dombes had to march there without him. When Elizabeth heard of the disagreement between Dombes and Norris, she threatened to withdraw her troops from Brittany, and blamed Henry for not sending reinforcements to Brittany. Henry said that Rouen and Normandy were more important than Brittany, and blamed Norris's lack of co-operation for the failure to capture Bloin.[28]

When Essex and Williams landed at Dieppe at the end of July 1591, and linked up with Henry's forces at Pont-de-l'Arche, they found to their surprise that Henry himself was not there. He had gone off with another force to link up in Lorraine with the German mercenaries who were coming to join him. On the way, he besieged Noyon, near Compiègne. When he heard that Essex had landed at Dieppe, he invited him to join him at Compiègne to discuss the campaign against Rouen. Essex decided to ride to Compiègne with an escort of fifty horsemen. This worried Williams, for there was no firm front line in the French civil war, and armed bands from both sides were roaming the countryside attacking enemy stragglers. He feared that Essex and his fifty horsemen would be attacked by the enemy; so Williams accompanied him to Compiègne with a total of three hundred horsemen.

Henry entertained Essex for a week at his headquarters at Atterly near Compiègne. They became good friends, and they and their gentlemen competed at tennis and riding at the ring. Henry explained that before beginning operations against Rouen, he intended to capture Noyon, to link up with the German mercenaries, and to go to Sedan for the wedding of the Duchess of Bouillon, who came from one of the leading Catholic families in France, with Henry's Huguenot general, Viscount Turenne. At the end of August, Essex and Williams rode back to Pont-de-l'Arche. Yate, who had been left in command of the English troops at Pont-de-l'Arche, heard that Villars, who held Rouen for the League, had sent out 2,500 horsemen to waylay Essex on his return journey; so Yate marched with the English army to meet Essex, and they all arrived safely at Pont-de-l'Arche.[29]

Elizabeth was very angry when she heard about Essex's journey to Compiègne. Henry had told her that he would besiege Rouen, and she had sent him troops for this purpose. Instead of beginning the siege, he had gone off to Noyon, and proposed to go from there to Sedan for a wedding. He had insulted her general, Essex, by summoning him to come to Noyon; and while Essex had been playing tennis with Henry at Atterly, her soldiers at Pont-de-l'Arche were being paid by her for doing nothing. Essex had risked being captured by the enemy on his foolhardy ride to Compiègne, and Yale had had to send the army to escort him back to Pont-de-l'Arche, again at her expense, instead of taking part in operations against Rouen.[30]

Essex was stung by suggestions that he had been wasting his time instead of fighting the enemy, and soon after returning to Pont-de-l'Arche he led an assault party in an attack on a fort at Rouen. His men fought valiantly, but their attack was repulsed, and Essex's brother, Walter Devereux, was killed. Williams thought that the operation was fully justified in order to give his untrained troops some fighting experience before they encountered Parma's veterans, who were expected to intervene again in the war in France;[31] but Elizabeth was angry, and wrote a reproachful letter to Essex. It was a great oversight 'that you would come so near Rouen, and there to make a bravado upon the enemy in sight of the town, where to your own greatest loss, as a reward of your unadvisedness, you lost your only brother'.[32]

Even by sixteenth-century standards, this was an insensitive way of referring to Devereux's death. When Essex received the letter, he was ill with an ague, and was deeply hurt by the letter. He was never afraid to state his mind about Elizabeth, and he wrote to Sir Robert Cecil asking him to 'judge uprightly between the Queen and me, whether she be not an unkind lady, and I an unfortunate servant'.[33]

Elizabeth told Essex that the two-month period of the troops' service expired on 26 September, and that on that day he and all his men were to return to England. Essex, Williams and other English officers wrote to Elizabeth beseeching her not to recall them; if she did, it would disgrace Essex in public estimation, and would probably lead to a break-up of Henry's army, because if the English left, many other soldiers would go home. In the end, she agreed to recall only Essex himself, and allow the other soldiers to stay; but she insisted that Essex should not be told until he reached England that the other soldiers were staying, in case this encouraged him to refuse to come home. When Essex reached England, he persuaded Elizabeth to change her mind and send him back to Dieppe to lead the English soldiers again.[34]

On the night of 9 November (N.S.) Rouen was invested by the English troops, and the siege began. A fortnight later, Henry himself arrived from the east. The English officers and soldiers greatly admired Henry's gallantry, but some of them questioned his generalship. He repeatedly ordered attacks on Fort St Catherine at Rouen, but never synchronised them with an attack on the forts on the other side of the town. On 3 January 1592 (N.S.), the English captured Fort St Catherine, but were afterwards driven out; and at the end of February they distinguished themselves in repulsing a sortie by the defenders.[35]

In January, the Margrave of Anhalt told Henry that he was withdrawing his mercenaries from the army at Rouen because their wages had not been paid. Elizabeth asked the Margrave to keep his men there for a little longer, because Henry would be able to pay them after he had captured Rouen; but she herself would not advance any more money to Henry to pay Anhalt's mercenaries. When Henry asked her to send more troops, because Parma was about to enter France, she ordered Burghley to inform Henry, on 12 December 1591, that she had received reliable intelligence from the Netherlands that Parma would not march next year.[36]

She was wrong, for Parma was already on his way, and twelve days earlier had reached St Quentin with 18,400 men. Passing to the north of Beauvais, he headed straight for Rouen. Henry, with part of his army, went to meet him and harried his line of march; but Parma ordered his men to march in very close formation, and Henry could do them very little harm. The rest of Henry's soldiers, including the English, remained at the siege of Rouen.

Elizabeth did not approve of this strategy, and wrote bluntly to Henry that he had made a mistake by dividing his army.[37]

On 20 April (N.S.), when Parma was twelve miles from Rouen, Henry abandoned the siege, and concentrated on bringing Parma to battle. Parma entered Rouen on 30 April (N.S.). A few days later, Henry succeeded in penning up Parma's army in the little peninsula between Yvetot and Caudebec, and prepared to annihilate the Spaniards in a decisive battle; but on the night of 5–6 May (N.S.) Parma crossed the Seine on a bridge of boats which he built at Caudebec, and marched his army back to Brussels. He had achieved his object of saving Rouen; but he received a wound in a skirmish at Caudebec which probably contributed to his death eight months later.[38]

Henry IV, who had also been wounded during the campaign and had had several of his best generals killed, received reproachful letters from Elizabeth, accusing him of bungling the siege of Rouen and wasting time, and Elizabeth's money, by going off to Noyon and Sedan in the previous autumn instead of beginning operations against Rouen as soon as Essex and the English soldiers arrived. Her anger had perhaps been fuelled, though she did not mention this to Henry, by a passage in code in one of the reports that she received, stating that people thought that Henry had besieged Noyon because the town belonged to the father of the beautiful Gabrielle d'Estrées, with whom Henry was madly in love, and that he wished to recover Noyon for her family in order to please Gabrielle. In his reply to Elizabeth, Henry vigorously defended his visit to north-east France. The capture of Noyon had won him control of all Picardy. If he had not gone to meet his German *reiters* in Lorraine, they might have been attacked and scattered by the enemy; and his presence at the wedding of the Catholic Duchess of Bouillon and the Protestant Turenne was politically important, for it would probably win over many Catholics to his side.[39]

A few days after Parma escaped from Caudebec, the extended term of service of the English troops expired. Elizabeth insisted on recalling them to England. All her generals were disappointed. 'If the King had had three thousand more English for ten days', wrote Yate to Burghley on 23 April 1592, 'France had been freed, Spain undone, and the Low Countries at liberty; for whilst there is a world, there will never be the like opportunity to ruin the King of Spain'. But the Council persuaded Elizabeth to change her mind, and Williams and his men were allowed to stay in France.[40]

The war in France continued for another year, during which time Henry captured a number of towns; but his failure to take Paris or Rouen, and the lack of any sign that he could win a decisive victory in the war, made him reconsider his attitude to the persistent requests from the Catholic officers in his army that he would convert to Catholicism and go to Mass. For four years he gave them the same reply: as King of France, he would uphold the Catholic Church, but he himself could not convert to Catholicism until he was sincerely persuaded of the truth of the Catholic faith. As soon as he had time, he would take instruction from Catholic priests; but at the moment he did not have time because he was unfortunately too busy fighting against his rebel subjects.

Henry was chary about appointing Protestants to high military or civil offices, and did not even repeal the edicts which Henry III had issued in 1585 prohibiting the exercise of the Protestant religion throughout France. This discrimination against the Protestants annoyed his most zealous supporters, and in July 1591 he issued an edict at Mantes which revoked Henry III's edicts of July 1585 on the grounds that the late King had been forced to issue them by his rebellious subjects.[41]

The Catholics who supported Henry were not happy about the Edict of Mantes; but Henry sent a Catholic herald to inform Elizabeth that he had issued the edict. Perhaps the herald said something which showed Elizabeth that he did not like it, for she told him that she thought that Henry had acted unwisely and precipitately in issuing it. Henry's Protestant representative in London, Du Plessis, was put out when he heard what Elizabeth had said to the herald, and on 3 January 1592 he wrote to Burghley to protest. He said that Elizabeth's words had encouraged the Catholics to increase their pressure on Henry to convert to Catholicism, for the herald had reported that Elizabeth would obviously not object if he did.[42]

On 23 July 1593 (N.S.) Henry announced that he had become a Catholic, and went to Mass in the abbey church of St Denis on the outskirts of Paris. The first reaction of the Pope and the diehard leaders of the League was to denounce his conversion as insincere; but after some successful political intrigues among the cardinals in Rome, in which Philip Neri played the leading part, the Pope granted him absolution for his heresies and received him into the Catholic Church. In March 1594 Paris surrendered to him on honourable terms.

If Henry, remembering Elizabeth's reaction to the Edict of Mantes, expected her to understand the reasons for his conversion to Catholicism, he was greatly mistaken, for she wrote him a reproachful letter denouncing him strongly for his apostasy.[43] Elizabeth, at the age of sixty, was now tending to blame everybody for everything they did; and just as she blamed Essex when he did not immediately send his troops into action at Rouen, and blamed him when he did, and blamed Henry for wishing to capture Rouen instead of the seaports of Brittany, and for campaigning at Noyon instead of capturing Rouen, so she condemned Henry for antagonising his Catholic supporters by issuing the Edict of Mantes and for placating them by becoming a Catholic himself.

But her position was not quite illogical. When it was a question of a sovereign exercising his right and his power to grant religious toleration or to enforce uniformity on his subjects, it was proper to judge it by the principles of political expediency; but we know from Elizabeth's devotional poems that she was a sincerely religious woman and a convinced Protestant. For a

Protestant to convert to Catholicism was an unpardonable act of apostasy which could never be justified, unless perhaps if it was done in obedience to the orders of the Prince, which was the reason why she herself had converted to Catholicism in her sister's reign. But this excuse was not, of course, open to a Protestant Prince who became a Catholic.

Elizabeth was so shocked at Henry IV's conversion that she decided to withdraw all her troops from France; but Burghley persuaded her to order them to go to the Channel Islands and to wait there for further developments. In the end, they remained in Brittany to fight the Spaniards.[44]

In France, Henry IV led a united nation of Catholics and Protestants in a national war against Spain. Elizabeth and her counsellors became alarmed when the Spaniards captured Amiens and Calais; but Henry regained both towns a few months later. At sea, the war continued without much success. The disaster of the Portuguese expedition of 1589 was followed by the repeated failure of the English ships to intercept the Spanish treasure-fleets from India and Peru, and by the defeat of the English expedition to the Azores in 1591, when the heroic sea-captain Sir Richard Grenville was killed. The English soldiers in Brittany failed to drive out the Spaniards, and in 1595 a Spanish raiding expedition, using the Brittany ports, landed in Cornwall and burned Penzance, Newlyn and Mousehole. Later in the year, when Drake went to sea for the first time for six years, the expedition which he led to the Spanish Main met with setbacks and bad luck, and Drake died of disease during the voyage. Elizabeth was not sparing in her criticism of those concerned when she heard of these failures.

These defeats were forgotten after the great victory at Cadiz in 1596. The plan was Essex's, for he had become the most prominent spokesman of the party that called for the continuation of the war against Spain until the final victory of the Protestant cause. This had made him a very popular figure with the people, especially with the Londoners. He suggested sending a powerful naval expedition to attack and capture Cadiz. Lord Howard of Effingham would command the fleet, with Lord Thomas Howard and Sir Walter Raleigh as his Vice-Admiral and Rear-Admiral, and Essex would command the land forces.

Elizabeth, of course, was reluctant to consent to the expedition, for she thought it might fail and be a waste of money; but she was at last persuaded by Essex to agree. The fleet of 93 English and 18 Dutch ships sailed from Plymouth on 1 June 1596, and arrived at Cadiz three weeks later. There had been a dismal failure of Spanish intelligence – Mendoza had retired, blind, to a monastery – and the Spaniards were sure that the English fleet was going to attack Lisbon. They had made no preparations to defend Cadiz. The English destroyed the Spanish ships in the harbour, and Essex and the soldiers landed and took the city by storm. Essex wished to leave a garrison to hold it, but was overruled by the other commanders, so they imposed a heavy fine on the inhabitants and burned the town. On the way home, they sacked Faro. Essex seized the books in the library of the Bishop of the Algarve, and presented them to the college libraries at Oxford. For King Philip, it was a profound humiliation.[45]

In the autumn of 1597, Henry IV entered into peace negotiations with Spain. England and the Dutch joined in the peace talks. Elizabeth and Burghley were in favour of peace with Spain if it could be made on satisfactory terms; but Burghley insisted that Philip should recognise the independence of the northern provinces of the Netherlands. Essex, Raleigh and the younger military men and the general public wished to continue the war against the Papists, and reminded the peace party that it was a principle of the Papists not to keep faith with heretics.[46]

In April 1598 Henry IV issued the Edict of Nantes, by which he granted the Protestants the right to worship in two towns in every district except Paris; elsewhere, Protestant religious services were banned, but the Protestants were allowed to worship in their houses, and were exempt from persecution. A month later, Henry made a separate peace with Philip II; but the war between England and Spain continued.

Elizabeth looked for allies against Philip II, and found some surprising ones. Sixty years before, Henry VIII and all his fellow-Kings in Christendom had paid lip-service to the idea of participating in a crusade against the Turk, though they had no real intention of doing so; and as late as 1571 Elizabeth had congratulated the Venetians on Philip's victory over the Turks at Lepanto.[47] By 1585 she was trying to enlist the support of the Sultan and his vassal-rulers of North Africa, and inciting them to make war on Spain. She was not very successful, for the Turks, having become involved in war with Persia, were not eager to renew hostilities with Spain.

Elizabeth sent envoys to the King of Morocco at Fez, and her merchants traded there; but although the King sent her friendly messages, and assured her that English traders would be welcomed in Morocco, she could not persuade him to enter into a military alliance with Don Antonio against Philip and his government in Portugal. The 'King of Fez' replied to Don Antonio's overtures by asking Don Antonio to deliver his son as a hostage to show his good faith. When Don Antonio did so, the King detained his son at Fez, but took no steps towards forming the alliance.[48]

Elizabeth's relations with the Sultan in Constantinople were more satisfactory, though she never succeeded in persuading him to go to war with Philip. She sent William Harborne, and afterwards Edward Barton, as her ambassador to the Great Turk. They had to make a long and difficult journey, as they could not sail through the Mediterranean for fear of capture by the Spaniards or their allies, the states of Italy; they therefore had to go overland through Germany, Bohemia, Hungary and the Balkans. It took between two and three months for the ambassador's letters from Constantinople to reach London.

Elizabeth and the Sultan Amurath III assured each other of their wish to maintain friendly relations and to encourage trade between their subjects. She warned him about the dangers of trusting his treacherous enemy, the King of Spain; and he congratulated her on her victory over the Armada. She persuaded him to use his influence with the King of Morocco to make him release Don Antonio's son, and to sort out troubles with the corsairs of Algiers and Tunis. After the assassination of Henry III, when the French ambassador in Constantinople became a supporter of the League, Barton persuaded Amurath and his viziers to refuse to recognise the ambassador and to receive instead a new ambassador from Henry IV.

For more than a century the Kings of Christendom had watched happily while the Turks and the Persian empire of 'the Sophy' fought each other in Anatolia and Azerbaijan, for they preferred to see the armies of the Great Turk besieging Tabriz rather than Vienna; but now Harborne and Barton tried unsuccessfully to persuade the Sultan's government to make peace with Persia, so that the Turkish forces would be free to attack the Spaniards in the Mediterranean.

Barton played a more active and successful role in 1590, when fighting broke out in Transylvania on the frontier between the Turkish empire and the kingdom of Poland. Amurath assembled an army and announced that he would punish the Poles for their insolence. Elizabeth offered to mediate in the dispute, hoping to prevent the Turks from becoming involved in a war with Poland so as to leave their hands free to fight Spain. Although the Turk's terms were hard, Barton persuaded the Poles to accept them. But Amurath always managed to find some excuse for not reopening hostilities with Spain.[49]

Elizabeth had greater difficulties in her dealings with the vast empire of Muscovy, whose Emperor could assemble an army of 150,000 men and send them against Poland, Sweden, or the Tartars of the Volga. In the last days of Edward VI's reign, an expedition under Willoughby and Chancellor set sail from London to find the north-east passage to China and India. Willoughby was shipwrecked and lost, but Chancellor reached Archangel, from where he travelled to Moscow to meet the Tsar Ivan Vasilievitch, whom future generations would call 'Ivan the Terrible'. Some English merchants established the Muscovy Company, and opened an English House in Moscow; they traded with Archangel and the west and with Astrakhan and the east. In 1568 Elizabeth recalled Randolph from Edinburgh and sent him on a five-month journey to Moscow by Archangel to pay a courtesy visit to Ivan and settle any problems about the merchants; and after 1570 she was permanently represented in Moscow on a semi-diplomatic basis by the spokesmen for the Muscovy Company.

The English ambassadors became involved in a great deal of friction with the Tsar and his courtiers. The English complained of the arrogance of the Russians, and they offended the Russians by sitting on the wrong side of the table at dinner and violating in other ways the unfamiliar rules of etiquette at the Tsar's court. The basic trouble was that the Tsar and his courtiers did not regard foreign sovereigns as being his equals, and expected their ambassadors to treat him with a deference which was not expected from foreign ambassadors in Western Europe. Ivan was always taking offence at something that the English ambassador, Sir Jerome Bowes, had done, or because he had received a letter from Elizabeth or her counsellors which he thought was not sufficiently respectful, or because she had sent him a gift which was less valuable than he expected; and he was angry when she stalled and played for time about his proposal to marry her maid-of-honour, the Earl of Huntingdon's sister, Lady Mary Hastings. Elizabeth was quite determined not to subject Lady Mary to the doubtful honour of living in Russia as the Tsar's bride.

Elizabeth handled Ivan and his rages very tactfully. She considered it essential to maintain her honour, as far as possible, in her relations with him; but she knew that her merchants in Moscow were at his mercy, and she did not wish to endanger their lives or their trading prospects in Russia. Bowes was not always so successful in handling the very difficult situation in which he was placed. In later years Hakluyt, Pepys and Dr Collins wrote accounts of his adventures in Russia, and his vigorous maintenance of Elizabeth's honour and of the privileges of her representative; but his letters from Moscow tell a very different story, of his forced submission to insults and humiliations, and his fear for his life.

Things became worse after Ivan died in 1584, and was succeeded by his weak-minded son, Tsar Feodor. The Tsar was completely dominated by his minister, Shalkan, one of the leading boyars at his court. Shalkan was bribed, or otherwise persuaded, by the representatives in Moscow of the Hansa towns to favour the Hansa merchants at the expense of the English; and Shalkan took advantage of every lapse in etiquette by Bowes, or other excuse, to cause difficulties for him and to discriminate against the English merchants.

The situation changed when Shalkan fell from power and was replaced by Boris Godunov, whose sister had married Tsar Feodor. Boris favoured the English against the Hansa merchants, and was on friendly terms with Elizabeth's new envoy, Horsey. He exchanged a number of courteous letters with Elizabeth. When Feodor died in 1598, Boris seized the throne, and as Tsar continued his friendly relations with her. He sent an ambassador to London, who was received with great honour by Elizabeth in October 1600. The ambassador assured her that Boris was the lawful heir to the throne of the Russian empire by hereditary descent. Boris did not die until two years after Elizabeth.[50]

THE OLD QUEEN

ELIZABETH was growing old, and did not like it. Sir John Harington, who was the son of her lady-in-waiting and was her godson, wrote after her death: 'There is almost none that waited in Queen Elizabeth's court and observed anything, but can tell, that it pleased her very much to seem, to be thought, and to be told that she looked young'.[1]

Anthony Rudd, the Bishop of St Davids, did not realise this when he preached before her at Richmond during Lent in 1597,* when she was aged sixty-three. He took his text from the 90th Psalm: 'So teach us to number our days, that we may apply our hearts unto wisdom', and then proceeded to preach about sacred and mystical numbers, how 3 was the number of the Trinity, 7 of the Sabbath, and 7 times 9 was the Great Climacterical Year. He then noticed that the Queen was looking very angry, and did not like this reference to the number 63. He hastily changed the subject to the number of the Beast, 666, which he proved was the Pope, and to the number 88, which the Queen's enemies had hoped would be the year of her overthrow, but had been the year in which she triumphed over the Armada.

Elizabeth, as usual, had listened to the sermon sitting behind a window, apart from the rest of the congregation. It was customary, when the preacher had finished, for her to open the window and thank him; but on this occasion she called out loudly that the bishop should have kept his arithmetic to himself, and added: 'But I see the greatest clerks are not the wisest men'.[2] Puckering, the Lord Keeper, realising how displeased she was, ordered Rudd to remain confined in his house for the time being; but when Elizabeth was told about this, three days later, she was angry that he had been placed under this restraint. Harington wrote that he was present when one of the ladies, in Elizabeth's presence, ridiculed Rudd's sermon. Elizabeth promptly scolded the lady for criticising it, but said that she was not as old at sixty-three

---

*Harington, who says that it was in Lent in 1596, was using the old style calendar, under which the year began on 25 March.

as the bishop supposed. She said that her appetite, her singing voice, and her eyesight were as good as ever. She proved this last point by producing a jewel on which an inscription had been engraved in very small letters. Neither the Bishop of Worcester nor Sir James Croft could read the inscription, but Elizabeth could do so.[3]

She looked immensely impressive, as she moved amid the pomp of her court. The German visitor, Heutzner, who saw her at Greenwich in 1598, described her as 'very majestic', with her oblong face, fair but wrinkled, her small dark eyes, her slightly hooked nose, her small hands and long fingers, and her red wig, though her teeth, like those of all other English ladies, were black as a result of eating too much sugar. She was dressed in white silk, and her bosom was uncovered, which was the fashion for unmarried English women. Her long train was carried by a Marchioness, and she wore many rich jewels. As she passed on her way to her chapel, she spoke graciously to her subjects and to the foreign visitors in the crowd in English, French or Italian, and they all knelt as she spoke to them. Heutzner was surprised at the ceremony with which her dinner was carried in by servants and tasted by a countess, all of whom knelt three times to the food on the royal table.[4]

She still ate heartily, and hunted, following the hounds on horseback several times a week; and she still went for energetic walks in the park at Hampton Court and in the grounds of her other palaces. She still danced, not only the stately *pavane*, but the more nimble *galliard*, though no longer the immodest *volta* which she had sometimes danced with Leicester, in which the gentleman put his arms around the lady's waist and lifted her up into the air.

She did not often travel as far afield as she had done when she was younger, though this had probably more to do with the risk of assassination than with her advancing years. After she accompanied Anjou to Canterbury when he left England to go to the Netherlands in 1582, she did not go further from London than Windsor during the next nine years, though she often travelled between Greenwich, Richmond, Nonesuch and Oatlands, and sometimes visited Burghley at his house at Theobalds in Hertfordshire. In August and September 1591 she went on a longer progress into Sussex, Hampshire and Surrey, by Cowdray and Chichester to Portsmouth and Southampton, returning to Richmond by Winchester, Basing House, Odiham, Farnham and Sutton Place near Guildford.[5]

In the summer and autumn of 1592 she went through Berkshire and Oxfordshire to Alderton and Sudeley Castle in Gloucestershire, to Woodstock again, and to Oxford, where the university had last entertained her twenty-six years before. She watched plays performed at Christ Church, attended a disputation on whether air or meat or drink did most change a man, and again charmed her audience, as she had done in 1566, by her speech to the university in St Mary's Church. While she was speaking, she noticed that Burghley, who was aged seventy-two, was standing, and she would not proceed with her speech until a stool had been brought for him.[6]

The morale of the English people was high in the last decade of the century. They gloried in the victory of their sailors – and of their Queen – over the Spanish Armada, which they saw as a sure proof that God was on their side. It was also a time when music and literature flourished, when the musical works of Morley, Byrd, Dowland and Weelkes were widely sold, when the dramas of Marlowe, Ben Jonson, Dekker, Middleton and Webster were performed, and of the first plays of Shakespeare, who could never have written them if he had been born, not in the sixth year of Elizabeth's reign, but fifty years earlier, before the drama had been freed from the straitjacket of the medieval morality plays in which it had been confined before the Reformation.

But it was also a difficult time. In the summer of 1594 it rained heavily throughout May, June and July, and, after a fine interlude in August, again in September, which ruined the harvest and sent food prices rocketing. Next year the summer was so cold, with so little sun, that it was said that no one would have known that it was summer if there had not been green leaves on the trees. 'Our summers are not summers', said a preacher, 'scant any day hath been seen that it hath not rained upon us'.[7] Prices rose again because of the heavy rains in the summer and autumn of 1596, after the third bad harvest in succession. In London food prices rose by forty-eight per cent during these four years, and wages did not increase at all. The government's attempt to remedy the situation by importing corn from abroad did not alleviate the food shortage, which led to riots in London in 1595 and in Oxfordshire next year.[8] The people found some consolation in a new pleasure, the smoking in long clay pipes of the tobacco which by the end of the century was being imported on a large scale from America.

The government was as vigilant as ever against attempts by Jesuits and other Papists to assassinate the Queen. In 1593 the arrest of some Portuguese, who were found to be Spanish agents, started a trail which led to Elizabeth's physician, the Portuguese Dr Roderigo Lopez, who was suspected of being involved in a plot to poison Elizabeth. Originally a Jew, he had for thirty-five years been living in London as a Christian and a Protestant, becoming house physician at St Bartholomew's Hospital and a fashionable society doctor. Unfortunately for him, he combined his medical practice with being the head of Don Antonio's intelligence service, and in this capacity got in touch with Spanish agents who were plotting to assassinate Don Antonio. There is no doubt that Lopez told the Spaniards that he would arrange to poison Don Antonio, and it is equally certain that he shielded and arranged for the escape of a spy who had betrayed to Mendoza the plans for the Portugal expedition of 1589; but according to Lopez he did all this, with Walsingham's knowledge, in order to double-cross the Spaniards.

He became involved in a struggle for influence at court between Essex and the Cecils. Philip II's Secretary of State, Antonio Perez, was arrested and charged with the murder of a prominent Spanish politician which he had carried out at Philip's orders and for which he was now to be made the scapegoat. He escaped, and fled to England, where he was welcomed as an important defector by Essex. Perez denounced Lopez as a Spanish agent, and convinced Essex of his guilt, while Burghley and his son Robert believed that he was innocent. Elizabeth at first believed Robert Cecil, and told Essex that he had made a fool of himself; but this only made Essex more determined to find more evidence to incriminate Lopez. He found enough in the confessions of Philip's Portuguese agents, and in some mysterious and ambiguous letters written to them by Lopez, to persuade Elizabeth to change her mind and believe in his guilt, though there was certainly more evidence that he intended to poison Don Antonio than the Queen.

His interrogators eventually induced him to confess without having to torture him, and he was convicted of high treason, and sentenced to be hanged, drawn and quartered. Elizabeth waited for four months before issuing the warrant for his execution, but the sentence was duly carried out in June 1594.[9]

There is no doubt that the people were prejudiced against him because he was a Jew, though this does not seem to have been a very important factor. It is questionable how far he was the prototype for Shakespeare's Jew, Shylock, in *The Merchant of Venice*; and certainly Lopez's character bore no resemblance to Shylock's. There is no reference to the fact that Lopez was a Jew in a broadsheet which, as usual in such cases, was published and circulated in London at the time of his execution, in which 'this wicked person Dr Lopez ... this perjured murdering traitor', who had plotted against 'the precious life of our sovereign sacred Princess, upon whose life so many lives do depend', is described as 'Dr Roger Lopez, a Portugal born', but not as a Jew.[10] But Camden described him as 'Roderigo Lopez of the Jewish sect', and wrote that when Lopez declared on the scaffold that 'he had loved the Queen as he had loved Jesus Christ', this statement 'from a man of the Jewish profession was heard not without laughter'. The English people probably hated Lopez more because he was a foreigner than because he was a Jew; and Camden warned about the dangers that had arisen from the presence of other Portuguese who had 'crept into England as retainers to the exiled Don Antonio'.[11]

The execution of Lopez consolidated Essex's position at court; but in June 1596, while Essex was fighting at Cadiz, Burghley persuaded Elizabeth to appoint Robert Cecil as Secretary of State. Two years later, on 4 August 1598, Burghley died at the age of seventy-eight. Elizabeth visited him when he was dying, and with her own hands fed him with soup from a spoon.[12]

As usual, there was trouble in Ireland. Hardly had the Spaniards from the Armada been dealt with than a revolt broke out in Connaught in the spring of 1589 under the leadership of the Bourkes. Several members of the Lord Deputy's Council in Dublin, including Thomas Jones, the Bishop of Meath, believed that it had been provoked by the oppressive rule of Sir Richard Bingham, the Governor of Connaught, and his subordinate officers. The bishop said that Bingham had executed several local Irish gentlemen without trial; he had hanged two children, aged nine and seven, as hostages because their father had joined the rebels; he had hanged without trial a one-legged man who was over eighty years old; and he had seized twenty cattle from each barony in order to provide a feast when Lady Bingham arrived from England. In Sligo, Bingham's agent, William Taaffe, seized cattle and horses, 'yea, if it be but a man's wife or daughter which Taaffe doth fancy, but so must have at his will'.[13]

Bingham said that these tales were lies disseminated by the rebels. He believed that 'without the sword be now and then severely used, it is impossible to govern the Irish people',[14] because an Irishman was no better than a ravening wolf.[15] Walsingham supported Bingham. He sharply reprimanded the Bishop of Meath and the Lord Deputy, Fitzwilliam, and told them that those who had libelled Bingham were either his personal enemies or traitors. Elizabeth eventually ordered an inquiry into the allegations against Bingham, but then announced that she considered that he had been completely vindicated.[16]

Bingham had no doubt what had caused the rebellion. It was the people's desire to recover their old doltish Irish customs,[17] particularly the Irish laws of inheritance which the English had abolished. Others thought that the root of the trouble was religion, and the laxity of the authorities in enforcing the law against Catholic recusants as it was enforced in England. How could a nation that did not know its duty to God be expected to obey its Prince? The Archbishop of Cashel in 1592, and Sir John Dowdall at Duncannon in Munster four years later, agreed about the alarming spread of Popery in Ireland.[18] Whereas in 1568 the people regularly attended the Protestant services in the churches, hardly anyone now came to church. First the women, and then the men, stayed away and attended Mass in secret. In every town and village there was a Papist school with an idolatrous schoolmaster, controlled by a Jesuit supervisor; there were secret routes from every town along which people passed to and from Papist centres in foreign countries; no Irishman could be induced to give evidence in court against another Irishman, for they were all devoted to 'the Romish religion, which they call the Catholic faith'.[19] In the reign of Edward VI there had not been six known Papists in Dublin; now there were not six score Protestants in the whole of Ireland.[20]

The English settlers hated the Irish as much as the Irish hated them. In Connaught it was common talk among the settlers that 'there could be no better service than to kill them all'.[21] Then the land could be divided up among the English. This was a favourite theme among the English Protestant commanders and the Anglican clergy in Ireland and England: God cannot have intended so fertile and agreeable a country as Ireland to be owned by

Papist savages: He had given it to the English as He gave the land of Canaan to the Israelites. John Bell, the vicar of Christchurch, who in 1597 sent an unsolicited memorandum on Ireland to Burghley, wrote that 'the Lord, having a special love unto us, God hath given the kingdom of Ireland to Her Majesty', and suggested that the Queen should give 300 acres of land in Ulster to every English colonist, at a rent of £5 a year.[22] Elizabeth did not follow his advice; but she gave 12,000 acres of land in Munster to Sir Walter Raleigh to console him for having been ousted by Essex as her chief favourite at court.[23]

The most serious threat came from Hugh O'Neill, Earl of Tyrone, who by 1588 dominated all Ulster from his castle at Dungannon. When it suited him, Tyrone professed to be an Irish patriot and a devout Catholic, and he always dated his letters in the Pope's new-style calendar; but no one was ever quite sure on which side he was going to be. He played an active part in killing the shipwrecked soldiers and sailors of the Armada in obedience to the Lord Deputy's proclamation;* but soon afterwards he seized Shane O'Neill's son and hanged him – he denied the story that he had strung him up with his own hands – because of a family feud.[24]

The Council in Dublin became alarmed at this violation of the law and the Queen's authority, especially as they received reports from their spies in Dungannon that Tyrone was in secret communication with Philip II. But they did not know what to do about it. Ulster had never been successfully invaded by a land army from the Pale, for an Irish leader who had the support of the people could withdraw into the forests of Tyrone and Fermanagh, out of reach of the invading army.[25] Elizabeth thought that it would be better if one of Tyrone's enemies, or some disloyal member of his bodyguard, could be bribed to kidnap him,[26] but the Council in Dublin could find no one to do the job, and they therefore advised Elizabeth to conciliate Tyrone.

Elizabeth's first reaction was to reject the advice of the Council in Dublin. She decided to send an army to Ireland, even if this cost her money; and in February 1595 she ordered that 2,000 English troops be withdrawn from Brittany to deal with Tyrone. Sir William Russell, who had succeeded Fitzwilliam as Lord Deputy, invaded Ulster; but Tyrone withdrew to the forests, and armed every shepherd with a pike.[27] Ulster seemed unconquerable. The Papist Bishop of Kildare wrote to Tyrone from Lisbon that if the last sparkles of the faith were extinguished in the other three provinces of Ireland, the most merciful God would allow it to survive in Ulster until it could spread again from there and win back the whole realm to the faith of St Patrick.[28]

Elizabeth decided to offer Tyrone a pardon on terms. On 12 August 1595 Cecil wrote that if his proud heart had so come down that he would submit

---

*A Spanish survivor of the Armada was told by an Irishman that 'the man who ordered all the [Spanish] soldiers to be murdered was an Irish earl named O'Neill.' (*Span. Cal. Eliz.*, iv.508–9).

absolutely to Her Majesty's mercy, it would not be denied him.[29] But Tyrone was not so come down that he did not keep his options open. On 27 September (N.S.) he and his son-in-law, Hugh Roe O'Donnell, the Lord of Tyrconnel, wrote to Philip II and his ministers and generals and asked for help, for now or never was the time to save the Catholic faith in the kingdom of Ireland; but a month later, as there was no sign of Spanish aid coming, Tyrone agreed to accept the Queen's pardon and pay a fine of twenty thousand cows.[30]

Elizabeth's agents had intercepted Tyrone and O'Donnell's letters to Philip; but she decided to pretend that she did not know about this act of treason. She would pardon Tyrone, and anyone else who would submit. But Tyrone and O'Donnell demanded that the Catholics in Ireland should be granted religious toleration.[31] This was unacceptable to the Protestants. 'They say they labour by Tyrone only for liberty of conscience', wrote the Anglican Bishop of Limerick, 'but if too much liberty had not been given heretofore, they had had no such conscience now'.[32]

In May 1596 Tyrone heard that an envoy from Philip II had arrived at the Liffey, and he rode forty miles to meet him and receive a letter of encouragement from Philip. He then sent the letter to Russell to prove his loyalty to Elizabeth, but asked Russell to return the letter to him and not to take a copy of it. He did not want the Spaniards and his Catholic supporters to know that he had sent it to Russell. Instead of returning the letter, Russell sent it to Elizabeth and ignored Tyrone's angry demands that it should be returned to him.

Elizabeth out-smarted Tyrone. She sent Philip's letter back to Philip, explaining that Tyrone had sent it to her because he had submitted, as the rebellion in Ireland had been finally suppressed. She thought that this would discourage Philip from intervening in Ireland, and would prevent him from trusting Tyrone and helping him in future. But Philip out-smarted Elizabeth. He wrote and told Tyrone that Elizabeth had sent him the letter, but that he was sure that Elizabeth was lying when she said that Tyrone had sent it to Russell; he was convinced that she had obtained the letter in some other way, as he trusted Tyrone completely. Tyrone wrote to Philip that the letter had been stolen by his secretary, and that it was the secretary who had sent it to Russell; he himself had always been loyal to Philip.[33] The result of the incident was to convince Tyrone that he could not trust Elizabeth or any Englishman, and he decided to start a new insurrection as soon as possible.

The English had left a garrison in the Blackwater Fort on the River Blackwater near Dungannon. In July 1598 Tyrone attacked and besieged the fort. A force of 3,500 foot and 300 horse was sent to relieve the besieged garrison. As they marched from Armagh to the Blackwater on 14 August, they were attacked by Tyrone near the Yellow Ford. Nearly half the men in the royal army were killed, and some of the Irish soldiers deserted to the rebels. Only 1,500 survivors made their way back to Armagh.[34]

The defeat at the Yellow Ford lifted the morale of the Irish rebels and shocked the English. Cecil and Lord Howard of Effingham, who had been created Earl of Nottingham after his victory at Cadiz, wrote to the Council in Dublin that 'Her Majesty's sense of dishonour doth greatly touch her'.[35] She wrote an angry letter to Ormond and the Council in Dublin, and decided to send to Ireland 2,000 English soldiers who were serving in the Netherlands and to enlist 2,000 men in England to replace them, even though it would cost her £12,000. She urged them not to enlist any more Irishmen into the army.[36]

Russell had no intention of doing this, for he and his officers were alarmed that two-thirds of the soldiers in the army in Ireland were Irish.[37] 'The rebel is Irish, the soldier is the same', wrote Sir George Clifford.[38] As he and his colleagues feared, there were several cases of Irish soldiers deserting to the rebels and giving them their weapons and ammunition. The government believed that in every town there were supporters of the rebels who arranged for food supplies to be sent to them; in Limerick, the Mayor and corporation did so quite openly. One English officer suggested that butchers should be forbidden to travel through the countryside to prevent them from taking meat to the rebels in the field. He also thought that small portable racks should be invented with which the local army commanders could torture the local inhabitants wherever they went in order to obtain information about rebel movements.[39]

When the rebels in Ireland were defeated, the Irish men, women and children in the district suffered. When the rebels won, it was Elizabeth's ladies-in-waiting who suffered. Sir John Harington admired the Queen, like all other loyal Englishmen, and he was personally grateful to her for the kindness that she had shown him over the years;[40] but he also saw the less agreeable side of her nature, and after her death he wrote about this in letters to his friends which he never imagined would be published by his descendants two hundred years later. He wrote that her courtiers, and above all her maids of honour, were often the victims of her angry tantrums. In May 1597 Sir William Fenton wrote to Harington that the Queen's behaviour towards her ladies had become much worse since the recent troubles in Ireland.[41]

Her mood could change very suddenly. 'When she smiled', wrote Harington, 'it was a pure sunshine, that everyone did choose to bathe in, if they could; but anon came a storm from a sudden gathering of clouds, and the thunder fell in wondrous manner on all alike'.[42] Her worst outbursts were often on the subject of marriage and sex. She had sound political reasons, as well as her innate sense of religious morality, for wishing to ensure that her court maintained the reputation for purity which it had possessed for a hundred years under Henry VII, Henry VIII, Edward VI and Mary. There were none of the flagrant love affairs in which the male and female members of the royal family and the nobility engaged at the French court under Francis I, Henry II and his three sons, and under Henry of Navarre. Anne Boleyn's heretical daughter had to be careful to avoid scandal, particularly after Amy Robsart's death. But her solicitude for her reputation and her duty to ensure that her maids of honour made suitable marriages do not account for the spite and petty vindictiveness with which she showed her displeasure if any of them dared to wish to get married. On these occasions, she spoke and acted not as a Queen but as an embittered old spinster who had not been able to marry the man she loved.

She often asked her maids of honour, when they were gathered together, if they had any wish to marry, and listened to their enthusiastic and oft-repeated assurances that they found the idea most repugnant. But the young daughter of Sir Robert Arundell was in love, and as she had only recently come to court, she did not realise the answer that the Queen expected. She hesitated, and looked embarrassed, and aroused Elizabeth's suspicions. Elizabeth took her aside, and encouraged her to confide, and discovered that she was in love with a young gentleman, whom she named, and that she hoped to marry him, but that they had not yet ventured to ask her father for his permission. Elizabeth told her to leave the matter in her hands, and she would obtain Sir Robert's permission.

Elizabeth had a private talk with Sir Robert Arundell, and told him that his daughter wished to marry the gentleman, and asked him if he had any objection. He replied that if the Queen favoured the match, he would willingly agree; and at her request he gave her his consent in writing. Then she summoned his daughter to her presence, and told her that she had obtained Sir Robert's consent to the marriage. 'Then I shall be happy, and please Your Grace', said the girl. 'So thou shalt', replied Elizabeth, 'but not to be a fool and marry. I have his consent given to me, and I vow thou shalt never get it into thy possession. So go to thy business. I see thou art a bold one to own thy foolishness so readily'.[43]

Lady Mary Howard's humiliation was more public; but she had behaved in a manner above her social station, and had annoyed the Queen by flirting with Essex. Elizabeth, like Henry VIII, dressed in rich garments and wore expensive jewels because she thought such clothes appropriate for a great Queen. She also expected her bishops to dress impressively, and not to succumb to the demands of the Puritans that they should avoid pomp and ostentation. In April 1594 Aylmer, the Bishop of London, who thirty-five years before had championed the rights of a woman sovereign against Knox, preached before Elizabeth. He spoke of the vanity of decking the body too finely. After the sermon, Elizabeth said to her ladies that if he continued to preach such sermons, 'she would fit him for Heaven, but he should walk thither without a staff and leave his mantel behind him'.[44] He went to Heaven sooner than she expected, for he died two months later.

Elizabeth believed that everyone should dress as richly as befitted their rank; but when she saw Lady Mary Howard wearing a rich velvet costume with a border powdered with gold and pearl, which was being admired by all the courtiers, she thought that Lady Mary was dressing above her rank. She took her aside and asked if she could borrow the costume. Lady Mary could not, of course, refuse, and Elizabeth put it on and appeared in it before the court; but the costume was too short for Elizabeth, because Lady Mary was smaller than the tall Queen. Elizabeth asked the courtiers and ladies how they liked the dress, and after everyone had praised it, she asked Lady Mary if it was not too short. With some embarrassment, Lady Mary admitted that it was. 'Why then', said Elizabeth, 'if it become not me, as being too short, I am minded it shall never become thee, as being too fine; so it fitteth neither well'. She did at least return the dress to Lady Mary, who took care not to wear it again during the Queen's lifetime, but kept it in her wardrobe and put it on after James I came to the throne.[45]

Lady Mary was not unduly overawed by the Queen's displeasure, and responded by a policy of passive resistance, absenting herself when the Queen wished to walk in the garden and to have Lady Mary behind her to hold her dress, and when she expected Lady Mary to pour out her wine at supper.[46] Essex was much bolder. In the summer of 1598 he became involved in an angry argument with Elizabeth in the presence of other courtiers, because she was reluctant to appoint one of his friends to some office. He angrily and ostentatiously turned his back on her. She was furious, and boxed his ears. He placed his hand on his sword, shouted out that he would not have tolerated such an insult even from her father, and left the room.[47]

Elizabeth placed him under house arrest, and waited for his letter of apology and submission. Instead, he wrote reproaching her for her unkindness. 'I have preferred your beauty above all things, and received no pleasure in life but by the increase of your favour towards me'; but 'Your Majesty hath, by the intolerable wrong you have done both me and yourself, not only broken all laws of affection, but done against the honour of your sex'.[48] She did not take any further action against him, and after a few weeks he was again back in favour. In the spring of 1599 she appointed him Lord General of her armies in Ireland with instructions to overthrow the arch-traitor Tyrone.

The defeat at the Yellow Ford had affronted English public opinion. The old soldier and author, Barnabe Rich, expressed the feelings of the people: how was it possible, after the Queen's armies had so often triumphed over the King of Spain in his own territories, 'yea, almost at his own court gates', that 'a base and barbarous nation, a beggarly people' could defeat the Queen in her own dominions, 'to the great dishonour of the whole English nation, and enough to make us contemptible and to be basely esteemed of amongst all the kingdoms of Christendom?'[49] But now a national hero was being sent to save the situation; the immensely popular Earl of Essex was going with an army of 16,000 foot and 1,300 horse, and 2,000 more men would soon be sent after him.[50]

Elizabeth complained about the cost, but for once she agreed to pay without argument, though the sum involved was not the £10,000 or £15,000 which she had so grudgingly agreed from time to time to lend to the Dutch and French Protestants, but £250,963. 10s. 10d., which was being spent at the rate of £15,738. 16s. 0¾d. a month.[51] She issued a proclamation in which she stated that she had always been a benign sovereign to the peoples of both her realms, and denied the falsehood spread by the rebel leaders that she intended to exterminate the Irish nation and treat Ireland as a conquered country.[52] She would show mercy to those who deserved it, but would 'extirpate the rest as enemies to God and traitors to our crown and dignity'.[53]

Essex was eager to win military glory in Ireland, but he did not wish to be exiled there for too long while his rival, Cecil, undermined his influence at court. He asked Elizabeth for permission to return home at any time he fancied, and persuaded her to agree to insert an unprecedented clause to this effect in his commission; but she added that she was sure that he would not return if this would be to the detriment of her service in Ireland.[54]

Essex, who embarked for Dublin at Chester, began his journey by riding through the city of London on 27 March 1599 amid cheering crowds who gave him the kind of reception which was usually reserved for the Queen. The nation was confident that he would soon return in triumph, having chastised the rebels. When Shakespeare's play *Henry V* was performed that year at the Globe Theatre in Southwark, with its stirring tale of an earlier episode of English military glory, the Chorus compared Henry V's arrival after his victory at Agincourt with the imminent return from Ireland of the victorious 'general of our gracious Empress';[55] and another poet, whose fame has been less enduring, wrote with equal enthusiasm:

Now Scipio sails to Afric far from home;
The Lord of Hosts and battles be his guide;
Now when green trees begin to bud and bloom
On Irish seas Eliza's ships shall ride. . . .
Right makes Wrong blush, and Truth bids Falsehood fly;
The sword is drawn, Tyrone's dispatch draws nigh.[56]

But the enthusiasm for invading Ulster was less marked among the officers and soldiers in Dublin than among the poets and the people in London. The difficulties of a land invasion from Drogheda to Armagh had always been appreciated by military men, and the defeat at the Yellow Ford had made Tyrone in his Ulster fastnesses into a bogeyman for the soldiers. Essex was influenced by their attitude, and doubtless remembered how he had been criticised by Elizabeth for his rashness at Rouen. As the rebels in Munster were active, he thought it wiser to deal with them rather than with Tyrone. He sailed from Dublin to Waterford with 3,000 foot and 300 horse, marched against the rebels at Clonmel, Cashel and Roscannon, and captured Cahir

Castle, hanging the rebels whom he took prisoner, although he was offered £2,000 to save the lives of some of them.[57]

Elizabeth was displeased. She congratulated Essex on his capture of Cahir Castle, but reminded him that his chief object was to march against 'the Northern traitor'.[58] She was also angry that he had created too many knights, for although the power to confer knighthoods for valour in the field was often granted to a Lieutenant-General, it was supposed to be used sparingly; by making thirty-nine knights, Essex seemed to be building up a party of political supporters rather than rewarding acts of conspicuous gallantry. She was angry that he had disregarded her orders by giving a high command in the army to his friend the Earl of Southampton, who had gone over to Ireland as a private individual; and she expressly ordered him not to return to England, despite the permission which she had previously given him to return at any time.[59]

When Essex returned to Dublin after his campaign in Munster, it was already the middle of July, and there was no time to be lost if the invasion of Ulster was to take place before the onset of autumn made campaigning difficult. But Essex, hearing of more trouble in Offaly, decided to go there and deal with it before marching against Tyrone. When Elizabeth heard this, she ordered him not to go to Offaly, but to invade Ulster immediately.[60] She blamed him for having done nothing against Tyrone, for having 'run out the glass of time, which hardly ever can be recovered', and for allowing 'these base rebels' to 'see their golden calf preserve himself without taint or loss as safe as in his sanctuary'.[61]

Essex then called all his senior officers to a Council of War in Dublin Castle, and finding them strongly opposed to invading Ulster, he obtained their signatures to a letter which he wrote to Elizabeth on 21 August, giving the reasons why it would be a serious military blunder to invade Ulster from Drogheda this year. The reasons were convincing, but Elizabeth was infuriated by the letter, and said that it was seditious of Essex to assemble the officers at a Council of War and canvass them to present a joint opposition to her orders. Neither Essex nor Elizabeth gave serious consideration to the suggestion of a few experienced officers that the way to defeat Tyrone was to send a military force by sea to Lough Foyle.[62]

On 28 August Essex, in obedience to Elizabeth's orders, left Dublin with his army and marched towards the borders of Tyrone's territory; but he then accepted an invitation from Tyrone to meet him to discuss peace terms. Essex and Tyrone met on 7 September without any attendants at the River Lagan between Ardee and Carrickmacross, with Tyrone sitting on his horse in mid-stream while Essex remained on horseback on the south bank. They agreed to make an immediate truce, and that Tyrone should be granted a pardon if he submitted to the Queen's authority.[63]

Essex then returned to England in defiance of Elizabeth's command. When he arrived at court at Nonesuch on 28 September, Elizabeth was friendly; then she changed her mind and on 2 October dismissed him from all his offices and ordered the Privy Council to publish a statement listing his offences. She considered that his actions amounted to a seditious defiance of her royal authority.[64] When, a few months later, Harington, who was one of the knights whom Essex had created in Ireland, came to her with a message from Essex, she burst into a rage, seized him by the girdle, and said: 'By God's Son, I am no Queen, this man is above me', and told Harington to go home. 'I did not stay to be bidden twice', he afterwards wrote. 'If all the Irish rebels had been at my heels, I should not have had better speed'.[65]

Elizabeth wrote to the Council in Dublin informing them of her action against Essex, but emphasised that she had disgraced him because he had disobeyed her by returning to England, and not because of his agreement with Tyrone. She confirmed his offer of pardon to Tyrone; but Tyrone would not submit and accept the pardon unless Elizabeth granted religious toleration to the Catholics in Ireland.[66] So the war continued.

Elizabeth appointed Lord Mountjoy to succeed Essex, and he persuaded her to allow him to send Sir Henry Docwra in May 1600 with four thousand men from Carrickfergus to Lough Foyle by sea, while he himself invaded Ulster by land from Drogheda as a diversion. Docwra's men suffered great hardships on the barren, treeless shore of Lough Foyle, but they built blockhouses, and made raids into Tyrone's territories which did great damage.[67]

The fighting continued all over Ireland, summer and winter, for two and a half years, at great expense to Elizabeth. By January 1600 the war had cost her £171,883 0s. 6½d. in nine months,[68] and the Privy Council complained that 'Her Majesty's treasure melteth like wax before the sun'.[69] The greatest ferocity was shown on both sides. The rebels killed the few English prisoners whom they captured. They also killed the English settlers whom they found, knocked out the brains of babies, and on one occasion left an English woman, naked, to die of cold in the bogs.[70] On the other side, Carew reported from Cork that in the districts between Youghal and Kerry he had killed twelve hundred armed rebels, 'besides husbandmen, women and children which I do not reckon'.[71] The Irish rebel, Tyrell, massacred the families of eighty English settlers in Munster. When he was captured and brought to Cork, he was sentenced to have his arms and thighs broken with a hammer and to hang alive in chains to die of exposure and hunger.[72]

But the English commanders realised that, to defeat the rebellion finally, they had to rely on the weapon of starvation, as they had done after Desmond's rebellion in Munster, when, as Ormond reminded the Privy Council, the Irish had been 'driven to eat one another'.[73] Mountjoy sent his horsemen to ride through the fields cutting down the corn with their swords, and to search the woods for the food that the Irish had hidden, and burn it.[74]

Philip II died in September 1598. His son, the young King Philip III, decided to send a small force to Ireland, which, if it succeeded in consolidating itself, could be followed by a full-scale invasion. In September 1601, 27 ships carrying 4,000 Spanish soldiers under the command of Don John of Aquila sailed from Lisbon to Kinsale. They captured the port, but were soon besieged there by Mountjoy with 6,000 of the 27,000 troops which Elizabeth had by now sent to Ireland to deal with Tyrone's 23,000 rebels. The siege continued through the coldest winter that had been known in Munster for many years, while Tyrone marched from Ulster to link up with his Spanish allies.[75]

On Christmas Eve – for Tyrone and the Spaniards it was 3 January 1602 – Tyrone tried to break through the English lines to reach the besieged Spaniards; but his untrained men were routed by the English, who killed over 1,600 of them. By February the Spaniards in Kinsale were starving, and Tyrone's defeat had shaken their faith in the Irish. On 22 February they surrendered on honourable terms, and after Don John had dined with Mountjoy they returned to Spain with their artillery and equipment.[76]

Shortly before the surrender, Elizabeth wrote an angry letter to Mountjoy, reproaching him for his failure to capture Kinsale and crush Tyrone. But when she heard of his success, she made amends with a warm letter of thanks. O'Donnell went to Spain to ask, unsuccessfully, for further aid, and died there. Tyrone withdrew to the forests of Ulster, pressed on both sides from Armagh and Lough Foyle. It was now only a question of waiting until the last rebels died of hunger; and in November 1602 Tyrone asked for a pardon. Elizabeth's first reaction was to refuse to forgive the arch-traitor once again; but after Mountjoy had pointed out what it would cost to defeat him, she agreed to pardon him and to allow him for the third time to escape the punishment which had been inflicted on so many of his followers.[77]

THE END

ESSEX lived quietly at his house in the Strand, in disgrace, for over a year. Then in February 1601 he planned an insurrection. The Queen was to be detained by his adherents at Richmond, while he arrested his rivals and seized control of London. As a preliminary attempt to influence public opinion in his favour, he paid the Lord Chamberlain's players, which was the name of Shakespeare's company, to perform a play about Richard II in London. It was almost certainly Shakespeare's play.[1]

This was a sensitive subject, dealing with the deposition of a King, and one which had been referred to recently in a book by Sir John Hayward, *The History of Henry IV*, which had worried Elizabeth. Hayward had dedicated the book to Essex and had written in the dedication; 'Most illustrious Earl, with your name adorning the front of our Henry, he may go forth to the public happier and safer'. Elizabeth thought that these words might have a sinister interpretation, even though they were written in Latin, not in English for the general public to read. She imprisoned Hayward in the Tower; but Sir Francis Bacon advised her that it would be impossible to prosecute him for high treason.[2]

The people of London did not rise in Essex's support, and the rebellion was suppressed. Essex and five of his followers were convicted of high treason, but astonishingly there were no other executions. Essex was beheaded in the Tower on 25 February, dying at the third stroke of the axe. Stories were afterwards told about Elizabeth's reluctance to sign the warrant for his execution; it was said that she had waited, hoping that he would send her the ring which she had once given him, which would be a sign that he was appealing to her for mercy, but that she never received the ring because Essex's servant negligently entrusted it to Lady Nottingham, the wife of his enemy the Lord Admiral, who did not send it on to Elizabeth. But although Elizabeth regretted having to put Essex to death, she hesitated much less than she usually did before reaching the decision. Essex was beheaded only seventeen days after the start of his insurrection.[3]

Elizabeth, despite her indecision, her rages and her personal prejudices, was a woman of strong principles. She never allowed personal feelings to deflect her from doing her duty. She knew that it was the duty of a Prince to punish rebellious subjects, and she emphasised this when she spoke to the French ambassador about Essex's treason and execution.[4] She was as sure of this as she was doubtful whether she was justified in putting to death another sovereign; and she signed the death warrant of Essex, for whom she had always felt great affection, without any of the hesitation which she had shown in authorising the execution of Mary Queen of Scots, whom she disliked and despised.

No action was taken against Shakespeare and his players, and his *Richard II* continued to be performed, though the scene in Westminster Hall, when Richard abdicates in favour of Bolingbroke, was cut out in later performances that year. But Elizabeth was still worrying about the play five months later. On 4 August 1601 she received the historian from Sevenoaks, William Lambarde, in her privy chamber at Greenwich, and he presented her with a copy of his book on English history. She was delighted, and, saying to him 'You shall see that I can read', read out sixty-four pages dealing with the period from 1199 to 1485, and asked very intelligent questions.

When she came to the passages dealing with Richard II, she said: 'I am Richard II, know ye not that?' Lambarde said that this wicked suggestion had been made by a most unkind gentleman. She replied, in that rather rambling manner that she sometimes adopted: 'He that will forget God will also forget his benefactors. This tragedy was played forty times in open streets and houses'. She then asked Lambarde if he had ever seen a portrait of Richard II, and showed him one which had been found for her after she had ordered that a search should be made for a portrait of this King.[5]

In ordinary circumstances, Elizabeth enjoyed the theatre. She had liked Shakespeare's *Merry Wives of Windsor* when it was written and performed at her request at the beginning of 1600.[6] The story of a lecherous old man being thwarted and tricked by two virtuous women was a much more congenial theme than the deposition of a king.

A few days after her talk with Lambarde, she left Greenwich on another long progress to Windsor and Oxfordshire and to the house of the Lord Chief Justice, Sir John Popham, at Littlecote in Wiltshire.[7] Her travels through her kingdom had taken her as far north as Norwich and Stafford and as far west as Bristol; but never in her life, either before or after her accession to the throne, did she go further than a hundred and fifty miles from London, or set foot in more than eighteen of the forty counties of England. While her seamen sailed from Plymouth to the Spanish Main, to Guinea, to California and the Philippines, she herself never went as far as their port of embarkation. There is something symbolical about this; it emphasises how far removed Elizabeth herself, as an individual, was from the adventurers, and from the spirit, of the period which we call 'the Elizabethan age'.

She had returned to Westminster before the new Parliament met in October 1601. It enacted legislation which completed the provisions for a new system of poor relief which had been introduced in the previous Parliament. The MPs did not like the monopolies which Elizabeth had granted to some influential courtiers and their friends, giving them the exclusive right to sell tobacco, salt and a number of other commodities; but she agreed, at their request, to cancel the monopolies, while asserting her right to grant them;[8] and she charmed them all with the speech that she made to them on 30 November 1601 when they came to her palace of Whitehall to thank her. Her speech was afterwards printed, and reprinted many times after her death, and became known as 'The Golden Speech of Queen Elizabeth'. She undoubtedly spoke the truth when she told them that she always saw, before her eyes, the last Judgement Day, when she would be judged by a higher Judge than herself, and that 'to be a King and wear a crown is a thing more glorious to them that see it, than it is pleasant to them that bear it'.[9] Elizabeth did not enjoy being a Queen, for it entailed the terrible duty of having to take decisions.

She made another speech when she came to the House of Lords to dissolve Parliament on 19 December. It was a justification of the policy which she had pursued towards Philip II, 'that potent Prince, the King of Spain, whose soul, I trust, be now in Heaven'. She accused him of ingratitude towards her – the offence which Mendoza had accused her of having committed towards Philip. It is significant that she should have spoken at such length to justify her intervention in the Netherlands. She referred to the events of thirty-five years before, when the first revolts had broken out in Brabant against the introduction of the Inquisition. 'Then I gave them counsel to contain their passions, and rather by humble petition than by violence or arms to seek ease of their aggrievances'. But instead of being grateful to her for this, the King of Spain encouraged the rebellion of the Earls of Northumberland and Westmorland, and later sent his navy against her realm. Now his son, the young King, whom she had never affronted, had sent troops to Ireland in an attempt to take away one of her two crowns.[10]

She did not go far from London in the summer of 1602, but stayed at the houses of several gentlemen in Middlesex and Buckinghamshire. When she moved to Sir William Clarke's house at Burnham, she travelled the ten miles on horseback, and hunted on the same day. She felt ill that night, but walked in the park next day to dispel any rumours about her health.[11] She seemed more cheerful than she had been in recent years.

On 18 September William Browne wrote to tell the Earl of Shrewsbury of an incident which had occurred when she was staying at her palace of Oatlands near Weybridge. She noticed that the young Countess of Derby – Elizabeth de Vere, the Earl of Oxford's daughter – had some ornament half-concealed in her bosom. Elizabeth asked to see it. Lady Derby was embarrassed, and asked to be excused from producing it; but Elizabeth insisted, and when Lady Derby reluctantly handed it over, Elizabeth saw that it was a locket which contained some love poems which had been written to the countess by Sir Robert Cecil. Elizabeth praised the verses, and tied the locket containing them to her shoe. She walked around with it for a little while, and then removed it from her shoe and tied it to her elbow; but in the end she apparently returned it to Lady Derby.[12]

She came from Richmond to Whitehall for the usual celebrations of her Accession Day on 17 November, changing her route and coming by water because of rumours of a plot to assassinate her. She was sixty-nine – a greater age than had hitherto been attained by any English sovereign. She spent Christmas and New Year's Day at Whitehall, and seemed to be in excellent health; but in the middle of January 1603 she caught a cold. It did not prevent her from travelling from Whitehall to Richmond on 21 January, though it was a very cold and wet day, and a few days later she had recovered from her cold; but on 28 February she felt unwell, and grew worse during the next three weeks.[12]

She seemed very depressed, heaving heavy sighs and sometimes telling her attendants how deeply she regretted the death of the Queen of Scots.[14] She complained bitterly to Cecil that he was advising her to pardon Tyrone for his seven years of treason against her, when she had been forced to execute Essex for one day's misconduct. The rumour spread in London that she was dying, but this was contradicted a few days later by another rumour that she was recovering.[15] On 20 March she suddenly collapsed when she was on her way to her chapel. They took her to her privy chamber, and as she refused to go to bed, they put cushions on the floor and laid her on them. She continued to refuse to go to bed, and remained lying on the cushions for four days. On 23 March she lost the power of speech.

For some years, her counsellors had tried from time to time to discuss with her the question of the succession to the throne. But as she refused to commit herself, or even to discuss it, Cecil had acted on his own responsibility, and had made all the arrangements for James VI to become King of England at her death. Now, as she lay dying and speechless, they went through the formality of pretending to consult her on the matter. They asked her if she wished the King of Scots to succeed her, and she raised her hand and touched her head, which they chose to interpret as a sign of her assent.

Sir Robert Carey, Lord Hunsdon's son, had come to court on a visit from Northumberland. He had become friendly with James VI some years before, when Elizabeth had sent him on a mission to Edinburgh. As early as 10 March he wrote secretly to James that Elizabeth would probably die soon, and now he decided to be the first to carry the news of her death to the King.

On Wednesday 23 March they lifted Elizabeth off the cushions and carried her to bed. They brought Whitgift to her, and he knelt and prayed at the bedside. After he had prayed for half an hour, he rose to go, but she made a sign to him to stay, and he prayed for another half hour. Again he rose to go, and again, at a sign from Elizabeth, he prayed for yet another half hour. Carey was in the anteroom, ready to leave for Scotland the moment the Queen died, though he feared that he would not be allowed to leave the palace, as the Council did not wish anyone to spread the news abroad without their authority. He heard Elizabeth's ladies weeping, and at about 1.30 a.m. on Thursday 24 March* a servant came and told him that she had died.

Carey immediately left the palace, though the porter at the gate tried to stop him and told him that he had orders to allow no one to leave. He rode from Richmond to Westminster, and waited at an inn near Charing Cross while he wondered if he dared to go to Edinburgh without authorisation from the Council. At 10 a.m. he decided to risk it, and rode north. He had arranged for relays of horses to be ready along the route, and late on 24 March he reached Doncaster, having ridden 155 miles from Richmond. It was the longest recorded journey that had ever been made in one day.

Next day he rode on, after a few hours' sleep, and by the late afternoon had covered 140 miles and reached his house at Widrington in Northumberland. He spent the evening and next morning arranging for the local gentlemen to uphold the authority of the new King, and then went on to Edinburgh. He rode 100 miles that day, and reached Holyroodhouse on the evening of 26 March just as James was sitting down to supper. He had ridden from London to Edinburgh in less than sixty hours. No one equalled his record until 1832.[16]

They brought the dead Queen's body from Richmond to Whitehall, and on 23 April carried it in state to Westminster and laid it to rest in the abbey. King James VI-and-I had already entered his new kingdom, and had reached Belvoir Castle in Leicestershire on his way to London.[17]

If Elizabeth, who enjoyed Shakespeare's plays, attended a performance of his *Twelfth Night* during the last two years of her life, she heard Malvolio read out the passage from Maria's letter: 'Some are born great, some achieve greatness, and some have greatness thrust upon them'.[18] If Elizabeth had not been born great, she would never have achieved greatness, and being a woman, she would not have been one of those unfortunate people, like Cranmer in her father's reign and Grindal in hers, who had greatness thrust upon them, although they tried hard to avoid it, knowing the risks which greatness entailed in the sixteenth century.

Elizabeth would not have achieved greatness, for she was not ambitious for power, and only upheld her royal authority so vigorously out of a sense of political and religious duty. She spoke the truth when she told her Parliament that she had not plotted to gain power during her sister's reign; and she really believed that a kingly crown was more glorious to behold than to wear.[19]

If we use the word 'great', not in Shakespeare's sense but in the meaning

---

*Carey wrote that she died between 1 and 2 a.m. Another account says at 3 a.m.

which history attaches to the term, can we rightly call Elizabeth a 'great Queen'? There is no doubt that her reign was a great and glorious era in English history, and it is not surprising that historians, like her contemporaries, have believed that the leader of the nation during a great epoch was a great ruler; though it might be argued that an ability to take decisions and adhere to them is a minimum requirement for a great ruler, and if this is so, Elizabeth falls at the first hurdle. The brilliant successes were often achieved, not by good policy and planning at the centre, but by luck, by muddling through, and above all by the courage, skill, initiative and improvisation of the many ardent patriots and Protestants who served their God and their Queen so devotedly.

There were the defeats as well as the victories. There are few examples in our history of such incompetence and blundering in wartime as those which were constantly recurring in Elizabeth's reign, and often because of her own errors of judgement. The famous war-time failures – Lord Aberdeen in 1855, Asquith in 1916, and Neville Chamberlain in 1940 – committed fewer mistakes than Elizabeth. No modern constitutional government could have survived the disasters and humiliations of Le Havre, Antwerp, Geertruidenberg, Lisbon and the Yellow Ford. The greatest defeat of all was Elizabeth's failure to recover Calais, which was lost so irretrievably that Englishmen today, who have long since ceased to think of Calais as an English town, find it difficult to appreciate what its loss meant to their ancestors in the sixteenth century.

But Elizabeth was not a modern constitutional Prime Minister. She was surrounded by the aura of royalty, and was regarded by all her subjects as the symbol of the glorious successes of her soldiers, sailors and statesmen. They did not know about her silly bickerings with her counsellors, her generals and her allies; that so many of the victories had been won against her advice; and how much more could have been achieved if she had not prevented it. Harington wrote that she always contrived to take the credit whenever anything turned out right, while her counsellors always took the blame on themselves when anything went wrong.[20]

Elizabeth's reputation may perhaps have benefitted from the fact that she was a woman. Male courtiers in the sixteenth century and male historians in the twentieth century have made allowances for her, as a woman, which they would not have made for a man. Her hesitation, indecision, petulance, emotionalism and petty-mindedness are vices which men throughout the ages have been pleased to regard as typically feminine. Not every woman has these characteristics, nor had every sixteenth-century Queen; there was no trace of them in Mary Tudor, Catherine de Medici or Mary of Hungary. But Elizabeth had them, and men have almost approved of such feminine faults in a woman. They might have been more critical if a King, and not a Queen, had changed his mind four times in a fortnight about whether to invade a neighbouring country, and had sent an admiral on active service three contradictory orders in the course of a few days as to whether he should or should not commit an act of war against a foreign power.

But Elizabeth's admirers who hail her as a great Queen are doing her an injustice. Their interpretation depends on seeing her as an utterly unscrupulous international power-politician, as ruthless and Machiavellian as her father. Her hesitation and changes of policy must then have been a clever diplomatic ruse. When she told Guzman de Silva that she hated the Protestants of the Netherlands as wicked rebels against their Prince a short while before she sent them financial and military aid, this must have been a deliberate lie in order to deceive him and Philip II; and when she agonised about authorising the execution of Mary Queen of Scots, this too was a trick so that she could disclaim responsibility for Mary's death and punish her secretary, Davison, for carrying out her secret wishes.

It might be possible to accept this interpretation were it not for the evidence of her counsellors and closest acquaintances. This evidence has survived in the letters which they were not afraid to write to each other, and makes it clear that the hesitations and changes of policy were genuine, and that Elizabeth's hatred of foreign Protestant rebels was as sincere as her reluctance to put Mary to death. This was not due so much to weaknesses in her character as to the contradictory political position in which she was placed as an absolute monarch depending on the support of a revolutionary movement, as the woman who, however much she prided herself on being the daughter of Henry VIII, could never escape the consequences of being the daughter of Anne Boleyn. The evidence shows her as a high-principled Queen who was prepared to devote her life, as she sacrificed her love for Leicester, to the performance of her duty to her people.

If Elizabeth deserves the blame for many failures, she must be given the credit for all the successes. It was ultimately she, and no one else, who decided in 1558 to make England a Protestant nation, and end the burning of heretics; it was she who decided, after all the hesitations, to send fourteen ships to the Forth through the winter gales and bring Scotland permanently into the English orbit of influence; it was she who, however reluctantly, dared to break the traditional alliance with Burgundy, to defy Philip and Alva, and to stand alone in a neutralist position between Spain and France, relying on the patriotism and religious fervour of her devoted subjects; and it was she who, despite the peace talks with Parma, stood firm against the Armada as the symbol of national independence.

She must also be given the credit for the relatively tolerant régime which she introduced, which may seem autocratic to twentieth-century democrats but seemed very free to people who had lived under Henry VIII and Mary. Her courtiers and maids of honour trembled when she flew into a rage, but they risked nothing worse than insults, slaps, or at worst a few weeks under house arrest. It is clear, from the way in which they wrote to each other, that they never feared that they would be beheaded or burned if they supported the wrong faction at her court; for although she sometimes wished that she could act as her father had done, she never seriously tried to do so.

There is something more to be said about Elizabeth. The prestige of kingship does not entirely explain the devotion which she inspired among her contemporaries. There must have been some other reason why the MPs in the House of Commons, who clashed with her in nearly every Parliament, were devoted to her; why Harington, after telling one discreditable story after another about her, repeatedly expressed his admiration for her; why John Stubbs called out 'God save the Queen!' when his hand was cut off at her orders; and why most of her subjects, and most historians for four hundred years, have given her the credit for every success and have been prepared to overlook all her faults. There must have been something which won them over but which we cannot easily grasp today – her charm, her courage, her charisma, and her magic – which fascinated her subjects and their descendants for twelve generations.

BIBLIOGRAPHY

MANUSCRIPT SOURCES

Public Record Office:
State Papers:
S.P.52/1, 10, 12, 13, 26.
S.P.63/50,52,68,72,76,78, 145, 151, 182, 184, 192.
S.P.70/9, 26, 124.
S.P.78/16, 19, 22, 25.
S.P.83/8, 11, 15, 18.
S.P.84/1, 28.

PRINTED WORKS

Accounts and Papers relating to Mary Queen of Scots (ed. A. J. Corsby and J. Bruce) (London, 1867).
Acts of the Privy Council. See Dasent.
ALLEN, J. W. – *A History of Political Thought in the Sixteenth Century* (London, 1928).
ALLEN, Cardinal W. – *An admonition to the Nobility and People of England and Ireland concerninge the present warres made for the execution of his Holines Sentence, by the highe and mightie Kinge Catholike of Spaine* (Antwerp, 1588).
ARBER, E. – *An English Garner* (London, 1877–96).
ASCHAM, R. – *The English Works of Roger Ascham* (ed. J. Bennet, and Dr. Samuel Johnson) (London, 1761).
ASKE, J. – *Elisabetha Triumphans* (London, 1588). See Nichols, J.
AUBREY, J. – *'Brief Lives' chiefly of contemporaries set down . . . between the years 1669 and 1696* (ed. A. Clark) (Oxford, 1898).
AYLMER, J. – *An Harborrowe for Faithful & Trewe Subiectes agaynst the late blowne Blaste concerninge the Gouvernmēt of Women* (Strasbourg, 1559).
BAGOT, W., Lord – *Memorials of the Bagot Family* (London, 1824).
BALE, J. – *Select Works of John Bale* (Cambridge, 1849).
The Bardon Papers: Documents relating to the imprisonment & trial of Mary Queen of Scots (ed. Conyers Read) (London, 1909).
BARONIUS, Cardinal C. – *Annales Ecclesiastici* (continued by O. Raynaldus) (ed. G. D. Mansi) (Lucca, 1738–59 edn.).

BATHO, G. R. – 'The Execution of Mary, Queen of Scots' (*Scottish Historical Review*, xxxix.35–42) (Edinburgh, 1960).

Bedingfield Papers – 'State Papers relating to the custody of the Princess Elizabeth at Woodstock in 1554, being letters between Queen Mary and Sir Henry Bedingfield, Kt., of Oxburgh, Norfolk". See *Norfolk Archaeology*.

BERTIE, Lady Georgina – *Five Generations of a Loyal House* (London, 1845).

BÈZE, T. de (BEZA) and DES GALLARDS, N. – *Histoire ecclésiastique des églises réformées au royaume de France* (ed. G. Baum and E. Cunitz) (Paris, 1883–9 edn.) (first published Geneva, 1580).

'Bishop Cranmer's Recantacyons' (*Miscellanies of the Philobiblon Society*, vol. xv) (London, 1877–84).

Booke of the Universall Kirk of Scotland: Acts and Proceedings of the General Assemblies of the Kirk of Scotland, Part I, 1560–1587 (Edinburgh, 1859).

BOR, P. – *Nederlandsche Oorloghen, beroerten, ende Borgerlijcke oneernicheyden*, (Leyden, 1621–30).

BOWES, R. – *The Correspondence of Sir Robert Bowes* (Durham, 1842).

BRAGHT, Thielman van – *Der blutige Schau-Platz oder Martyrer Spiegel* (Ephrata, Penn., 1748).

BROOK, V. J. K. – *A Life of Archbishop Parker* (Oxford, 1962).

BRYCE, T. – *A Compendious Register in Metre conteigning the names and pacient suffryngs of the membres of Jesus Christ* (London, 1559). See Farr.

BUCHAN, J. – *A Book of Escapes and Hurried Journeys* (London, 1922).

BURGHLEY, W. CECIL, LORD – *Iustitia Britannica (The Execution of Justice in England)* (London, 1584).

BURGON, J. W. – *The Life and Times of Sir Thomas Gresham* (London, 1839).

Cabala: Mysteries of State and Government in letters of Illustrious Persons (London, 1654).

Calendar of Letters and Papers relating to the affairs of the Borders of England and Scotland (ed. J. Bain) (Edinburgh, 1894–6).

Calendar of Letters and State Papers relating to English Affairs preserved principally in the Archives of Simancas (1558–1603) (ed. M. A. S. Hume) (London, 1892–9) (cited as 'Span. Cal. Eliz.').

Calendar of Letters, Documents and State Papers relating to the Negotiations between England and Spain in Simancas and elsewhere (1485–1558) (ed. P. de Gayangos, G. Mattingly, R. Tyler, etc.) (London, 1862–1954) (cited as 'Span. Cal.').

Calendar of Scottish State Papers relating to Mary Queen of Scots 1547–1603 (ed. J. Bain, W. K. Boyd, etc.) (Edinburgh, 1898–1952) (cited as 'Sc. Cal.').

Calendar of State Papers and Manuscripts relating to English Affairs in the Archives of Venice and other Libraries in Northern Italy (ed. Rawdon Brown, Cavendish Bentinck, etc.) (London, 1864–1947) (cited as 'Ven. Cal.').

Calendar of State Papers (Domestic) of the Reign of James I 1603–1610 (ed. Mary Everett Green) (London, 1857) (cited as 'Dom. Cal. Jas. I').

Calendar of State Papers (Domestic Series) of the Reigns of Edward VI, Mary, Elizabeth (1547–1603) (ed. R. Lemon, Mary Everett Green, etc.) (London, 1856–70) (cited as 'Dom. Cal.').

Calendar of State Papers (Foreign Series) of the reign of Edward VI 1547–1553 (ed. W. B. Turnbull) (London, 1861 (cited as 'For. Cal. Edw. VI').

Calendar of State Papers (Foreign Series) of the reign of Elizabeth (1558–1589) (ed. J. Stevenson, R. B. Wernham, etc.) (London, 1863–1950) (cited as 'For. Cal. Eliz.')

Calendar of State Papers (Foreign Series) of the reign of Mary 1553–1558 (ed. W. B. Turnbull) (London, 1861) (cited as '*For. Cal. Mary*').

Calendar of State Papers relating to English Affairs preserved principally at Rome (ed. J. M. Rigg) (London, 1916–26) (cited as '*Rom. Cal.*').

Calendar of the Carew Manuscripts (ed. J. S. Brewer and W. Bullen) (London, 1867–70) (cited as '*Carew Cal.*').

Calendar of the State Papers relating to Ireland of the reigns of Henry VIII, Edward VI, Mary and Elizabeth (ed. H. C. Hamilton, E. G. Atkinson, etc.) (London, 1860–1912) (cited as '*Irish Cal.*').

Cambridge Modern History: vol. ii, The Reformation; vol. iii, The Wars of Religion (ed. A. W. Ward, G. W. Prothero, S. Leathes) (Cambridge, 1907). See *New Cambridge Modern History*.

CAMDEN, W. – *Annales, The True and Royall History of the famous Empresse Elizabeth Queene of Englande, France and Ireland etc.* (London, 1625 edn.).

— *The Historie of the most renowned and virtuous princesse Elizabeth, late Quene of England . . . Composed by way of Annals* (London, 1635 edn.)

— *Annalium rerum Anglicarum et Hibernicarum regnante Elisabetha* (ed. T. Hearne) (Oxford, 1717). (Unless otherwise stated, all references are to the 1625 English edition).

CAMUSAT, N. – *Meslanges historiques* (Troyes, 1619).

Carew Cal. – See Calendar.

CASTELNAU DE LA MAUVISSIERE, M. de – *Les mémoires de Messire Michel de Castelnau* (ed. J. Le Laboureur) (Paris, 1731).

CATHERINE DE MEDICI – *Lettres de Catherine de Médicis* (ed. H. de La Ferrière-Percy and B. de la Puchesse (Paris, 1880–1909).

CHAMBERLAIN, J. – *Letters written by John Chamberlain during the reign of Queen Elizabeth* (ed. Sarah Williams) (London, 1861).

CHAMBERLIN, F. – *The Private Character of Queen Elizabeth* (London, 1922).

CHRISTY, M. – 'Queen Elizabeth's Visit to Tilbury in 1588' (*English Historical Review*, xxxiv.43–61) (London, 1919).

Chronicle of Queen Jane and of Two Years of Queen Mary (ed. J. G. Nichols) (London, 1850).

CLAPHAM, J. – 'Certain Observations concerning the Life and reign of Queen Elizabeth', sub. tit. *Elizabeth of England* (ed. Evelyn P. Read and Conyers Read) (Philadelphia, 1951).

CLIFFORD, H. – *The Life of Jane Dormer, Duchess of Feria* (London, 1887).

COBBETT, W. – See Howell.

COLLINSON, P. – *Archbishop Grindal* (London, 1979).

— *The Elizabethan Puritan Movement* (London, 1967).

CONINGSBY, Sir T. – 'Journal of the Siege of Rouen 1591' (ed. J. G. Nichols) (in *Camden Miscellany*, vol. i) (London, 1847).

CORBETT, Sir J. S. – *Drake and the Tudor Navy* (London, 1898).

— *Papers relating to the Navy during the Spanish War 1585–1587* ((London, 1898).

CRANMER, T. – *The Works of Thomas Cranmer* (Cambridge, 1844–6).

DASENT, J. R. (ed.) – *Acts of the Privy Council of England (New Series)* (London, 1890–1907).

DAWSON, JANE E. A. – 'Mary Queen of Scots, Lord Darnley, and Anglo-Scottish Relations in 1565' (*The International History Review*, viii.1–24) (Burnaby, B.C., 1986).

A Declaration of the Lyfe and Death of John Story, late a Romish Canonicall Doctor by Profession (London, 1571). See *Harleian Miscellany.*

DEE, M. . – *British Ballads* (Wedgwood Selections) (London, 1926).

DELONEY, T. – *The Queen . . . at Tilbury* (London, 1588). See Arber.

DENNIS, J. – *The Comical Gallant: or the Amours of Sir John Falstaffe* (London, 1702).

DEVEREUX, W. B. – *Lives and Letters of the Devereux, Earls of Essex* (London, 1853).

Dictionary of National Biography (Oxford, 1885–1900).

A Diurnal of Remarkable Occurrents that have passed within the country of Scotland since the death of King James IV till the year MDLXXV (Edinburgh, 1833).

DIXON, R. W. – *History of the Church of England* (London, 1875–1902).

Dom. Cal. – See Calendar.

Dom. Cal. Jas. I – See Calendar.

DREWES, J. B. – *Wilhelmus van Nassouwe* (Amsterdam, 1946).

DURENG, J. – 'La complicité de l'Angleterre dans le complot d'Amboise' (*Revue d'histoire moderne et contemporaine*, vi.249–56) (Paris, 1904–5).

DURO, C. F. – *La Armada Invincible* (Madrid, 1885).

E.H.R. – *English Historical Review.* See under names of authors of articles.

ELIZABETH I – *Letters of Queen Elizabeth* (ed. G. B. Harrison) (London, 1935).

— *Letters of Queen Elizabeth and James VI* (London, 1849).

Elizabethan Government and Society: Essays presented to Sir John Neale (ed. S. T. Bindoff, J. Hurstfield, C. H. Williams) (London, 1961).

ELLIS, H. *Original Letters illustrative of English History* (London, 1824–46).

ELTON, Sir G. R. – *England under the Tudors* (Cambridge, 1969).

— *The Parliament of England 1559–1581* (Cambridge, 1986).

— *The Tudor Constitution* (Cambridge, 1968).

Encyclopaedia Britannica (11th edition, London, 1910).

Epistre envoiee au Tigre de la France (no place, 1560). – See *Tigre.*

ERICKSON, Corally – *The First Elizabeth* (London, 1984).

FARR, E. – *Select Poetry chiefly devotional of the reign of Queen Elizabeth* (Cambridge, 1845).

FENELON – *Correspondance diplomatique de Bertrand de Salignac de La Mothe Fénélon* (ed. A. Teulet) (Paris, 1838–40).

FORBES, P. – *A Full View of the Public Transactions in the Reign of Q. Elizabeth* (London, 1740–1).

For. Cal. Edw. VI – See Calendar.

For. Cal. Eliz. – See Calendar.

For. Cal. Mary – See Calendar.

FOXE, J. – The Book of Martyrs.

　　The Acts and Monuments of John Foxe (ed. J. Pratt) (London, 1877; New York, 1965).

　　First edition. *Actes and Monuments of these latter and perillous dayes touching matters of the Church* (London, 1563).

　　Second edition. *The Ecclesiasticall History, contayning the Actes and Monuments of thynges passed in every kynges tyme in this realm, especially in the Church of England* (London, 1570). Reprinted with minor alterations in 1576, 1583, etc.

　　Unless otherwise stated, all references are to the 1877//1965 edition.

FRASER, Antonia – *Mary Queen of Scots* (London, 1969).

FROUDE, J. A. – *History of England from the Fall of Wolsey to the Defeat of the Spanish Armada* (London, 1870 edn.).

GACHARD, L. P. – *Collection des voyages des souverains des Pays-Bas* (Brussels, 1876–82).

GAYANGOS, P. de – *Viaje de Felipe Segundo a Inglaterra* (Madrid, 1877).

GEE, H. – *The Elizabethan Prayer-Book and Ornaments* (London, 1902).

GOODMAN, C. – *How Superior Powers ought to be obeyed* (New York, 1931, reprint of first edition, Geneva 1558).

Granvelle Correspondence – See Poullet; Weiss.

Greyfriars Chronicle – *Chronicle of the Greyfriars of London* (ed. J. G. Nichols) (London, 1852).

GRIMSTONE, E. – See Meteren.

GRINDAL, E. – *The Remains of Archbishop Grindal* (Cambridge, 1843).

HAKLUYT, R. – *The principal navigations, voyages, traffiqves and discoveries of the English nation at any time within the compasse of these 1600 yeres* (London, 1599).

HALL, E. – *Chronicle* (London, 1809 edn.).

HALLER, W. – *Foxe's Book of Martyrs and the Elect Nation* (London, 1963).

Hamilton Papers (ed. J. Bain) (Edinburgh, 1890–2).

Hardwicke Papers – Miscellaneous State Papers from 1501 to 1726 (London, 1778).

HARINGTON, Sir J. – *Nugae Antiquae* (London, 1779).

The Harleian Miscellany (London, 1809 edn.).

HAYNES, S. – *A Collection of State Papers . . . left by William Cecill Lord Burghley* (London, 1740).

HAYWARD, Sir J. – *Annals of the first four years of the reign of Queen Elizabeth* (London, 1840).

HEARNE, T. – *Titi Livii . . . accedit, Sylloge Epistolarum a variis Angliae Principibus scriptarum* (Oxford, 1716).

HENRY IV, KING OF FRANCE – *Recueil des Lettres missives de Henri IV* (ed. B. de Xivrey and J. Gaudet) (Paris, 1843–76).

HILL, C. – *Intellectual Origins of the English Revolution* (Oxford, 1965).

— *Society and Puritanism in Pre-Revolutionary England* (London, 1964).

HILLYARD, N. – *A Treatise concerning the Arte of Limning* (ed. P. Norman) (Edinburgh, 1912).

Historical Manuscripts, Reports of the Royal Commission on, Twelfth Report, Part iv – The Manuscripts of the Duke of Rutland, vol. 1 (London, 1888).

— *Calendar of the Manuscripts of the Marquess of Salisbury* (London, 1883–5) (cited as 'H.M.C., Cecil').

— *Report on the Pepys Manuscripts* (London, 1911).

HOLINSHED, R. – *Chronicles of England, Scotland and Ireland* (London, 1807–8 edn.).

HOLT, M. P. – *The Duke of Anjou and the Politique Struggle during the Wars of Religion* (Cambridge, 1986).

HOTMAN, F. – *Franco-Gallia* (London, 1711 edn.)

HOWELL, T. B. – *Cobbett's State Trials* (London, 1809–26).

HUDSON, W. S. – *John Ponet: Advocate of Limited Monarchy* (Chicago, 1942) (includes facsimile reprint of Ponet, *A shorte treatise of politike power* (Strasbourg (?), 1556).

HUGGARDE, M. – *The Displaying of the Protestantes* (London, (?), 1556).

HUME, M. A. S. – *The Courtships of Queen Elizabeth* (London, 1904 edn.).

HURSTFIELD, J. – *Elizabeth I and the Unity of England* (London, 1960).

Irish Cal. – See Calendar.

IVES, E. W. – 'Faction at the court of Henry VIII: the fall of Anne Boleyn' (*History*, lvii,1–15) (Glasgow, 1972).

JENKINS, Elizabeth – *Elizabeth the Great* (London, 1958).

JENSEN, J. de L. – 'On the phantom will of Mary Queen of Scots' (*Scotia*, iv.1–15) (Norfolk, Va., 1980).

JOHNSON, P. – *Elizabeth I, a study in power and intellect* (London, 1974).

A Justification of Queen Elizabeth in relation to the affairs of Mary Queen of Scots – see *Accounts and Papers relating to Mary Queen of Scots*.

KAULEK, J. – *Correspondance politique de MM. de Castillon et de Marillac 1537–1542* (Paris, 1885).

KEITH, R. – *History of the Affairs of Church and State in Scotland* (Edinburgh, 1844–50 edn.).

KNOX, J. – *The Works of John Knox* (ed. D. Laing) (Edinburgh, 1846–64).

L.A. – See *Lists and Analysis*.

LABANOFF, Prince A. – *Lettres, instructions et mémoires de Marie Stuart, reine d'Ecosse* (London, 1844).

LAUGHTON, Sir J. K. – *State Papers relating to the Defeat of the Spanish Armada Anno 1588* (London, 1894).

LEE, M. – *James Stewart Earl of Moray* (New York, 1953). – 'The Fall of the Regent Morton: a Problem in Satellite Diplomacy' (*Journal of Modern History*, vol. xxviii) (Chicago, 1956).

Leicester Correspondence – Correspondence of Robert Dudley Earl of Leicester during his government of the Low Countries (ed. J. Bruce) (London, 1844).

LETI, G. – *La vie d'Elizabeth reine d'Angleterre, traduite de l'Italien de Monsieur Gregoire Leti* (Amsterdam, 1714 edn.).

LETTENHOVE, Baron Kervyn de – *Relations politiques des Pays-Bas & de l'Angleterre sous le règne de Philippe II* (Brussels, 1882–1900).

Letters and Papers (Foreign and Domestic) of the Reign of King Henry VIII (ed. J. Brewer and J. Gairdner) (London, 1862–1920) (cited as '*L.P.*').

List and Analysis of State Papers Foreign Series Elizabeth I preserved in the Public Record Office (ed. R. B. Wernham) (London, 1964–84) (cited as '*L.A.*').

LLOYD, C. – *Formularies of Faith put forth by authority during the reign of Henry VIII* (Oxford, 1856 edn.).

L.P. – See *Letters and Papers*.

MACHYN, H. – *The Diary of Henry Machyn* (ed. J. G. Nichols) (London, 1848).

MANNINGHAM, J. – *Diary of John Manningham* (London, 1868).

MARLOWE, C. – *The Plays and Poems of Christopher Marlowe* (London, 1905).

MARY QUEEN OF SCOTS – See Labanoff; Pollen.

MATTINGLY, G. – *The Defeat of the Spanish Armada* (London, 1959).

MAXWELL, Constantia – *Irish History from Contemporary Sources 1509–1610* (London, 1923).

METEREN, E. van – *A generall historie of the Netherlands* (translated by E. Grimstone) (London, 1608).

MILTON, J. – *The Tenure of Kings and Magistrates* (London, 1649) reprinted in *Complete Prose Works of John Milton* (New Haven and London, 1953–66).

MOREY, A. – *The Catholic Subjects of Elizabeth I* (London, 1978).

MORRIS, J. – *The Troubles of our Catholic Forefathers revealed by themselves* (London, 1872–7).

MOTLEY, J. L. – *History of the United Netherlands* (London, 1860).

— *The Rise of the Dutch Republic* (London, 1861 edn.).

MOZLEY, J. F. – *John Foxe and his Book* (London, 1940).

MUMBY, F. A. – *The Girlhood of Queen Elizabeth* (London, 1909).

MURDIN, W. – *A Collection of State Papers . . . from the Year 1571 to 1596 . . . left by William Cecill Lord Burghley* (London, 1759).

NAUNTON, Sir R. – *Fragmenta Regalia* (ed. J. S. Cerovski) (Washington, London and Toronto, 1985).

NEALE, SIR J. E. – *Elizabeth I and her Parliaments 1559–1581* (London, 1953) (cited as 'Neale, *Eliz. & Parliaments*, vol. i.').

— *Elizabeth I and her Parliaments 1584–1601* (London, 1957) (cited as "Neale, *Eliz. & Parliaments*, vol. ii.').

— *Essays in Elizabethan History* (London, 1958).

— *Queen Elizabeth* (London, 1934) (reprinted sub. tit. *Queen Elizabeth I* (London, 1953) (cited as 'Neale, *Queen Elizabeth*').

— 'Sir Nicholas Throckmorton's Advice to Queen Elizabeth on her Accession to the Throne' (*English Historical Review*, lxv.91–98) (London, 1950).

— 'The Elizabethan Acts of Supremacy and Uniformity' (*English Historical Review*, lxv.304–32) (London 1950).

— *The Elizabethan House of Commons (London, 1949).*

The New Cambridge Modern History:

    vol. ii. *The Reformation 1520–1559* (ed. G. R. Elton) (Cambridge, 1958).

    vol. iii *The Counter-Reformation and Price Revolution 1559–1610* (ed. R. B. Wernham) (Cambridge, 1968).

    See *Cambridge Modern History.*

NICHOLS, J. *The Progresses and Public Processions of Queen Elizabeth* (London, 1823).

NICHOLS, Sir J. G. – *Literary Remains of King Edward VI* (London, 1857).

NICOLAS, Sir N. H. – *Life of William Davison, Secretary of State to Queen Elizabeth* (London, 1823).

NOAILLES, A. de – *Ambassades de MM. de Noailles en Angleterre* (ed. Vertot) (Leyden, 1763).

Norfolk Archaeology, vol. iv (Norwich, 1855).

O'RAHILLY, A. – *The Massacre at Smerwick* (Cork, 1938).

OUTHWAITE, R. B. – 'Royal borrowing in the reign of Elizabeth I: the aftermath of Antwerp' (*English Historical Review*, lxxxvi.251–63) (London, 1971).

PARKER, G. – *Philip II* (London, 1979).

— *The Dutch Revolt* (London, 1977).

PARKER, M. – *The Correspondence of Matthew Parker* (Cambridge, 1853).

PARSONS, R. – *Leicester's Common-Wealth* (London, 1641 edn.).

PEARS, E. – "The Spanish Armada and the Ottoman Porte' (*English Historical Review*, viii.439–66) (London, 1893).

PEEL, A. – 'A Conscientious Objector of 1575' (*Baptist Historical Society*, vii.78–128) (London, 1920).

PETRIE, SIR C. – 'The Hispano-Papal landing at Smerwick' (*The Irish Sword*, ix.82–94) (Dublin, 1969).

POLLEN, J. H. – *A Letter from Mary Queen of Scots to the Duke of Guise, January 1562* (Edinburgh, 1904).
— *Mary Queen of Scots and the Babington Plot* (Edinburgh, 1922).
— *Papal Negotiations with Mary Queen of Scots* (Edinburgh, 1901).
— *The English Catholics in the reign of Queen Elizabeth* (London, 1920).
PONET, L. – See Hudson.
POULLET, E. and PIOT, C. – *Correspondance du Cardinal de Granvelle 1565–1586* (Brussels, 1878–97).
POWER, M. J. – 'London and the Control of the "Crisis" of the 1590s' (*History*, N.S., lxx.371–85) (Glasgow, 1985).
Queen Elizabeth I: Most Politick Princess (ed. S. Adams) (London, 1986).
The Quenes Maiesties passage through the Citie of London to Westminster the day before her coronation (ed. J. M. Osborn and J. E. Neale) (facsimile reprint of the 1559 London edition).
RAIT, R. S. and CAMERON, Annie – *King James's Secret* (London, 1927).
RAPPAPORT, S. – 'Social structure and mobility in 16th Century London', Part I (*London Journal*, ix.107–35) (London, 1983).
READ, Conyers – *Lord Burghley and Queen Elizabeth* (London, 1960) (cited as 'Read, *Burghley*').
— *Mr Secretary Cecil and Queen Elizabeth* (London, 1955) (cited as 'Read, *Cecil*').
— *Mr Secretary Walsingham and the policy of Queen Elizabeth* (Oxford, 1925) (cited as 'Read, *Walsingham*').
— 'Queen Elizabeth's Seizure of the Duke of Alva's Pay-Ships' (*The Journal of Modern History*, v.443–64) (Chicago, 1933).
— *The Bardon Papers*. See Bardon.
— 'The Fame of Sir Edward Stafford' (*American Historical Review*, xx.292–313) (Lancaster, Pa., 1915).
READ, Evelyn and READ, Conyers – *Catherine, Duchess of Suffolk* (London, 1962).
— *Elizabeth of England*. See Clapham.
RIDLEY, J. – *John Knox* (Oxford, 1968).
RODRÍGUEZ-SELGADO, M. J., and ADAMS, S. – 'The Count of Feria's Dispatch to Philip II of 14 November 1558' (*Camden Miscellany*, xxviii.302–44) (London, 1984).
ROEDER, R. – *Catherine de' Medici and the Lost Revolution* (London, 1937).
ROGERS, T. – *History of Agriculture and Prices* (Oxford, 1872).
Rom. Cal. – See Calendar.
ROMIER, L. – *La conjuration d'Amboise* (Paris, 1923).
ROWE, N. – See Shakespeare.
ROWSE, A. L. – *Ralegh and the Throckmortons* (London, 1962).
— *The Elizabethans and America* (London, 1959).
— *The Expansion of Elizabethan England* (London, 1955).
RYMER, T. W. – *Foedera, Conventiones, Et . . . Acta Publica inter Reges Angliae* (London, 1704–17).
Sadler Papers – *The State Papers and Letters of Sir Ralph Sadler* (ed. A. Clifford) (Edinburgh, 1809).
Satirical Poems of the time of the Reformation (ed. J. Cranstoun) (Edinburgh, 1891).
Sc. Cal. – See Calendar.
SHAKESPEARE, W. – *The Complete Works of William Shakespeare* (ed. W. J. Craig) (Oxford, 1905 edn.).

— *The Works of Mr William Shakespeare, in six volumes, adorn'd with cuts* (ed. N. Rowe) (London, 1709).

SITWELL, Edith – *The Queens and the Hive* (London, 1962).

SPADDING, J. – *The Letters and the Life of Francis Bacon* (London, 1861–74).

Span. Cal. – See Calendar.

Span. Cal. Eliz. – See Calendar.

SPENSER, E. – *The Complete Works of Edmund Spenser* (ed. A. B. Grosart) (London, 1882–4).

Statutes of the Realm (London, 1810–24).

STEVENSON, J. – *Selections from unpublished Manuscripts . . . illustrating the reign of Mary Queen of Scotland* (Glasgow, 1857).

STOW, J. – *Annales, or A Generall Chronicle of England* (London, 1631 edn.).

STRACHEY, Lytton – *Elizabeth and Essex* (London, 1928).

STRICKLAND, Agnes – *Lives of the Queens of England* (London, 1840–8).

STRYPE, J. – *Annals of the Reformation . . . during Queen Elizabeth's happy reign* (Oxford, 1824 edn.).

— *Ecclesiastical Memorials . . . of the emergence of the Church of England* (Oxford, 1822 edn.).

— *The Life and Acts of John Whitgift* (Oxford, 1822 edn.).

STUBBS, J. – *The Discoverie of a Gaping Gvlf wherein England is like to be swallowed by an other French marriage if the Lord forbid not the banes by letting her Maiestie see the sin and punishment thereof* (London, 1579).

SUTHERLAND, N. M. – 'Queen Elizabeth and the Conspiracy of Amboise, March 1560' (*English Historical Review*, lxxxi.474–89) (London, 1966).

— *The Massacre of St Bartholomew and the European Conflict 1559–1572* (London, 1973).

TEULET, A. – *Papiers d'État, pièces et documents relatifs à l'histoire de l'Ecosse au XVIᵉ siècle* (Paris, 1851–60).

THOMSON, G. M. – *Sir Francis Drake* (London, 1972).

Le Tigre de 1560 (ed. Chas. Read) (Paris, 1875).

The true Report of the lamentable death of William of Nassayre, Prince of Orange, who was trayterouslie slayne with a Dagge, in his owne Courte, by Balthazar Serack, a Burgunion . . . Whose Death was not of sufficient Sharpness for such a Caytiff, and yet too soure for any Christian (Middelburg, 1584). See *Harleian Miscellany*.

Two Missions of Jacques de la Brosse (ed. Gladys Dickinson) (*Edinburgh, 1942*).

TYNDALE, W. – *Works* (Cambridge, 1848–9).

TYTLER, P. F. – *England under the reigns of Edward VI and Mary* (London, 1839).

UNTON, H. – *Correspondence of Sir Henry Unton, Knt., Ambassador from Queen Elizabeth to Henry IV, King of France* (ed. J. Stevenson) (London, 1847).

UNWIN R. – *The Defeat of John Hawkins* (London, 1960).

Ven. Cal. – See Calendar.

WALDMAN, M. – *Elizabeth and Leicester* (London, 1944).

WALDSTEIN, BARON Z. B. – *The Diary of Baron Waldstein* (ed. G. W. Groos) (London, 1981).

WARNICKE, ROTHA M. – 'The Fall of Anne Boleyn: a reassessment' (*History*, N.S., lxx.1–15) (Glasgow, 1985).

WEDGWOOD, C. V. – *William the Silent* (London, 1941).

WEISS, C. H. – *Papiers d'État du Cardinal de Granvelle* (Paris, 1841–53).

WERNHAM, R. B. – *After the Armada: Elizabethan England and the Struggle for Western Europe 1588–1595* (Oxford, 1984).
— *Before the Armada: The growth of English Foreign Policy 1485–1588* (London, 1966).
— 'Queen Elizabeth and the Portugal Expedition of 1589' (*English Historical Review*, li.1–26, 194–218) (London 1951).
— *The Making of Elizabethan Foreign Policy 1558–1603* (Berkeley, Ca., 1980).
WHITEHEAD, A. W. – *Gaspard de Coligny, Admiral of France* (London, 1904).
WILKINS, D. – *Concilia Magnae Britanniae et Hiberniae* (London, 1737).
WILLIAM OF NASSAU, PRINCE OF ORANGE *Apologie de Guillaume de Nassau* (ed. A. Lacroix) (Brussels, 1858).
WILLIAMS, G. H. – *The Radical Reformation* (London, 1962).
WILLIAMSON, J. A. – *Hawkins of Plymouth* (London, 1969).
— *Sir John Hawkins: the time and the man* (Oxford, 1927).
WILSON, C. – *Queen Elizabeth and the Revolt of the Netherlands* (London, 1970).
WILSON, E. P. – *The Plague in Shakespeare's London* (Oxford, 1963).
WRIGHT, T. – *Queen Elizabeth and her Times* (London, 1838).
WRIOTHESLEY, C. – *A Chronicle of England during the reigns of the Tudors* (ed. W. D. Hamilton) (London, 1875–7).
Zurich Letters (Cambridge, 1852–5).

REFERENCES

References to *For. Cal. Eliz.*, vols. i–xviii; *L.P.*; and *Sc. Cal.* are to numbers of documents; all other references (including to *For. Cal. Eliz.*, vols. xix–xxiii) are to page numbers.

Chapter 1 – The Protestant Child

1. Foxe, *Acts and Monuments*, iv.706–7.
2. Baronius (Raynaldus), *Annales Ecclesiastici*, xii.428–9.
3. Cranmer, *Works*, ii.246; Hall, *Chronicle*, 794.
4. Camusat, *Meslanges historiques*, ii.17–18; *L.P.*, vi.585.
5. *L.P.*., vi.142, 152, 324, 508, 556, 568, 570, 808, 1249.
6. ibid., vi.1069–70.
7. ibid., vi.1065.
8. ibid., vi.1112, 1125; Hall, 805–6.
9. *L.P.*., vi.918.
10. ibid., vii.83.
11. ibid., vii.393.
12. ibid., vi.733; vii.939; Ellis, *Original Letters illustrative of English History*, iii(ii).332–3.
13. *L.P.*, x.601.
14. ibid., x.908; Wriothesley, *Chronicle*, i.189–226.
15. *L.P.*, x.888, 956, 1043; xi.41.
16. Rymer, *Foedera*, xiv.467; Wilkins, *Concilia*, iii.803.
17. *L.P.*, x.1187.

Chapter 2 – The Lady Elizabeth

1. Lloyd, *Formularies of Faith*, 311–20.
2. Nichols, *Literary Remains of King Edward VI*, cclv.
3. *L.P.*, xii(ii).1060.
4. Leti, *La vie d'Elizabeth, reine d'Angleterre*, 135–6; Hearne, *Sylloge*, 149.
5. *L.P.*, xvi.804.
6. ibid., xviii(i).873.
7. Historical Manuscripts Commission, *Rutland Papers*, i.30.
8. *L.P.*, xii(i).816.
9. Kaulek, *Correspondance politique de MM. de Castillon et de Marillac*, 327.

10. *L.P.*, xiii(ii).484.
11. *Hamilton Papers*, i.501; *Sadler Papers*, i.129, 139.
12. Sadler, i.248.
13. *L.P.*, xx(i).90–91, 451, 667, 677(2), 904; xx(ii).639, 764, 1038.
14. ibid., xv.543; xvi.204, 306; xxi(ii).466.
15. ibid., xxi(i).469.
16. Foxe, v.486–94.
17. Foxe, vi.537–50.
18. ibid., v.553–61.

Chapter 3 – The Lord Admiral

1. Leti, 160–3.
2. Haynes, *Burghley Papers*, 96, 99.
3. Mumby, *Girlhood of Queen Elizabeth*, 38.
4. Read, *Cecil*, 63.
5. Mumby, 37.
6. Haynes, 103.
7. Dasent, *Acts of the Privy Council*, ii.251.
8. Haynes, 70.
9. ibid., 71.
10. ibid., 102–3; Mumby, 57.
11. Haynes, 108.
12. Mumby, 57–59.
13. Leti, 182.
14. Dasent, iii.350.
15. *Span. Cal.*, x.6.
16. ibid., x.186, 203, 213.
17. Foxe, viii.604.
18. *Span. Cal.*, x.299, 325, 369, 394, 493; Machyn, *Diary*, 16.
19. *Chronicle of Queen Jane*, 89–102.
20. Wriothesley, ii.88–89.
21. ibid., ii.91; *Greyfriars Chronicle*, 80–81; Machyn, 38.
22. Leti, 193–5.
23. Camden, *Annales*, 'Preparation' (unpaginated) 18.
24. Wriothesley, ii.92–96; Greyfriars, 81–82; Machyn, 38.
25. Gachard, *Voyages des souverains des Pays-Bas*, iv.92.

Chapter 4 – The Tower

1. Foxe, vi.712–14.
2. Noailles, *Ambassades*, ii.141; *Span. Cal.*, xi.188, 196.
3. Gachard, iv.94–106.
4. Foxe, vi.390–1.
5. ibid., vi.391–2; Gachard, iv.98; Dasent, iv.320–1.
6. Dasent, iv.320–2, 328, 333, 335, 337–8, 345–7.

7. See, e.g., Huggarde, *The Displaying of the Protestantes*, passim.
8. Weiss, *Papiers d'Etat du Cardinal de Granvelle*, iv.68.
9. Gachard, iv.117–18; Noailles, ii.155.
10. Gachard, iv.111.
11. ibid., iv.126.
12. ibid., iv.118.
13. ibid., iv.241; *Span. Cal.*, xi.259–63.
14. Gachard, iv.130.
15. Noailles, ii.191–6, 204–7, 248.
16. Gachard, iv.159; *Span. Cal.*, xi.281.
17. *Span. Cal.*, xii.220.
18. ibid., xi.352; Gachard, iv.245.
19. Gachard, iv.140–1, 158, 170, 180–3, 252, 255–7.
20. Clapham, *Elizabeth of England*, 68.
21. Gachard, iv.140–1, 175, 180–3, 241; Noailles, ii.273.
22. ibid., iv.226–7.
23. ibid., iv.158, 170, 182, 241; Noailles, ii.307–12.
24. Gachard, iv.252.
25. Mumby, 98.
26. Gachard, iv.241.
27. Mumby, 99.
28. Weiss, iv.193–4.
29. *Span. Cal.*, xii.56, 80, 119; Noailles, iii.77–79.
30. *Span. Cal.*, xii.154–5.
31. Weiss, iv.198.
32. *Span. Cal.*, xii.125; Foxe, viii.606–7.
33. *Span. Cal.*, xii.157, 165–6; Foxe, viii.607–8.
34. Mumby, 115–17.
35. *Span. Cal.*, xii.167.
36. Foxe, viii.609.

Chapter 5 – The Heir to the Throne

1. Foxe, viii.612–13; 'Bedingfield Papers', in *Norfolk Archaeology*, iv.141–4.
2. Mumby, 105.
3. Gachard, iv.371–2, 375; *Span. Cal.*, xii.220.
4. Weiss, iv.249.
5. Foxe, viii.614–15.
6. *Norfolk Arch.*, iv.149–50; Foxe, viii.615.
7. *Norfolk Arch.*, iv.147.
8. ibid., iv.150.
9. ibid., iv.150–3; Foxe, viii.615–16.
10. *Norfolk Arch.*, iv.157–9, 163–4.
11. ibid., iv.166.
12. ibid., iv.164, 168, 172, 175, 178.
13. ibid., iv.208, 213–16, 218.
14. ibid., iv.163, 180–1, 183–4, 193, 198, 221–4; Foxe, viii.617–18.

15. *Norfolk Arch.*, iv.182–3, 185–6, 203–4, 209, 217, 221–3; Gachard, iv.414; Foxe, viii.617.
16. Foxe, viii.619.
17. Gayangos, *Viaje de Felipe II a Inglaterra*, 108, 120.
18. *Ven. Cal.*, vi.1074–5.
19. Foxe, vi.609.
20. *Span. Cal.*, xiii.138–9.
21. Foxe, vi.658–9; vii.26.
22. *Span. Cal.*, xiii.151–2, 165–7, 169; *Ven. Cal.*, vi.44–45, 57, 107, 218.
23. *Span. Cal.*, xiii.171–2; *For. Cal. Mary*, 165.
24. Information from Major Peter Watson.
25. *Norfolk Arch.*, iv.225; Weiss, iv.432.
26. *Ven. Cal.*, vi.70, 82, 475.
27. Strype, *Ecclesiastical Memorials*, iii(ii).352; Strickland, *Lives of the Queens of England*, v.417–19; Parker, *Philip II*, 18–20, 82–87.
28. *For. Cal. Eliz.*, xi.1236.
29. Noailles, iii.85, 122–3, 126; *Ven. Cal.*, vi.148, 218; Machyn, 94.
30. Foxe, viii.550–1.
31. Bryce, *Compendious Register*, in Farr, *Select Poetry*, i.162.
32. Foxe, viii.84–90; *Bishop Cranmer's Recantacyons*, 94–108; Cranmer, *Works*, ii.563–6; *Ven. Cal.*, vi.386.
33. Farr, i.166.
34. *Ven. Cal.*, vi.475, 479–80, 484, 718.
35. Foxe, viii.140–1, 247–50.
36. Farr, i.167.
37. Mumby, 212–13; *Ven. Cal.*, vi.571.
38. Mumby, 214–15.
39. *Ven. Cal.*, vi.809, 836, 848, 887; Machyn, 120.
40. *Ven Cal.*, vi.836.
41. ibid., vi.1115–17.
42. ibid., vi.1105; *Span. Cal.*, xiii.293; *For Cal. Eliz.*, xxi(iii).319.
43. *Ven. Cal.*, vi.1151.
44. *Span. Cal.*, xiii.330–3, 340, 346–7, 352; *For. Cal. Mary*, 361–2.
45. Ponet, *A shorte treatise of politike power*, E.viii (in Hudson, *John Ponet*); Rogers, *History of Agriculture and Prices*, iii.629–32, 634; Rappaport, 'Social structure and mobility in 16th Century London' (*London Journal*, ix.127).
46. Farr, i.169.
47. Foxe, viii.468; Dixon, *History of the Reformation of the Church of England*, iv.708; Strype, *Eccl. Mem.*, iii(ii).130–1.
48. Foxe, viii.491–2.
49. Machyn, 166–7.
50. Lettenhove, *Relations politiques des Pays-Bas et de l'Angleterre*, i.180–1, 229; *Span. Cal.*, xiii.372–3, 380–1, 390; Mumby, 236–8.
51. *Ven. Cal.*, vi.1538.
52. Foxe, viii.504–6, 528–30, 535.
53. *Camden Miscellany*, xxviii.319–38.
54. Mumby, 246–7; *Ven. Cal.*, vi.1559.
55. Farr, i.173.

Chapter 6 – The Coronation

1. Camden, 2.
2. Strype, *Annals*, i(ii).389–90.
3. *Ven. Cal.*, vi.1559.
4. Read, *Cecil*, 104–5, 109–11.
5. Haynes, 202.
6. Strype, *Annals*, i(i).14; Dasent, vii.5, 7–8.
7. *Zurich Letters*, i.4–5.
8. Harington, *Nugae antiquae*, i.67–68; Strype, *Annals*, i(i).154.
9. Waad, 'The Distresses of the Commonwealth' (in Gee, *The Elizabethan Prayer Book*, 206–15).
10. Goodrich, 'Divers points of Religion contrary to the Church of Rome' (in Gee, 202–6).
11. Lettenhove, i.365.
12. Strype, *Annals*, i(ii).391–2.
13. Pollen, *English Catholics in the Reign of Elizabeth*, 24.
14. Lettenhove, i.338.
15. ibid., 1.399–401.
16. Camden, 5–8.
17. *The Quenes Maiesties passage through the Citie of London to Westminster*, passim.

Chapter 7 – The Protestant Realm

1. Neale, *Eliz. & Parliaments*, i.38–39.
2. ibid., i.49.
3. Strype, *Annals*, i(ii).399–407; and see also, ibid., i(ii).403, 408–9.
4. ibid., i(i).115; *Declaration of the Lyfe and Death of John Story* (Harleian Miscellany, iii.102).
5. Gee, 255–7.
6. Neale, *Eliz. & Parliaments*, i.67–71.
7. Lettenhove, i.494.
8. ibid., i.483.
9. Parker, *Correspondence*, 375.
10. *Statutes of the Realm*, 1 Eliz., c.1.
11. ibid., 1 Eliz., c.3, 23; Neale, *Eliz. & Parliaments*, i.44–45.
12. Lettenhove, i.496.
13. *Span. Cal. Eliz.*, 1.41.
14. ibid., i.116–17; Clifford, *Life of Jane Dormer, Duchess of Feria*, 108–9; Lettenhove, i.572–3.
15. Morey, *The Catholic Subjects of Elizabeth I*, 27.
16. Lettenhove, i.520–1.

Chapter 8 – John Knox

1. Knox, *Works*, vi.86, 88–89, 144, 147, 529, 541–2; *Sc. Cal.*, i.1136, 1139, 1152, 1155.

2. Knox, 'Appellation to the Nobility and Estates of Scotland'; 'Letter to the Commonalty of Scotland' (Knox, *Works*, iv.463–520, 523–38).
3. Knox, *Works*, vi.47–50; Knox, *History of the Reformation in Scotland*, i.291–4.
4. Parker, 61.
5. *Ven. Cal.*, vii.102–4; *Rom. Cal.*, i.22.
6. Forbes, *Public Transactions in the Reign of Q. Elizabeth*, 160; *Ven. Cal.*, vii.112.
7. Parker, 105.
8. PRO/SP 52/1/f.185 (8 July 1559).
9. Sadler, i.377–83.
10. Forbes, i.163, 171, 182, 212, 216; Sadler, i.417, 430, 437, 439, 447, 471; *For. Cal. Eliz.*, i.1274; Lettenhove, i.544, 605; Teulet, *Papiers relatifs à l'histoire de l'Écosse*, i.357–60.
11. *Sc. Cal.*, i.508, 529, 571, 588; *For. Cal. Eliz.*, ii.4.
12. Lettenhove, i.595, 604.
13. ibid., ii.58; Teulet, i.365; *For. Cal. Eliz.*, iv.151, 892; *Ven. Cal.*, vii.80–81.

Chapter 9 – The Victory in Scotland

1. Forbes, i.219, 228, 240, 252, 254; Sadler, i.516, 532; *For. Cal. Eliz.*, ii.59, 333.
2. Keith, *History of Church and State in Scotland*, i.246; *Sc. Cal.*, i.582.
3. Gee, 207–8; *Sc. Cal.*, i.848; Sadler, i.438, 478, 528, 531, 536.
4. Sadler, i.528, 530, 536.
5. ibid., i.566.
6. ibid., i.604.
7. ibid., i.532.
8. Gee, 211; *For. Cal. Eliz.*, i.1300; ii., p. 197–8n.
9. Sadler, i.532.
10. Wright, *Queen Elizabeth and her times*, i.24–25.
11. Sadler, i.638; Keith, i.408.
12. *Span. Cal. Eliz.*, i.117–18; *For. Cal. Eliz.*, ii.633.
13. PRO/SP 70/9/f.111A (25 Dec. 1559).
14. *Span. Cal. Eliz.*, i.118–19.
15. *For. Cal. Eliz.*, ii.385; Lettenhove, ii.116–23.
16. Haynes, 212.
17. Teulet, i.462–6.
18. *For. Cal. Eliz.*, ii., p. 197–8n, No. 483; Keith, i.408; *Sc. Cal.*, i.670(3).
19. Forbes, i.263, 274, 299; Lettenhove, ii.135–6, 178–9; *For. Cal. Eliz.*, ii.333, 408.
20. *Sc. Cal.*, i.620(3), 629.
21. Rymer, xv.589.
22. *For. Cal. Eliz.*, ii.504.
23. Forbes, i.352. For Throckmorton's part in the Conspiracy of Amboise, see Sutherland, 'Queen Elizabeth and the Conspiracy of Amboise' (*English Historical Review*, lxxxi.474–89); Dureng, 'La complicité de l'Angleterre dans le complot d'Amboise' (*Revue d'histoire moderne et contemporaine*, vi.249–56); Romier, *La conjuration d'Amboise*, 73–76.
24. Forbes, i.376; *For. Cal. Eliz.*, ii.952; *Ven. Cal.*, vii.156–66, 169–74.
25. Haynes, 268.

26. Lettenhove, ii.212–15n.; *Span. Cal. Eliz.*, i.132–3, 156; *For. Cal. Eliz.*, ii.971, 1082; *Ven. Cal.*, vii.154; *Sc. Cal.*, i.869; Pollen, *Papal Negotiations with Mary Queen of Scots*, 456–8.
27. Lettenhove, ii.242–5n., 299–305n.; *Span. Cal. Eliz.*, i.132; Haynes, 280.
28. Forbes, i.408.
29. *For. Cal. Eliz.*, ii.1020; *Sc. Cal.*, i.803, 829; Teulet, i.381–92.
30. Lettenhove, ii.336–8, 442–4; *For. Cal. Eliz.*, ii.524, 1066; Burgon, *Life of Sir Thomas Gresham*, i.308–9.
31. Haynes, 304; *Sc. Cal.*, i.777–8.
32. Forbes, i.455.
33. ibid., i.494.
34. Hist. MSS. Comm., *Cecil*, i.764; *Sc. Cal.*, i.857.

Chapter 10 – Lord Robert

1. Read, *Cecil*, 198–9.
2. Lettenhove, i.541.
3. Waldman, *Elizabeth and Leicester*, 68.
4. ibid., 71.
5. Lettenhove, i.505, 513, 530; *Span. Cal. Eliz.*, i.141; Camden, 32.
6. Haynes, 364–5.
7. Lettenhove, i.505.
8. Neale, *Queen Elizabeth*, 85.
9. Huggarde, *The Displaying of the Protestantes*, 74, 76.
10. Lettenhove, ii.15, 19–20; *Span. Cal. Eliz.*, i.112.
11. Lettenhove, ii.530–2.
12. Waldman, 78–90.
13. *Hardwicke Papers*, i.121.
14. *For. Cal. Eliz.*, i.690.
15. *Span. Cal. Eliz.*, i.177, 182; Neale, *Queen Elizabeth*, 88.
16. *Span. Cal. Eliz.*, i.178–84, 187–91, 199–201.
17. Teulet, i.620–2; *Sc. Cal.*, i.903; *For. Cal. Eliz.*, iii.784–6.
18. *For. Cal. Eliz.*, iii.534, 796; iv.73, 136; vi.548; Forbes, i. 339–40; Keith, ii.40–54.
19. *For. Cal. Eliz.*, iv.265, 321, 336; Keith, ii.33, 40–54.
20. Keith, ii.40–54.
21. *For. Cal. Eliz.*, iv.243–5.
22. ibid., iv.337.

Chapter 11 – Defeat in France

1. Forbes, i.216.
2. Baronius (Raynaldus), xv.73.
3. *For. Cal. Eliz.*, iv.362; Beza, *Histoire des églises protestantes*, i.294.
4. *For. Cal. Eliz.*, iv.155, 169, 197, 612, 617, 660, 750, 758, 783, 789, 997; *Ven. Cal.*, vii.311.

5. *For. Cal. Eliz.*, iii.451.
6. ibid., iv.151.
7. ibid., iii.1000; v.233.
8. PRO/SP 70/26/f.57 (15 Jan. 1560/1).
9. Haynes, 366.
10. *For. Cal. Eliz.*, iii.1030.
11. PRO/SP 70/26/f.49 (7 May 1561).
12. *For. Cal. Eliz.*, iv.926; *Hardwicke Pap.*, i.180–6.
13. Pollen, *Papal Negotiations*, 113–39; Pollen, *Letter from Mary Queen of Scots to Guise*, 3–28.
14. Lethington's report, in Pollen, *Letter from Mary Queen of Scots to Guise*, 41–42.
15. *Sc. Cal.*, i.1070, 1083, 1117, 1119, 1125; Read, *Cecil*, 236–7; *For. Cal. Eliz.*, v.170, 381, 440.
16. *For. Cal. Eliz.*, iv.934.
17. ibid., iv.934, 943.
18. ibid., iv.967.
19. ibid., v.207–12, 214, 245, 309; *Sc. Cal.*, i.1126; Dasent, vii.110.
20. Forbes, ii.8; *For. Cal. Eliz.*, iv.997, 1013, 1019, 1043, 1074; v.11, 28, 68, 101, 174, 189, 238, 264, 303, 340, 361, 387, 601, 617; *Ven. Cal.*, vii.341.
21. *For. Cal. Eliz.*, v.246, 255.
22. ibid., iv.965.
23. ibid., v.337, 435, 707; Forbes, ii.2.
24. *For. Cal. Eliz.*, v.491.
25. ibid., v.268, 398, 663; Forbes, ii.48–51.
26. *For. Cal. Eliz.*, v.187, 214; *Sc. Cal.*, i.1126.
27. Haynes, 392–3; *Sc. Cal.*, i.1127.
28. Haynes, 391–2.
29. *For. Cal. Eliz.*, v.264, 303, 354, 361, 387; Forbes, ii.8, 195, 323.
30. Forbes, ii.93.
31. *For. Cal. Eliz.*, v.875.
32. ibid., v.1014, 1053; Lettenhove, iii.165–7; *Span. Cal. Eliz.*, i.263.
33. *For. Cal. Eliz.*, v.920, 944, 952, 969; Forbes, ii.160, 166.
34. *For. Cal. Eliz.*, v.1140; Forbes, ii.230, 271; Beza, ii.121.
35. *For. Cal. Eliz.*, v.1172.
36. Forbes, ii.219–21.
37. ibid., ii.224–5.
38. *For. Cal. Eliz.*, vi.428–31.
39. ibid., vi.687; Forbes, ii.404.
40. *For. Cal. Eliz.*, vi.171, 242, 977; Forbes, ii.332, 369, 452.
41. *For. Cal. Eliz.*, vi.1017; Forbes, ii.467, 475–81, 487, 489–90, 497.
42. *For. Cal. Eliz.*, vi.1156.

Chapter 12 – The Tolerant Queen

1. Camden, 10.
2. PRO/SP 52/1/f.455 (26 Oct. 1559).
3. Foxe, viii.226–41.

4. ibid., viii.600.
5. ibid., v.235; cf. 1563 edn., p. 533 and 1570 edn., p. 1284.
6. ibid., i.502.
7. ibid., viii.510–13.
8. *Stat. of Realm*, 5 Eliz., c.1; Strype, *Annals*, i(ii).2–8.
9. Neale, *Eliz. & Parliaments*, i.107.
10. *Span. Cal. Eliz.*, i.296.
11. Parker, 224.
12. ibid., 223–30, 235, 237.
13. ibid., 235; *Span. Cal. Eliz.*, i.405.
14. *L.P.*, v.216, 266, 941.
15. Foxe, vi.722–9; vii.118–19; viii.397.
16. Neale, *Eliz. & Parliaments*, i.129–30.

Chapter 13 – Mary Queen of Scots

1. Hist. MSS. Comm., *Cecil*, i.854.
2. *Span. Cal. Eliz.*, i.313; Read, *Cecil*, 303.
3. *Span. Cal. Eliz.*, i.312–18; Read, *Cecil*, 302; *For. Cal. Eliz.*, vii.980.
4. *Sc. Cal.*, ii.23; Keith, ii.205–8.
5. *Sc. Cal.*, ii.67.
6. ibid., ii.45.
7. ibid., ii.60, 68–69, 93, 104.
8. ibid., ii.78.
9. ibid., ii.112, 127.
10. ibid., ii.97, 108.
11. ibid., ii.123, 146–8.
12. Antonia Fraser, *Mary Queen of Scots*, 220-ln.
13. *For. Cal. Eliz.*, iv.40.
14. Camden, 60; Read, *Cecil*, 309–15. See also Dawson, 'Mary Queen of Scots, Lord Darnley and Anglo–Scottish Relations in 1565' (*International History Review*, viii.1–24).
15. *Sc. Cal.*, ii.186.
16. ibid., ii.156.
17. PRO/SP 52/10/f.64 (29 Apr. 1565).
18. *Sc. Cal.*, ii.172.
19. ibid., ii.183.
20. PRO/SP 52/10/f.125 (8 June 1565).
21. *Sc. Cal.*, ii.246, 257, 259.
22. ibid., ii.270, 272; *For. Cal. Eliz.*, vii.1441.
23. *Sc. Cal.*, ii.286–7, 291, 302, 345; *Span. Cal. Eliz.*, i.496–7, 499–502.
24. *Sc. Cal.*, ii.343–4, 346, 349, 352, 360.
25. Fraser, 236–7.
26. Pollen, *Papal Negotiations*, passim.
27. For Mary's account of Riccio's murder, see Keith, ii.411–28; and see *Diurnal of Occurrents*, 89–93; Fraser, 250–4.
28. PRO/SP 52/12/No.28 (6 Mar. 1565/6).
29. *Sc. Cal.*, ii.353.

30. *Span. Cal. Eliz.*, i.539–40.
31. *Sc. Cal.*, ii.365, 369, 382, 395, 400, 405, 415, 458, 462.
32. *Diurnal of Occurrents*, 103.

Chapter 14 – In Defence of Monarchy

1. *Span. Cal. Eliz.*, i.574.
2. *For. Cal. Eliz.*, vii.1147.
3. Neale, *Eliz. & Parliaments*, i.136–43.
4. *Span. Cal. Eliz.*, i.589–90.
5. Neale, *Eliz. & Parliaments*, i.145–50.
6. ibid., i.156–8, 160–1.
7. ibid., i.173–6.
8. Pollen, *Papal Negotiations*, 272, 278, 321, 323.
9. *Sc. Cal.*, ii.477.
10. ibid., ii.709.
11. ibid., ii.529.
12. PRO/SP 52/13 (Part I)/No.83 (30 June 1567).
13. Stevenson, *Selections from unpublished manuscripts*, 203–4, 210–11, 237–41, 247–52, 267–8, 297–301.
14. ibid., 203–4.
15. ibid., 219–23.
16. ibid., 237–41.
17. *Sc. Cal.*, ii.600.
18. Keith, ii.702.
19. *Sc. Cal.*, ii.586.
20. ibid., ii.593; *Span. Cal. Eliz.*, i.667–71.
21. *For. Cal. Eliz.*, viii.1558–9.
22. PRO/SP 85/14/f.109 (11 Aug. 1567).
23. *Sc. Cal.*, ii.593; Read, *Cecil*, 385–7.
24. Keith, ii.741–7.
25. ibid., ii.747–9; Stevenson, 297–301.
26. *For. Cal. Eliz.*, viii.1719.
27. ibid., viii.1805, 1816.
28. ibid., viii.1836, 1864; *Span. Cal. Eliz.*, i.684.
29. *Span. Cal. Eliz.*, i.678–9, 682–4.
30. *For. Cal. Eliz.*, viii.1919.
31. ibid., viii.1864.
32. *Sc. Cal.*, ii.1702, 1723, 1772, 1778, 1808.
33. ibid., ii.628.
34. Haynes, 462.

Chapter 15 – The Revolt in the Netherlands

1. Pollen, *Papal Negotiations*, 465.
2. Bor, *Nederlandsche Oorloghen*, i.5–9.
3. Lettenhove, iv.283–4; *Span. Cal. Eliz.*, i.541–2.
4. *Span. Cal. Eliz.*, i.552–3.

5. ibid., i.571.
6. ibid., i.577.
7. *For. Cal. Eliz.*, viii.935.
8. Lettenhove, v.17, 33, 717–20.
9. *Span. Cal. Eliz.*, i.610.
10. ibid., ii.13–14.
11. ibid., ii.51.
12. *Sc. Cal.*, ii. 656.
13. *Span. Cal. Eliz.*, ii.36.
14. See Fraser, 385–408, 556–68.
15. *For. Cal. Eliz.*, viii.2249, 2256–7, 2273, 2333.
16. Lettenhove, vi.124–6; *Span. Cal. Eliz.*, ii.54–55, 59–61.
17. *For. Cal. Eliz.*, ix.409.
18. ibid., ix.495.
19. *For. Cal. Edw. VI*, 87, 138, 166–7.
20. *For. Cal. Eliz.*, viii.2098, 2109, 2139; *Span. Cal. Eliz.*, ii.19.
21. *Span. Cal. Eliz.*, ii.9–10.
22. ibid., ii.3.
23. ibid., ii.18–20.
24. ibid., ii.29.

Chapter 16 – The Contest with Alva

1. *Stat. of Realm*, 1 Edw. VI, c.3; 3 & 4 Edw. VI, c.16.
2. Shakespeare, *Merchant of Venice*, Act iv, scene i, lines 90–98.
3. Camden, ii.417; Thomson, *Sir Francis Drake*, 13–15.
4. Unwin, *The Defeat of John Hawkins*, 48–49, 71–109; Thomson, 21–22; Read, *Cecil*, 427–30.
5. Unwin, 189–311; Thomson, 24–40; Read, *Cecil*, 429–30.
6. *Span. Cal. Eliz.*, ii.81.
7. ibid., ii.84, 88, 93–94, 104; Lettenhove, v.198–205, 417–19, 738–43; *For. Cal. Eliz.*, ix.44; Read, *Cecil*, 432–3; Read, 'Queen Elizabeth's seizure of Alva's pay-ships' (*Journal of Modern History*, v.443–64).
8. Lettenhove, v.242–4, 253–63, 297; *Span. Cal. Eliz.*, ii.106–10, 112–14, 132–7, 159–63; *For. Cal. Eliz.*, ix.226.
9. Lettenhove, v.270–96; *Span. Cal. Eliz.*, ii.122–37.
10. Lettenhove, v.743–4; *Span. Cal. Eliz.*, ii.133–7, 155–6, 186, 188, 215–17.
11. *Span. Cal. Eliz.*, ii.133–40.
12. ibid., ii.137.
13. ibid., ii.171–2, 195–200; Lettenhove, v.421–2, 429–30.
14. Haynes, 565.
15. ibid., 555; *Rom. Cal.*, i.626.
16. *Span. Cal. Eliz.*, ii.187, 210, 217.
17. Haynes, 556.
18. ibid., 559.
19. *Sc. Cal.*, iii.36.
20. ibid., iii.76, 80, 86–87, 202; *For. Cal. Eliz.*, ix.613, 627, 1232; x.186, 200, 232,

250, 302, 327, 355–6, 364, 367, 369, 384, 402; *Span. Cal. Eliz.*, ii.406.

21. *Ven. Cal.*, vii.448–51.
22. Labanoff, *Lettres de Marie Stuart*, iii.211–17.
23. *Sc. Cal.*, iii.119, 123, 178.
24. *For. Cal. Eliz.*, ix.96.
25. *Sc. Cal.*, iii.169.
26. *For. Cal. Eliz.*, ix.805.
27. *Correspondance diplomatique de La Mothe Fénélon*, iii.188.
28. *Sc. Cal.*, iii. 289.
29. ibid., iii.214–15.
30. For the King's lords' propagandist view of Grange and Lethington, see Robert Sempill's poem 'The Crooked leads the Blind' (in *Satirical Poems of the time of the Reformation*, 132–7).
31. *Sc. Cal.*, iii.518.
32. ibid., iii.523.
33. ibid., iii.672.
34. For the Ridolfi plot, see Read, *Burghley*, 38–50, and authorities cited there.
35. *Sc. Cal.*, iv.55, 63–64, 78, 117; *For. Cal. Eliz.*, x.179, 186, 272.
36. Neale, *Eliz. & Parliaments*, i.250, 259, 264, 269, 271–3.
37. ibid., i.281–3, 307–9.
38. See supra, p.83.
39. *Declaration of the Lyfe and Death of John Story* (*Harleian Miscellany*, iii.100–8); *Dom. Cal.* i.389–93, 395, 411, 415.
40. *Span. Cal. Eliz.*, ii.326–7.
41. Lettenhove, vi.600–5, 601n., 618–22; *For. Cal. Eliz.*, x.936, 1021; Read, *Burghley*, 97–102.
42. *Span. Cal. Eliz.*, ii.376.

Chapter 17 – The Massacre of St Bartholomew

1. Wilson, *The Plague in Shakespeare's London*, 114, 193; Collinson, *Archbishop Grindal*, 163.
2. Nichols, *Progresses of Queen Elizabeth*, i.87, 92–103, 149–89.
3. ibid., i.192–8, 204–17, 229–47.
4. ibid., i.207.
5. ibid., i.257–9, 307–21.
6. Read, *Burghley*, 86.
7. PRO/SP 70/124/f.137 (22 Aug. 1572).
8. For an exhaustive analysis of the conflicting evidence of the responsibility for the massacre, see Sutherland, *The Massacre of St Bartholomew and the European Conflict*, 312–46. See also *For. Cal. Eliz.*, x.538, 584; Whitehead, *Coligny*, 255–84; Read, *Walsingham*, i.220–2; Read, *Burghley*, 86.
9. *Rom. Cal.*, ii.68; Wright, i.438; Parker, 398; *For. Cal. Eliz.*, x.741; *Book of the Universal Kirk*, 252–4.
10. Fénélon, v.112–19.
11. ibid., v.120–31.
12. *For. Cal. Eliz.*, x.622, 755.

13. ibid., x.682, 779, 1065, 1083.
14. ibid., x.1271.
15. ibid., x.996; Lettenhove, vi.411–13, 458.
16. Lettenhove, vi.390, 411, 429, 458; *For. Cal. Eliz.*, x.488.
17. Lettenhove, vi.658–9.
18. Penshurst MSS.
19. Lettenhove, vi.796.
20. *Sc. Cal.*, iv.240, 272, 309, 319, 474, 486, 491, 507, 509, 576.
21. *For. Cal. Eliz.*, x.699, 740, 744.
22. ibid., x.872.
23. *Diurnal of Occurrents*, 331–3; *Sc. Cal.*, iv.664–7.
24. *Sc. Cal.*, iv.686.
25. ibid., iv.712; *Diurnal of Occurrents*, 335–6.

Chapter 18 – Puritans and Anabaptists

1. Lettenhove, vii.24–25.
2. ibid., vii.100, 109, 531–4.
3. ibid., vii.532–3.
4. ibid., viii.399–404.
5. ibid., viii.338–42, 386–9, 413–19, 433–54, 462–3, 467–72.
6. Read, *Walsingham*, ii.136, 140–1, 145–6.
7. *For. Cal. Eliz.*, xi.275.
8. ibid., xi.244.
9. ibid., xi.260, 276, 283–4, 290, 296–7, 299.
10. ibid., xi.311.
11. ibid., xi.351, 394, 404, 438.
12. Collinson, *The Elizabethan Puritan Movement*, 168–76; Read, *Burghley*, 236–7.
13. Parker, 418–19.
14. For the case of the Anabaptists, see Holinshed, *Chronicles*, iv.326–8; Braght, *Der blutige Schau-Platz oder Martyrer Spiegel*, 789–91; Williams, *The Radical Reformation*, 784–6; Mozley, *John Foxe and his Book*, 86–89.
15. Mozley, 86–87.
16. Holinshed, iv.328.
17. Collinson, *Grindal*, 221–2.
18. Grindal, *Remains*, 376–90.
19. Collinson, *Grindal*, 246–52.
20. ibid., 252.
21. Grindal, 467.
22. Neale, *Eliz. & Parliaments*, i.322.
23. ibid., i.329–30.

Chapter 19 – The Rift with Spain

1. Lettenhove, vii.382–6, 410–13, 432–6.
2. ibid., vii.454–5.

3. *For. Cal. Eliz.*, xi.49.
4. ibid., xi.989, 1056, 1083, 1085, 1228, 1283, 1438; Lettenhove, viii.82–83; ix.85–90, 116–19, 233–4, 236–8, 240–1, 335–8.
5. Lettenhove, viii.118–25, 127–31.
6. ibid., ix.85–90, 138; *For. Cal. Eliz.*, xi.1024.
7. *For. Cal. Eliz.*, xi.1236.
8. ibid., xii.700, 830; Lettenhove, ix.466; *Span. Cal. Eliz.*, ii.600–1.
9. *For. Cal. Eliz.*, x.1423, 1431; xi.365.
10. ibid., xi.771.
11. PRO/SP 70/144 (4 Mar. 1576/7).
12. *For. Cal. Eliz.*, xii.21, 41.
13. ibid., xii.90.
14. ibid., xii.109.
15. Lettenhove, ix.567; x.9, 14–15.
16. ibid., x.163–4.
17. ibid., x.334.
18. ibid., x.438–9.
19. ibid., x.448–9, 486–9, 494–500; *For. Cal. Eliz.*, xii.803.
20. Nichols, *Progresses*, i.331–54, 391–410, 417–599; ii.6–7, 55–60; Strype, *Annals*, ii(ii).539–44.
21. Nichols, *Progresses*, ii.92–222.
22. Lettenhove, x.595.
23. ibid., x.659–61.
24. ibid., x.661–2.
25. ibid., x.696–7.
26. PRO/SP 83/8 (7 Aug. 1578).
27. Lettenhove, x.710.
28. ibid., xi.65–66; *For. Cal. Eliz.*, xiii.163, 215.
29. *For. Cal. Eliz.*, xi.199, 545, 1024.
30. ibid., xi.71, 1508; *Span. Cal. Eliz.*, ii.578, 580, 586–7; Unwin, 272–3.
31. *Span. Cal. Eliz.*, ii.491–2.
32. *For. Cal. Eliz.*, xi.981.
33. ibid., xi.1436.
34. *Span. Cal. Eliz.*, ii.550–2.
35. ibid., iii.133.
36. ibid., ii.553–8.
37. Thomson, 98–105.
38. *Span. Cal. Eliz.*, ii.545.
39. ibid., iii.74–75, 93–95; Thomson, 151, 155–6, 161; Read, *Burghley*, 270.

Chapter 20 – The Virgin Queen

1. Clapham, 68.
2. *Span. Cal. Eliz.*, i.589.
3. *For. Cal. Eliz.*, ix.1968; Read, *Burghley*, 51–64.
4. Stubbs, *The Discovery of a Gaping Gulf*, (unpaginated), 1, 22–23, 63–66, 80.
5. Strype, *Annals*, ii(ii). 641–52.

6. Camden, iii.14.
7. *Stat. of Realm*, 1 & 2 Ph. & Mary, c.3.
8. Froude, x.502.
9. Strype, *Annals*, ii(ii). 232–8.
10. Dasent, xi.270; Harington, iii.98–103.
11. *Ven. Cal.*, vii.621.
12. Camden, iii.16.
13. ibid.; Harington, iii.180–3.
14. Neale, *Queen Elizabeth*, 243.
15. Camden, Latin edn., 379; cf. 1625 English edn., iii.16, and 1635 edn., 239.
16. Harington, iii.202–7.
17. ibid., iii.213.
18. *Span. Cal. Eliz.*, ii.702–3; Murdin, *Burghley Papers*, 322–37; Read, *Burghley*, 217–18.
19. *Span. Cal. Eliz.*, ii.704.
20. ibid., ii.705.
21. *For. Cal. Eliz.*, xv.225, 487.
22. ibid., xv.413–14; *Span. Cal. Eliz.*, iii.226–8, 251–3; Read, *Burghley*, 268.
23. *For. Cal. Eliz.*, xv.415, 553, 570, 616; xvi.183; Read, *Burghley*, 271.
24. *Span. Cal. Eliz.*, ii.664.
25. Clapham, 68.

Chapter 21 – Ireland

1. *Irish Cal.*, iv.155.
2. ibid., i.179.
3. *Carew Cal.*, i.312.
4. ibid., i.352, 362–4; *Irish Cal.*, i.202, 222–4.
5. *Irish Cal.*, i.299, 325.
6. ibid., i.248, 304–5, 324.
7. ibid., i.335.
8. ibid., i.353.
9. ibid., i.446–7, 449, 469–70, 472; *Ven. Cal.*, vii.479.
10. *Irish Cal.*, i.490.
11. ibid., i.424.
12. ibid., i.493–4, 499–501, 503; ii.14–15, 19.
13. ibid., ii.19, 32; Devereux, *Lives of the Devereux*, i.63–67, 74; *Carew Cal.*, i.467–71, 526.
14. *Irish Cal.*, ii.53; *Carew Cal.*, ii.2–3.
15. Devereux, i.98–99.
16. PRO/SP 63/50 (31 March 1575).
17. Devereux, i.104–6, 108–13.
18. Thomson, 96.
19. Devereux, i.113–17; PRO/SP 63/52/f.204 (31 July 1575); Froude, x.529–30.
20. *Irish Cal.*, i.447; ii.106, 113, 130, 132, 134–6, 150, 163, 167, 172–3, 178, 181; xi.590; *For. Cal. Eliz.*, xiii.685.
21. *Irish Cal.*, ii.173–6.
22. PRO/SP 63/68/f.5 (3 Aug. 1579).

23. *Irish Cal.*, ii., p.lix, 174, 178, 186–7, 196, 206, 216, 262, 268.
24. ibid., ii.195.
25. ibid., ii.310.
26. PRO/SP 63/72/f.56 (31 Mar. 1580).
27. *Irish Cal.*, ii.274.
28. *Carew Cal.*, ii.314.
29. PRO/SP 63/76/No.30 (8 Sept. 1580).
30. *Irish Cal.*, ii.243.
31. ibid., ii., p.lxvi.
32. ibid., ii.187, 265, 362, 403, 451.
33. ibid., ii.255, 259.
34. ibid., ii., p. lxix–lxxiii.
35. PRO/SP 63/78/f.85 (14 Nov. 1580).
36. ibid., ff.59, 85 (11 and 14 Nov. 1580); O'Rahilly, *The Massacre at Smerwick*, 7–8, 17, 21.
37. *Span. Cal. Eliz.*, iii.69; and see the commemorative stone on the site of Fort del Oro at Smerwick.
38. Spenser, *Works*, ix.166–7.
39. Petrie, 'The Hispano-Papal landing at Smerwick' (*The Irish Sword*, ix.92); O'Rahilly, 1–34.
40. O'Rahilly, 5–6.
41. Camden, ii.409.
42. *Span. Cal. Eliz.*, ii.686; iii.20–21, 28, 33, 41–42.
43. ibid., iii.28.
44. *Irish Cal.*, ii., p. ci–cii.
45. Spenser, ix.162; and see *Irish Cal.*, ii., p. lxxxix–xc, 416.
46. *Irish Cal.*, ii.299.
47. ibid., ii.300–1; see also ibid., ii.318, 321, 362, 377.
48. ibid., ii.318.
49. ibid., ii., p. xxxvi–xxxvii.
50. ibid., ii.300.
51. ibid., ii., p. lxxxv–lxxxviii.

Chapter 22 – The Jesuits

1. Read, *Walsingham*, ii.149–50.
2. ibid., ii.141.
3. ibid., ii.145–8.
4. For the overthrow of Morton and subsequent events in Scotland and Elizabeth's attitude, see ibid., ii.164–227.
5. ibid., ii.168.
6. ibid., ii.170.
7. ibid., ii.171.
8. Bowes, *Correspondence*, 199.
9. Read, *Walsingham*, ii.190.
10. Pollen, *English Catholics*, 244–98.
11. *Stat. of Realm*, 1 Eliz., c.2.
12. Pollen, *English Catholics*, 331–72; Read, *Burghley*, 244–55.

13. Spadding, *Letters and Life of Bacon*, i.97–98.
14. Pollen, *English Catholics*, 293–8.
15. *Stat. of Realm*, 23 Eliz., c.1; Neale, *Eliz. & Parliaments*, i.378–92.
16. Pollen, *English Catholics*, 371.
17. *Span. Cal. Eliz.*, iii.68, 173.
18. ibid., ii.573–5, 593–4, 602–4, 607, 617–18, 624–5, 629–30, 651–2, 654, 656, 665, 667, 673–4, 676.
19. *For. Cal. Eliz.*, xiv., p. xxii–xxiii, Nos. 459, 476; xv.46, 57, 126, 170, 235, 239; xvi.194, 252, 416; xix.53.
20. ibid., xv.170, 235.
21. ibid., xiv.248, 295, 345, 450.
22. ibid., xiv.402; xv.206, 208, 241, 387.
23. ibid., xv.406; xvi.402.
24. ibid., xvi.112, 115, 213, 338, 340, 353, 365, 383.
25. ibid., xvi.368; and see ibid., xv.459.
26. ibid., xv.314; xvi.59.

Chapter 23 – Intervention in the Netherlands

1. *Apologie de Guillaume de Nassau*, 5–26.
2. *For. Cal. Elix.*, xv.615, 618, 621, 628, 630–1, 636, 640, 642, 646, 649–50, 655, 658, 662, 671, 691.
3. ibid., xv.624.
4. *Span. Cal. Eliz.*, iii.331, 342.
5. ibid., iii.362–3, 370–3, 377–9.
6. ibid., iii.382–4.
7. ibid., ii.574; iii.10–12; *For. Cal. Eliz.*, xxi(i).464–7.
8. *For. Cal. Eliz.*, xiv.339, 344.
9. ibid., xv.397, 415, 616.
10. PRO/SP 83/11/f.6 (2 Jan. 1578/9).
11. PRO/SP 83/15/f.21 (6 Feb. 1581/2).
12. *For. Cal. Eliz.*, xv.574.
13. ibid., xvi.274.
14. ibid.
15. ibid., xvi.405–6.
16. ibid., xvii.21, 24, 40.
17. ibid., xvii.19, 24, 28, 30, 35, 38, 42, 46.
18. ibid., xvii.45, 48, 58–59, 71, 80.
19. ibid., xvii.41, 85, 87, 90, 98.
20. PRO/SP 83/18 (1 Feb. 1582/3, O.S.).
21. *For. Cal. Eliz.*, xvii.80.
22. ibid., xvii.98.
23. ibid., xvii.58–59, 61–62, 65–66, 77, 84–85, 103, 110, 120–1, 302.
24. ibid., xvii.210, 306.
25. ibid., xvii.25.
26. ibid., xiv.474; xv.478; *Span. Cal. Eliz.*, iii.406.
27. *Span. Cal. Eliz.*, iii.513–15.

28. *For. Cal. Eliz.*, xvi.181, 231, 323, 396, 423, 434, 441, 484.
29. ibid., xviii.716; xix.67, 103–6, 378–80, 516–17, 574–5.
30. ibid., xx.429–31.
31. For the assassination of William and the execution of Gérard, see Motley, *Rise of the Dutch Republic*, iii.458–72; *For. Cal. Eliz.*, xviii.715, 721, 725, 728, 768.
32. Motley, *Rise of the Dutch Republic*, iii.472.
33. *Harleian Miscellany*, iii.200; *For. Cal. Eliz.*, xix.68.
34. *For. Cal. Eliz.*, xix.86, 101–2, 129–32, 176–81.
35. ibid., xix.96–98, 149–51.
36. ibid., xix.228–31, 233–41.
37. ibid., xix.176, 354–5, 370–3, 380, 391, 408, 411, 423, 462, 516, 541, 549.
38. ibid., xix.292, 333, 336–7, 365–7, 395–6, 400, 402, 465; xx.8, 28.
39. ibid., xix.413.
40. PRO/SP 84/1/f.103 (22 Apr. 1585, O.S.).
41. *For. Cal. Eliz.*, xix.474–81, 488–90, 531–2, 535, 542, 558, 568–9, 579–80; *Correspondance de Granvelle*, xii.280–1.
42. *For. Cal. Eliz.*, xix.477, 497, 519, 618, 705–6, 708.
43. ibid., xix.604–5, 630, 634, 659, 690.
44. ibid., xix.641, 661, 667.
45. ibid., xx.204, 710; Read, *Walsingham*, iii.107–10.
46. *For. Cal. Eliz.*, xix. 668, 691; xx.6, 23, 215.
47. ibid., xix.671–3.
48. For the negotiations, see ibid., xx.329–30, 360–1, 368, 370, 379–82, 391–2, 398–400, 448–9, 513–14, 516–17, 538–9, 553–4, 595, 616–17.
49. ibid., xxi(iii).83, 227–9.
50. ibid., xx.146, 166–7, 171.
51. ibid., xx.172.
52. ibid., xx.126.
53. ibid., xx.219.
54. ibid., xx.176–7, 180.
55. ibid., xx.8, 205.
56. ibid., xx.213.
57. ibid., xx.231, 243–5.
58. ibid., xx.322–4.
59. ibid., xx.319, 326; Bor, xxi. 6–8.
60. *For. Cal. Eliz.*, xx.364–5, 371–2, 376–7; *Leicester Correspondence*, 105–10.
61. *For. Cal. Eliz.*, xx.364–5.
62. *Leicester Correspondence*, 117–26.
63. Motley, *United Netherlands*, i.432.
64. *Leicester Correspondence*, 105–10; *For. Cal. Eliz.*, xx., p. xxvi–xxxiii, 371–2, 376–7, 445–6; Waldman, 178–85.
65. *For. Cal. Eliz.*, xx.409.
66. ibid., xx.366–7, 385–6, 402–3, 445–7, 450–4, 457.
67. ibid., xx.500–1.

Chapter 24 – Execution of a Queen

1. Collinson, *The Elizabethan Puritan Movement*, 243–70; Neale, *Eliz. & Parliaments*, ii.19–23; Read, *Burghley*, 294–6; Strype, *Whitgift*, i.275.
2. Neale, *Eliz. & Parliaments*, ii.69.
3. ibid., ii.16–18.
4. ibid., ii.120.
5. ibid., ii.32–53, 98.
6. ibid., ii.44–48.
7. Read, *Walsingham*, iii.1–28, 65–70.
8. *Bardon Papers*, 36.
9. ibid., 45; Read, *Burghley*, 346–7; Camden, iii.142–3.
10. *For. Cal. Eliz.*, xxi(i).118–20; *Cal. Border Papers*, i.249–51; Hist. MSS. Comm., *Cecil*, iii.228–30; *Ven. Cal.*, viii.266; Neale, *Eliz. & Parliaments*, ii.134–5.
11. Camden, iii.144.
12. Read, *Walsingham*, iii.49–52; Read, *Burghley*, 348.
13. Howell, *State Trials*, i.1161–1228.
14. Read, *Walsingham*, iii.54.
15. Neale, *Eliz. & Parliaments*, ii.105.
16. PRO/SP 78/16/f.67 (1 Nov. 1586, N.S.).
17. Read, *Walsingham*, iii.54–55.
18. Neale, *Eliz. & Parliaments*, ii.109.
19. ibid., ii.105, 114–21; Read, *Walsingham*, iii.56.
20. Neale, *Eliz. & Parliaments*, ii.126–9.
21. ibid., ii.131–5; *For. Cal. Eliz.*, xxi(ii).251–2; *E.H.R.*, xxxv.103–13; Holinshed, iii.1386.
22. Read, *Walsingham*, iii.57.
23. *For. Cal. Eliz.*, xxi(i).184.
24. ibid., xxi(i).189–90; Read, *Walsingham*, iii.60–63.
25. *For. Cal. Eliz.*, xxi(i).190–4.
26. Cf. Hume's Preface to *Span. Cal. Eliz.*, iv., p. xii–xvi; Read, *Burghley*, 386–90; Read, *Walsingham*, iii.212; Read, 'The Fame of Sir Edward Stafford' (*American Historical Review*, xx.292–313); Neale, *Essays in Elizabethan History*, 146–69.
27. Nicolas, *Life of Davison*, 232–6, 259–61, 269–74; *For. Cal. Eliz.*, xxi(i).241.
28. Nicolas, 243–7, 277–80; Morris, *Troubles of our Catholic Forefathers*, ii.359, 361; Neale, *Eliz. & Parliaments*, ii.139–41.
29. *For. Cal. Eliz.*, xxi(i).241–2; Read, *Burghley*, 366–78; Neale, *Eliz. & Parliaments*, ii.141–2.
30. Neale, *Eliz. & Parliaments*, ii.142; and see Batho, 'The Execution of Mary, Queen of Scots' (*Scottish Historical Review*, xxxix.35–42).
31. Froude, xii. 268–74; Read, *Burghley*, 375–9, 466, 575; Nicolas, 168–200, 302–49.
32. *For. Cal. Eliz.*, xxi(i).199, 203–14, 217–18.
33. ibid., xxi(i).227, 236, 240, 243, 248, 257.
34. ibid., xxi(i).227.
35. ibid., xxi(i).254.
36. ibid., xxi(i).186, 236, 252.
37. *Span. Cal. Eliz.*, iv.41.

38. ibid., iv.38.
39. *For. Cal. Eliz.*, xxi(i).249, 257, 266, 274, 276.
40. ibid., xxi(i).236.
41. ibid., xxi(i).242, 275, 278–9, 291–2.
42. ibid., xxi(i).241–2.
43. Neale, *Eliz. & Parliaments*, ii.148–65; Collinson, *The Elizabethan Puritan Movement*, 310–15.
44. Neale, *Eliz. & Parliaments*, ii.163.

Chapter 25 – Cadiz

1. *For. Cal. Eliz.*, xix.541–2, 550–4.
2. ibid., xix.447–8, 499, 534–5, 556–7, 561–2, 584–5, 587–9, 596–7; xx.107, 109–10, 364–5, 377–8.
3. ibid., xxi(i).124, 138–42, 417–21, 427, 430–1, 436, 478–83, 491–3.
4. ibid., xxi(i).478–83, 510; Mattingly, *The Defeat of the Spanish Armada*, 146–7.
5. Dee, *British Ballads*, 27–36.
6. *For. Cal. Eliz.*, xxi(ii).15–16, 407–9; xxi(iii).6–8, 12–13, 48–50, 123–4.
7. ibid., xx.618; xxi(ii).274, 279, 336, 340–1; *Irish Cal.*, ii.190, 238, 247, 296–7, 315, 320–1.
8. *For. Cal. Eliz.*, xxi(ii).326, 328–32; *Span. Cal. Eliz.*, iv.15–17.
9. *For. Cal. Eliz.*, xxi(ii).287; xxi(iii).341, 489; *Span. Cal. Eliz.*, iii.689.
10. *For. Cal. Eliz.*, xxi(ii).332–6, 340–2, 345, 355, 361–2, 387; xxi(iii).224; Meteren, *General History of the Netherlands*, 945–9.
11. *For. Cal. Eliz.*, xx.231; xxi(ii).357, 369–70, 373.
12. ibid., xix.713; *Span. Cal. Eliz.*, iii.544, 547–8; Thomson, 173, 176.
13. *For. Cal. Eliz.*, xx. 64–65.
14. ibid., xx.551, 575, 595, 598, 601, 610, 635, 643, 662; xxi(i).56–59, 88; *Span. Cal. Eliz.*, iii.444; Labanoff, vi.296, 432; Thomson, 173–93.
15. *For. Cal. Eliz.*, xx.240, 329–30, 391–2, 513–14, 635; xxi(ii).223, 277, 388–9, 396–9, 435–7; xxi(iii).28, 41–42, 51–55, 117.
16. Labanoff, vi.310; Jensen, 'On the phantom will of Mary Queen of Scots' (*Scotia*, iv.1–15).
17. *For. Cal. Eliz.*, xxi(i).278.
18. *Span. Cal. Eliz.*, iv.126, 139, 189, 198, 213, 256–7, 261, 278.
19. ibid., iv.74, 352.
20. ibid., iv.60–61.
21. *For. Cal. Eliz.*, xxi(iii).186.
22. Read, *Walsingham*, iii.233.
23. *Span. Cal. Eliz.*, iv.65–67, 83.
24. Thomson, 199–213; *For. Cal. Eliz.*, xxi(i).658–9.
25. *Span. Cal. Eliz.*, iv.83, 97.
26. Thomson, 206–7.
27. *For. Cal. Eliz.*, xxi(i).573.
28. ibid., xxi(iii).161, 185–6, 218, 483.
29. ibid., xxi(iii).83, 91, 95, 162, 227–9, 302–3, 361–3, 371–4, 392.
30. ibid., xxi(iii).367.
31. ibid., xxi(iii).370.

32. ibid., xxi(i).389–90; xxi(iii).390–1.
33. ibid., xxi(iii).335.
34. ibid., xxi(iii).272.
35. ibid., xxi(i).451.
36. ibid., xxi(iii).399–400.
37. ibid., xxi(iii).246.
38. *Span. Cal. Eliz.*, iv.106.
39. ibid., iv.101–5.
40. ibid., iv.105–6, 111–12.
41. ibid., iv.106.
42. ibid., iv.112.

Chapter 26 – The Armada

1. *Span. Cal. Eliz.*, iv.135–7.
2. ibid., iv.200; *For. Cal. Eliz.*, xxi(iii).394, 401, 409–10, 413, 415, 420, 428, 430–1, 446–7, 450, 453–4, 464–5.
3. *For. Cal. Eliz.*, xxi(iii).461; xxii.2–3, 15, 152.
4. ibid., xxii.118.
5. *Span. Cal. Eliz.*, iv.199–201, 211, 237–8, 300, 348.
6. *For. Cal. Eliz.*, xxi(iv).222–3.
7. ibid., xxi(iv).273–4.
8. ibid., xxi(iv).323–4, 333, 370–1, 386–7, 403; xxii.73; *Span. Cal. Eliz.*, iv.307–8.
9. *For. Cal. Eliz.*, xxi(iii).459; xxi(iv).425–7, 471–2, 485–8; xxii.71–74.
10. ibid., xxi(iv).520, 522.
11. ibid., xxi(iv).472–4; xxii.29.
12. *Span. Cal. Eliz.*, iv.275–6, 280–5, 309, 314–19, 321–2.
13. *For. Cal. Eliz.*, xxi(i).611, 633–7, 643–4.
14. *Span. Cal. Eliz.*, iv.184–6.
15. ibid., iv.212–13.
16. Allen, *Admonition to the Nobility and People of England*, especially pp. 8, 11, 15, 25, 27, 53–54.
17. *For. Cal. Eliz.*, xxi(iv).528–9; xxii.32–34, 47, 51–52; Motley, *United Netherlands*, ii.399–406.
18. *Span. Cal. Eliz.*, iv.250–2.
19. ibid., iv.358, 362–6; Mattingly, 273.
20. *Span. Cal. Eliz.*, iv.240–1, 421.
21. ibid., iv.354.
22. Camden, iii.280–3; Mattingly, 290–1, 294.
23. Mattingly, 228–68; *Span. Cal. Eliz.*, iv.393.
24. Laughton, *State Papers relating to the Defeat of the Spanish Armada*, i.305–6.
25. Nichols, *Progresses*, ii.530.
26. Mattingly, 260–84; Thomson, 262–76.
27. *E.H.R.*, xxxiv.44; *Span. Cal. Eliz.*, iv.270, 404, 502.
28. *For. Cal. Eliz.*, xxii.99–100, 121–2; *Span. Cal. Eliz.*, iv.381.
29. *Span. Cal. Eliz.*, iv.371.
30. *E.H.R.*, xxxiv.43–61; Neale, *Essays in Elizabethan History*, 104–6.

31. *E.H.R.*, xxxiv.46.
32. Neale, *Queen Elizabeth*, 297–8.
33. Laughton, ii.59, 96, 164, 183, 303–8.
34. *E.H.R.*, xxxiv.55.
35. *Span. Cal. Eliz.*, iv.394, 432, 439, 450; Mattingly, 307–13.
36. *Irish Cal.*, iv.43, 47, 49–50, 58, 63–64, 66, 69, 72, 78; *Span. Cal. Eliz.*, iv.411, 456–7, 487.
37. *Irish Cal.*, iv.47, 53, 62, 65, 76, 93; *Span. Cal. Eliz.*, iv.489, 492, 501; *For. Cal. Eliz.*, xxiii.132.
38. *Span. Cal. Eliz.*, iv.506–10.
39. *Sc. Pap.*, ix.547, 554, 587–8, 600; x.15, 22, 33–34, 125, 128–9, 150, 156–7; *List and Analysis of State Papers*, i.91; Duro, *La Armada Invincible*, ii.337–70.
40. *Irish Cal.*, iv.58–59; *Span. Cal. Eliz.*, iv.502–3.
41. *Span. Cal. Eliz.*, iv.438, 455, 482, 486; Dasent, xvi.205, 347.
42. *Span. Cal. Eliz.*, iv.519, 548–51; *For. Cal. Eliz.*, xxii.214; Dasent, xvi.210–11.
43. *Irish Cal.*, iv.37, 43; Dasent, xvi.288.
44. *Irish Cal.*, iv.53, 66, 73, 76.
45. ibid., iv.65.
46. ibid iv.49, 68; Laughton, ii.299–301.
47. ibid. iv.93, 99.
48. Camden, iii.286; Nichols, *Progresses*, ii.538–42.
49. Camden, iii.288–9; Neale, *Queen Elizabeth*, 301; Waldman, 199–200.

Chapter 27 – Mutinies and Failures

1. *For. Cal. Eliz.*, xxi(ii).430; xxi(iii).21; xxii., p. xxxiv–xxxv.
2. ibid., xix.443; xx.195, 280, 469–71, 489; xxi(iii).85, 103–4, 110–11, 223–4, 465; xxii.87, 360, 368; *L.A.*, i.184–5, 241, 417–18, 420–1, 423–30; ii.177, 223; iii.131–2, 162, 476–82.
3. *For. Cal. Eliz.*, xxi(iv)., p. xxv.
4. ibid., xxii.167.
5. For the events at Geertruidenberg, see ibid., xxi(iv).246, 318–19, 335, 350, 356–61, 364–7, 401, 447–8, 492–3, 501–2, 518, 531; xxii.15, 19, 25, 44, 49–50, 55–57, 59, 63–68, 82–83, 90.
6. ibid., xxi(iv).501, 503, 518, 526–8; xxii.55, 65, 83.
7. ibid., xxii.189.
8. ibid., xxii.168.
9. ibid., xxii.168, 202.
10. ibid., xxii.188–91, 202–3.
11. ibid., xxii.190–1.
12. ibid., xxii.167.
13. ibid., xxii.190–4, 205–6, 218–19, 238–40, 279, 284.
14. PRO/SP 84/28/f.124 (19 Nov. 1588, O.S.).
15. For the betrayal of Geertruidenberg and the ensuing events, see ibid., xxii.140, 154, 183–4, 234, 241, 248, 254, 283–4, 303, 312, 319–20, 328–9; xxiii.154–5, 157, 159–60, 164, 166–8, 171–4, 186–7, 194–6, 200, 205–8, 212–13, 216–19, 221, 235, 237–8.

16. ibid., xxiii.254–6, 304–8, 327–9; *L.A.*., i.240.
17. *For. Cal. Eliz.*., xxiii.84.
18. *Span. Cal. Eliz.*, iv.473, 482, 486–7, 490–1, 514–16, 522–3, 529–30, 532–3, 536; Thomson, 278–81.
19. For the Portuguese expedition, see *For. Cal. Eliz.*, xxiii.353–4, 360–3, 383–4, 410–11; *Span. Cal. Eliz.*, iv.537–8, 542, 546–7, 549, 553–6; Thomson, 284–97; Wernham, *The Making of Elizabethan Foreign Policy*, 64–69.
20. Thomson, 298–9.
21. Mattingly, 317–21.
22. *For. Cal. Eliz.*, xxiii.17, 47.
23. ibid., xxii.405.
24. ibid., xxii.391–3; xxiii.16, 19, 24–25, 33, 49–50, 96.
25. PRO/SP 78/19/f.40 (12 Feb. 1589, N.S.).
26. ibid., f.1 (2 Jan. 1589, N.S.).
27. *For. Cal. Eliz.*, xxiii.7.
28. ibid., xxiii.91.
29. ibid., xxiii.93–94.
30. ibid., xxiii., p. liii–lix, 227–9, 236–7, 334–6, 340–3, 351–2, 357–8, 360, 375–6, 385–90, 393.
31. PRO/SP 78/19/f.197 (31 July 1589, N.S.).
32. *For. Cal. Eliz.*, xxiii., p. lvi, lviii.
33. Dasent, xvii.419–20.
34. *For. Cal. Eliz.*, xxiii.394.
35. *Plays and Poems of Marlowe*, 398.
36. *L.A.*., i.245–6; iii.302.

Chapter 28 – Essex

1. Neale, *Eliz. & Parliaments*, ii.196–7, 199.
2. Collinson, *The Elizabethan Puritan Movement*, 405.
3. Neale, *Eliz. & Parliaments*, ii.249.
4. ibid., ii.251–65.
5. ibid., ii.259.
6. ibid., ii.274.
7. Collinson, *The Elizabethan Puritan Movement*, 406–7.
8. Neale, *Eliz. & Parliaments*, ii.321–2.
9. ibid., ii.326.
10. Bagot, *Memorials of the Bagot Family*, 31.
11. Thomson, 293.
12. Neale, *Eliz. & Parliaments*, ii.219–20; and see Collinson, *The Elizabethan Puritan Movement*, 444–6.
13. Strachey, *Elizabeth and Essex*, 5–6.
14. *L.A.*, i.250, 292.
15. ibid., i.292–5.
16. ibid., i.250, 295, 298.
17. ibid., i.254, 259, 262, 276–7, 296–8, 306–7, 321–6, 330–1; Georgina Bertie, *Five Generations of a Loyal House*, 288–90.

18. *L.A.*, i.285, 287; ii.232–41, 243, 275–6, 289.
19. ibid., ii.275–6, 285.
20. ibid., ii.241–6, 252, 256–8.
21. ibid., ii.289–91.
22. ibid., ii.418–35.
23. PRO/SP 78/22/f.189 (20 Dec. 1590, N.S.).
24. *L.A.*, ii.269, 297, 299, 301–2, 315, 319–20, 323, 325, 327.
25. *L.A.*, ii.328–9, 339; iii.187, 317, 324; *Unton Correspondence*, 8–10.
26. PRO/SP 78/25/f.70 (21 July 1591, O.S.).
27. *L.A.*, iii.349.
28. ibid., ii.337, 339, 341–6, 355–6; iii.271–81, 284–6, 288–97, 336, 345, 347–8; Unton, 12–16, 159–62, 269–74, 283–6; *Lettres missives de Henri IV*, iii.832–9.
29. Unton, 32–34, 106; *L.A.*, iii.196, 200–3.
30. Unton, 55–57, 72–75, 95; *L.A.*, iii.342.
31. *L.A.*, iii.204–5, 209.
32. Unton, 73.
33. Devereux, i.234.
34. Unton, 80–82; Devereux, i.245–6; *L.A.*, iii.340–2, 345.
35. Unton, 146–8, 214–16, 222–3, 233–5, 337, 345–6; Devereux, i.256–60; *L.A.*, iii.218–19, 224, 229, 246, 366.
36. Unton, 143–5, 159–61, 183–6, 195–6, 212–16; *L.A.*, iii.225, 357, 366–8.
37. Unton, 190–2, 233–5, 269–73, 283–6, 295–8, 303–4, 306–11, 341–6, 353–8, 360–3, 400–4; *L.A.*, iii.243, 248, 251, 374–7.
38. Unton, 413–20, 423–30, 432–7, 440–2, 444–6; *L.A..*, iii.260–8.
39. Unton, 106; *L.A.*, iii.209–10, 345, 374–7, 379–81.
40. *L.A.*, iii.268.
41. ibid., i.267; iii.298, 300–1, 304, 309; Unton, 3–4, 116–17, 134–5, 180, 302, 310, 352, 354, 357, 361–2.
42. *L.A.*, iii.368–9.
43. Hist. MSS. Comm., *Cecil*, iv.343; Camden, (1635 edn.) 422.
44. Read, *Burghley*, 483.
45. ibid., 516–21; Strachey, 95–105.
46. Camden, (1635 edn.), 490–1; Read, *Burghley*, 537–45.
47. *Ven. Cal.*, vii.479; *Span. Cal. Eliz.*, ii.350.
48. *For. Cal. Eliz.*, xii.179; xx.411; xxiii.193; *L.A.*, i.441; ii.454, 466–7; Nichols, *Progresses*, iii.516.
49. *For. Cal. Eliz.*, xiv.70, 305; xv.234; xviii.634; xix.313–14, 441–2, 482–3; xxi(i).344–5, 508–9, 562–3, 647–9; xxii.101–3, 138–9, 165–6, 172–5, 281–2, 334–5, 404; xxiii.12–13, 132–5, 164, 346–9, 401–2; *L.A.*, i.440–54; ii.452–3, 457–71; iii.494–6, 499–501, 504.
50. *For. Cal. Eliz.*, viii.2414; ix.384; x.1525; xi.116, 588, 978; xvii.74, 340–1, 374; xix.83–86, 692–3; xx.54–56; xxiii.246–7; *Span. Cal. Eliz.*, ii.189; *L.A.*, i.430–5; ii.441–5; iii.483–6; Nichols, *Progresses*, iii.515.

Chapter 29 – The Old Queen

1. Harington, i.186.
2. ibid., i.189.
3. ibid., i.186–90.
4. Nichols, *Progresses*, iii.424–6.
5. ibid. iii.90–122.
6. ibid., iii.129–48.
7. Neale, *Eliz. & Parliaments*, ii.335.
8. ibid., ii.335–6; Rappaport (*London Journal*, ix.127); Rogers, v.664–5.
9. Strachey, 69–90; Read, *Burghley*, 497–8.
10. Murdin, 669–75.
11. Camden, (1635 edn.) 430–1.
12. Read, *Burghley*, 521–3, 545–6.
13. *Irish Cal.*, iv.172, 263–6; PRO/SP 63/145/f.32 (20 June 1589, O.S.).
14. PRO/SP 63/145/f.12 (10 June 1589, O.S.).
15. PRO/SP 63/192/f.79 (27 Aug. 1596, O.S.).
16. *Irish Cal.*, iv.202, 219, 266–7, 270–2; v.122–3.
17. PRO/SP 63/151/f.168 (7 Apr. 1590, O.S.).
18. *Irish Cal.*, iv.491, 493; v.487–8.
19. ibid., vii.435.
20. ibid., ix.295.
21. PRO/SP 63/192/f.40 (9 Aug. 1596, O.S.).
22. *Irish Cal.*, vi.499.
23. ibid., iv.214.
24. ibid., iv.54, 65, 312–13, 319–21; *Span. Cal. Eliz.*, iv.508–9.
25. *Irish Cal.*, iv.132; v.280–2, 285, 291, 294–5, 323–6.
26. *Carew Cal.*, iii.101.
27. ibid., iii.99–100, 111–12; *Irish Cal.*, v.299, 305, 314, 332–5.
28. *Irish Cal.*, v.341–2.
29. PRO/SP 63/182/f.106 (12 Aug. 1595, O.S.).
30. *Irish Cal.*, v.406–9, 442; *Carew Cal.*, iii.125–6.
31. *Carew Cal.*, iii.133.
32. PRO/SP 63/184/f.141 (Nov. 1595).
33. *Irish Cal.*, v.523, 526–7, 534–6, 541–2, 544; vi., p.xvi, 352; vii.50.
34. ibid., vii.227–8.
35. ibid., vii.239.
36. ibid., vii.239, 379; xi.607.
37. ibid., vi.231–2, 255, 257, 372; vii.254–6.
38. ibid., vi.372.
39. ibid., ix.12, 106–7.
40. Harington, i.77; ii.133, 210.
41. ibid., ii.234.
42. ibid., ii.140–1.
43. ibid., ii.137–9.
44. ibid., ii.215.
45. ibid., ii.139–40.
46. ibid., ii.232–5.

47. Strachey, 168–9.
48. ibid., 173–4.
49. *Irish Cal.*, viii.48.
50. ibid., viii.13.
51. ibid., vii., p. lxviii, 483.
52. ibid., xi.608–9.
53. ibid., vii.468–9.
54. ibid., vii.502.
55. Shakespeare, *Henry V*, Act v, Chorus, lines 24–33.
56. Nichols, *Progresses*, iii.434.
57. *Irish Cal.*, viii.16–17, 37–40, 123–5.
58. ibid., viii.106.
59. ibid., viii.61–62, 80–81, 98–101, 150–3, 218.
60. ibid., viii.98–102.
61. ibid., viii.106.
62. ibid., viii.116, 126–7, 153.
63. ibid., viii.136, 144–7.
64. ibid., viii.150–3, 177–9; Strachey, 210–15.
65. Harington, ii.134–5.
66. *Irish Cal.*, viii.177–9, 215–21, 227–30, 279–81, 327; xi.614–15.
67. ibid., viii.232; ix.192, 226, 380–1; x.7–12, 334, 411; xi.43, 92–95.
68. ibid., viii.448.
69. ibid., viii.308.
70. ibid., vii.300–2, 355.
71. ibid., ix.369.
72. ibid., vii.322.
73. ibid., viii.431.
74. ibid., ix.338, 394.
75. ibid., xi.83, 634–5; *Span. Cal. Eliz.*, iv.684–5.
76. *Irish Cal.*, xi., p. xxviii, 175, 198, 202–5, 208–13, 220, 234–5, 238–42, 270, 276, 641–3; *Span. Cal. Eliz.*, iv.699–703, 707–8.
77. Nichols, *Progresses*, iii.575–7; *Irish Cal.*, xi., p. lix, 274, 286–7, 335, 406–7, 412–13, 417, 514–17, 535, 551–2, 584.

Chapter 30 – The End

1. Strachey, 234–41; Neale, *Queen Elizabeth*, 366–73; *Irish Cal.*, x.198–200.
2. Strachey, 192–3.
3. ibid., 242–54, 259–63; Neale, *Queen Elizabeth*, 373–8; Nichols, *Progresses*, iii.544–50; *Irish Cal.*, x.200–1.
4. Neale, *Queen Elizabeth*, 373.
5. Nichols, *Progresses*, iii.552–3.
6. Rowe's edition of Shakespeare's *Works*, i., p. viii–ix; Dennis, *The Comical Gallant* ('Epistle Dedicatory to the Hon. George Granville'), A2.
7. Nichols, *Progresses*, iii.564–8.
8. Neale, *Eliz. & Parliaments*, ii.337–67, 372–88.
9. ibid., ii.388–91.

10. ibid., ii.428–32.
11. *Dom. Cal.*, vi.232.
12. Nichols, *Progresses*, iii.596–8.
13. ibid., iii.600–2, 607–8; Chamberlain, *Letters*, 162–3, 174.
14. Nichols, *Progresses*, iii.603.
15. *Dom. Cal.*, vi.299, 302.
16. For Elizabeth's death and Carey's journey, see Nichols, *Progresses*, iii.603–9; and see Buchan, *Escapes and Hurried Journeys*, 254–5.
17. Nichols, *Progresses*, iii.614–24; *Dom. Cal. Jas I*, i.5.
18. Shakespeare, *Twelfth Night*, Act ii, scene v, lines 139–40.
19. See supra, pp. 147, 332.
20. Harington, ii.135–6.

INDEX

Mary Tudor (Mary 1) – *cont.*
55–8; sends Elizabeth to Tower, 58–9, 60; and Elizabeth's further imprisonment, 61, 62, 63, 64; imagined pregnancy, 65–6; conflict with Pope, 69–70; declares war on France, 70; unpopularity, 71; last meeting with Elizabeth, 72; death, 72–3, 74; funeral, 77; Knox's *Blast* against, 91
Mary Tudor, Queen of France, Duchess of Suffolk, 36
Mary of Guise, Queen Regent of Scotland, 30, 43, 90, 91; and civil war, 92–3, 94, 95, 96, 97, 98, 99, 103; death, 106
Mary of Hungary, 43, 70, 72, 91
Mason, Sir John, 102
Massacre at Paris, The (Marlowe), 299
Maude, Barnard, 255n
Maurice, Count of Nassau, and Geertruidenberg mutiny, 291–2, 293–4
Mauvissière Michel de Castelnau, Sieur de la (French ambassador), 212, 231, 258, 259, 261, 263, 265, 277
Maximilian II, Emperor, 157
Mayenne, Charles, Duke of, 228, 268, 296, 298, 304, 305
Meaux, 182
Medina Sidonia, Duke of, and Armada defeat, 281, 282–3, 284, 285, 286–7, 288
Mendoza, Don Bernardino de (Spanish ambassador), 204–5, 234, 235, 247, 285, 312; and Elizabeth's proposed marriage to Anjou, 212, 213; and Spanish intervention in Ireland, 226, 244; secret correspondence with Mary Queen of Scots, 238, 239, 244; expulsion, 244; secret contacts with Catholics in England, 244, 255, 261; use of English spies, 261, 269, 272–3, 274, 295, 318
Mercoeur, Philip Emmanuel of Lorraine, Duke of, 307
Merchant of Venice, The (Shakespeare), 164–5, 319
Merry Wives of Windsor, The (Shakespeare), 331
Milan, Christina, Duchess of, 30
Mildmay, Sir Walter, 302
Mina, Abbé, 154
Moncontour, battle of (1569), 160
Monson, Robert, Justice of the Court of Common Pleas, 193, 210
Mont, Christopher, 101
Montaigne, Michel de, 268
Montauban, 184

Montfaucon, 184
Montpellier, 117
Montpensier, Catherine, Duchess of, 229, 296
Montpensier, Louis of Bourbon, Duke of, 229
Montrose, John Graham, 3rd Earl of, 230
Moray, James Stewart (q.v.), Earl of, 29, 92, 118, 140, 142, 143, 145, 151; objections to Mary Queen of Scots' proposed marriages, 137, 138; rebellion against Mary, 140–2; secret meeting with Elizabeth, 141, 150; pardoned by Mary, 144; as Regent for James VI, 150, 153, 158; private correspondence with Cecil, 153; measures against Mary, 158, 170; assassination, 171, 172
More, Sir Thomas, 19, 23, 24, 87
Morice, James, 301–2, 303
Morley, Henry Parker, 8th Baron, 28
Morley, Thomas, 318
Morton, James Douglas, 4th Earl of, 173; and murder of Riccio, 143, 144; pardon, 145; forces Mary's abdication, 150; as Moray's second-in-command, 150, 174; as Regent, 187–8, 190–1, 229; quarrel with Elizabeth over Border incident, 191–2, 228; seeks anti-Catholic alliance with England, 228; ousted as Regent, 229; accused as accessory to Darnley's murder, 229–30; execution, 231
Moscow, 314–15
Mountjoy, Charles Blount, 8th Baron, 328, 329
Munster, 321; revolts in (1569–73) 218, 219, (1579–81) 222–7, 269; famine, 226, 227, 328; campaign in (1599–1601), 326–9; Spanish forces in, 329
Muscovy Company, 314

Nantes, Edict of (1598), 313
Nassau, Count Justin of, 279
Nassau, Count Louis of, 155, 159, 189
Nemours, Anne d'Este, Duchess of, 182
Nerac, 199
Neri, Philip, 311
Nevers, Louis de Gonzaga, Duke of, 182
Newcastle, 103, 106, 119, 141, 142, 143, 144
Newdigate, Sir Francis, 115
Nieuport, 244, 278, 279, 284, 285
Nîmes, 184
Noailles, Antoine de (French ambassador), 47, 50, 51, 54, 56, 57, 67, 96, 104